# THE CHINESE CONNECTION

STUDIES OF THE EAST ASIAN INSTITUTE · COLUMBIA UNIVERSITY

Warren I. Cohen

# THE CHINESE CONNECTION

## Roger S. Greene, Thomas W. Lamont, George E. Sokolsky and American-East Asian Relations

1978 COLUMBIA UNIVERSITY PRESS NEW YORK

**Library of Congress Cataloging in Publication Data**

Cohen, Warren I
The Chinese connection.

(Studies of the East Asian Institute)
Bibliography: p.
Includes index.
1. United States—Foreign relations—China.
2. China—Foreign relations—United States. 3. United States—Foreign relations—Japan. 4. Japan—Foreign relations—United States. 5. Greene, Roger Sherman, 1881–1947. 6. Lamont, Thomas William, 1870–1948.
7. Sokolsky, George Ephraim, 1893–1962. 8. Diplomats—United States—Biography. I. Title. II. Series: Columbia University. East Asian Institute. Studies.
E183.8.C5C623 327.73′051 77-18101
ISBN 0-231-04444-5

COLUMBIA UNIVERSITY PRESS
NEW YORK—GUILDFORD, SURREY

PRINTED IN THE UNITED STATES OF AMERICA

THE EAST ASIAN INSTITUTE OF COLUMBIA UNIVERSITY

The East Asian Institute of Columbia University was established in 1949 to prepare graduate students for careers dealing with East Asia, and to aid research and publication on East Asia during the modern period. The faculty of the Institute are grateful to the Ford Foundation and the Rockefeller Foundation for their financial assistance.

The Studies of the East Asian Institute were inaugurated in 1962 to bring to a wider public the results of significant new research on modern and contemporary East Asia.

For

**DOROTHY BORG**

and

**W. STULL HOLT**

Teachers and Friends

# Acknowledgments

Dorothy Borg, John K. Fairbank, W. Stull Holt, Richard W. Leopold, and Ernest R. May helped me with my conception of this book. Dorothy Borg, John Fairbank, Ned Greene, Nancy Hennigar, Akira Iriye, Dick Leopold, and Peter Levine read the manuscript and were unsparing in their criticism—the best evidence of genuine friendship, I also benefited greatly from the comments of an anonymous reader, at whose suggestion I prepared the appendix. Waldo Heinrichs, Fred Hoyt, Jerry Israel, Charles Neu, Noel Pugach, and Morty Rozanski proposed additions to my original list.

Sylvia Anderson spent a good part of a summer typing the manuscript, assisted cheerfully by Marilyn Wilcox. They could easily have found better things to do. My research was made possible by annual grants from the Michigan State University All-University Research Fund and by a special grant from the Michigan State University Center for International Programs that enabled me to spend spring term, 1971, at Harvard. The Director of the Asian Studies Center, William T. Ross, always found money to cover my expenses, allowed me to commandeer his secretaries, his copy machine, and whatever else was needed to complete my work.

Members of the staff at the Houghton Library, Harvard University, and of the manuscript division of Baker Library, Harvard, were kind and supportive beyond the call of duty. My favorite place to work remains the Diplomatic Branch of the National Archives, where the efficiency of Pat Dowling, Milt Gustafson, and Kathy Nicastro provides a striking contrast with the frustrations suffered time and again when attempting to work with the Modern Military Branch in the same building. The librarians of the manuscript division at Princeton and the custodians of the oral history collection at Columbia also served me exceptionally well. I hope I can find something kind to say about the manuscript librarians at the Hoover Institution next time I try to work there.

I owe a special debt to the family of Roger Greene—to his lovely wife Kate, to his son Ned, who I have claimed as a friend, and to his daughter Katharine, who reviewed the manuscript patiently. The Greenes gave unstintingly of their time, found material for me, and answered my many questions. Corliss Lamont was cordial in our one conversation. Regrettably, Dorothy Sokolsky chose not to respond to my letters.

And finally, to return to my dedication. Stull Holt, historian and poet, directed me toward the study of American–East Asian relations and tried, years ago, to turn a sailor into a scholar. Later, as I drifted on my own, Dorothy Borg provided a compass. I hope I have the opportunity to do as much for a few of my students and friends.

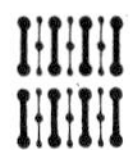

# Contents

# THE CHINESE CONNECTION

# INTRODUCTION

In *1066 And All That,* Sellar and Yeatman concluded with a single chapter summing up the world after the Paris Peace Conference of 1919. That chapter, entitled "A Bad Thing," contained but one sentence: "America was thus clearly top nation and History came to a ."

In the years that followed the Great War, while the United States remained outside the League of Nations, allegedly "isolationist," its citizens appeared everywhere, not least of all in East Asia. The kind of sojourners Jonathan Spence has labeled "China's Helpers" were more likely than before to be Americans, heralding the blessings of democracy and free enterprise, fulfilling the national mission abroad as well as at home. Although American business and missionary interest in China long antedated the emergence of the United States as "top nation," only the missionaries had developed an important stake there. British traders dominated the market and treaty port life generally. Little American capital was available for export and most of that was invested in areas closer to home. After 1919, however, the financial center of the world crossed the Atlantic to New York, suggesting that the potential existed for a major expansion of American economic interests in East Asia—and the government of the United States was not remiss in its efforts to promote opportunities for its citizens.

This is a study of one element in the process of formulating American policy toward East Asia: of the way in which individuals outside the government convey their ideas, directly or through their ability to rally segments of the public, to the men responsible for policy decisions. My fundamental assumption is that in the first half of this century the number of Americans who had both the desire and the ability to transmit their opinions on the affairs of China and Japan was extremely small—a tiny group of missionaries, educators, businessmen, journalists, and former diplomats. Judging by the number of people who published books and articles, wrote to or were consulted by the Department of State, testified before Congressional committees, or were active lobbyists, fewer than 100 American men and women regularly had the opportunity to offer their opinions on issues relating to East Asia. I will not discuss all of them in this book, but I have appended a list with brief sketches.

This is also a story of three men who participated in the intensification of America's relationship with East Asia. They were men whose lives coursed through very different channels, rarely meeting. The currents did not run evenly. One was deeper, one was stronger than the others, one darker. And yet, when the experiences of these men are pooled, they reflect much of the American encounter with China and Japan in the first half of the twentieth century: efforts to assist in the modernization of China, responses to the rise of nationalism and communism in China, and to Japanese imperialism.

The purpose of this book, then, is twofold. First, it is a study of the way in which categories of people James N. Rosenau has designated as "opinion-submitters," "opinion-makers," and "opinion-leaders" function. My aim is not to measure the elusive quality of *influence* but rather to chart lines of *access* to decision-makers and to the public. As Rosenau has explained most succinctly, the ability to transmit one's views does not guarantee influence, but there can be no influence without the ability to convey opinions to policy-makers or without access to the media. Second, it is important to learn something about the men themselves: the substance of their opinions, how they became involved in the affairs of China and Japan, how they emerged from the larger mass of men and women who held opinions but lacked the will or the means to communicate them.[1]

1. See Rosenau's *Public Opinion and Foreign Policy* (New York, 1961) and *National Leadership and Foreign Policy* (Princeton, 1963). "Opinion-leader" and "opinion-maker" are used interchangeably to designate persons able to transmit opinions regularly to unknown persons through impersonal channels such as the mass media. "Opinion-submitter" is used to designate someone with access to decision-makers. When Lamont speaks to a secretary of state he is an opinion-submitter. When he writes an article for a popular magazine, he is an opinion-maker or leader.

My interest in this subject began with the discovery of the efforts of Roger S. Greene to shape American opinion and policy during the years 1938 to 1941. An earlier study of the role of private groups in Japanese-American relations led me to conclude that Greene, through an intricate maze of family, school, and professional connections, and especially as a result of positions as chairman of the American Committee for Non-Participation in Japanese Aggression and as associate chairman of the Committee to Defend America by Aiding the Allies, had been the most important nongovernmental advocate of American intervention in the war in Asia.[2]

I had intended to write a biography of Greene, but other scholars persuaded me to write a composite biography comparing Greene, a former diplomat with close ties to missionary and educational circles, with a businessman and a journalist. The choice of a businessman was obvious: Thomas W. Lamont of J. P. Morgan and Company, chairman of the American Group of the International Banking Consortium for China, financial agent for the government of Japan, and confidant of presidents from Wilson through Franklin D. Roosevelt. My selection of a journalist, however, was clearly idiosyncratic, eliciting wrinkled brows—and noses. But years ago, when George E. Sokolsky was still alive and peddling hate in his syndicated columns, I discovered that he had been in China during the May Fourth Movement and, as an informant for American military intelligence, had provided quite useful analyses of student radicalism. Subsequent research on other projects had revealed that his writings for newspapers in China during the 1920s were regularly praised and forwarded to Washington by American diplomats—and that Sokolsky had developed friendships and corresponded at various times with J. V. A. MacMurray and Stanley K. Hornbeck, central figures in the Far Eastern Divison of the Department of State in the 1920s and 1930s respectively. Perhaps of greatest fascination for me was his role as Jewish reactionary, his ties to Joe McCarthy's Roy Cohn and to Alfred Kohlberg, "the China Lobby Man," in the American Jewish League Against Communism. How did the son of a New York rabbi get to China, gain access to decision-makers, become a reactionary, and serve as one of the extreme Right's most widely read experts on East Asia?

Part one of this book introduces the main characters, Greene, Lamont,

2. See my "Role of Private Groups in the United States," in Dorothy Borg and Shumpei Okamoto (eds.), *Pearl Harbor as History: Japanese-American Relations, 1931–1941* (New York, 1973), 421–58.

and Sokolsky, and examines their origins, identities, and involvements in Chinese and Japanese affairs up to the early 1920s, to the eve of the Nationalist revolution in China. Part two explores the further evolution of their ideas and their actions in response to developments in East Asia, specifically the Nationalist revolution, the Sino-Japanese conflict, the Pacific War, and the ascendancy of the Chinese Communists. Throughout I am concerned with their respective roles in American-East Asian relations and with the larger question of how private citizens interact with the process of determining foreign policy.

# PART 1

# In the Beginning

# 1

# THE EDUCATION OF ROGER SHERMAN GREENE

"AMERICAN of Americans, with Heaven knew how many Puritans and Patriots behind him," Henry Adams found himself superfluous in late nineteenth-century America—cast off like "the Indians or the buffalo who had been ejected from their heritage by his own people." Jews, "still reeking of the Ghetto, snarling a weird Yiddish," had a surer instinct and a freer hand in the new industrial America. E. L. Godkin, gentleman reformer, brooded about the waste of young men, educated and of good family, in an industrial democracy in which social connections had yielded to the spoils system. A leading anti-imperialist forced to come to terms with his country's acquisition of an overseas empire, Godkin conceived of an American colonial service, after the British model, as a haven for the best and the brightest. Some middle- and upper-class Americans dedicated their mature years to reform movements, most notably the Progressive movement that followed the turn of the century. A handful considered revolution, but many more young Americans went to remote and backward lands, especially to China, to carry out the "evangelization of the world in this generation," and in this task fulfilled the demands of a tradition of service for which they had been bred.[1]

Roger Sherman Greene, born in Westboro, Massachusetts in 1881,

1. Henry Adams, *The Education of Henry Adams* (New York, 1931), 238; David Healy, *US Expansionism* (Madison, 1970), 107–8.

could not match Henry Adams' Presidential lineage, but Puritans and Patriots were not lacking among his forebears. If the Greene, Sherman, Evarts, Forbes, and Crosby families did not shine as brightly as the Adams, Cabot, and Lodge families, they were nonetheless visible in the firmament.[2] Yet Roger Greene was not like other young men from prominent families. At Harvard he worked alongside Frank Roosevelt, Joe Grew, and other luminaries of the *Crimson*, but he never felt a part of their world, for he was a sojourner in the land of his birth.

Although born in New England, Roger Greene grew up in Japan, the fourth son and sixth of eight children of Daniel Crosby and Mary Jane Forbes Greene. His parents were among the earliest American missionaries to Japan, deeply involved in bringing modern Western education to the Japanese during the Meiji era. Born toward the close of a rare family furlough in the United States, he spent all but two of his precollege years in Japan, where he developed a profound sense of himself as different and isolated. And, like his older brothers (Evarts Boutell, who became a distinguished historian, DeWitt Clinton Professor of American History at Columbia University; Daniel Crosby, a noted laryngologist; and Jerome Davis, best known for his work with Harvard and the Rockefeller Foundation), Roger Sherman Greene experienced enough of Christian missions to prefer some other form of service to mankind.

At Harvard, Greene prepared himself for a position in the administration of his country's new empire in the Philippines—an unconscious step toward the fulfillment of Godkin's vision and a conscious secularization of his father's mission. The alternative of a career within the United States had no appeal for him. He had been leavening his study of the science of government with the study of Spanish and Portuguese, and already had some knowledge of Japanese and Russian. When no opening could be found in the Philippines, Greene went off to Brazil in 1902 as secretary to Minister Charles P. Bryan. Within a year he was serving as deputy consul general in Rio de Janeiro.

Greene's entrance into the consular and diplomatic service paralleled that of many young men of good family in the years before the Progressives had reformed and bureaucratized the pattern of American overseas represen-

2. Information on the Greene family comes from Evarts B. Greene, *A New Englander in Japan: Daniel Crosby Greene* (New York and Boston, 1927) and from correspondence with Professor Edward Forbes Greene.

tation. Social connections were still basic to obtaining secretarial posts. Consular posts, low in salary, were generally doled out as a form of patronage—rewards for favors of a lesser magnitude. The young aristocrats often supplemented their incomes with allowances from home and, after a few years abroad, returned to take over their fathers' businesses. For the lowly politicians, opportunities for extracurricular activities, occasionally extralegal as well, promised supplementary income. Greene's Harvard connections and the willingness of his cousin, Senator George F. Hoar, to use his influence, opened the necessary doors, but then financial problems began. His family had bequeathed him high standards of performance and intense honesty, but little means. Unable to meet the demands of Rio society on his purse, Greene sought the post of consul at Buenos Aires, but the support of his brother Jerome and of Senator Hoar were to no avail. There was no vacancy.

Greene liked his work in Rio and performed ably, winning accolades from Bryan's successor as Minister, David E. Thompson, and from the American consul-general.[3] Had his income allowed him to live as well as his status within the community permitted, Greene might have joined the revelers, learned to dance all night, and developed an identity in keeping with the popular stereotype of a diplomat. But his financial straits, combined with his New England missionary background and sense of personal isolation, kept him aloof from the social pleasures available—and left him generally unhappy in Rio. A missionary wife suggested that he find his way to the countryside, where he would like the people better, but he concluded that he had best go home, to Asia.[4]

In February 1904 Roger Greene left Rio without regrets and headed for Nagasaki, Japan, where he was to be Vice Consul and Interpreter. He could not read Japanese and his spoken Japanese was rusty, but his superiors in the Department of State did not share his concern. Americans who could speak *any* Japanese were rare. He enjoyed Nagasaki immensely. Not only were his parents closer, in Tokyo, but he felt comfortable in a small Japanese city. Living there was inexpensive—there were none of the feelings of inadequacy that had plagued him in Brazil, none of the financial or social de-

3. D. E. Thompson to John Hay, November 21, 1903, and Eugene Seeger to Herbert H. D. Peirce, III, February 15, 1904. Papers of Roger Sherman Greene, Houghton Library, Harvard University, hereafter RSG ms.

4. Ella Tucker to Greene, undated, RSG ms.

mands. He could save money to pay off debts incurred at Harvard and while travelling to his posts, and there was good walking. A good walk, the satisfaction of a job well done and of a debt repaid—what more could a man ask of life?

Again, in Nagasaki as in Rio, his superior thought well of Greene and, as pressures on the post increased during the Russo-Japanese War, asked the Department to increase his salary. He was reported to be "thoroughly capable," "by training and education exactly such a person as is required at a consulate at a strategic and central point . . . where matters of importance are constantly arising." The Department was slow to respond. Struggling in face of war-borne inflationary pressures, Greene became interested in an opening in Kobe, largely because of the higher salary involved and the consul's willingness to share the fees collected for consular services. His good reputation, made known by family connections, won him the Kobe position, but Greene remained in Kobe only a few months before the Department decided that a man of his ability, able to speak Russian, was precisely the man for a commercial office in Vladivostok.[5]

Greene was not quite 25 when he arrived in Vladivostok—the tumultuous Far Eastern frontier of the Tsar's empire. The young man's first days on Russian soil were anything but auspicious. First, his hotel burned down with the loss of all his possessions. Then, when the Department of State titled him Consul as opposed to Commercial Agent, the Russians refused to recognize his official rank. After months of frustrating negotiations and rumors of a transfer to Seoul, the Russians relented, recognizing him as American Consul in October 1906. Again, he distinguished himself by the quality of his performance, gaining the respect of the community and high praise from the Department official responsible for inspecting his work. From Vladivostok he was sent in 1907 to Dalny (Dairen or Talien) in Russian-controlled Manchuria, and in 1909, when a crisis in Russian-American relations developed at Harbin, Greene was sent to look after American interests there.[6]

As the professionalization of the Consular Service progressed, especially after 1906, it became clear that the Service could provide a promising

5. Charles B. Harris to Assistant Secretary of State, March 18, 1905, Consular Despatches, Nagasaki, National Archives (microfilm); Lloyd Griscom to Greene, February 28, 1906, RSG ms.

6. Charles B. Harris to Greene, September 22, 1906, RSG ms; Inspection Report, American Consular Office, Vladivostok, May 30, 1907, by Fleming D. Cheshire, National Archives.

and satisfying career for able young men like Greene. Pressures from American business for higher quality commercial representatives abroad led to decent salaries and to the implementation of the merit system for both admission to the Service and for promotion. Biennial inspections led to the elimination of incompetent or corrupt officials, and almost immediately the Willard Straights and the Roger Greenes shot to the top. Straight became consul-general at the Mukden outpost at the age of 26 and Greene became consul-general at Hankow, a major city, at the age of 30. And yet both of these young men, with great opportunities for advancement before them, left the Service. For Straight, the pattern followed was familiar. A wealthy young man spent some years abroad, found the world of high finance more stimulating, found greater access to power on Wall Street, and left the Department of State. As Straight went off to associate himself with bankers and railroad magnates, Greene tied himself to the Rockefellers, but the parallel was more apparent than real. Unlike Straight, Greene gradually became uncomfortable in his role as agent of the interests of the United States, came to feel that his duties in the service of the Department of State conflicted with his sense of America's mission and his own. He found it painful to represent his country and his countrymen as they betrayed, cheated, and manipulated the Chinese. When offered an opportunity to join in the philanthropic activities of the Rockefeller Foundation, he perceived an opportunity to serve in a way that would fulfill his inherited mission. It was an opportunity he could not resist. This first chapter in the education of Roger Greene is, then, the story of the unmaking of an American diplomat.[7]

As America became an imperial power, acquiring an overseas empire at the close of the nineteenth century, the Adams brothers, both Henry and Brooks, Alfred Mahan, and others who watched the course of American expansion across the Pacific, foresaw a test of power between the United States and Russia. Conflicting policies toward China and especially China's Manchurian provinces produced serious tensions in Russo-American relations in the early years of the twentieth century. President Theodore Roose-

7. See Waldo H. Heinrichs, Jr., "Bureaucracy and Professionalism in the Development of American Career Diplomacy," in John Braeman et al., *Twentieth-Century American Foreign Policy* (Columbus, Ohio, 1971). For Straight's career, see Herbert Croly, *Willard Straight* (New York, 1924); Charles Vevier, *The United States and China, 1906–1913* (New Brunswick, New Jersey, 1955); and an important reassessment in Michael H. Hunt, *Frontier Defense and the Open Door* (New Haven, 1973).

velt expressed a desire to "go to extremes" with the Russians. When war came between Russia and Japan in 1904, American sympathies appear to have been with Japan. Roosevelt argued that Japan was fighting "our fight." But once Japan had defeated Russia, American military planners, writers on geopolitics, and others who found their pleasure in the search for a credible enemy, began to focus their attention on Japan. As the Japanese became more assertive in their relations with the Great Powers, tensions between Japan and the United States developed, most obviously over American discrimination against Japanese immigrants, but also over the treatment of American economic interests in Japanese-controlled regions of Manchuria. Roosevelt had shied away from a confrontation with Japan, convinced that no American end in East Asia was important enough to justify challenging the Japanese. His successor, President William Howard Taft, launched an aggressive campaign designed to undermine Japanese influence in Manchuria and to improve the competitive position of the United States.

Roger Greene did not move, with his countrymen and the relevant authorities within the Department of State, into the new milieu of suspicion of and hostility toward Japan. There was nothing in Greene's experience to justify adopting a new attitude toward the people among whom he had lived so many years of his life. On the other hand, his experiences with the Russian bureaucracy reinforced his hostility to the Tsarist regime. He concluded that Russia, not Japan, posed the greatest threat to China and to American interests in China.

Complaints of American businessmen about Japanese obstacles to the development of markets in Manchuria angered Greene. From Manchuria, as from Vladivostok, he argued constantly that there was a market for American goods that required only the study of local needs and the presence of business representatives familiar with local language, customs, and laws. In Vladivostok, the Germans were doing well, despite all obstacles, because of the seriousness with which they met the challenge. In Manchuria, he insisted that it was not discrimination on the part of the authorities but aggressive practices by hungry Japanese businessmen that was allowing them to take over the market in cotton goods. Although Japanese goods were of inferior quality, they were better packaged, more attractively presented, and cheaper. Cotton mills in Japan had combined to use the giant Mitsui holding company as an agent in Manchuria, where Mitsui had an office in every city. American goods could not compete largely because they could not sell by themselves. No one representing American textile interests was there to keep the goods moving. If American textile manufacturers wanted to retain a share of the market in Manchuria, Greene contended that better business practices, not the intervention of the American government, would provide the means.[8]

An attack on consular officials for offering inadequate protection to American cotton interests led Greene to reiterate his argument and to demonstrate that foreign firms that followed the pattern he advised had been successful. There was money coming into Manchuria and purchasing power was developing rapidly. The British-American Tobacco Company and Standard Oil of New York had good men on the scene, dealing with local firms and making profits. As for John Foord and his fellow lobbyists for the textile industry, "those people in New York prefer to lie back and imagine that the Japanese owe all their success to discrimination and none to hustle. Anybody that suggests the homely remedy of work for a declining business deserves to be kicked."[9]

To his brother Jerome, Greene explained that businessmen whose profits had soared during 1905 and 1906 were unrealistic in assuming those years were normal. The Russo-Japanese War had kept two major competitors out of the market, permitting a temporary increase in American sales. Now sales had returned to the prewar average. Again he explained that while some local discrimination did exist, its import was difficult to assess in the absence of a strong American commercial effort in Manchuria. Jerome's task, as always, was to use the contacts he had as Secretary of the Harvard Corporation to get important businessmen to understand that a powerful American firm could get better freight rates, could force an end to discrimination. "In short," Roger reminded his brother, "what is wanted is for our people to come out and work for their trade."[10]

As Americans interested in East Asia grew worried about Japanese intentions, Greene made occasional forays to counter this tendency. He had some luck convincing an important American scholar, George H. Blakeslee, to view the Japanese more sympathetically. He was less successful with

8. Summary of Greene reports on trade conditions in Vladivostok, in Cheshire Inspection Report, May 30, 1907; Roger to Jerome Greene, April 6, 1909, RSG ms.

9. Greene to P. S. Heintzleman, February 17, 1910, and Heintzleman to Greene, April 1, 1910, RSG ms.

10. Roger to Jerome Greene, March 23, 1910, RSG ms.

Frederick McCormick, Associated Press correspondent in Peking, whose sensitivity to Japanese aggressiveness and unsurpassed access to American readers threatened to stimulate unfriendly attitudes toward Japan throughout the United States. At least as troublesome was his inability to smooth over the mutual feelings of hostility between the Japanese in Manchuria and Willard Straight—and it was Straight whose anti-Japanese maneuvers were tied closely to the blunders of the Taft Administration's policies in Manchuria.[11]

In 1908 Willard Straight returned to Washington to head the recently created Far Eastern Division of the Department of State. He teamed up with Huntington Wilson, Assistant Secretary of State, in a series of ambitious plans to force American capital into Manchuria and China proper. Rebuffed during the Roosevelt administration because of Roosevelt's insistence on giving priority to good relations with Japan, Straight, Wilson, and their associates found Taft and his secretary of state, Philander Knox, more than eager to endorse their program. Against this array in Washington, Greene and Fred Fisher, another American consular official who thought Russia rather than Japan posed the gravest danger to China and ultimately to American interests there, were overmatched. A Russian-American controversy over the municipal administration of Harbin illustrated the shift in the policy of the United States and the shift in the Department of State's perception of its opposition in Manchuria. It also led to Greene's initial disillusionment with his role as representative of the United States.[12]

The main contestants for control of Manchuria included not only the Russian and Japanese governments, but the Chinese as well. In the last years of the Roosevelt administration, the Chinese government determined to end its benign neglect of Manchuria and to tie those northeastern provinces more tightly to China proper. Fear of dismemberment by Japan, Russia, or both provided the impetus for Chinese action. On one front the Chinese sought aid, especially from the United States, but from Germany and Great Britain as well, to counter Russian and Japanese pressures. The basic Chinese plan was to draw the less feared Western countries, those without territorial and political ambitions in Manchuria, into the region, to Balkanize Manchuria as

11. Blakeslee to Greene, September 9, 1907; Greene to McCormick, January 31, 1908; Greene to Straight, May 12, 1908, RSG ms.

12. For the background of the Harbin controversy, see Walter and Mary Scholes, *The Foreign Policies of the Taft Administration* (Columbia, Missouri, 1970), especially 160–63.

a means of preserving Chinese sovereignty. To this end, T'ang Shao-i had approached Roosevelt in 1908, hoping the United States would join in China's efforts to develop Manchuria, and hoping to give the United States a greater stake in a Chinese-controlled Manchuria. Similarly T'ang had interested Straight in plans for Sino-American railroad developments in Manchuria.[13]

On another front, the Chinese attempted to resist imperialist encroachments directly. In December 1907 the management of the Russian-controlled Chinese Eastern Railway established a municipal adminstration for Harbin, a town that had sprung into existence on the railway line, largely as a result of Chinese Eastern operations. The Chinese Viceroy for Manchuria, Hsü Shih-chang, supported by T'ang Shao-i, and Alfred Sao-ke Sze, both American-educated, called upon the Chinese Foreign Office, the Wai-wu Pu, to protest against this Russian usurpation of Chinese sovereignty—the establishment by Russians of a political administrative unit on territory recognized as belonging to China.[14]

The Russian Government rejected the Chinese protest and complained angrily to the Department of State about the apparent collusion between the Chinese and the American Consul in Harbin, Fred Fisher. In a surly memorandum the Russians asked that Fisher be directed to tell the Chinese that the government of the United States "does not wish to meddle in this matter." Careful consideration of the problem in Washington led Secretary of State Elihu Root to conclude that the Russian action in Harbin would provide a dangerous precedent for Japanese as well as Russian infringements upon Chinese sovereignty, to the potential detriment and even exclusion of American interests in Manchuria. At the same time, Root was not eager to antagonize the Russians in an area where American interests were relatively minor—indeed hardly existed. Gently, in April 1908, he assured the Russian Ambassador in Washington of his sympathy for Russian efforts to establish order in Harbin and of his confidence that no problem would arise between Russia and the United States. At the same time, however, Root questioned the basis of the Chinese Eastern's action, denying, as had Fisher, that the

13. Robert Irick, "The Chinchow-Aigun Railroad and the Knox Neutralization Plan in Ch'ing Diplomacy," *Papers on China* (Cambridge, Massachusetts, 1959), XIII, 80–112, and Hunt, *Frontier Defense*, 152–166.

14. Scholes, *Foreign Policies of the Taft Administration*, 160–62; Chang Tao-hsing, *International Controversies over the Chinese Eastern Railway* (Taipei, 1971), 70–74.

business contract the railway company had entered into with the Chinese government granted the right of political administration. Such a claim threatened Chinese sovereignty and was therefore unacceptable to the United States. Root suggested, however, that the Russians might claim the right to administer Harbin on the basis of extraterritorial privileges to which *all* foreigners were entitled by treaty. The formula proposed by Root guaranteed Americans—and all other foreigners—opportunity to share in the administration of Harbin. By internationalizing the municipal administration, it might ease Chinese fears that Russia intended the permanent separation of the region from China.[15]

Root's subtleties were wasted on the Russians who, once noting Japanese acquiescence in their plans, proceeded to establish a municipal administration in Harbin and began to levy taxes on the inhabitants of the town. The Chinese, prodded by the Americans, in turn supported by the British and Germans, protested against the Russian infringement of Chinese sovereignty. Fisher, in Harbin, continued to protest and the Russian government became increasingly irritated by the role of the United States. Within the Far Eastern Division of the Department of State plans for an offensive in Manchuria began to take shape as Willard Straight was ordered home and Roger Greene sent to Harbin. William Phillips, a young foreign service officer who helped to create the Division, assured W. W. Rockhill, the Department's leading authority on East Asia, that the Department wanted to avoid conflict with either Russia or Japan in Manchuria. Nonetheless, it could not concede the Russian demand that Americans yield their extraterritorial privileges in Harbin and on all railway property. Such a blow to China could not easily be tolerated.[16]

Nothing came of the Department of State's plans during 1908 or 1909. Roosevelt and Root opposed ambitious plans in regions remote from vital interests and those functionaries with grander visions were forced to mark time. In Harbin, Greene almost single-handedly tried to hold off the Russians. To his delight, the Standard Oil Company of New York opened an office early in 1909. In those happy days when most of the world's oil was

15. Memorandum from Russian Embassy for Department of State, February 4, 1908, and Secretary of State to Russian Ambassador, April 9, 1908, U. S. Department of State, *Foreign Relations of the United States, 1910* (Washington, 1915), 202–5, hereafter cited as *FRUS*.

16. Memorandum from Russian Embassy for Department of State, June 9, 1908, *FRUS, 1910,* 205–8; Phillips to Rockhill, September 19, 1908, Papers of W.W. Rockhill, Houghton Library, Harvard University.

produced in the United States, Rockefeller's representatives wandered throughout the world, bringing "oil for the lamps of China" and a host of other nations. Standard Oil was precisely the kind of firm Greene wanted to see in Manchuria: aggressive, powerful—ideal for pressing American rights against Russian infringements. Greene urged the company to go all out to support its representative in Harbin, to make clear that Americans had the right to do business there on the same basis as at any treaty port, subject to no Russian restrictions. The time was right for a stand by an American firm and Greene assured Standard Oil that Washington was interested.[17]

Greene, like Fisher, Straight, and so many of his contemporaries, was driven at this time by an assumption of American liberal exceptionalism—the idea, hardly debatable and shared by the Chinese, that a strong American presence, unlike a strong Russian or Japanese presence, would be salutary for China. On the one hand Greene urged American businessmen to come to Manchuria, to compete vigorously for the opportunities there. On the other, he tried to awaken the American government and people as to the meaning of Tsarist oppression—as to what kind of government the Russians would impose on Manchuria if left unchecked. Greene was employed by his government to promote American economic interests—the aim of the consular service to which he had been appointed. But the intensity of his feeling while stationed at Harbin did not derive from a zeal to promote business opportunities for Americans. It came rather from an assumption that such business not only made money for Americans but also halted the extension of Tsarist tyranny and was thus benevolent in its effect on China. When, during the course of the Taft administration, Greene realized that the American government and American business would continue to seek advantage at the expense of the Chinese, the conflict between conscience and duty soured the joy he found in his work.

In May 1909 the general manager of the Chinese Eastern reached a preliminary agreement with the Wai-wu Pu to permit the railroad to establish a municipal government in Harbin while specifically recognizing China's sovereignty over the leased area. The Chinese were satisfied that they had obtained the best terms possible—reassurance as to Chinese sovereignty and an opportunity to participate in the administration of Harbin—and announced the terms of the agreement to the diplomatic corps in Peking. Neither Prince

17. Greene to Lyman, March 20, 1909, RSG ms.

Ch'ing nor any other member of the Wai-wu Pu indicated a willingness to jeopardize the agreement to obtain a role in the administration of Harbin for Americans or any other foreigners. In the months that followed, however, the representatives of Great Britain, Austria, Germany, and the United States urged the Chinese to repudiate the preliminary agreement. They insisted that any regulations for the city of Harbin be drawn up in consultation with the consuls of the various powers represented there. By the end of the year, goaded by the United States and other powers, and angered by the arbitrary proceedings of the Russians, the Chinese announced that the treaty rights of the powers would have to be considered in the framing of municipal regulations for Harbin. Without abrogating the agreement of the previous May, the Chinese took the offensive, protesting not only Russian actions in Harbin, but the whole structure of Russian justifications as well.[18]

The Department of State was pleased to find the Chinese responsive to American wishes. But for Huntington Wilson, William Phillips, and Willard Straight, this moment of satisfaction was only the beginning. No longer would the Chinese or anyone else in East Asia view the United States as a second-rate power, unworthy of being considered in the great affairs of state. Where Rockhill and Hay had failed with their Open Door notes, where Roosevelt had feared to try, the Department was now prepared to assert American power, fight for American interests, and obtain justice for China. The Chinese were presumably responding to American pressure on the Harbin question in recognition of the new role the United States was prepared to play. Underlying the bold new policy of the United States was the conviction that American economic power could be used in lieu of military power to give the United States the controlling hand in East Asia—dollars instead of bullets, or "dollar diplomacy."

For the men back in Washington, Japanese activities in south Manchuria had become the primary focus of activity. Somehow the power the Japanese exercised through the South Manchuria Railway (SMR) had to be curtailed, and Straight came up with a program. Freeing himself of official shackles by resigning from the Department, he returned to China as the representative of a group of American bankers brought together by the Depart-

18. Scholes, *Foreign Policies of the Taft Administration,* 161–62; Rockhill to Secretary of State, enclosure, May 19, 1909, and Fletcher to Secretary of State, enclosure, July 3, 1909, *FRUS, 1910,* 208–13; Sir John Jordan to Sir Edward Grey, January 31, 1910, Great Britain, Foreign Office, 405/195, 26–30, Confidential Prints (microfilm), hereafter cited as FO; Fletcher to Secretary of State, November 11 and December 6, 1909, *FRUS, 1910,* 221.

ment to supply the dollars for dollar diplomacy. In October 1909 he signed a draft agreement with Chinese officials in Manchuria to have the American banking group finance a trans-Manchurian railroad from Chinchow to Aigun. The Chinese had long dreamt of having the United States and Great Britain build such a railroad, giving those countries a stake which would preclude their acquiescence in any Japanese or Russian scheme to take Manchuria away from China. For the United States such a railroad provided an important interest in Manchuria that would require American participation in any decisions the great powers contemplated for the area—a role sought rather than avoided by the Taft administration. To the Japanese and Russians, however, the proposed Chinchow-Aigun railroad posed a threat to vital interests. Straight understood all this and was exhilarated. The Russians could probably be pacified if they were offered a share in the venture. E. H. Harriman had found the Russians interested in his offer to buy the Chinese Eastern, so presumably some arrangement for a detente with the Russians could be devised. The Japanese would then be isolated and forced to bring the source of their power in Manchuria, the SMR, into the system Straight had conceived.[19]

Straight's ideas, modified slightly after Harriman's death, were the foundation of Philander Knox's well-known plan for the internationalization of Manchurian railways. Directed primarily against Japanese expansion, the operation rested heavily upon the success of the United States in winning over Russia, the other major power in Manchuria. And in 1909, as Knox and Straight strove to bring their complicated plans to fruition, they found the United States embroiled in a bitter quarrel with Russia over the municipal administration of Harbin, where Roger Greene held forth.

One historian viewed the record of the following months with near disbelief: "With almost tragic persistence, Washington continued its dispute with Russia over the Harbin municipality." Knox was not unaware of Russian anger. The Russians made no pretense of being polite, either in their protests to Washington about the attitude of Fisher and Greene in Harbin or in Foreign Minister Alexander Izvolski's tirades to the American and British Ambassadors in St. Petersburg. Nor was the Department determined to insist on the principle at stake in Harbin. Early in January 1910, the Acting Secre-

19. Scholes, *Foreign Policies of the Taft Administration,* 148–73; Irick, "The Chinchow-Aigun Railroad . . ."; Hunt, *Frontier Defense,* 177–80, 198; Edward H. Zabriskie, *American-Russian Rivalry in the Far East, 1895–1914* (Philadelphia, 1946), 157.

tary of State informed Rockhill that the railway internationalization plan would resolve the Harbin question, and was more important. Knox was quite ready to retreat, to concede the administration of Harbin to the Chinese Eastern, but apparently hoped to find a way to retreat without being humiliated and embarrassing those nations that had followed the American lead—and whose support might be needed for the internationalization plan. Not only Greene, but Henry Fletcher, the chargé at Peking, Huntington Wilson, assistant secretary of state, Knox himself, and his predecessor, Root, had gone on record in opposition to Russian pretensions in Harbin. The United States had obtained the support of Great Britain, Austria and Germany for its position. It had pushed the Chinese into a confrontation with the Russians on the issue. Repudiation of the American position was a matter of some delicacy, therefore, and Knox's efforts to retreat were complicated by Greene's intransigence.[20]

January 1910 was the first turning point in American policy toward the Chinese Eastern's administration of Harbin. While Wilson, Fletcher, and Greene continued to oppose Russian efforts to control schools or collect taxes or register foreigners in Harbin, Knox was entertaining Russian claims that they were doing nothing more than the Japanese had been doing for years along the SMR. He was grasping at any and all opportunities to end the controversy without appearing to surrender. When the Wai-wu Pu assured Fletcher that the American consul at Harbin would be notified when the municipal regulations were ready, Knox purported to be pleased and cabled Rockhill, in St. Petersburg, to defer any further discussion with Izvolski of American objections. Greene was advised to watch quietly, taking no action without instructions from the Department or the Legation.[21]

Although the British reported that there were only two other Americans with Greene in Harbin, both employed by the Imperial Maritime Customs Service and thus exempt from Russian imposed taxes, Greene stood firm on the principle that the Chinese Eastern could not assume rights of political administration. He insisted that Americans would not pay taxes. He warned the Department that the Russians were attempting to mislead in their claim

20. Vevier, *US and China,* 147; Scholes, *Foreign Policies of the Taft Administration,* 167; A. Nicholson to Grey, December 29, 1909, FO 405/202/11; Wilson to Rockhill, January 3, 1910, *FRUS, 1910,* 226.

21. Wilson to Rockhill, January 3, 1910; Adee to Fletcher, January 5, 1910; Wilson to Fletcher, January 7, 1910; and Knox to Fletcher, February 7, 1910, *FRUS, 1910,* 225–29.

that other foreigners were paying. Many Japanese were not and the Japanese consul-general was not enforcing payment. No Germans were paying and no Frenchmen were paying. But he acknowledged his orders to take no official action. In May, the dreaded instructions came from Knox via the Legation. The Department considered it ''no more than equitable'' that Americans in Harbin pay provisionally at the same rates that Russians and Chinese paid, pending the adoption of satisfactory regulations. Greene immediately cabled directly to the secretary of state strongly opposing the reversal of policy, asking for authority to hold firm until Russia conceded the principle. He argued that once the tax question had been settled, the Russians would have no incentive to revise the regulations and ''recent unsatisfactory administration conditions will probably continue indefinitely.'' He noted that even the French, most closely tied to Russia of any of the powers represented in Harbin, had deferred payment of taxes pending settlement of the principle. Fisher cabled from Mukden with a strong endorsement of Greene's position, but they could not prevent Knox from informing the Russian ambassador of American willingness to pay taxes in Harbin and to meet the Russians half way.[22]

Greene was not through, however. When the Russian consul-general in Harbin called on him to gloat over Greene's defeat, Greene informed him that he had *not* been instructed to require American residents in Harbin to pay taxes. As he explained later to the Legation, he did so, among other reasons, because the Department's telegram ''stated an opinion without giving any instructions.'' In a 21-page letter to the Minister, Greene argued that payment of taxes to a municipal administration established by the Chinese Eastern would be disastrous—a peril to Chinese sovereignty over Harbin. He readily conceded Russian commercial domination of the region and the indifference of American manufacturers to the possibility of a market there, but insisted that the United States had to stand by its rights and oppose the undermining of China's sovereignty. He followed this letter with an analysis of Russian press articles which he found indicating that the ''aggressive party'' in Russia interpreted the reported American reversal on Harbin as a

22. H. E. Sly to Max Müller, March 27, 1910 FO/405/199/135; Greene to Assistant Secretary of State, December 27, 1909, *FRUS, 1910,* 224–25; Greene to Secretary of State, March 24, 1910, State Department Decimal File, 893.102 Harbin/276, hereafter cited as SD; Knox to American Legation, May 24, 1910, SD 893.102 Harbin/281A; Greene to Secretary of State, May 27, 1910, SD 893.102 Harbin/282; Fisher to Secretary of State, May 27, 1910, SD 893.102 Harbin/283.

sign of weakness. The only way to deal with the men shaping Russian policy in the Far East, Greene contended, "is to stand on our rights, as quietly as possible, but uncompromisingly." But from Washington came a cable to the legation: "Make it plain" to Greene that the earlier telegram "was an instruction to be carried out without delay."[23]

Greene was convinced that the surrender of the American position on Chinese sovereignty and foreign treaty rights in Harbin derived from Straight's machinations on behalf of his railroad schemes—and he was not alone. The British Legation in China professed to be astonished by the reversal of American policy and the British were angered by the failure of the United States to consult with them, leaving them out on the limb of opposition to the Russians where Root had urged them only two years before. The British Foreign Minister, Sir Edward Grey, contended that the American treatment of the Harbin question showed "an absence of purpose, coupled with a disregard of us, which cannot be ignored." The British chargé in Peking reported that the diplomatic community there considered the American retreat an attempt by Knox to smooth the way for Straight's negotiations in St. Petersburg on behalf of the Chinchow-Aigun railroad—although the Russian chargé in Peking insisted that the Americans could not have hoped to succeed with so transparent and meaningless a bribe. But the Russians had hinted in February 1910 that they might be more amenable on the Chinchow-Aigun line if the United States ceased to be disagreeable about Harbin. The German Ambassador in Washington, Count J. H. von Bernstorff, reported that Knox admitted conceding the Harbin question in hope of a favorable outcome for Straight's efforts.[24]

The result of American maneuvers in Manchuria was, of course, the Russo-Japanese agreement in July 1910 for a demarcation of their spheres of influence in China—a drawing together of those two powers to defend their interests against the threat of American intrusion. Of all the possible results of the Taft administration's offensive in Manchuria, this was the one most feared by the British, and most likely to occur, in the eyes of experienced

23. William J. Calhoun to Knox, July 5, 1910, SD 893.102 Harbin/290; Greene to Knox, enclosing Greene to Calhoun, June 7, 1910, SD 893.102 Harbin/291; Greene to Secretary of State, June 27, 1910, SD 893.102 Harbin/295; Wilson to Calhoun, July 6, 1910, SD 893.102 Harbin/290.

24. Greene to Nelson T. Johnson, July 4, 1910, RSG ms; Sir Edward Grey to James Bryce, September 22, 1910, FO 405/200/142–43; British Legation Annual Report for 1910, dated March 5, 1911, FO 405/201, 107; Scholes, *Foreign Policies of the Taft Administration,* 183.

students of East Asian affairs. Knox's decision to yield on Harbin may have been a desperate effort to stave off the Russo-Japanese accord, rumored several weeks before it was consummated.

But Greene had still not surrendered. Throughout the summer of 1910, he continued his argument with the Legation at Peking and continued to be offensive to his Russian colleague at Harbin. E. T. Williams wrote to explain the Department's view to Rockhill in Russia, confessing that the United States had been "just a bit too literal and too logical" on the Harbin question, and sanctioning more "flexibility", a treating of such questions "in a practical way." Lewis Einstein, the new First Secretary at Peking, tried to explain the virtues of "realism" to Greene. He advised Greene to follow the Department's instructions "literally and without interpretation," but for a while Greene preferred to court dismissal rather than obey instructions contrary to his principles. Curiously, instead of the "order of the boot" he anticipated, and in face of his threat to resign, the Department indicated regret at his embarrassment in Harbin, offering to transfer *and* promote him. Despite his obstreperousness, word came from the Legation that "your work is simply splendid and the Legation's only regret is that all our consuls in China do not more closely approximate the standard fixed by you."[25]

The Harbin dispute continued without Greene and in modified form for several more years, with the British fighting a rear guard action until after the beginning of World War I. In December 1914, an agreement was reached between Russia and Great Britain, to which Denmark, France, Italy, Japan, Spain, and Belgium adhered. The United States, having once surrendered the substance of the dispute, and conceding the Russian right to set up a municipal administration and to tax foreign residents toward its support, remained "a notable exception."[26]

The story of the Harbin dispute reinforces the existing assumption of the incompetence of the Taft administration in its efforts to have the United States assert itself in East Asia. It demonstrates the separate standard of behavior which that administration reserved for itself in foreign affairs. While decrying the inadequacy of the support it was receiving for its railway

25. Calhoun to Knox, September 9, 1910, SD 893.102H/298; Williams to Rockhill, June 7, 1910, Rockhill ms; Einstein to Greene, July 10, September 10, and October 11, 1910, Greene to Gordon Paddock, July 9, 1910, Heintzleman to Greene, December 6, 1910, RSG ms.

26. Chang, *International Controversies Over the Chinese Eastern,* 78.

schemes in Manchuria, it abandoned its position on Harbin without warning or apology to the nations that had followed the American lead on that issue. And, however much a "realist" might applaud the willingness to sacrifice the principles at stake at Harbin for a more important cause, no one today and few diplomats at the time, foreign or American, considered the Taft-Knox-Straight plan for Manchuria realistic. The British in particular considered it silly at best and dangerous to the interests of all but the Russians and Japanese who they early warned would be driven together. The action of the Department of State, tolerating and even rewarding Greene's disobedience, suggests that having failed to appease the Russians with Harbin, the Department developed reservations of its own about the wisdom of its course.

Of Greene, the incident is perhaps more revealing. If a diplomat is "an honest man sent abroad to lie for his country," he demonstrated himself to be a less than willing or committed diplomat. Convinced of the correctness of the policy he was sent to Harbin to defend, the lowly consul chose to defy his own government when visions of grand triumphs enticed the men in Washington away from their inherited faith. Forced to yield on the issue, after higher authorities had yielded repeatedly at Washington, St. Petersburg, and Peking, he submitted his resignation—and found himself vindicated, answered with promotion instead of reprimand or "the boot." And yet, if this was a triumph for conscience, is it possible that, as Lewis Einstein argued, the problem was not that important; that there was too little at stake for a man to choose the Harbin question as one on which to make a stand for conscience? Whatever the historian may think, Roger Greene made his first stand against his superiors on the Harbin issue in 1910. He lost on the policy at issue and was hurt and angry for months. But the failure of Straight's schemes, to which Harbin had been sacrificed, the demonstration of his own courage, and the consolations and rewards that followed, left him with a sense of triumph, conviction in his judgment, and all the delights of a clear conscience.

From Harbin, Greene was sent to Hankow as consul-general, arriving late in the summer of 1911—in time to witness the opening shots of the Chinese Revolution. Racing to the scene of the conflict, he recognized the seriousness of the uprising at Wuchang and saw to the evacuation of American missionaries and their students. Gratefully the missionaries described his assignment to Hankow as "nothing less than providential." As he watched events unfold, looked after Americans and their interests, and analyzed developments for the Legation and for Washington, praise for his performance came from a wide variety of Americans. Among the Chinese he was reported to be the only consul in Hankow who remained genuinely neutral, treating revolutionists and Imperialists with equal courtesy.[27]

All were agreed that Greene was an excellent consular official and Nelson T. Johnson, who served under him at Harbin and Hankow, credited Greene for much of his own subsequent success. Greene's scholarly ways deeply impressed the younger man. He had a mind such as Johnson had never encountered before, "and he . . . inspired me, because everything that he came to, he learned something about." It was under Greene, Johnson claimed, "that I discovered that a consular officer, a foreign service officer, if he was going to perform his work efficiently, had to be a kind of walking encyclopedia, and know something about everything that went on around him."[28]

Praise from superiors and peers, reinforced by the adulation of his subordinates, strengthened Greene's determination to be guided by his own judgment. When the British, Russian, and German governments attempted to extend their concessions in Hankow, allegedly to defend their nationals during the revolution, Greene denied the need and prodded the American Legation to support the Chinese. When Americans in China intervened in Chinese politics, he opposed them indignantly, arguing that they were playing a game in which they, protected by extraterritoriality, had nothing to lose, while the Chinese had not only their property but their lives at stake. He insisted that few foreigners were close enough to the Chinese people, or sufficiently experienced in political affairs, to advise wisely. If they felt so deeply interested in China's future "that they must participate in its political life, let them lay aside the privileges they enjoy as foreigners and become naturalized citizens . . . then they can join in the game fairly and honestly, if they will." Throughout this first stage of the revolution, he insisted that there be no foreign interference, that the Chinese be allowed to work out their own solution.[29]

The policies of his government also came under attack, especially the

27. S. H. Littell to Greene, October 14, 1911; E. T. Williams to Greene, November 6, 1911; F. D. Cheshire to Greene, November 16, 1911; Straight to Greene, February 23, 1912; Einstein to Greene, June 11, 1912, RSG ms.

28. Nelson T. Johnson, Oral History Collection, Columbia University, 257.

29. Greene to Legation, October 23, 1911, SD 893.102 Hankow/-; Greene to Williams, November 2, 1911, SD 893.00/834; Greene to Williams, enclosure, July 25, 1913, SD 893.00/1845.

Taft administration's refusal to grant recognition to the Chinese Republic. Greene, close to the center of the revolutionists' strength, harbored no illusions about them. Opposition to the Manchus was widespread and apparent, but the revolutionists were disorganized and poorly disciplined. He found that the people's interest in the revolutionary cause was generally overestimated. Although he did not believe a Manchu restoration likely, by mid-December he considered a restoration of government authority an easy matter in Hunan and Hupei, given one or two more victories by Imperialist forces. But after Yüan Shih-k'ai had demonstrated his power to the revolutionaries, manipulated the abdication of the Manchus, managed to have himself selected as President of the Republic of China, Greene saw no reason to delay recognition. Throughout the spring and early summer of 1912 he called for early action by the United States.[30]

His call for recognition of the Chinese government focused principally on the double standard the great powers were applying. Having exceeded the limits of proper diplomatic behavior, interfering to prevent the Chinese from finishing their war and perhaps leaving one side firmly in command, the powers were now being extraordinarily legalistic about the conditions for recognition. He noted the promptness with which the United States had recognized the Republic of Panama—not because its government had demonstrated control of its territory or an ability to meet its obligations, but because it suited American ends. With the fighting over in China, a coalition government in existence, why wait any longer? How could the United States continue demanding that local authorities provide protection for American interests and refuse recognition in the absence of conflict? Greene insisted that the Chinese deserved great credit for their success in protecting foreigners and their interests during the revolution. He feared that continued withholding of recognition would weaken the government, conceivably leading to renewed civil war.[31]

Unable to achieve his ends in correspondence with middle echelon officials, Greene turned to the American Minister in Peking, reporting on a variety of problems for Americans in China that he attributed to the failure of the United States to recognize the Republic of China. Acknowledging the existence of "weighty reasons" for delay, he expressed hope that recogni-

30. Greene to Calhoun, January 20, 1912, SD 893.00/1122, and December 18, 1911, SD 893.00/953.

31. Greene to Williams, April 17, 1912, to Einstein, June 11, 1912, RSG ms.

tion would come soon. He noted the absence of other claimants to supreme power and the inconsistency of having representatives of the Six Power Banking Consortium negotiate with Yüan while their governments withheld recognition from him. But Greene's campaign failed, and it required another year and another administration before the United States recognized the government of the Republic of China. By then, the unrest he feared had begun as the opposition to Yüan Shih-k'ai's rule was encouraged by his inability to obtain the blessings of the powers.[32]

The Consortium's negotiations with China also irritated Greene. His experience with the workings of dollar diplomacy in Manchuria had left him skeptical of this approach. Not even Straight's praise of his work at Hankow during the revolution changed his low regard for Straight's judgment. Greene mistrusted the efforts of the Consortium to monopolize loans to China, and worried about the additional conditions Consortium representatives tried to impose on Yüan with each installment of the loan. In general he held his government responsible, rather than the bankers it sent forth as its agents.[33]

Greene's discontent mounted in 1913 and another failure to have his advice heeded led to a second offer to resign—a second show-down with the Department and a second vindication, with offer of promotion. During the outbreak of hostilities in China in July 1913, a Kuomintang-led uprising in the south, Greene requested that a military guard be sent to Kuling to protect about 1,000 foreigners—mostly American women and children on summer vacation. Many of the women were reported pregnant and not easily moved. But the American and British admirals responsible for the deployment of forces in the area refused, insisting that the people Greene sought to protect come to the coast instead. Greene was infuriated, deeply worried about the numbers of deserters and stragglers reportedly converging on Kuling. He demanded that the Legation go to Washington, over the American admiral's head. Otherwise he could not be responsible for the safety of the Americans at Kuling and would be obliged to resign. Angrily, he argued that if American sailors could be used at Chapei, "practically to interfere in a conflict between the Government and a band of rebels," there could be no objection to using them to protect American lives at Kuling. E. T. Williams, American

32. Greene to Calhoun, June 25, 1912, SD 893.00/1422.

33. Greene to Williams, March 26, 1912, RSG ms.

chargé at Peking, cabled Washington immediately, concurring with Greene, but first withholding and then asking the Department to ignore his statement of intent to resign, contending that "the Consular Service cannot afford to lose so efficient a member."[34]

Williams wrote personally to Greene, urging him not to resign. He recognized that Greene was upset by his difficulties with the Navy, with the Department's failure to promote Nelson Johnson, and with poor pay. He agreed with Greene on all points, but the former missionary appealed to the misionary's son's sense of duty—the service needed him. Two months later, when Williams learned he was to become Chief of the Division of Far Eastern Affairs, he asked Greene if he would serve as Assistant Chief—an opportunity that pleased Greene, despite the salary reduction it might involve. But the death of Greene's father, further disillusionment with his government's role in China, and other more promising opportunities for service intervened.[35]

Michael Hunt has scraped away the coating of altruism generally spread over the American remission of the Boxer indemnity, noting that remission was not an act of generosity but derived from American claims that were originally excessive. Toward the close of 1913, Greene was horrified to find the government of the United States backing its nationals in a myriad of preposterous claims for damages incurred during the Chinese revolution. Expressing his outrage to the new American Minister, Paul Reinsch, Greene argued that the United States was supporting claims on the basis of principles that "would not be accepted by any of the great nations of the world as binding in international law between themselves." The secrecy of the report of the claims commission established by the diplomatic body in Peking he considered tantamount to a "confession that the policy it embodies is unjustifiable in international law." Contending that the American government had not in the past, during its civil war, nor would ever in the future consider paying claims such as China was being asked to indemnify, he insisted that the same standard be applied to China. Disgusted with the American position, Greene wrote that "there seems something pitifully small in the great nations of the world demanding of China in her present impoverished state

34. Williams to Secretary of State, enclosures, July 29, 1913, SD 893.00/1831; Greene to Williams, August 4, 1913, SD 893.00/1902.

35. Williams to Greene, July 31 and September 26, 1913, Greene to Williams, October 1, 1913, RSG ms.

that she give out of her poverty what we would never dream of giving out of our easy wealth." Arguments that the United States had to cooperate with the other powers, stand with them in hope of restraining them, he dismissed contemptuously. Solidarity with the powers had put no limit on their demands—the United States should do what was right.[36]

Reinsch forwarded Greene's criticism to Washington, but misrepresented him as contending the Chinese had "no" liability, and then went on to dissent from that fictitious position. To Greene he explained that purely legal principles did not suffice, for the Chinese "voluntarily" accepted broad liability. In addition, Reinsch explained that he could not ask American citizens to take less than other nationals. Nonetheless, he conceded that some of the items that had upset Greene were unfair and that he had asked the Department to authorize him to stress direct claims. Ultimately, the Department of State authorized Reinsch to press for direct claims only, dropping the others, provided he stood by the other powers—and Greene may have felt some sense of satisfaction at finding that his efforts were not wholly in vain.[37]

While Greene waited for word from Washington as to whether he would be appointed the assistant to Williams, decisions were being made in New York that led to the end of his career as a diplomat, providing an alternative and, for years, more satisfying form of service. In May 1913, the Rockefeller Foundation had been incorporated and Frederick T. Gates, adviser to John D. Rockefeller for philanthropic concerns, was eager to introduce modern medicine into China. The Harvard Medical School of China appealed to the Foundation for money and one of the trustees, Jerome D. Greene, was very much interested in both East Asia and Harvard. He was also an older brother of Roger S. Greene. But although Jerome Greene supported the medical project in China, he was not responsible for the Foundation's decision to approach Roger to join in its work. Indeed Jerome, sensitive to the issue of nepotism, was the only trustee to object to inviting Roger Greene to participate. The initial suggestion had come from President Charles W. Eliot of Harvard and was warmly seconded by John D. Rocke-

36. Michael H. Hunt, "The American Remission of the Boxer Indemnity: A Reappraisal," *Journal of Asian Studies,* XXXI (May 1972), 539–59; Greene to Reinsch, December 6, 1913, *FRUS, 1914,* 81–84.

37. Reinsch to Greene, December 31, 1913, to Secretary of State, January 2, 1914. Secretary of State to Reinsch, February 14, 1914, *FRUS, 1914,* 84–86, 89.

feller, Jr. As a result, when the Foundation created a China Medical Commission to study conditions in China, Roger Greene was asked to serve as one of its three members, as its specialist on China.[38]

The offer from the Rockefeller Foundation was most attractive, carrying a salary considerably higher than that of a consul-general and a promise of permanent association with the work of the Foundation. Jerome Greene, overcoming his reservations, made it difficult for his brother to decline by tying the Foundation's work in China to their late father's vision of an international institute for general education in East Asia—a dream of a great university to facilitate the modernization of China and Japan. Moreover, Jerome wrote, "your enlistment with me in an enterprise having such vast capabilities and such immediate certainties of influence in humanitarian directions, would be a consummation immensely gratifiying to Father had he lived. I hope you will consider the matter partly in this light, for it seems to me that the Foundation offers a real opportunity for a continuation of the missionary tradition to the fourth generation of our family."[39]

Thirty-three years old, Greene realized he was making a decision that would probably determine his identity, launch him on the path he would follow the rest of his life—and he vacillated. He was irritated with the Department of State for its delay in deciding whether to call him to Washington as Williams' assistant, and bored with some of the bureaucratic ledgerdemain of his consular duties. Moreover, he was disturbed by the "narrowing effect" of the consular service "with its unnatural emphasis on nationality." His interest in relations between East and West reconciled him to his work in East Asia, but he saw the possibility of the Rockefeller Foundation's proposal allowing him to develop this interest further, along more direct and practical lines, without "the break in the continuity of my life that I want to avoid." Yet he also felt a sense of commitment to the service, to E. T. Williams in particular. He felt guilty about leaving before he had mastered his position, before he had gotten his office in order—though Jerome sent a copy of a letter he had received from Williams, assuring him there would be no dishonor if Roger joined the Rockefeller Foundation. But Williams also urged that Roger Greene stay with the service, insisting "he is

38. Mary E. Ferguson, *China Medical Board and Peking Union Medical College* (New York, 1970), 13–18; Jerome to Roger Greene, February 16, 1914, RSG ms.

39. Jerome Greene to Roger Greene, February 25, 1914, and Roger Greene to Reinsch, February 26, 1914, RSG ms.

one of the best men we have anywhere.'' From Peking Reinsch wrote to ask Greene to stay with the Department, insisting that he was needed, that he had ''an enviable record as a consular officer,'' that his work was ''appreciated most highly, not only by the Legation but by the Department.''[40]

To be needed, to be *the* man, perhaps the only man, for a job—could there be a moment more gratifying in a man's life?—and Roger Greene was being called twice, toward two lines of service, two missions at the same time. Finally, the Department of State offered him a temporary respite from his dilemma by offering him a leave of absence for an indefinite period to work with the China Medical Commission. In April 1914, he joined Harry Pratt Judson, President of the University of Chicago, and Dr. Francis Weld Peabody on a four month tour of medical facilities in China.[41]

The choice of careers, however, could no longer be delayed. In July, the Department of State made its bid to retain Greene by promoting him to the post of Consul General at Large for the Far East, responsible for the supervision and inspection of all consulates in the region. For an administration that had become notorious for impeding the process of developing a professional foreign service by filling posts with ''deserving Democrats,'' Democrats hungry for patronage after sixteen years out of power, the appointment of Greene, whose original sponsors were Republicans, came as a surprise. The *Philadelphia Record* expressed its approval editorially, praising President Wilson for ''showing his entire accord with the principles of the merit system.'' The *Record* considered Greene to be admirably qualified, with long experience and excellent performance, ''but he is without political backing, and there were strong influences in support of Democrats for this appointment.'' Happily, ''the good of the service and not the reward of a useful member of the Democratic party moved the President.''[42]

Greene, however, was enjoying his work with the Commission and ambivalent about the attractions of the newly proffered post. To a former subordinate he wrote that he would rather stay in China if he remained in the service. To his brother Jerome, he explained the attractions of the Department's appointment, but largely as a means of eliciting a definite offer from the Rockefeller Foundation—a prerequisite to declining the appointment.

40. Jerome Greene to Roger Greene, February 26, 1914; Roger to Jerome Greene, March 1, 1914; Reinsch to Greene, March 4, 1914; Greene to Reinsch, March 10, 1914, RSG ms.

41. Ferguson, *CMB and PUMC,* 18–21.

42. Editorial note, *Philadelphia Record,* July 28, 1914, RSG ms.

Jerome assured him that the original invitation had been for a permanent position and that Judson's "enthusiastic report of your ability and personality leaves no doubt about your future with the Foundation." And so, Roger Greene resigned from the service of his government, hoping to fulfill his mission in the philanthropic work of the Rockefeller Foundation in China.[43]

The coming of war in Europe caused a twinge of conscience in Roger Greene. He wondered if the needs of his country required him to postpone his resignation from the Department of State. But Secretary Bryan had made other provisions for filling the Consul General at Large post and Greene was free to concentrate his efforts on the work of the Rockefeller Foundation's newly created China Medical Board, of which he was appointed Resident Director in China. He busied himself especially with plans for the development of Peking Union Medical College, starting with the facilities of an old missionary medical school purchased by the Board. After a few months in the United States participating in plans for the new operation, he returned to China to begin his new life in Peking.[44]

Greene was 34, a bachelor with a successful past and an extraordinarily promising future. He was eligible, and the ladies of good family who passed through Peking pursued him. They found him aloof, serious, unable to return their overtures. To one young woman who wrote a moving, mystical letter offering him friendship, he replied with an unflattering self-portrait:

> I wish that we might be friends indeed. Real friends are not so common in this world, but I fear that when you come to see the reality, an old-young man, who has never really done anything or created anything in his more than ten years of grown-up life, and yet lacks the freshness and vigor which a man should have when he is about to embark on his real life's work, you should not think me worthy of such a friendship as I believe you meant to offer. In fact I sometimes wonder whether real blood runs in my veins. . . .

Unlike his situation in Rio de Janeiro, finances were not an obstacle to high living, but he could not become, as one young lady begged, a little more frivolous. Instead, he studied Chinese for an hour every morning with a tutor, and for another hour every afternoon. For diversion he skated at the Peking Club, where his companions were generally missionaries or Chinese

43. Greene to Jameson, August 2, 1914; to Jerome Greene, August 4, 1914; Jerome to Roger Greene, August 6, 1914, RSG ms.

44. Roger to Jerome Greene, undated, RSG ms.

returned from studying abroad. Apart from the American Legation, with which he was very close, he found the Legation quarter revelers unappealing, and preferred the company of missionaries to that of diplomats.[45]

Despite the obvious comfort he felt among missionaries and the apparent sharing of values, Greene had serious reservations about their role in China—particularly within the scope of his work for the Rockefellers. He was uneasy about "sectarian medicine," disturbed because he found "the more old-fashioned" missionaries impatient with demands for better trained personnel and better equipment in the missionary hospitals: "they justify education, medical work, etc. merely as baits to catch the people so they can be preached to." He found others, more broad-minded, apparently gaining the upper hand within the missionary movement. But even they were often "afraid that their constituencies at home are not ready for such strong meat as the theory that missionaries are justified in teaching schools and healing the sick without any ulterior motive, however high, but merely because they want to help the people in that way. . . ."[46]

John D. Rockefeller, Jr., as Chairman of the China Medical Board, did not share Greene's reservations. His advisor, Frederick Gates, saw the Board's work as an extension of the work of Christian missions, and Rockefeller was personally committed to maintaining the Christian character of any institutions built by the Board. In 1915 he wrote to all of the American missionary organizations involved in medical work in China, telling them of the China Medical Board and its intended role—and assuring them that in choosing personnel for any institutions that came out of the Board's work, they would select only persons "sympathetic with the missionary spirit and motive." Greene was aware of the attitudes of Gates and Rockefeller, but apparently underestimated the depth of the latter's conviction while assuming correctly that the quality of the Board's work would not be adversely affected. A confrontation over the Christian character of Peking Union Medical College was far in the future.[47]

Greene clearly saw missionaries coming in two varieties: modernists who came primarily to help the Chinese people—as his father had the people of Japan—and "old fashioned" types, coming to save the heathen Chinee.

45. Greene to Miss R——, October 16, 1915; to "Peabo" (probably Francis Peabody), January 26, 1916, RSG ms.

46. Greene to Family, March 9, 1916, RSG ms.

47. Ferguson, *CMB and PUMC*, 22–23.

He wanted no part of the latter. This atittude reflected Greene's acceptance of the Chinese as a people with legitimate traditions and national aspirations of their own. He respected Chinese pride even as he came to give help. Both he and Dr. Wallace Buttrick, who directed the Board's work in New York, were very careful to avoid indications that they were preparing their program in China because the Chinese were desperate, in *need* of help. They wanted to avoid offending Chinese sensibilities. Greene perceived the old-style missionaries, with their implicit contempt for the Chinese, as poor instruments for this approach. He went further and argued that missionaries coming to China from the United States could learn a great deal about international and interracial relationships. To Robert Speer, a leader in the mission movement, Greene contended that Americans should no longer limit themselves to the goal of social justice for all within the United States, "but we shall also have to consider whether the peasant in China should not have as square a deal as the farmer at home, and an equal share of the good things of this world." This was the lesson he wanted Speer's emissary to Peking to learn and bring back to the United States.[48]

Similar thoughts dotted his writings on a variety of subjects. To an old friend in Harbin he indicated his preference for his new philanthropic work over his earlier consular duties, declaring his skepticism about the value of "national commercial propaganda," of efforts to promote American trade. He had come to believe that such efforts were founded on a "very vicious principle," which he considered largely to blame for the war in Europe. The nationalist approach angered him again when consular officials tried to force Peking Union Medical College and mission hospitals to use only Americans as head pharmacists. Deliberate nationalist bias troubled him, as did interference and involvement in Chinese affairs based on ignorance and condescension. When a bank with which his brother Jerome was affiliated lent money to the Chinese government amidst internal strife, he did not hesitate to berate Jerome. He did not share the widespread admiration for the Imperial Maritime Customs Service. Indeed, he charged it with being corrupt and paying excessive salaries to lazy foreigners. Greene was convinced that the Chinese could run their own customs service and do it cheaper, yet they were not being trained for responsible positions within the service.[49]

48. Greene to Rev. Robert W. Speer, October 20, 1917, RSG ms.

49. Greene to Jacques Klemantaski, February 2, 1916, RSG ms; Greene to Nelson Johnson, December 21, 1922, SD 893.1283/28; Roger to Jerome Greene, May 18, 1916, to Family, April 3, 1917, RSG ms.

And as Japan's role in China changed in the second decade of the twentieth century, Greene's attitude toward the land of his childhood changed also. Japanese economic hegemony in Manchuria had not troubled him as he watched it develop from Dairen and Harbin. Beginning with no hostilities toward the Japanese, experiencing first-hand the apathy and incompetence of American businessmen, he concluded that the Japanese were dominating the market because it was important to them and they were therefore willing to work hard for it. His views did not prevent Knox, Straight, and their followers from assaulting the Japanese position in Manchuria—an assault which did much to bring about the Japanese-American estrangement that endured through World War II. It was not the arguments of Knox or Straight, but rather overt Japanese imperialism, beginning with the annexation of Korea, that altered his view of Japan.[50]

By 1911 Greene was worried about the possibility of Manchuria also being annexed by Japan. He believed the United States could and should prevent such an occurrence. Like many of his contemporaries, including Knox, he perceived an alternative between war and appeasement—apparently one based on world public opinion, which the Chinese could organize effectively if they could conciliate the British. Japan's notorious 21 Demands on China, in 1915, troubled him further. Again, he thought reasoned diplomacy and appeals to Japanese and world public opinion might help. But he did not want the American government to scold the Japanese government when it seemed "unlikely that any very effective steps can be taken against Japanese aggression." He did not think American interests justified taking a strong stand and he suspected friendly measures were more likely to bear fruit. Most of all, he believed it important for third parties to avoid involvement.[51]

Greene's hopes for containing Japanese aggression never came to anything, despite modest encouragement from Williams at the Far East desk of the Department of State. Slowly he tried to reeducate his family and friends. As a critical friend of Japan he found himself hopelessly in a minority between those bitterly anti-Japanese and those uncritically pro-Japanese. Basically, he felt that Japan's policies were unjust to China, short-sighted from the standpoint of Japanese interest, but not so different from the policies of the United States and Europe to justify considering Japan a pariah. He could

50. Greene to Nelson Johnson, August 30, 1910 RSG ms.

51. Greene to Heintzleman, March 9, 1911; to E. T. Williams, March 18, 1915; to Bishop Logan Roots, March 18, 1915, RSG ms.

apologize for Japanese discrimination against American mission schools in Korea on the grounds that they were subversive; that they were teaching the Koreans their own language in an atmosphere of American liberal ideas—in opposition to the Japanese policy of attempting to assimilate the Korean people. He insisted that "China had herself largely to blame for her troubles, since she is often unreasonable in her dealings with foreign powers." He could continue to insist that the extension of Japanese influence in China could be salutary for the Chinese and benefit rather than hurt American economic interests. But he would not accept his brother Jerome's conception of Japanese self-restraint. He would not surrender the conviction that Japan was doing a great injustice to China, was more dangerous to China during and immediately after World War I than any other nation, and that the friends of Japan should not defend the actions of the Japanese government.[52]

Japan was not the only source of Chinese misery during the years of World War I. In the autumn, 1917, shortly after the cornerstone of Peking Union Medical College's first new building was laid, the traditional twin scourges of flood and famine struck heavy blows on North China. The American Red Cross, though heavily committed to war relief, found $200,000 for China. In the same telegram in which the availability of funds was announced, the Red Cross asked the secretary of state to designate Roger Greene as its representative, responsible for administering relief with the advice of the American Minister in Peking. Greene accepted the appointment and devoted the next four months to the most urgent need he perceived: the employment of homeless, starving Chinese on public works. Like an early version of Harry Hopkins, Greene set the Chinese to work building roads. Unlike Harry Hopkins, he returned the last $75,000 provided by the Red Cross, indicating that no new projects were advisable.[53]

Once again there was fulsome praise in China and the United States for Roger Greene and once again he felt inadequate to the praise. He was disturbed by the corruption and inefficiency he had witnessed, among Americans as well as Chinese. He had neglected his work with the China Medical

52. Williams to Greene, March 19, 1915; Roger to E. B. Greene, August 15, 1915; to Jerome Greene, September 21, 1916; to Family, January 14 and April 3, 1917; to M. F. Denton, December 16, 1919, RSG ms.

53. W. Frank Persons to Secretary of State, October 5, 1917, SD 893.48/68; Reinsch to Greene, October 8, 1917, RSG ms; *New York Times,* October 10, 1917, p. 10; Greene to Persons, October 29, 1917, SD 893.48/76; Persons to Secretary of State, November 1, 1917, SD 893.48/78.

Board and most of all, when he thought of the war in Europe, "of the splendid activity of so many men in Europe and at home, I feel ashamed that I have not risen to the occasion more adequately." To do his share, he registered for the draft, offered himself for work in Siberia, and served the Legation as a Russian expert.[54]

In July 1918, as the United States prepared to intervene in Siberia, ostensibly to rescue Czechs eager to fight the Germans, J. V. A. MacMurray at the Legation in Peking cabled the secretary of state to advise him of Greene's availability for use by the American command in its dealing with both Japanese and Russians. Few, if any, Americans matched his language competence and MacMurray declared that in view of his "long experience and exceptional ability and character . . . his assignment to such duty would be of the utmost value in furthering cooperation and eliminating possible friction." The Legation's idea for utilizing Greene's skills was not picked up in Washington, and a few months later the American Ambassador to Japan, Roland Morris, asked Greene if he would be willing to serve on a council to oversee temporarily the Trans-Siberian and Chinese Eastern railways. Morris was profoundly concerned over mounting friction between the United States and Japan and worried about the hostility of the American railway men toward the Japanese. He apparently saw Greene as the man for the job and Greene was attracted to it. The position Morris outlined was one for which he was well suited and the idea of playing the role of pacifier in an international operation including Japan, China, Russia, France, Great Britain, and the United States had great appeal. Success might well mean lasting peace in East Asia.[55]

Greene went to Washington early in 1919 to discuss the position Morris had outlined with the Department of State. He found that position no longer available, but William Phillips, now First Assistant Secretary of State, urged him to stay with the Department in the Division of Far Eastern Affairs. He was tempted, not only out of a genuine sense of duty, but also perhaps because of more mundane conditions of job insecurity. Brother Jerome had become involved in a power struggle within the Rockefeller Foundation and had lost, forced subsequently to sever most of his connections with Rockefeller enterprises. Would these frictions ultimately drive the younger brother

54. Greene to Dr. Wallace Buttrick, April 19, 1918, RSG ms.

55. J. V. A. MacMurray to Secretary of State, July 22, 1918, SD 861.00/2314; Greene to Dr. Henry Houghton, January 16 and 20, 1919, RSG ms.

out as well? Once again, the trustees of the Foundation expressed a decided determination to keep Roger Greene with the China Medical Board, explaining to Phillips that his work for the Board was of greater importance than the work for which Phillips needed him. Having yielded the services of Willard Straight to J. P. Morgan and the American Group a decade earlier, Phillips was apparently amenable to the request of the Rockefeller Foundation.[56]

Having decided that he could serve best by remaining with the China Medical Board, Greene wrote a long letter to Phillips recommending a new course for American policy toward the Bolsheviks. In the process he offered a devastating critique of the policy the Wilson administration had pursued. Indicating an awareness that Wilson's policy had been modified because of a perceived need to defer to Britain and France, he still questioned the taking of sides between factions in the Russian revolution—was this not a complete departure from traditional diplomatic practice? Extreme as the radicals were, despite their withdrawal from the war, wouldn't it have been better to have remained aloof so long as the outcome of the struggle was in doubt, dealing frankly with the Soviet government as the de facto government in the areas they controlled? Greene contended that the American government was too inclined to view the conflict from the point of view of Russian elites, "without sufficient understanding of the situation of the peasant and the workman, and is it not unfortunate that we now find ourselves ranged on the side of the relics of the old bureaucracy and military machine?" The Russian masses, he explained, yearned for decent, orderly government, but could not be expected to trust Horvath and Kolchak, the representatives of the old regime in whom the United States seemed interested. If his experiences in China had taught him the value of impartiality in revolutionary situations, his experience in Russia left him feeling that the Russian peasant had good reason to mistrust the conservatives: "I certainly felt very rarely that I could attach any importance to the unsupported word of a Russian general, diplomat or ordinary civil servant."[57]

Greene, the Rockefellers' man in Peking, might have astonished the Bolsheviks by his sympathy for their cause. He noted that some of the Soviet leaders had personally experienced "some of the less successful features of the Anglo-Saxon democratic regime, as exemplified in the east sides of London and New York." He recalled that even bourgeois Russians had en-

56. Greene to Houghton, March 4, 1919, RSG ms.

57. Greene to Phillips, March 7, 1919, RSG ms.

joyed Upton Sinclair's *The Jungle* and were convinced something was wrong with capitalism. "Can we blame the Soviets," he asked, "for groping towards something different in the hope that it may prove to be better?" He argued that the military interventions were increasing Bolshevik use of violence and concluded by demanding to know if the government knew "what those American boys who are still fighting in Russia are dying for, and is it a consistent policy that we can and will fight through to the end?" Greene's hope was that the United States would withdraw its forces and come to terms with Soviet leaders.[58]

Phillips responded politely, perfunctorily, welcoming Greene's views, but disagreed about the possibility of coming to terms with Lenin and his colleagues. A few weeks later, his conscience tormented by a letter from Jerome, Roger Greene wrote again to Phillips, convinced "that it is my duty to offer my services to the Department. It is the only thing the government has asked me to do in this crisis when other men have sacrificed so much, and I want to respond." He volunteered for a place in Russian affairs at a substantial reduction from his salary with the China Medical Board. Phillips expressed his appreciation for Greene's spirit, but "there does not seem to exist, however, in the Russian Division quite the same need of additional help which confronted us a little while ago." And so Roger Greene was free to return to China, to serve as Resident Director of the China Medical Board.[59]

In Peking, Greene enjoyed an unusual status derived in large part from his position with the China Medical Board and association with the Rockefeller name, but also stemming from his outstanding reputation with the Department of State, and his missionary parentage. His position with the Board guaranteed a prominent role in community affairs, a place on the councils of churches, schools, and the usual civic associations. As one of the most important Americans in Peking, he had a place at the American Minister's table whenever countrymen of note were passing through. Presiding over the work of Peking Union Medical College, he was in frequent contact with Chinese government authorities, Chinese educators, and the Chinese intellectual elite of Peking. When he was in New York or Washington

58. *Ibid.*
59. Phillips to Greene, March 17, 1919; Greene to Phillips, April 2, 1919; and Phillips to Greene, April 8, 1919, RSG ms.

he was assured of an audience with or on behalf of the powerful men with whom he was associated in the Rockefeller Foundation. His years in the consular service provided him with another range of contacts through the middle echelons of the Department of State. Three chiefs of the Division of Far Eastern Affairs, from 1914 to the late 1920s—E. T. Williams, J. V. A. MacMurray, and Nelson T. Johnson—had worked with him in China and were on record in praise of his ability, judgment, and character. MacMurray was Minister to China from 1925 to 1929 and was replaced by Johnson, who headed the Legation, then Embassy, until 1940. These were men to whom he had unusual access and through whom he came to know and have access to other diplomats. Finally, the fact that his parents had been missionaries, combined with the staid ways that led him to enjoy missionaries as social companions, kept him in touch with the missionary movement in China and its administrators back in the United States. In the years that followed, his past and present reinforced each other, leaving him with an incredible web of contacts in the small world of people concerned with the affairs of East Asia. His contacts provided him with extraordinary opportunities for making his opinion on these affairs known to the interested American public and especially to the few who determined American policy.

2

# THOMAS W. LAMONT DISCOVERS EAST ASIA

WHEN, after World War II, Thomas Lamont looked back to his boyhood in the 1870s, he remembered lean, hard years in a parsonage. Like Roger Greene, Lamont was the son of an ordained minister, but there were few other parallels in their early years. Lamont's father, a Methodist, spent his ministry in the United States, in a number of small churches around the Catskills in the Hudson Valley of New York. His recollections of early readings and interests include no reference to East Asia. Perhaps most revealing was his sharp memory of the relative prosperity of the Presbyterian communities of his childhood, of the higher social position of people that attended the Presbyterian Church and the higher standard of living of the family of the Presbyterian ministers. Years later he married a Presbyterian and became active in his wife's church rather than that of his father.[1]

But if Lamont's family did not prosper relative to others in its environment, a broader standard would suggest that the Lamonts had fared reasonably well. Poverty, even of a genteel sort, was hardly a threat. Following in his brother's path, young Tom went off to Harvard, by way of Phillips Exeter Academy. School finances were a bother, but there were, after all, some Americans for whom preparatory schools and Harvard were just fantasies, if indeed ever dreamt of.

1. Lamont's memories of his childhood are collected in his *My Boyhood in a Parsonage* (New York and London, 1946).

At Harvard Lamont was an editor of the *Crimson,* ten years before Greene's arrival. After graduation in 1892, he followed his brother into journalism, obtaining a position in the *New York Tribune.* He spent several years as a journalist and then a decade in a commercial enterprise where Henry P. Davison, a partner in J. P. Morgan and Company, discovered him and led him off to the world of high finance. Rising rapidly within the banking world, ultimately chairman of the board of J. P. Morgan and Company, Lamont insisted "I did not know then, nor do I know to this day, the techniques of banking." Though he may have been excessively modest, Lamont's description of his role was inherently accurate. His genius was in diplomacy, in the relations between the firm and the businessmen, bureaucrats, journalists, and political leaders whose good will and wise policies were so important to Morgan's vast empire.[2]

Lamont's emergence as spokesman for the House of Morgan, as J. P. Morgan, Jr.'s public persona, is explicable in terms of Morgan's abrasiveness, Lamont's charm, and the death of Davison in 1922. Morgan, once described as "the most undiplomatic man in America," was supercilious and acerbic in his rare public appearances. Davison was viewed as the "real fighting edge" of the firm, as Morgan spent more time than his father had enjoying the good life great wealth permitted. Like Davison, Lamont was a man of unusual breadth, as comfortable with intellectuals and diplomats as with businessmen. A description of the Morgan partners published in 1914 referred to Lamont's "engaging personality," as revealed by "even a glance at his photograph." He was portrayed as "as a good mixer, unassuming, unpretentious, unconventional. . . ." With the younger Morgan aloof and considered unsafe for public relations, first Davison and Lamont, then Lamont alone, treated with the world beyond the portals of 23 Wall Street.[3]

During his college days Lamont had no apparent interest in foreign affairs, sharing the narrower concerns of most Americans, confident that the world in which he lived could be at peace forever. As his horizons grew, as he travelled abroad in the early years of the twentieth century, he was deeply impressed with the cultural ties between the United States and Western

2. *Ibid.,* and Thomas W. Lamont, *Across World Frontiers* (New York, 1951), 36. See also George Kibbe Turner, "Morgan's Partners," *McClure's Magazine,* XL (April 13, 1913), 31.

3. W. M. Walker, "J. P. The Younger," *American Mercury,* XI (June 1927), 129–36; "Personal Equations in the House of Morgan and What They Signify," *Current Opinion,* LVI (February 1914) 105–7.

Europe, ties "that must never be broken." Whether derived from these travels or from the teachings of his colleagues on Wall Street, he was also very much aware of the economic interdependence of Europe and the United States. In particular, Lamont, like Morgan, considered the well-being of Great Britain of tremendous importance to the United States, economically as well as politically. When war came to Europe in 1914, there was no pretense of neutrality within the firm. J. P. Morgan and all his associates were certain of the importance of a British victory and determined to do all they could to assist the Allies against the Central Powers. They took over purchasing arrangements for the British and, with the grudging acquiescence of the Wilson administration, helped the Allies with loans when their cash ran out. Unquestionably, Morgan and Company developed an important stake in an Allied victory btween 1914 and 1917. Equally certain was the firm's commitment to England's cause before the wartime loans.[4]

Once the United States intervened in the war, Wall Street's connections with the British were less awkward for the American government. The Wilson administration found it useful to have Lamont "volunteer" to accompany Col. House on a mission to London in the autumn of 1917. At the Paris Peace Conference, Lamont, at the request of the Secretary of the Treasury, represented the Treasury Department on the American Commission to Negotiate the Peace. Along with Bernard M. Baruch, Oscar S. Straus, Norman Davis, and Vance McCormick, he served on the Supreme Economic Council. At Paris he tried unsuccessfully to convince Lloyd George and Wilson to cooperate with, perhaps even aid, Lenin and Trotsky, and became devoted to the League of Nations. Indeed, in 1920, Lamont parted temporarily from the proper Republicanism into which he had been raised and voted for Cox and the League, choosing international cooperation and collective security rather than the irresponsibility for which Harding appeared to stand.[5]

At the war's end and after the peace conference, Lamont, in his late forties, stood out as a distinguished diplomat-financier—a partner in one of the world's leading banking institutions. He and his colleagues had worked closely with their government during the war and had participated in the making of the peace. Although he disagreed with a number of Wilson's decisions at Paris and his handling of the Treaty of Versailles afterward, he

4. *Across World Frontiers*, 21–22, 66–71, *passim*.
5. *Ibid.*, 75–97, 107 ff; *New York Times*, January 18, 1919, p. 4, and February 10, 1919, p. 2.

had demonstrated to Wilson and to the Departments of State and Treasury that he shared much of the Wilsonian vision. He was committed to a course of international cooperation, especially with Great Britain. Lamont was, therefore, an obvious choice when the Department of State wanted an American banker to negotiate on its behalf in the creation of a new international banking consortium for China—all the more so since the House of Morgan had dominated the American Group in an earlier organization of like purport.

J. P. Morgan had entered the investment field in China in 1905 by purchasing a Belgian syndicate's majority interest in the ill-fated American China Development Company. The company's concession for building a railroad between Canton and Hankow had come under attack as a result of its violation of the terms of the initial contract and because of rising opposition among the Chinese gentry to foreign control of Chinese railroads. Supported by the protests of the American government, Morgan was able to defer cancellation of the concession until assured by the Chinese of a substantial profit on his investment. Although President Roosevelt asked him to hold on to the concession, considering it important to American prestige and economic interests in China, Morgan refused. His stockholders were satisfied with the Chinese offer and the exigencies of state were not sufficient to override the profit motive.[6]

For the remaining years of the Roosevelt administration, American economic interests in China continued to be negligible. After the Russo-Japanese War, Roosevelt was quite prepared to abandon the field to the Japanese, as a price for friendly relations between the United States and Japan. Japan's victory over Russia had convinced him that good relations with Japan was America's only vital interest in East Asia. But Willard Straight, described by Lamont as "a perfectly corking fellow, delightful in every way," succeeded in infecting his contacts on Wall Street with his vision of fortunes to be made by investing capital in Chinese plans for countering Japanese influence in Manchuria. In the summer of 1908, Straight was called back to the United States because, William Phillips explained to Rockhill, " 'Wall Street' is feeling confident again and looking for the investment of

6. See William R. Braisted, "The United States and the American China Development Company," *Far Eastern Quarterly*, XI (1952), 147–65, and Howard K. Beale, *Theodore Roosevelt and the Rise of America to World Power* (Baltimore, 1956), 200–11.

capital in foreign lands. It has turned to Manchuria and wants the latest advice on the situation up there. . . ." Straight and his friends in New York financial circles weathered Roosevelt's resistance to their operations, found the Taft administration receptive—and then failed utterly in their various schemes for investing in Manchurian railroads.[7]

But where the Taft administration's economic offensive failed in Manchuria, it met with a degree of success in China proper. The Chinese and an existing syndicate of British, French, and German bankers reluctantly accepted American participation in a loan to finance the Hukuang Railway. To this end, the United States brought into being an American Group, headed by J. P. Morgan and Company, formally admitted into what became a four-power banking consortium in May 1910.[8]

Taft's men perceived of the Consortium as a means of implementing John Hay's Open Door notes, of arresting the scramble for concessions and spheres, preserving both opportunities for the growth of American economic interests and the integrity of China. Japanese encroachments had to be checked in the interest of both the United States and China, as well as the European nations involved. The Chinese would have to understand that political cooperation among the powers would be built on financial cooperation, through the Consortium. Such ties with other powers would make the United States more useful to China.

In practice, however, this consortium, enlarged by the admission of Japan and Russia in 1912, acquired a sinister image in China and the West as a consequence of its efforts to force loans upon the Chinese government and to monopolize all loan business with China. By 1913, when Taft ended his tenure in the White House, the state of negotiations with Yüan Shih-k'ai for a "reorganization" loan suggested that both ends of the Consortium policy, cooperation among the powers and a benign involvement in the modernization of China, were beyond reach.[9]

7. See Raymond A. Esthus, *Theodore Roosevelt and Japan* (Seattle, 1966), and Charles E. Neu, *An Uncertain Friendship* (Cambridge, Massachusetts, 1967); Lamont to E. L. James, December 20, 1946, file 127–7, Papers of Thomas W. Lamont, Baker Library, Harvard University, hereafter TWL ms; Phillips to Rockhill, July 16, 1908, Rockhill ms.

8. The standard work on the first consortium is Frederick V. Field, *American Participation in the China Consortiums* (New York, 1931). See also Scholes, *Foreign Policies of the Taft Administration*.

9. See Calhoun to Secretary of State, October 25, 1910, SD 893.51/208, and Jordan to Gregory, August 26, 1913, FO 371/1594/501 (from unpublished manuscript by John Cunningham).

The day after Woodrow Wilson was inaugurated President of the United States, the American Group asked if he wanted them to continue in the Consortium. The bankers were prepared to maintain their involvement only at the express request of the administration and with assurances of support. A young foreign service officer, J. V. A. MacMurray, wrote to Rockhill describing dissension within the American Group, irritation over the long negotiations with the Chinese, and general apathy toward doing business with China. MacMurray was himself irritated by the bankers' demand that Wilson ask them to continue their operations and saw "no likelihood that this rather peremptory assumption of a philanthropic attitude in their chafferings will be humored by the Administration." He assumed the end of American involvement in the Consortium was at hand—and his old professor at Princeton did not disappoint him. Without consulting China or the other participants in the Consortium, Wilson announced to the press that the American Group would no longer have the support of its government.[10]

Wilson mistrusted the Wall Street bankers and their foreign partners, suspecting all involved in the Consortium of seeking to take advantage of China's weakness, to infringe upon China's sovereignty and to make a profit at China's expense. A better way to help China had to be found. Reporting Wilson's decision to Rockhill, MacMurray expressed his approval. Two years before, he would have considered withdrawal from the Consortium "a great and quixotic renunciation of our opportunities," but the American Group had gotten out of hand and was leading the government around "like a trick dog." There would probably be a temporary loss of trade opportunities, but MacMurray considered such sacrifice a reasonable price for freeing the State Department "from a false position into which the bankers had led it by their unwillingness to play the game fairly in return for the political support given them."[11]

Thomas Lamont's views did not deviate from the American Group's line which, indeed, he promulgated with the help of Willard Straight. As MacMurray had noted, the bankers were remarkably unwilling to concede

10. Roy Watson Curry, *Woodrow Wilson and Far Eastern Policy, 1913–1921* (New York, 1957), 21–24, and Arthur S. Link, *Wilson: The New Freedom* (Princeton, 1956), 284–86. See also J. V. A. MacMurray to W. W. Rockhill, March 18, 1913, Rockhill ms.

11. E. David Cronon (ed.), *The Cabinet Diaries of Josephus Daniels, 1913–1921* (Lincoln, Nebraska, 1963), 8; P.S. dated March 20, 1913, MacMurray to Rockhill, Rockhill ms.

the profit motive a place in their decision to enter the Consortium. Lamont carefully stressed the point that the government had come to the bankers, appealing to their patriotism. He insisted that the bankers had never wanted to be involved, had quite enough to do at home, would not have gone in on a purely business basis, and were glad to get out. Nonetheless, his analysis of Wilson's decision to withdraw support from the Consortium left no doubt that Lamont considered Wilson mistaken. He found Wilson and Bryan acting on two principles: 1) fear of entanglement in foreign affairs; 2) belief that if American businessmen could not penetrate the market in China, they would have to operate without it. "To sum up," Lamont suggested, "Taft and Knox wanted to sit around the table in the Council of Nations about China. Wilson and Bryan don't." He purported to leave the question to posterity, but clearly preferred dollar diplomacy to the approach of the Wilson administration. When he asked "shall this country take a practical interest in helping China—not by sending a few missionaries—but by lending her money and helping develop her resources?"—he allowed for only an affirmative answer. Many years later, he offered a totally different explanation for his concern over Wilson's decision: "It was not because of prospective profits that the American Group was concerned by this sudden announcement, because Chinese Government business in itself had small attraction, but rather because the State Department had administered a wholly uncalled-for affront to the British, French, and German Foreign Offices, and because of the manifest concern shown in China by the withdrawal of America, which it had regarded as its staunchest friend."[12]

The Japanese government was indeed irritated by Wilson's unilateral action, but the European Powers were generally less perturbed. The Chinese, contrary to Lamont's allegations, seemed genuinely pleased. Yüan Shih-k'ai sent Wilson a note of appreciation, and the Chinese government turned to the American Group and other American bankers as a preferable source of financing. They hoped, given Wilson's attitude, that loans on a less restrictive basis, with fewer controls over expenditure and fewer infringements upon Chinese sovereignty, would be forthcoming. But the American Group would not compete against its recent partners. Other American bankers and industrialists found investor indifference to China and inad-

12. Typescript of speech, misdated February 3, 1913, 183–2, TWL ms; and Lamont, *Across World Frontiers*, 229.

equate government support in the face of Russian, French, and British governmental pressures on the Chinese.[13]

In the absence of American participation and, with the coming of the war in Europe, the absence of European participation, Japan was left as the only nation both willing and able to supply China with capital desperately needed for development. But by 1914, the Japanese government no longer shared the American estimate of the value of a strong, independent China. The Japanese had demonstrated to themselves and to the world that they were worthy of great power status. They were far less fearful of the effect of Russian imperialism on their own interests than they had been at the turn of the century. Indeed, Japan had emerged as the leading predator in China. Economic assistance was offered not to help the Chinese cast off their chains but to enlarge and consolidate Japan's empire. With Europe at war, only the United States could provide China with an alternative.

Domestic affairs, problems with Mexico, and the coming of war in Europe preoccupied Woodrow Wilson in the first years of his presidency. The problems of China, where the United States had no vital interests, were remote from his concerns. His sympathy for Chinese aspirations was expressed in uncomplicated acts like withdrawing support from the American Group and by extending recognition to the Republic of China. The "better way" of helping China, to which he had referred when arguing against support of the American Group, was left to be defined by private interests, by missionaries and by businessmen rather than by the government of the United States.

By mid-April 1915, however, the reality of Japan's intent to dominate China, as evidenced by the 21 Demands, penetrated Wilson's consciousness and forced him to reconsider his policy toward China. During and after the crisis over the 21 Demands the Wilson administration followed another tack in opposing Japanese imperialism in China, its own version of dollar diplomacy. Wilson and his Minister to China, Paul Reinsch, were hostile to the American Group because of its presumed monopolistic practices and the attempts of the Consortium to infringe on Chinese sovereignty. Nonetheless, they remained very much interested in the use of American capital to further the process of Chinese modernization. Wilson's initial interest was in ex-

13. Japanese Embassy to Department of State, March 24, 1913, E. T. Williams to Bryan, and A. A. Adee to Wilson, March 25, 1913, *FRUS, 1913,* 173–75; Field, *China Consortiums,* 118–29.

tending the economic interests of the United States in a way that would not be detrimental to Chinese interests. Reinsch was deeply convinced that American trade could be expanded in a mutually profitable partnership with China. Japanese pretensions in China obviously threatened more than Chinese sovereignty. They threatened American visions of preserving for the United States a share of the potential market in China.[14]

Failing to arouse interest among other American bankers and in response to a direct request from the Chinese government in 1916, the Wilson administration asked the American Group if it would consider a loan to China. The American Group refused to consider any proposition that would place it in competition with the Consortium. Morgan and his associates indicated that they would consider a loan outside the scope of the Consortium only if specifically secured *and* if the American government would offer a guarantee that China would fulfill its obligations. The government would not offer any such guarantee, appealing to the sense of patriotism the bankers had exuded in 1913. The bankers, however, would participate in a loan to China only as a strict business proposition—and the matter was dropped.[15]

Two banks outside the American Group ultimately responded. Lee, Higginson, and Company sought to arrange a loan, but found no buyer interest. A representative of the firm informed Reinsch that the effort to sell Chinese Treasury notes had uncovered "such an absolute lack of knowledge about, and interest in, China that it was evident that more time must be taken for a campaign of education before anything could be accomplished." In November 1916, the Chicago Continental and Commercial Trust and Savings Bank entered into a loan agreement with the Chinese, evoking a strong protest from the remaining Consortium bankers. The President advised Lansing to make it known to the Russian, Japanese, British, and French governments that the United States would not tolerate "any strained construction of existing agreements between the Chinese government and their bankers or any attempt to exclude our bankers from a fair participation in Chinese affairs." With most of the governments involved eager to avoid conflict with the United States while involved in a life and death struggle with the Central Powers in Europe, their bankers could count on little support against a potential invasion of American bankers. There was one hope.

14. Noel Pugach, "Making the Open Door Work: Paul S. Reinsch in China, 1913–1919," *Pacific Historical Review,* XXXVIII (1969), 157–75.

15. Field, *China Consortiums,* 129–30; Curry, *Wilson and FE Policy,* 152.

British, French, Russian, and Japanese bankers expressed a strong desire to see the United States rejoin the Consortium, to co-opt the United States and to contain the financial offensive the American bankers were capable of launching.[16]

In March 1917, the American Group notified the Department of State that it favored accepting the invitation to rejoin the Consortium, contending that the time was ripe for advancing American commercial prestige. But representatives of the American Group who met with Lansing found that the administration had not changed its position. Wilson favored loans to China, but insisted that they be made directly to the Chinese rather than through the Consortium. Wilson, Lansing, and Reinsch recognized the overtures from the Consortium for what they were—a hope of preventing independent American action. Reinsch in particular saw the Consortium as an instrument of Japanese policy. Certainly the Terauchi Cabinet saw it as a useful means of outmaneuvering the United States. For a while the administration toyed with the idea of a direct loan from the American government to the Chinese government, encouraging the Chinese to declare war on Germany to facilitate such a loan—but nothing came of this scheme as the war in Europe consumed Wilson's attention.[17]

Throughout the first half of 1918, the State Department still hoped to find a way to arrange loans to China without having to ask the American Group to rejoin the Consortium. But Lansing and Wilson failed, and were forced to recognize the fact that the Japanese banks would offer better terms than independent American banks. Clearly American banks would not make any offers without security and a promise of government support to protect that security. And the administration suspected that the future of American trade and investments was at stake. Unopposed, the Japanese would use the opportunity to exclude American economic interests from China. In addition, Reinsch and Lansing feared Chinese resentment. China had entered the war against Germany at the invitation of the United States and expected financial support in return. But only the Japanese were offering loans. To

16. Field, *China Consortiums,* 128–34; Curry, *Wilson and FE Policy,* 152–54; Lee, Higginson and Company to Reinsch, August 21, 1916, SD 893.51/1679; Wilson to Lansing, December 5, 1916, SD 893.51/3010.

17. Field, *China Consortiums,* 133–34; Frank Langdon, "The Japanese Policy of Expansion in China, 1917–1928," Ph.D. dissertation, University of California (1953), 57; Lansing to Wilson, April 12, 1917, SD 893.51/3007a and Wilson to Lansing, April 13, 1917, SD 893.51/3008.

Wilson, Lansing proposed a new cooperative arrangement, ultimately a new consortium. On June 21, 1918, Wilson approved the course Lansing recommended, assuming "that everything necessary would be done to protect the Chinese government against such unconscionable arrangements as were contemplated by the former consortium." As a result, Lamont recorded, the American Group was asked to create a new consortium and "wonder of wonders," promised "full diplomatic support."[18]

Wilson recognized that China, left to the mercies of the "free market," was in fact left to the mercies of the none too benevolent Japanese, with effects almost certain to be detrimental to American economic prospects. He agreed, therefore, to allow the American Group to reassociate itself with the British, French, and Japanese members of the Consortium. The American Group in turn accepted the administration's condition that it become more inclusive, admitting to membership interested banking groups throughout the country. In return for the American Group's pledge not to undermine Chinese sovereignty, the administration agreed to announce that the Group would offer capital to China at the suggestion of the government. With the monopolistic appearance of the earlier American Group altered and with the Group's assurance that it would work in the interests of the Chinese people, Wilson rested and Thomas Lamont took over. To Lamont fell the task of convincing the British, French, and Japanese banking groups—and their governments—to create a new consortium on American terms.

Lamont was in Paris in the spring of 1919, serving as an adviser to the American Commissioners at the Peace Conference. Meeting with representatives of the British, French, and Japanese banking groups, he proposed and reached rapid agreement on the American plan for pooling all future business in China. They also agreed to pool all existing loan agreements and options involving public subscription *except* those relating to industrial undertakings "upon which substantial progress has been made." The efficiency of cooperation rather than competition, with the expectation of the exclusive support of their governments, was attractive to the bankers.[19]

18. Field, *China Consortiums,* 143–45; Curry, *Wilson and FE Policy,* 191–96; Breckinridge Long to Lansing, February 12, 1918, SD 893.51/1894; Lansing to Wilson, June 20, 1918 and Wilson to Lansing, June 21, 1918, *FRUS, 1918,* 171; Lamont, *Across World Frontiers,* 229–30.

19. Field, *China Consortiums,* 154–56.

The British government responded eagerly to the American plan, sharing American perceptions of the situation in China and of the need to restrain Japan's drive toward commercial hegemony and railway control. Cooperation with the United States was attractive to British leaders, despite frequent irritation in the Foreign Office with American "unreliability." They concluded that the regulation of Chinese finances through an international consortium was an excellent means of working with the Americans toward ends they shared in opposition to Japan in China. The men responsible for Great Britain's policy were also aware of the danger of having to compete with American capital if a cooperative policy could not be fashioned.[20]

In June, however, Anglo-American reveries were interrupted by a letter from Odagiri Masunosuke, for the Japanese Group, to Lamont. Odagiri reported that his government insisted upon excluding from the consortium agreement "all the rights and options held by Japan in the regions of Manchuria and Mongolia, where Japan has special interests." This position, Odagiri explained, was based on "the very special relations which Japan enjoys geographically, and historically with the regions referred to, and which have been recognized by Great Britain, the United States, France and Russia on many occasions." Officials of the Gaimusho apparently expected the United States to consent to the exceptions on the basis of Lansing's recognition of Japan's "special interests" in his 1917 agreement with Ishii. Once Japan's sphere in Manchuria and Inner Mongolia was thus protected, the Hara Cabinet viewed the Consortium with favor. It could serve as a means of improving relations with the United States—as well as an instrument for checking the anticipated torrent of American capital.[21]

The purpose of the Consortium, as understood in Washington and in London, however, was to *eliminate* special claims in spheres of influence and to open all of China to cooperative international development. Not only the Wilsonians, but also Lord Curzon, Great Britain's Secretary of State for

20. Jordan to Balfour, December 23, 1918, FO 405/226/16; Jordan to Curzon, February 12, 1919, FO 405/227/29; Memorandum by W. G. Müller, February 1919, FO 405/227/18. See also Ian Nish, *Alliance in Decline* (London, 1972), 258, 277–78.

21. Field, *China Consortiums,* 156; Asada Sadao, "Japan and the United States, 1915–1925," Ph. D. dissertation, Yale (1962), 86; John W. Young, "Japanese Military and the Hara Cabinet," Ph.D dissertation, University of Washington (1972), 116–17; Mitani Taichiro, *Nihon Seito Seiji no Keisei* (Establishment of Party Politics in Japan) (1967), 287–89 (translated for me by Hiramatsu Tetsuji).

Foreign Affairs, considered economic imperialism an anachronism in the face of the nationalist movement that was sweeping over China. When the French government expressed fear that refusal to grant the reservations Japan requested would result in the Japanese finding friends outside the circle of their wartime allies, Curzon insisted that the Japanese request was inadmissible. He expressed confidence that they would back down in face of the unanimity of the British, French, and American Groups supported by their governments.[22]

Replying to Odagiri, Lamont insisted that Mongolia and Manchuria were important parts of China and could not be excluded from the Consortium. In private conversations with Odagiri, Lamont was informed that the Japanese bankers shared his view and would do everything possible to modify their government's policy. Both the American and British governments protested against the Japanese reservations, but Tokyo was unresponsive. Finding the Japanese Ambassador to Great Britain unapproachable, unwilling to press his Japanese ally further, Curzon allowed the initiative in the negotiations to rest with Washington, where the proposal for the new Consortium had originated.[23]

Throughout the summer and autumn of 1919, while the President, Congress, and the American people worried over the Treaty of Versailles and the League of Nations, the Department of State, working closely with the British Foreign Office, tried to convince Japan to surrender its reservations to the consortium plan. Similarly Thomas Lamont, including support for the League among his civic activities, kept in close touch with Breckinridge Long and J. V. A. MacMurray, respectively Assistant Secretary of State and Chief of the Bureau of Far Eastern Affairs, as they schemed to bring the Japanese into line.

In late August, the Japanese Ambassador to the United States reported that his government had narrowed its position. His superiors were prepared to accept the consortium proposal provided it did not prejudice the special interests and rights possessed by Japan in South Manchuria and Eastern

22. W. Roger Louis, *British Strategy in the Far East, 1919–1939* (London, 1971), 20–21; Curzon to Beilby Alston, November 20, 1919, FO 405/227/164; Curzon to French Ambassador, London, July 29, 1919, Great Britain, Foreign Office, *Documents in British Foreign Policy* (hereafter *DBFP*), *1919–1939,* First Series, VI, 1919 (London, 1956), 650.

23. Field, *China Consortiums,* 156–57; Lamont, "Memorandum as to Chinese Consortium," June 28, 1919, *DBFP, 1919–1939,* First series, VI, 1919, 625; Nish, *Alliance in Decline,* 258; Louis, *British Strategy,* 31–32.

Inner Mongolia. With Wilson campaigning for the League and ultimately suffering a debilitating stroke, two months passed before Lansing rejected the Japanese move. He argued that "it would be a calamity if the adoption of the consortium were to carry with it the recognition of a doctrine of spheres of interest more advanced and far-reaching than was ever applied to Chinese territory even in the period when the break-up of the Empire appeared imminent." He sought to allay Japanese fears by insisting that no one intended to encroach upon "existing vested Japanese interests in the region indicated." The consortium agreement would apply only to undertakings where there had been no substantial progress. It would not apply to the South Manchuria Railway.[24]

During the two months before Lansing replied to the Japanese overture, the Department of State fretted over China's urgent need for money and the need to prevent that money from coming exclusively from Japanese sources. For a moment the idea of proceeding with a three-power consortium without Japan was considered, but neither the British nor the French were interested. Both preferred to lure Japan into the Consortium with half a loaf—South Manchuria. The State Department rejected this compromise, but there was agreement within the Department that a three-power consortium was desirable only if agreement with Japan proved impossible. Indeed, the three-power consortium was conceived primarily as a device with which to threaten the Japanese—a spectre of what might follow if they failed to accept the American plan.[25]

Long and MacMurray also made a pilgrimage to York Harbor to discuss with Lamont a Chinese proposal that the American Group become the sole financial agency of the Chinese government. They explained China's urgent need and the Department's hope of using a loan from the American Group for the twofold purpose of checking the growth of Japanese influence and of assisting the Chinese to demobilize their armies, to end civil war and to enhance their credit. They also indicated that they expected a threat of independent action by the American Group to bring a change of policy in Tokyo, with the Japanese government quickly approving partici-

24. Japanese Ambassador to Department of State, August 27, 1919, and Lansing to Japanese Ambassador, October 28, 1919, SD 893.51/2405.

25. Curry, *Wilson and FE Policy*, 200–1; Lamont to Long, September 18, 1919, SD 893.51/2430; Jordan to Curzon, June 16, 1919, FO 405/227/77; Curzon to Jordan, October 4, 1919, FO 405/227/112; Sir Charles Addis to Foreign Office, October 14, 1919, enclosure from French Group, FO 405/227/129; Grey to Curzon, November 19, 1919, *DBFP, 1919–1939*, First series, VI, 828.

pation of the Japanese Group in the Consortium on the original American terms.[26]

After consulting with Morgan, Lamont expressed the willingness of the American Group to help, but doubted that it could come up with a large loan that would appeal to the American investor. At the very least a strong statement from the government, indicating its desire that Americans subscribe to the loan to spare China from Japanese imperialism, would be necessary. It is unlikely that Lamont expected the admnistration to issue any such statement. On the contrary, Lamont and his Morgan partners were not interested in lending money to China, especially for patriotic purposes. The main thrust of Lamont's reply to the Department's overtures to the American Group was his argument that the American *government* lend the money to the Chinese government. Brushing aside State Department reservations about the legality of such a procedure, he insisted that the President could authorize the Treasury Department to lend money to the Chinese government. Morgan's lawyers were all agreed on the legality of such a procedure. As a commercial venture, loans to China were virtually impossible until China ironed out its financial difficulties. However, China could not settle her financial difficulties until she could pay off her troops. Lamont argued that since the Chinese had mobilized at the request of the United States, a Treasury loan to finance demobilization "would be clearly admissible." A disingenuous argument given the insignificant relationship between the existence of Chinese armies and the American invitation to China to declare war against Germany, Lamont's proposal did offer a way out of the dilemma—but it was a way out of the banker's dilemma rather than that of the United States government. The bankers, to no one's surprise, wanted to invest their time and money in those ventures likely to provide the highest profits. On the other hand, they realized that it was important to develop markets in countries like China—important to the expansion of the market economy of which their operations were an integral part. Ideally, private capital would be used in direct profit-generating operations of minimum risk, such as investment in modern economies, like that of Japan. The government would provide the funds necessary for less attractive but nonetheless important ventures such as the development of China and the reconstruction of Europe. But Lamont's vision was one war ahead of its time.[27]

26. Lamont to Long, September 18, 1919, SD 893.51/2430.
27. Lamont to Long, September 23, 1919, SD 893.51/2437.

In October, the administration was paralyzed by Wilson's stroke, unable to undertake any major initiatives such as lending money directly to the Chinese government, and Lamont was stalling in the hope that the American Group could exude civic virtue without having to underwrite a loan to China. Then a Chicago banker, John J. Abbott, came forward. As Lamont reported to his partners, the State Department was "exceedingly" eager to have the American Group make a loan, for "by so doing we should at once force Japan to come into the Consortium without reservations." The loan itself would probably be safe, Lamont thought, because there was an ample margin on the revenues pledged, but it would not "listen" well because of prior liens on those revenues. Abbott was willing to arrange the loan if the American Group still refused, and this disturbed Lamont on two counts. First, he did not want the administration to think Abbott's bank had more power than the whole American Group—the value of the Group's prestige with the administration could not be underestimated. Second, he was contemptuous of Abbott, convinced he would botch the arrangements "and spoil the way for permanent Chinese financing here." But given the choice between letting Abbott arrange the loan or having the American Group exercise its option, Lamont chose to step aside and let Abbott have the business. Basically, his conviction that the American investing public would not touch the loan dictated his reluctance. A loan to China was a worthy venture and he hoped someone would undertake it, but as a business proposition it would be too bothersome to underwrite.[28]

Left to his own devices, Lamont was prepared to forget about East Asia, to concentrate exclusively on his primary concerns within the Atlantic community. In his speeches and writings in the summer and autumn of 1919, he focused his attention on the problems of European recovery. An article he prepared for the *Atlantic Monthly* was entitled "The World Situation," but it contained not a single mention of Asia. Lamont wrote exclusively about problems of European recovery and the need for the United States to find a way to help Europeans to purchase what they needed from the United States. But his role as chairman of the American Group permitted no escape from the affairs of China and Japan. Reinsch wrote to insist that Chinese securities offered by reputable bankers with the approval of the United States government would be well received by the American public.

28. "Note for Harry and Dwight," undated, 183–5, TWL ms.

From Shanghai, the young American manager of the China Bureau of Public Information, George E. Sokolsky, informed Lamont of Japanese efforts to discredit the new Consortium in China, and insisted that the Consortium was China's only hope. And the State Department was unrelenting in its pleas, with Breckinridge Long finally begging Lamont to go to Tokyo to bring Japan into the Consortium. Implying that the alternative might mean war with Japan or the elimination of American economic and political interests in China, and appealing to Lamont as perhaps the only man who could carry the day, Long prevailed. In February 1920 Lamont left for Japan.[29]

With Lamont in Tokyo to negotiate with the Japanese Group, theoretically representing only the American Group, negotiations continued between the American and Japanese governments. The positions of the two sides were clear. The Japanese government, firmly supported—perhaps even driven—by its people, insisted that Japan had vital economic and strategic interests in Manchuria and Mongolia that could not be compromised. The Japanese were apprehensive about Bolshevism, the rise of Chinese nationalism, and American hostility to Japan's expansion on the Asian mainland. Protection for Japan's interests in Manchuria and Mongolia was the essential prerequisite to Japanese cooperation with other powers in the Consortium or any other affairs affecting Japan's position on the mainland. Japanese political leaders, bankers, militarists, and intellectuals were united in their unwillingness to compromise Japan's vital interests in Manchuria and Mongolia. The American government, with virtually no concern for East Asia among its people, was nonetheless determined not to concede a Japanese sphere of influence in Manchuria or Mongolia, determined not to allow the Japanese a veto over activities in a region the United States recognized as part of China. With fewer present interests in China than the Japanese enjoyed, the American government was more sympathetic to Chinese national aspirations. At the same time, officials of the Department of State were convinced that checking the Japanese surge toward hegemony over China was essential to preserve the opportunity for the expansion of American interests there.[30]

29. *Atlantic Monthly,* CXXIV (September 1919), 420–29; Reinsch to Lamont, October 23, 1919, Sokolsky to Lamont, October 20, 1919, 183–6, and Long to Lamont, December 20, 1919, 185–15, TWL ms.

30. For Japanese attitudes see Asada, Langdon, and Young dissertations, cited above, and Mitani, *Party Politics in Japan.*

One area for possible compromise between the American and Japanese positions existed and the State Department had focused on it in the fall of 1919. Japan's existing *economic* interests, "vested" interests in Manchuria and Mongolia, could be conceded, excluded from the scope of the Consortium. Toward this position both sides moved slowly. During the first few days of Lamont's visit to Tokyo, the Japanese government presented a new proposal, but it still contained a formula for giving Japan a veto over Consortium activities in Southern Manchuria and Eastern Inner Mongolia. Lamont, in consultation with the British as well as the American Ambassador, concluded that the Japanese were taking a bargaining position from which they would retreat. His talks with Japanese bankers convinced him that they strongly favored participation in the Consortium and, if the United States and Great Britain held firm, would be able to press their government to move toward the American position. Lamont found the bankers eager to cooperate with the United States, sharing his vision of a world in which trade and investments would grow and in which the only expansion would be economic. To push the Japanese government a little harder, President Wilson authorized a threat to reveal the secret protocol of the Lansing-Ishii agreement in which Ishii had committed Japan not to seek privileges in China at the expense of other powers.[31]

Although the British and American governments decided to reject the Japanese formula in markedly similar terms, Lamont and the American Ambassador to Japan, Roland Morris, began to edge toward the Japanese position. The British Ambassador to Japan, Beilby Alston, similarly urged a more conciliatory course upon the Foreign Office. Morris cabled Lansing to report that he and Lamont were agreed that there was "a measure of reason and justice" in Japan's determination to protect her continental interests. A way had to be found to provide the Japanese with assurances, otherwise chances for reaching an agreement were remote. Lamont had come up with an idea Morris and Alston thought worthy of consideration: an exchange of notes between the American and Japanese Groups defining the attitude of foreign *bankers* toward Japanese *economic* interests in Manchuria and Mongolia, specifying what would or would not come within the scope of the

31. Long to Lamont, December 20, 1919, 185–15, TWL ms; Curry, *Wilson and FE Policy*, 201–2; Mitani, *Party Politics in Japan*, indicates that exclusion of specific interests had been the Hara government's original alternative to the more desirable exclusion of the region, 292; Morris to Secretary of State, March 8, 1920, SD 893.51/2703; Frank L. Polk to Wilson, March 9, 1920, SD 893.51/2856a and enclosure, /2856b.

Consortium. Lamont's plan would allow for the acceptance of existing economic realities without giving official governmental recognition—which might be construed as recognizing a sphere of economic influence. Only the Consortium would recognize Japan's economic interests.[32]

Initially, the State Department balked at Lamont's proposal. The pretense that the American Group functioned independently of the government of the United States might be carried too far. The idea that Lamont could recognize the existence of a Japanese sphere of influence in Manchuria and Mongolia without compromising the principle for which the Department was fighting was beyond comprehension. Instead the Department suggested that Lamont reach an agreement on the basis of the specific enterprises the Japanese wanted to exclude from the Consortium's focus, indicating a willingness to accept the entire Japanese list. But the Department would not countenance reference to the exclusion of any *region* of China in the proposed agreement between the American and Japanese banking groups.[33]

The State Department's scruples irritated Lamont. To his partners at J. P. Morgan and Company he contended that Manchuria was in fact dominated by Japanese trade and investment and unattractive to nationals of the other banking groups. The Japanese government could not resist pressures to protect Manchuria. He was convinced that the exclusion of Manchurian railroads from the Consortium was sensible economically, because the railroads were a poor investment, and valuable politically because exclusion would ease the domestic situation in Japan. Several days later he cabled Morgan, asking him to make personal calls on Long and Undersecretary Frank Polk, and to urge upon them the importance of accepting Lamont's proposed exchange of notes. He contended that for the first time, the problem seemed to be resolved. He thought the Japanese government would withdraw its reservations, participate in the Consortium whole-heartedly, "provided only at this juncture our own government is not too obstinate." Blaming the difficulty on MacMurray, whose attitude he deemed "stiff and academic" and whom he considered "very anti-Japanese", he expressed his concern lest MacMurray's views influence the final attitude of the United States. "This," he insisted, "must be avoided at all costs." Concluding his

32. Department of State to Japanese Embassy, March 16, 1920, SD 893.51/2695 and Wright, London, to Secretary of State, March 20, 1920, SD 893.51/2725; Morris to Secretary of State, March 11, 1920, SD 893.51/2707; Louis, *British Strategy*, 33–34.

33. Polk to Morris, March 16, 1920, SD 893.51/2695.

cable he asked Morgan to remind Long that he had taken the trip at Long's request "and that I look to him especially for sympathetic approval of solution worked out here with great difficulty and now offered."[34]

MacMurray, however, resisted all pressure and was able to prevail as Lansing departed from State and the administration seemed immobilized by Wilson's prolonged disability. After another round of exchanges with Tokyo, MacMurray drafted a cable for Secretary of State Bainbridge Colby approving Lamont's proposed exchange of notes—modified to list only specific railroads and without any expression of understanding of Japanese concerns in Manchuria and Mongolia. In return for the Japanese government's approval of the agreement between the two banking groups, the American government would ask the British to waive their protest against the exclusion from the Consortium of three railway lines west of the South Manchuria Railway. And confident that the Japanese government would approve the agreement, having bluntly warned Japanese officials that approval was the price they would have to pay for needed American financial assistance, Lamont sailed for China.[35]

Lamont wanted to look around China, speak to its "men of affairs," consult with American diplomats and businessmen—to determine for himself how much time and energy China was worth. In addition, he had two specific tasks to perform, only one of which had the complete support of the American government. First, he wanted to counter a torrent of anti-Consortium sentiment building up among Chinese students and intellectuals, the vanguard of the May Fourth Movement, guardians of China's sovereign rights. Second, and of paramount importance, he wanted to convince the Chinese to pay for coupons on German-issued Hukuang Railway bonds.

Fearful that the Consortium was an imperialist device for the economic exploitation of China, perhaps a means by which the Japanese could control all financial assistance to the Chinese government, the student movement opposed it and generated opposition among Chinese officials and journalists. In addition, the Japanese community in China opposed the Consortium, fearful that it would block the expansion of Japanese interests, and thus rein-

34. Lamont to J. P. Morgan and Company, March 20, 1920 and to J. P. Morgan, Denkstein, March 26, 1920, 185–19, TWL ms.

35. Colby to Morris, March 30, 1920, SD 893.51/2738; Lamont's warning to the Japanese *antedated* Colby's cable. See Alston to Curzon, March 28, 1920, *DBFP, 1919–1939,* First series, VI, 1057; and Louis, *British Strategy,* 32.

forced the nationalist agitation. Lamont, like most Americans with a superficial understanding of his country's past role in China, could not conceive of a genuine suspicion of American purposes on nationalist grounds. He assumed that the Japanese were largely responsible for the campaign against the Consortium. The longer he stayed in China, and the more aware he became of opposition to the Consortium, the angrier he became with the Japanese.[36]

In Shanghai, George Sokolsky brought local student leaders to meet with Lamont. Lamont was favorably impressed with Sokolsky, who gave him advice on how to combat Japanese propaganda and how to reassure the students. After a week of speeches and meetings, all widely publicized, in which he assured his audiences that he had not come to impose a loan on the Chinese government and promised that the Consortium would undertake only constructive operations desired by the Chinese people, Lamont believed he had blunted the force of the opposition's propaganda. The report from the American Legation, prepared much later in the year, was less sanguine. Conceding that Lamont had made a favorable impression, especially in his first speech at Shanghai, the Legation nonetheless found Chinese officials "cool" toward the Consortium. The American Minister's report suggested that fear of Japanese influence in the Consortium might explain continued Chinese reservations. It also noted that the Chinese government was discouraged by Lamont's statements that loans would be limited to nonpolitical purposes and had to be preceded by payment of the Hukuang bond coupons.[37]

Lamont's insistence that the Chinese pay for coupons on German-issued Hukuang bonds was of questionable fairness and had only the reluctant support of the Department of State. In 1917, after declaring war on Germany, the Chinese government repudiated its obligations to the subjects of an enemy country, including its obligation to pay off the German-issued share of the Hukuang loan. Such repudiation was accepted international practice in time of war and was matched by British and American treatment of enemy-owned securities and properties. The customary prerequisite to sustaining a wartime decision to repudiate obligations was victory—and the

36. U.S. Army, Military Attaché Reports, hereafter MA, "Opposition to Consortium," March 25, 1920, Record Group 165, hereafter RG 165, 2655-I-25, National Archives; Tenney to Secretary of State, April 25, 1920, SD 893.51/2797; Lamont, *Across World Frontiers,* 237–44.

37. Diary entry for March 31, 1920, 270–3, TWL ms; Crane to Secretary of State, December 16, 1920, SD 893.00/3731.

Chinese had emerged from the war on the winning side. All might have been well had it not been for the fact that between 1914 and 1917—*and after*—American investors had bought heavily from hard-pressed Germans. In short, some of the bonds on which the Chinese were refusing to make payment were owned by Americans, who were furious with not only the Chinese, but also the American Group bankers who had facilitated their purchases. The American Group had stipulated therefore, from the outset of negotiations for a new consortium and talk of new loans for China, that payment on the German-issued bonds was a prerequisite.

The Department of State Solicitor examined Chinese policy and concluded that the United States had no grounds for objection. The issue was strictly between the Chinese and German governments. The only legitimate American interest was in protecting Americans who had bought German-issued bonds in good faith—before the Chinese Government had repudiated them. The Chinese had agreed to pay any Americans or nonenemy nationals who could prove that they owned the bonds prior to repudiation. According to the Department Solicitor, the United States could only ask that the Chinese be more lenient in their requirements for proof of prewar ownership. The American Legation at Peking was instructed to conform to the Solicitor's decision.[38]

Morgan and Lamont kept pressing the Department of State for support for the American investor, replying to Departmental references to China's urgent need for a loan by demanding prior Chinese agreement to pay the coupons on the German bonds. They insisted that a refusal would seriously injure Chinese credit, making it impossible to float a new loan. The Solicitor's contention, that China's actions did not constitute default and that such practices did not necessarily reflect on a government's credit, was brushed aside. Long and MacMurray resisted intense pressure from the American Group all through January. In early February, the Department sent word to the Chinese Vice-Minister of Finance, stating the American Group's position, indicating that only China's refusal to pay coupons on bonds of German issue prevented an immediate advance. As desperately as the Chinese needed money, they would not yield on the issue.[39]

38. G. H. Hackworth to MacMurray, January 9, 1920, SD 893.51/2637; Polk to Legation, January 24, 1920, SD 893.51/2639a.

39. J. P. Morgan and Company for American Group to Lansing, January 17, 1920, SD 893.51/2620; Reinsch for Pan Fu via Lansing, February 6, 1920 (drafted by MacMurray), SD 893.51/2635; International Banking Corporation to J. P. Morgan and Company, March 4, 1920, SD 893.51/2701.

When Lamont left Japan enroute to China, Morgan cabled him, via the Department of State for maximum impact, warning that "we cannot too strongly impress upon you that it will, in our opinion, be wholly impossible make any issue Chinese securities in this market unless Government restores complete pre-war status to all coupons Hukuang loan." But despite Lamont's powers of persuasiveness, despite the very powerful weapon for extortion Morgan had put at his disposal, he could not get the Chinese to change their attitude on the Hukuang coupons. On the eve of his return to Tokyo, he cabled the Department of State, referring to Chinese obstinacy, reporting that he was "obliged to decline to renew negotiations or make any fresh loan proposals." He believed he had the "good will and confidence of the government and men of affairs generally," and that most Chinese favored the Consortium and American leadership in it. When the Chinese were ready to put their house in order—when they were ready to pay the Hukuang coupons—money could be made available, but not before.[40]

Lamont's rigidity on the Hukuang bond question was fortified by investment conditions within the United States. He had ample evidence of the American investor's lack of interest in Chinese securities. In addition, Morgan had advised him of the American Group's desire that he note the high levels of interest at which "sound domestics" were being offered. Morgan warned that high interest rates on domestic securities created a market situation that all but precluded any loan to the Chinese, even of an emergency nature, "on terms previously considered."[41]

In the spring of 1920 capital available for investment was insufficient to satisfy the demands of American industry. In the consequent struggle for the investor's eye, Chinese securities could not compete with American offerings bearing higher interest and apparently involving fewer risks. Against this setting, Lamont's position on the Hukuang bonds may be seen as the deliberate stipulation of an unacceptable condition to spare the American Group the necessity of having to underwrite a loan to China. In this manner, blame for the inability to float a loan could be attributed to the insensitivity of the Chinese to their credit rating, allowing Lamont and Morgan to retain the good will of the Department of State for their public service in forming the American Group and for all Lamont's efforts. If, on the other hand, the Chinese would accept the unacceptable, paying off the German-issue

40. J. P. Morgan and Company to Department of State, March 26, 1920, SD 893.51/2737; Lamont via Tenney to Secretary of State, April 29, 1920, SD 893.51/2807.

41. J. P. Morgan and Company to Lamont, April 13 and May 5, 1920, 185–19, TWL ms.

bonds—if the moon were blue—the potential for profit would be infinitely greater, and the bankers *might* be able to consider the entire venture as something more than "public service."

While Lamont toyed with the Chinese, the agreement he had sewn together in Tokyo began to unravel. Although the British were grumbling about Lamont having conceded too much, they notified the Department of State of their willingness to accept the compromise over railway construction in Manchuria and Mongolia. But the Japanese government, very likely in a last effort to strengthen the consensus within the leadership, bid once more for veto power over any railway construction in Manchuria. As the American Embassy in Tokyo reported, Japanese editorial opinion was divided on the agreement, with severe opposition developing. One of the editors who saw the Japanese government selling out to the United States argued that "if the present government stays in power for another year the Empire's rights abroad will be surrendered, and all that will remain of the work of the great Emperor Meiji will be a dream." If the Japanese government could win further concessions from its prospective partners, it might still the opposition. The effort alone might satisfy dissidents within the cabinet that the government had done all that was possible.[42]

Japanese efforts to hedge on the agreement which he had spent a month spinning, using all of his charm and much of his considerable power to bring both the Japanese and American governments into line, infuriated Lamont. What could be more unsettling to a busy man of affairs than to have a venture concluded, even applauded, with bows already taken, collapse—the praise unearned, the work to begin anew? And Lamont's fury was intensified by the hostile propanganda with which the Japanese in China were meeting his visit there. Having earlier pressed the Department of State to concede more than it had desired to, Lamont could ask nothing further of it. Instead, he argued that the Department should stand firm and threaten the Japanese with the prospect of a three-power consortium. He suggested that the Department send the Japanese government a message indicating that if the Japanese were "unable after the assurances that have been given in principle by both the United States and the American Banking Group to authorize the Japanese Banking Group to proceed at once with the proposed

42. British Ambassador, Washington, to Secretary of State, April 7, 1920, SD 893.51/2762; Japanese Ambassador, Washington, to Secretary of State, April 3, 1920, SD 893.51/2754; Morris to Secretary of State, April 1, 1920, SD 893.51/2748.

exchange of letters . . . then the United States Government will consider that it is useless to continue the discussions further and will suggest to the American Group that they so advise Mr. Lamont.'' He insisted that it would be ''poor policy to give the Japanese Government any further leeway in this matter.'' In his judgment, ''they ought to be down on their knees in gratitude to the American, British, and French Groups for inviting the Japanese Group to become a partner and for being so patient about it.''[43]

The British and American governments did not need Lamont's urging to stand firm. Nor was the Department of State unaware of the relationship between Lamont's new enthusiasm for a three-power consortium and his interest in a Chinese proposal for involving American finance in the Chinese Eastern Railroad. Neither the Department nor J. P. Morgan was interested in touching the proposal, and Morgan cabled Lamont that the managing committee of the American Group was unanimous in opposition to a three-power consortium: ''all feel that Japanese co-operation or acquiescence in these matters essential to success.'' Quickly the matrix in which a solution would be sought had been narrowed. The Japanese could obtain no more than had been conceded by Lamont before he left Tokyo at the end of March and there could be no threat of a three-power consortium used against them. All the American government and Lamont could do was to hold the line and hope the Japanese government would accept the terms of the March agreement. The British were confident that the Japanese would yield.[44]

As Lamont became annoyed with the Japanese government, he retained the conviction that the Japanese bankers were on the side of the angels, working toward the common good, in opposition to sinister influences within the Japanese government. He was especially confident of the support of Inoue Junnosuke, Governor of the Bank of Japan, and he did what he could to strengthen Inoue's hand. To the American Ambassador in Tokyo he sent a cable expressing his faith in Inoue, his disgust with the Japanese government, and hints of a three-power consortium. He informed Ambassador Morris that he was at liberty to show the cable to Inoue. Morris urged Lamont to be patient, shuddering at the prospect of a three-power consor-

43. Morris to Colby repeating Lamont to Morris, April 8, 1920, SD 893.51/2765; Tenney to Secretary of State with Lamont supplementary remarks, April 12, 1920, SD 893.51/2766; Tenney to Secretary of State with Lamont comments, April 16, 1920, SD 893.51/2775.

44. Colby to Lamont, April 21, 1920, SD 893.51/2775; J. P. Morgan and Company to Lamont, April 21, 1920, SD 893.51/2788; American Embassy, London, to Secretary of State, April 21, 1920, SD 893.51/2789.

tium competing against Japan, destroying his own efforts to bring Japan into a cooperative relationship with the United States. Hoping that the American refusal to make further concessions would help Inoue and lead to the withdrawal of the conditions imposed by "the powerful military group," Morris begged Lamont to "join me in one final drive."[45]

Throughout April, Lamont travelled in China, in constant cable communication with the Department of State and his partners on Wall Street. As the cables crossed back and forth across the Pacific, the Department orchestrated its movements with the British Foreign Office. Toward the end of the month the Japanese government was informed officially of the refusal of the American, British, and French governments to consider its last set of proposals. The American note was replete with Wilsonian references to a new order about to dawn, expectations of harmonious and friendly cooperation instead of competition, and the unambiguous statement that the "granting to any one party to the consortium of the power to veto the possible construction of a railway would appear to be contrary to the principles upon which the idea of the consortium is based."[46]

As anticipated, the Japanese government retreated—or did it? On May 5 the Ministry of Foreign Affairs gave the American Ambassador a "draft reply" to the American rejection of Japan's last set of reservations. The Gaimusho claimed that the earlier note had not been presented for the purpose of raising new conditions but simply to avoid future misunderstandings. The Japanese government would not insist on "explicit assurance or consent of the American government" but would accept the "general assurances" offered previously. It would refrain from insisting upon discussion of the veto power it sought over railway construction in Manchuria. The Japanese were satisfied to make known to the American government their interpretation of the questions at issue. Forwarding the Japanese draft, Ambassador Morris described it as a "complete and sincere acquiescence in the position taken by the other three powers." He was certain that Lamont would approve—and he was correct. When Lamont saw the draft, Morris reported that he was pleased with the Japanese decision to meet the State Department's views so completely. At last the way was clear for the final

45. Morris to Secretary of State, April 19, 1920, repeating Lamont to Morris and Morris to Lamont, SD 893.51/2785.

46. Colby to Morris, April 29, 1920, SD 893.51/2754.

exchange of notes and the four-power banking consortium for China could become a reality.[47]

In Washington, however, MacMurray read an entirely different meaning into the Japanese note. He insisted that the note retracted nothing: "on the contrary, it re-emphasizes Japan's claim to a veto upon railway construction which might compete with existing Japanese lines in Manchuria, and (what is more significant) places on record that the Japanese Government interprets as meaning precisely *that* the assurances which we have given them regarding our willingness to respect Japan's rights of self-preservation." Disagreeing sharply with Morris' interpretation of the Japanese note, MacMurray argued that the Japanese were not accepting the same terms as were the Americans, British, and French. Instead they were simply repeating their effort to enter the Consortium "only upon conditions which assure to Japan an actual and recognized monopoly in Manchuria." If the United States accepted the Japanese note, it could never dispute Japan's right to forbid undertakings which might compete with Japanese holdings in Manchuria. Rather than agree that the Japanese note was satisfactory, MacMurray recommended a message to Morris warning that the United States might have to readjust its policy in recognition of the impossibility of obtaining Japanese cooperation.[48]

To Lamont, MacMurray's concerns were academic. No Americans or Europeans would try to build railways in competition with Japan in Manchuria. To concede this region to Japan in an agreement was to concede nothing more than the reality of the economic conditions existing in Manchuria. Lamont realized the inability of the Department of State or of the European Foreign Offices to grant an explicit veto to Japan. This would be tantamount to recognizing a Japanese sphere of influence in Manchuria, inconsistent with the "new era" to which the Wilsonians hoped to serve as midwives. Once the Japanese withdrew their demand for explicit assurances, however, Lamont had no tolerance for MacMurray's legalism. If the Japanese were on record, unchallenged by the United States, as understanding that American assurances of concern for Japan's self-preservation meant the Consortium would finance no railways in Manchuria without Japanese approval, what did it matter? A test of the meaning of American assurances, of

47. Morris to Colby, May 5, 1920, SD 893.51/2815.
48. MacMurray memorandum for Long, May 6, 1920, SD 893.51/2815.

the difference in the Japanese and American interpretations of those assurances, would never come because there would never be any effort to build competing railroads in Manchuria. Lamont had already asked J. P. Morgan to warn the top echelons of the Department against MacMurray's legalism—and now Lamont's view prevailed. On May 7 the secretary of state cabled his acceptance of the Japanese draft. On May 8, he sent congratulations to Morris and Lamont for the success of their efforts to organize the Consortium, foreseeing "a new era in our relations with Japan" and a prospect of "permanent peace in the Far East." On May 10, Lamont received congratulations from his colleagues at J. P. Morgan and Company, with an added note of perhaps central import: "relieved in view existing market conditions that no loan to China is to be considered at present time."[49]

MacMurray was probably correct. The Japanese, in addition to receiving explicit acceptance by the United States of all their existing and some of their projected economic interests in Manchuria and Mongolia—economic interests recognized to have political and strategic importance as well—had established a strong basis for arguing that the United States had conceded to Japan veto power over railway construction in Manchuria. Certainly that was implicit in the view that prevailed in Japanese official circles. Of the several reasons for the Department's hurried decision to reject MacMurray's argument, perhaps the most obvious was the fact that it was very much at the mercy of its chosen instrument, Thomas Lamont. Lamont had left Wall Street for more than two months in response to urgent pleas from the Department. Now, as he claimed success, supported by the American Ambassador to Japan, the Department was faced with taking upon itself responsibility for failure if it rejected the Japanese position. Lamont, with easy access to the press, would almost certainly charge that the success of his mission had been snatched away at the very last moment by petty bureaucrats in Washington—and with a real likelihood that the Ambassador would resign and stand behind Lamont.

Of greater importance in choosing Lamont's view over that of MacMurray may have been its inherent realism. The Department's goal in resurrecting the Consortium idea had been to preserve American interests in China—that is, to preserve American economic opportunity in China—by checking Japanese expansion and assisting in the modernization of China.

49. Colby to Morris, May 7, 1920, SD 893.51/2815; Colby to Morris, May 8, 1920, SD 893.51/2819; J. P. Morgan and Company to Lamont, May 10, 1920, SD 893.51/2821.

By May 1920, it was readily apparent that little if any money was available in the United States for economic assistance, for development projects of any kind, in China. Lamont had provided, through his negotiations in Tokyo, a basis for cooperation with Japan in the Consortium. It was not as happy a set of conditions for co-opting Japan as MacMurray and Long had desired, but the conditions that Lamont had obtained were the only ones available to the Department. With Lamont's departure from Japan imminent, the Department had to choose between a Consortium on the terms Lamont and Morris considered adequate—or no Consortium at all. For the United States, the idea of a three-power consortium without Japan or no consortium would be a negation of the Department's efforts in East Asia for two years. The British could face such an alternative with relative equanimity—they might be able to use their alliance with Japan as a basis for cooperation in China. The United States had no alternative to the Consortium, especially after March 1920, when American participation in the League of Nations was rejected for the third time by the Senate. Finally, the Department could not easily escape the correctness of Lamont's underlying assumption. There would never be a test of Japan's right to veto railway construction in Manchuria because there was no likelihood of the Consortium ever undertaking any such venture. And thus began Wilson's new order for East Asia.

In passing, it should not be forgotten that Lamont's ends in East Asia were not identical to those of the Department of State. First, Lamont undertook the mission as a public service, seeking good-will and prestige for himself and his firm. The act of going provided the image of the banker as public servant, but at least the appearance of success was important for prestige and ultimately influence. Lamont was interested in cooperating with Japanese bankers, but not for the reasons that appealed to MacMurray and Long. He was not interested in preserving economic opportunities in the abstract, in some distant future—or even in China. He was much more concerned with seizing existing opportunities and these were not in China, certainly not in Manchuria, but more likely in Japan. For Lamont, then, his mission was an unmitigated triumph. An editorial in the *New York Times* ranked the Consortium agreement as a world settlement second only to the one at Paris.[50] Praise of his efforts filled Washington and he became, in the American business world, the leading authority on East Asian affairs. And

50. *New York Times*, June 17, 1920, p. 10.

his good relations with Japanese bankers did not go unrewarded, as the Japanese men of affairs turned to him for the next decade in their quest for money and advice. Only the Chinese seemed to emerge empty-handed as Lamont and the Department celebrated their success in bringing Japan into the new Consortium—although it should be noted that giving nothing to the Chinese was soon described as the Consortium's most valuable contribution to China.

# 3

# GEORGE E. SOKOLSKY: A JEW WANDERS TO CHINA

GEORGE SOKOLSKY's father was also a man of the cloth. That much of their heritage he shared with Roger Greene and Thomas Lamont. But none of Sokolsky's relatives had come close to catching the *Mayflower* and Rabbi Sokolsky did not find his way from Bialystok to America until the 1880s. Although his son George was born in Utica, New York, in 1893, the rabbi raised his family in New York City—in Jewish ghettos on the East Side and in Harlem. There young Sokolsky grew up conscious of radical ideas that permeated the Jewish intellectual community. In later years he claimed to have studied socialism and to have known Emma Goldman and Leon Trotsky before he went to college.[1]

Although Sokolsky's origins were more removed from the establishment mold than those of Greene and Lamont, he nevertheless was able to obtain a decent education. Although he settled for a Bronx high school, he found his way to Columbia University where he studied journalism, and became a leader among student radicals. He also developed an interest in a young woman whose family disapproved of him. Sokolsky left Columbia under duress in 1917, but it is not clear whether his antiwar stand or his sex-

1. George E. Sokolsky, 1956 transcript, 1–10, Oral History Collection, Columbia University.

ual activities were responsible for his trouble with the authorities. The pain of his departure was eased by an irresistible offer to go to Russia to cover the Russian Revolution for a New York news service. He subsequently suspected the offer had been arranged by his lady-friend's relatives as a means of getting him out of the United States, a theory given substance by the collapse of the news service shortly after his arrival in Russia. Sokolsky left for Petrograd in the summer of 1917 and did not see New York again for thirteen years. Most of the first year of his exile was spent in Russia, where he was miserable, feeling oppressed by the filth and disorder he came to associate with Russians and revolutions. He found no Washingtons, Jeffersons, and Hamiltons among the revolutionaries—only a sordid mess. And he was lonely.[2]

One day in March 1918, Sokolsky found himself on a train headed for China, allegedly deported by the Bolsheviks for being hostile to the regime, but very likely departing voluntarily to seek his fortune in more promising surroundings. Indeed, American and British authorities in China long suspected that he had been sent by the Bolsheviks to stir up trouble among the Chinese. Arriving in Tientsin, Sokolsky was able to obtain employment writing for the *North China Star,* an English language paper owned by Edward Fox, a British subject. More than Fox or most Westerners, Sokolsky plunged into Chinese society, becoming both professionally and socially more involved with Chinese than with other Americans or Europeans. Conceivably this pattern was a response to the contempt in which he, as a Jew—a "half-Oriental"—was held by many of his countrymen in China. To the Chinese, his religious eccentricities were less offensive, and he could assume a higher place in the pecking order. He soon developed an unusual connection with the local police, describing himself as an adviser to the police chief.[3]

2. *Ibid.; New York Times,* May 31, 1915, p. 6, February 22, 1916, p. 7, March 30, 1917, p. 4; fragment of draft autobiography, undated, 94–102, Box 15, Papers of George E. Sokolsky, Butler Library, Columbia University. Sokolsky was dismissed from Columbia for "immoral conduct," after complaints by the parents of the young woman with whom he was living, but his antiwar stand had previously angered President Nicholas Murray Butler, who ordered the dismissal; Professor Richard T. Baker to author, September 5, 1974. Sokolsky's papers are divided between Columbia and the Hoover Institution. Materials at Columbia are primarily scrapbooks, containing his published writings and transcripts of speeches. What remains of his correspondence is at Hoover, access controlled by his second wife and not granted to me.

3. Sokolsky transcript (1956), Oral History, Columbia; Sokolsky, "These Days," (syndicated column, 1941–1962, from scrapbooks), September 23, 1962. Hereafter cited as GES ms.

By 1919, Sokolsky had drifted down to Shanghai, where most of the action could be found. He picked up odd jobs and, at the time of the May student outbreaks, was managing American motion picture shows. As unrest mounted in China, Sokolsky became associated with student leaders of the May Fourth Movement and with members of Sun Yat-sen's Kuomintang (Nationalist Party). He joined the *Shanghai Gazette,* controlled by Sun's party, in an editorial capacity. Before long, "the paper became very secondary to me, and I became part of Sun Yat-sen's group." On the fringes of the Kuomintang, Sokolsky served as a publicist and "literary assistant," helping to promulgate the Canton group's views among Westerners and, according to the American consul-general in Shanghai, "injecting numerous of his own views into Chinese procedure relative to student and other activities." Soon Sokolsky had a new title: Manager, Bureau of Public Information. As such he produced pro-Sun and anti-Japanese propaganda releases for Western consumption and generally worried American authorities in Shanghai who feared him as a subversive—a man whose activities would at very least embarrass the government of the United States. In the United States, Sokolsky was little known, but his information bulletins were dutifully filed by the Department of State and he published an article in *Current History* and a letter to the editor of *The New York Herald.*[4]

In 1920, Sokolsky's status with American authorities changed and his services were in greater demand. British intelligence estimates continued to list him as a probable Bolshevik agent, but for the American government he became an important source of information on Chinese radicalism and Kuomintang politics. Although he remained on the suspect list until September 1920, he had developed a close friendship with an American military attaché, Col. Walter Drysdale, and a good working relationship with the new consul-general in Shanghai, Edwin Cunningham. When Lamont visited China, it was Sokolsky who arranged the contacts with student leaders. In addition to his work with the Bureau of Public Information and his role as informant for the American government, Sokolsky wrote under assumed names—G. Gramada, George Rappaport, George Soks—for various newspapers in China and Japan. Before the end of the year he had also joined

4. Sokolsky transcript (1956), Oral History, Columbia, 20–21; Thomas Sammons to Paul Reinsch, May 9, 1919, SD 893.4016/1; Sammons to Secretary of State, May 20, 1919, SD 893.911/32, August 8, 1919, SD 893.912/2, and September 22, 1919, SD 893.91/3; Sokolsky, "Shantung Under General Ma Liang," *New York Times Current History,* XI (November 1919), 350–51; *New York Herald,* November 30, 1919, GES ms.

W. H. Donald's Bureau of Economic Information, an organ of the Peking government.[5]

Of service to two major contenders for power in China—and the United States government—writing for several newspapers with conflicting editorial policies, advising the student movement while simultaneously aiding the American Chamber of Commerce in its efforts to bypass the student-directed boycott, Sokolsky's sole commitment was, obviously, to himself. He was a pen for hire, a man with more information about Kuomintang politics than the American government could get elsewhere, a man with the desire and the ability to ingratiate himself with those who had the power to advance his interests. To this end he was even willing to infiltrate a group of Jewish refugees from Siberia, to report on their activities to American military intelligence.[6]

Writing under his own name in 1918 and 1919, Sokolsky's main theme was opposition to Japanese imperialism in China. Two items that reached audiences in the United States were critical of Japan's role in Shantung. A third presented a sympathetic and simplistic analysis of the May Fourth Movement, interspersed with nonsense designed to win the support of American readers, i.e.: "the fourth of July was nationally celebrated by the Chinese as a tribute to our great Republic."[7]

As an informant to the American government and when writing under various pseudonyms in 1920, Sokolsky focused primarily on Chinese internal affairs. For American officials he reported on factional politics within the Kuomintang and was generally critical of Sun Yat-sen and those closest to him. He assuaged American anxieties about Bolshevik activities by insisting that there was little Bolshevik propaganda in Shanghai and that none of

5. Memorandum on Bolshevism prepared by C. C. Denham, April 7, 1920, FO 405/228/157. Sokolsky was believed to be the intermediary between the Russians and the Chinese; Sokolsky transcript (1956), Oral History, Columbia; A. B. Ruddock to Secretary of State, enclosing Gauss to Crane, November 13, 1920, SD 893.911/121; Lamont, *Across World Frontiers,* 238; Cunningham to Secretary of State, March 30, 1920, SD 761.93/142, May 26, 1920, 893.00/3376, and October 14, 1920, SD 893.00/3609. See examples by G. Gramada in *Japan Advertiser,* August 28, 1920; *North China Daily News,* December 23, 1920; *Trans-Pacific,* April 1921; and by George Rappaport in *North China Star,* December 19, 1920, GES ms. Earl Albert Selle, *Donald of China* (Sydney, Australia, 1948).

6. Cunningham to Secretary of State, April 7, 1920, SD 693.1117/22; MA "Accommodations for Jewish Refugees from Siberia" (informant is *not* named), September 15, 1919, RG 165, 2657-I-6.

7. "Shantung under General Ma Liang," and letter to editor, *New York Herald,* cited above; "China's Defiance of Japan," *The Independent,* XCIX (September 20, 1919), 388–90.

it emanated from Moscow—there were only a lot of Russian refugees pretending to be Bolshevik agents. He did indicate, however, that Sun was in contact with Soviet authorities, seeking aid in his obsession with unifying China by force.[8]

Sokolsky's writings were often in the realm of political theory—analyses of the failure of the Chinese revolution and suggestions for improvement. One theme that emerged was that of federalism, of the need for a new constitution in which the provinces would be granted autonomy more in keeping with reality than the fanciful centralized regime of the constitution adopted in 1912. The idea of a Chinese federation, attractive to a few Chinese intellectuals and warlords at the time, was opposed by Sun—perhaps explaining Sokolsky's negative view of the Chinese leader. Another concept Sokolsky offered was that of China as an emerging middle-class democracy. Arguing that "every important step in the progress of the human race was made either by the middle class or under its direction," he contended that China was in the process of undergoing a middle class revolution. Uneasy about student leadership of the May Fourth Movement, the Chinese Chambers of Commerce had come forth to temper the movement. Now students, merchants, and industrialists were all working together for representative, stable government—internal peace on a federative basis.[9]

Sokolsky's criticism of Sun and praise of middle-class virtues suggested that he was moving toward a new identity. The image of Sokolsky the dangerous radical or the visionary socialist faded quickly, to be replaced by Sokolsky the realist, the old China hand to whom American businessmen and American diplomats could turn for reliable information and sound advice. Lamont had been favorably impressed with him and a sporadic correspondence grew between the two men. If not yet one of them, Sokolsky now moved more easily among the Respectables.

If being a Jew was not sufficient to limit Sokolsky's upward mobility in Shanghai's international settlement, his marriage to a Chinese woman in October 1922 posed an insurmountable barrier. His wife, the former Rosalind Phang, had been born in Jamaica, educated in England—"a licentiate of the

8. Cunningham to Secretary of State, May 26, 1920, SD 893.00/3376, October 14, 1920, SD 893.00/3609, and March 30, 1920, SD 761.93/142.

9. "G. Gramada," *Japan Advertiser*, August 28, 1920, GES ms; Li Chien-nung, *Political History of China, 1840–1928* (Princeton, 1956), 402–4; "George Rappaport," *North China Star*, December 19, 1920, GES ms.

Royal Academy of Music, London''—but to no avail. Though her family was wealthy and she was far more cultivated than the average western woman in Shanghai, Mrs. Sokolsky and her husband were not welcome in western homes. Even more than before, Sokolsky's social life centered in Chinese circles. His American and European male associates became mere business acquaintances because social contacts could not be extended to include their wives.[10]

There were compensations, however. Rosalind Phang was given in marriage by another Jamaican Chinese, Eugene Chen, increasingly prominent in Kuomintang politics. One of her friends—one of their circle—was Soong Mei-ling, whose sister had married Sun Yat-sen and whose family was perhaps the most powerful family in Kuomintang circles. Sokolsky grew closer to the leading western-educated, English-speaking Chinese who were rising to the top in Chinese politics, particularly in the south.[11]

In the early 1920s, years of instability and disorder in China—the heyday of the warlords—Sokolsky's opportunities to write for a wide variety of newspapers and journals increased. He wrote extensively for the *North China Daily News* (Shanghai), *North China Star* and *Japan Advertiser,* and contributed frequent articles to the *Weekly Review* (formerly *Millard's Review*) and *Trans-Pacific*. His unsigned articles appeared occasionally in papers in the United States, most notably the *Philadelphia Public Ledger*. He became one of the best-known foreign journalists in China, a source of information and contacts for transient and newly arrived journalists—a man worth knowing, ''a clever Jew.''

Throughout 1921, he published under the pseudonym G. Gramada, while using his own name to front for Chinese friends interested in operating Chinese-language newspapers under American auspices. The trust in which he was held in Shanghai was slow to permeate the American Legation in Peking, where his connections with Chinese of doubtful repute reinforced earlier impressions of Sokolsky as a shady if not subversive operator. The Legation and ultimately the Department of State supported Clarence Gauss, American consul at Tsinan, in his refusal to register Sokolsky's paper as American-owned. At approximately the same time, Sokolsky associated himself with C. T. Wang (Wang Cheng-t'ing) in Wang's efforts to gain sup-

10. Clipping of wedding announcement, undated, GES ms; Sokolsky, ''My Mixed Marriage,'' *Atlantic Monthly*, CLII (August 1933), 137–46.

11. Sokolsky, ''My Mixed Marriage''; Sokolsky transcript (1956), Oral History, Columbia.

port within the foreign community and among Kuomintang politicians. "G. Gramada" found Wang an attractive alternative to the "erratic and wild" Sun Yat-sen. Sokolsky's ties to Wang were short-lived, but in the next decade he put his pen to similar use for Wang, T. V. Soong, and others able to attract his support.[12]

Apparently, long before the Comintern promulgated its call for bourgeois revolution in China, Sokolsky had concluded that middle-class leadership was the answer to China's ills. Men of substance—with money and business experience—had to come forth and carry out the political reforms necessary to create a modern China. His sympathies were with the Kuomintang, but with its more conservative elements. The Kuomintang would have to unify China and the bankers and industrialists aligned with the party would have to rule in its name. China needed stability and the replacement of warlords with wild radicals would not suffice. Despite his ties to young Chinese political leaders, Sokolsky's views were in 1921 already moving rapidly toward agreement with American businessmen and diplomats impatient with adolescent Chinese nationalism.

Writing about the Consortium, Sokolsky reflected Chinese suspicions of Japan, tempered with a faint hope that American participation might protect China. He considered the participation of a Chinese banking group essential and noted that Lamont was supposedly willing to accept such a group. Consistent with the thought of both Lamont and Kuomintang leaders, Sokolsky argued that the Consortium should withhold money from China—money that could only go to the Peking government, strengthening the warlords in control there. Like the Consortium bankers, he insisted that stability had to precede a loan. But though the Consortium had issued no loans—had done nothing—by May 1921, he professed to see its demise. The American Group's effort "to help China and save her from chaos" had been defeated by the Japanese—and British and French imperialists. Analyzing American trade prospects at approximately the same time, he disposed of the myth of Chinese preferences for American goods. The Chinese merchant bought where he got the best deal—and the Japanese offered lower prices and more reliable credit. Opportunities for expanding American trade in China existed, but American firms would have to study the market and adapt to local practices—and the Chinese were skeptical about American

12. Ruddock to Secretary of State, enclosures, July 29, 1921, SD 893.911/121; "G. Gramada," *Japan Advertiser*, April 13, 1921, GES ms.

seriousness of purpose, with an attendant loss of American commercial prestige.[13]

In the spring of 1921, Sokolsky prepared a series of memoranda for American authorities in China. Forwarding them to Washington, to the secretary of state, Consul General Edwin Cunningham testified to Sokolsky's reliability as an observer and contended that his memoranda were "of greater interest than any of the political comments that appear editorially in the foreign newspapers." Sokolsky described an apathetic populace among whom neither Sun Yat-sen nor Wu P'ei-fu, one of the most prominent warlords, could attract much support. He considered the student leadership of the May Fourth Movement adrift, becoming decadent in the quest for sex reforms, neglecting politics for social change. Reporting an increase in antiforeign sentiment, he suggested that Americans were less disliked than other foreigners, but claimed that the outcome of the Consortium was crucial. If the Consortium failed or became either a British or a Japanese tool—events which, as G. Gramada, he had already called into being—American prestige would be hurt. He warned that Chinese friendship for the United States was being eroded by unkept American promises.[14]

In July 1921 the American government, in response to domestic pressures and British overtures, invited nations with interests in the Western Pacific, including China, to a conference designed to prevent a naval arms race and to settle a wide range of East Asian problems. The Chinese responded with enthusiasm—and with dreams of using the conference to rid China of foreign spheres of influence, of extraterritoriality and tariff restrictions.

As the hour neared for China and the powers to meet at Washington, Sokolsky became increasingly less sympathetic to the demands of Chinese nationalists. He was irritated by their antiforeign outcries, by their demands for the abolition of the "unequal treaties." To be sure, they were entitled to have their lost territories restored and spheres of influence returned to Chinese control. An end to these foreign infringements on Chinese sovereignty would not affect the quality of George Sokolsky's life in China, and would have little impact on the exalted status of foreigners in the treaty ports. But a restoration of tariff autonomy would threaten the profits of his friends in the American Chamber of Commerce, Shanghai—and an end to extraterri-

13. "G. Gramada," *North China Daily News,* December 23, 1920; unsigned article in *Philadelphia Public Ledger,* despatched from Shanghai, May 19, 1921; "G. Gramada," *Trans-Pacific,* April, 1921, GES ms.

14. Cunningham to Secretary of State, June 3, 1921, enclosures, SD 893.00/3963.

toriality, to foreign concessions in the treaty ports—would mean the end of the good life.

Despite his Chinese wife and Chinese friends, Sokolsky's writings reflected the fears of the white man who saw his privileged status threatened. Like all friends of China, he decried the continuing skirmishes among the warlords, the "childish internecine strife," "make-believe wars for make-believe principles." Despite his closeness to Kuomintang politics, he seemed unimpressed by *any* claims to be fighting for principle. But he was angry at the Chinese people who "are ready enough to quarrel and threaten foreigners, but before their coolie generals they tremble and hand over the lucre." If the Chinese did not end the nonsense by the time the conference met in Washington then the powers had to threaten intervention. Most of all, he was unyielding in his opposition to the Chinese demand for the abolition of extraterritoriality. If one doubted his contentions of Chinese weakness at administration as compared to foreign, "one need only go from the modern city of Shanghai to the filth of the native city to realize the difference." Apart from the questionable relevance of his example, it was clear that the position of Rosalind Phang's husband was not far from the stereotypical treaty port resident and his expressed contempt for "the filthy Chinese."[15]

At the Washington Conference the major seapowers reached an agreement to limit the size of their navies and committed themselves, under the Nine Power Treaty, to refrain from interfering in the internal affairs of China. At Washington the great powers found a way to resolve conflicts among them, a way to coexist peacefully in East Asia. But the results of the Conference were bitterly disappointing to the Chinese. The sovereign rights the Chinese had been forced to surrender over the previous eighty years were not regained. Foreign troops remained on Chinese soil and foreign warships patrolled Chinese waters. In response to China's request for tariff autonomy, the powers offered only an interim surcharge and a promise of future discussions. In answer to China's demand for an end to extraterritoriality, the powers promised a commission to study the problem. The new order in East Asia contained few attractions for Chinese nationalists—and few threats to the Old China Hands in the treaty ports.

Civil strife continued in China through the early 1920s. The fortunes of Sun Yat-sen and the Kuomintang waxed and waned with little to indicate

15. "G. Gramada," *Weekly Review*, October 1, 1921, and *North China Daily News*, August 24, 1921; "G. Gramada," *Japan Advertiser*, November 4, 1921, GES ms.

that they would prevail over the Northern warlords who dominated the Peking regime—or over the undependable Southern warlords who provided the military power Sun needed for his vision of unifying China. Soviet agents circulated through the contending camps in China, seeking friends among warlords, bourgeois revolutionaries, and intellectuals. As well as anyone else in China, George Sokolsky understood what was happening, retained a vestigial sympathy for the Chinese, but was disgusted with Chinese politics and the intensification of antiforeignism among Chinese politicians. In general he found himself outside the mainstream of political activity, welcomed as an adviser by lesser warlords but without access to the more prominent leaders. Increasingly he was forced to fall back on writing for a livelihood and increasingly, he wrote for and became affiliated with newspapers and journals unfriendly to Chinese nationalism, reflective not only of treaty port old China hands, but of Japanese propaganda as well.

In 1921 and 1922 Sokolsky was still associated with ardent defenders of China like W. H. Donald and Thomas F. Millard. During those years, George Bronson Rea, whose *Far Eastern Review* had become notorious for its pro-Japanese propaganda, once complained to the American consul-general at Shanghai that Donald, Millard, and Sokolsky were agitating for war between the United States and Japan. By 1923, Rea was considered not only pro-Japanese but anti-American as well, and all American advertising was withdrawn from the *Far Eastern Review*. Nonetheless, Sokolsky began to write for him and two years later became Rea's second-in-command.[16]

With the exception of his writings for the *Far Eastern Review*, Sokolsky generally signed or initialed his articles after 1921. George E. Soks made an appearance in 1922, but George Rappaport and G. Gramada vanished. "Soks" criticised Sun for the Tokyo-based American newspaper, the *Japan Advertiser*, writing him off as a good critic and revolutionary, but a poor administrator—a judgment few historians would dispute. He reported that Sun and his intimates were feared by businessmen, merchants, and bankers—by the middle class to whom Sokolsky sought to award leadership in the modernization of China. The returned students who flocked to Sun's banner did not know the Chinese people, did not understand the life—or even the language of the villagers. Writing for the pro-Sun *Weekly Review*, Sokolsky developed this argument into a call for Chinese intellectuals to go

16. Cunningham to Secretary of State, December 15, 1924, SD 893.00/5929, to Legation, July 11, 1921, SD 893.911/118.

to the villages to educate the Chinese people, to democratize education.[17]

Resuming his original focus on the returned Chinese students—the Chinese to whom because of language, values, and finances he had always been closest—Sokolsky concluded that it was wrong to continue the American system of allowing Chinese to attend scattered universities, never becoming part of the community, becoming an entity neither Chinese nor American. He contended that they became accustomed to standards of living that were too high. They became unfit for service in China. Sokolsky argued instead for a system closer to British practices of supporting schools in China, keeping students in a Chinese environment during their formative years, skimming off a few of the best for post-graduate work in England. The rest remained Chinese, able to communicate with their own people and to work among them. These again were ideas with which later historians might agree—and which educators gradually accepted in the interwar period. As Sokolsky noted, returned students, perhaps especially those from the United States, remained a part of urban China, not always understanding or even sympathizing with the plight of rural China. They did not move among the masses like fish through the water, but were more likely to be in their element at the Harvard Club. The problem Sokolsky recognized haunted China throughout the Republican era—and its ultimate resolution by Mao Tse-Tung did not come in a form acceptable to him.[18]

In the early 1920s, fear of Bolshevism permeated Western capitals and the foreign community in China. As Chinese intellectuals and a few political figures pondered the meaning of the Russian Revolution, weighing its lessons for their own cause, occasionally parroting Lenin, there was concern among Westerners and Japanese about the extent of Soviet influence on Chinese nationalism. Sokolsky was remarkably sanguine about the situation, ridiculing foreigners who blamed the increasing assertiveness of the Chinese upon Lenin. He foresaw that the privileged position of foreigners in China would be undermined within the decade and praised the missionaries for encouraging the emergence of Chinese leadership within an indigenous church—evidence that missionaries "understand conditions in China better than businessmen and better even than the experts in the legations and consulates."[19]

17. "George E. Soks," *Japan Advertiser*, March 23, 1922; *Weekly Review*, June 24, 1922, GES ms.

18. *Japan Advertiser*, March 31, 1923, GES ms.

19. *Japan Advertiser*, May 22, 1922, GES ms.

When Adolph Joffe led a Soviet mission to Peking in 1922, Sokolsky remained confident that the mission's presence would change little. Joffe might establish contacts with Chinese intellectuals, but he would find that they resented Soviet meddling no less than that of other foreigners. More significantly, he reminded his readers, China was an agrarian country for which Bolshevism, the concept of leadership by industrial laborers, was irrelevant. He argued that the Chinese peasant would be as adverse to Bolshevism as the Russian peasant, that "any system of life which is not premised upon the ownership of property by families in China cannot hold." For thoughtful students of Chinese affairs, unwilling to be frightened by the bogey of Bolshevism, the conviction that Marxism was irrelevant and could not take root in China became conventional wisdom—a source of comfort in the face of Chinese abrasiveness in the 1920s.[20]

At approximately the same time that Joffe reached Peking, Sun Yat-sen was driven out of Canton by his erstwhile ally, Ch'en Chiung-ming, and fled to Shanghai. With his career at low tide, Sun renewed negotiations with Soviet agents. Sokolsky, writing for the *China Review,* argued that Sun was too clever to be fooled into seeing Bolshevism as the answer to China's needs. He did note, however, that the Russians, like the Germans, had surrendered the privileges of the unequal treaties and were considered by the Chinese to be less grasping than other powers. Even after Sun's alliance with the Russians and his acceptance of the Chinese Communists into the Kuomintang with the consequent great growth of his power in 1923 and 1924, Sokolsky defended him and the Chinese nationalist movement generally against charges of Bolshevism. Writing for the *North China Daily News,* a paper not known for its sympathy to Sun, Sokolsky claimed that Northern warlords, specifically the notorious Anfu clique, were trying to deceive foreigners by labelling their enemies Bolsheviks. Conceding that Sun's political thinking was "never very clear" he insisted that his main demand was for the abrogation of the unequal treaties—which was not Bolshevism. Sokolsky warned that calling Sun a Bolshevik was not only erroneous but would likely increase the popularity of Bolshevism. He concluded that foreign diplomats were confusing economic and social doctrines prevalent in Russia with "anti-foreign Pan-Asianism," which was developing rapidly in China.[21]

20. *Philadelphia Public Ledger,* October 22, 1922, GES ms.

21. "Nobody Can Make Chinese Bolshevik," *China Review,* November 1922; "Bogey of Bolshevism," *North China Daily News,* December 29, 1924, GES ms.

Having disposed of Bolshevism to his own satisfaction, understanding the desire of Chinese nationalists to be free of the burdens imposed by the unequal treaties, Sokolsky was nonetheless impatient with Chinese antiforeignism. He contended that the American open door policy had been of tremendous value in preserving China's sovereignty and integrity. Especially after it was embodied in the Nine Power Treaty at the Washington Conference, American policy gave China "time to grow strong." But he later noted that the Chinese were not grateful to the United States or to their American advisors for the achievements of the Washington Conference. Similarly he professed not to understand Chinese hatred for the Japanese "since the return of Shantung." He suggested that baiting the Japanese had become habitual, regardless of Japanese efforts to win favor with the Chinese. Similarly, while Leo Karakhan was in Peking representing Moscow in negotiations to normalize Sino-Soviet relations, Sokolsky claimed (with little regard for the facts) that the Chinese had turned down Karakhan's offer to renounce the unequal treaties in exchange for recognition. Although Karakhan was actually driving a very hard bargain, inconsistent with the generosity of his famed memorandum of 1921, Sokolsky contended that the Chinese government wanted to keep the unequal treaties, to keep a foreign presence in China, as a means of confusing the masses and obscuring China's real problems.[22]

Sokolsky was profoundly aware of the appeal of antiforeignism to the Chinese, of the value of this appeal as a means of transcending disunity. One part of him seemed to identify with his Chinese friends, with their desire to throw out warlords, corrupt politicians, and overbearing foreigners, to unite and modernize China, and to free their land of those who impinged on their peace, their freedom, and their sovereignty. He wrote critically of the warlords and their civilian puppets. He wrote critically of arrogant foreigners—of men of little stature in their own country finding instant status by patronizing the Chinese. He defended the Chinese resistance to Westernization, arguing that it was "a racial desire to maintain itself" and not opposition to modernization. If young people had stopped imitating Western styles and were "going back to China," wonderful—"those who understand China can see in this tendency nothing but good, since it is developing a national consciousness, a desire to understand the people and the country and a will to serve both." The Chinese were becoming their own masters again,

22. *Weekly Review,* August 19, 1922; *Japan Advertiser,* June 15, 1923; *Philadelphia Public Ledger,* July 13, 1923; *North China Daily News,* April 26, 1924, GES ms.

"learning to do modern things in a Chinese way." And he was confident that this new assertiveness of Chinese officials was "wholesome" for Chinese *and* foreigners.[23]

But there was also the other part of Sokolsky—the part that identified with beleaguered foreigners struggling to maintain the good life, the life of privilege, the life George Sokolsky had come to enjoy. In June 1924 he turned on the Chinese publicists who attacked the treaty system. Sun was preparing his Northern Expedition to drive out warlords and foreign imperialists and denunciations of these twin evils resounded through the treaty ports. Sokolsky would not defend the warlords, but "to couple the Chinese militarists and foreign imperialists in one sentence, to say that one supports the other, to ask Chinese to rid the country of both military officials and foreigners, is the logic of ignorance." He wrote off the propaganda flowing from Canton as undigested Marx, ideas unrelated to Chinese thought or to the reality of the Chinese experience. Offering his own image of reality, he declared:

> The foreigner offers China his best: he brings his methods of production and distribution which teach the Chinese merchants and industrialists how to make things efficiently and speedily and less expensively. He brings here his physicians and teachers to strengthen the body and make virile the mind. He offers China an example of methods which someday will make China one of the great and strong countries of the earth. . . .

Angrily, in tones that surely brought cheers in every bar where white men gathered in China—perhaps there would be room for a Jew now—Sokolsky damned the Chinese for rejecting the foreigner's gifts: "You reject these . . . You care nothing for the future of China. Your only interest is the present noise. . . ." And he concluded with the advice that the Chinese radicals *work* for China instead of circulating stupid pamphlets.[24]

How account for the two minds of George Sokolsky? The evidence provides no clear answer. His writing in the early 1920s reflected less sympathy for the behavior and aspirations of Chinese nationalists than it had in his first three years in China—during part of which he was employed as a propagan-

23. *North China Star,* August 28, 1923; "The Changing Chinese," *Far Eastern Review,* January 1924, GES ms.

24. *North China Daily News,* June 6, 1924, GES ms.

dist by Chinese nationalists. To some extent, his position in the early twenties was sounder, more balanced—no longer uncritical, special pleading. Perhaps his analyses of events and personalities in the years between the Washington Conference and the Northern Expedition reflected the more mature judgment of an independent journalist. Surely it is as reasonable to assume that his critical analyses of Chinese nationalism led to employment by newspapers and journals opposed to Chinese nationalism as it is to assume that he modified his views to suit his employers. But the knowledge that in his early years in China and again in later years Sokolsky wrote as a publicist rather than a journalist leaves doubt as to his integrity as a reporter. Perhaps there were really three George Sokolskys: paid partisan of the Chinese nationalists, detached analyst of the Chinese scene, paid partisan of the enemies of Chinese nationalism—and perhaps it is possible that on a given occasion he assumed more than one of these identities. Clearly, however, by the time Sun died in 1925, by the time the Soviet-supported Northern Expedition, led by Chiang Kai-shek, began to move northward, George Sokolsky had completed the transition toward his acceptance by the enemies of the Chinese Nationalist revolution.

As the staging for the Chinese Nationalist revolution began, Sokolsky took a clear stand on the two issues of greatest importance to the Chinese and to the foreigners concerned with China's course. He opposed treaty revision and he opposed the kind of leadership Sun Yat-sen offered. Denying Chinese claims that new conditions allowed for revision of the treaty system, he argued that they could not yet provide security for life or property—that conditions for foreigners in China might well be worse in 1924 than when the treaty system had developed in the middle of the 19th century. He expressed doubt that the Chinese would benefit from the freedom they hoped to gain from treaty revision, offering an invidious comparison between Chinese and Japanese capacities for modernization. Sokolsky also contended that Chinese living in foreign concessions did not want change, that even the most patriotic Chinese in Shanghai realized the time was not ripe because of the "utter corruption of the courts and their incapacity to render fair decisions." On a barbed note of hope he remarked that although China was "cursed with a particularly vile set of officials who are directed by overkeen American returned students," there were better men on the horizon who would try to undo the wickedness of the existing regime. Perhaps they would call George Sokolsky to his rightful place in their inner councils.[25]

Criticizing Sun's leadership, Sokolsky focused on the Canton regime's interference with trade. Sun's government had failed to provide the business leadership expected of its modern young men. On the contrary, the unending political troubles they stirred prevented stability and threatened the financial order and regularity upon which trade depended. Sokolsky recognized the attractiveness of Sun's policies, including his ties to Soviet Russia, to some Chinese intellectuals, "but responsible Chinese, merchants, bankers, etc., are naturally opposed. . . . they want no more disturbances. They want peace and a chance to continue their business." As is apparent in some of his earlier writing, Sokolsky had concluded that China's salvation depended on the rise to power of the merchant prince, the enlightened capitalist—some bright young man with Western training who would emulate Thomas Lamont. His subsequent attraction to T. V. Soong is not difficult to understand.[26]

The evolution of Sokolsky's thought during his formative years in pre-Kuomintang China would be an academic matter but for the fact that he was involved intermittently in Chinese politics and, more significantly, he became an important source, the most important source, of information on Chinese politics for some American diplomats and journalists. When someone like Edna Lee Booker credits Sokolsky with putting her in touch with student groups, alerting her to the formation of the Chinese Communist Party, generally telling her what the news was and where to find it, she can be written off as a minor figure; but Hallett Abend of the *New York Times* presents the same image of Sokolsky. He arrived in China with a letter of introduction to Sokolsky. It was Sokolsky who provided the contacts with the Canton regime. It was Sokolsky alone of the men he met in Shanghai who insisted that the Canton revolutionaries had to be taken seriously.[27]

Similarly, Sherwood Cheney, who replaced Drysdale as American military attaché, relied on Sokolsky as Drysdale had. Cunningham not only elicited memoranda from Sokolsky but frequently sent clippings of So-

25. "G.E.S.," *Transpacific Notes,* July 19, 1924; *Japan Advertiser,* August 28, 1924, GES ms.

26. *North China Daily News,* August 20, 1924; *Japan Advertiser,* November 28, 1924, GES ms.

27. Booker, *News Is My Job* (New York, 1940), 209, 217; Abend, *My Life in China* (New York, 1943), 8, 17, 21.

kolsky's analyses back to the Department of State. Ferdinand Mayer of the American Legation (close confidant of the Chief of the Far Eastern Division of the Department of State, J. V. A. MacMurray) wrote to tell MacMurray of the value of talks with Sokolsky, whom he considered "a very clever Jew. Sherwood Cheney thinks very highly of him and I must say that most everything he said checked up."[28]

Sokolsky was not yet an important source of the American public's information on East Asian affairs, although his writings were beginning to appear in newspapers and journals in the United States. Whatever impact he had on public opinion—and it must have been extremely limited—probably came indirectly through the writings of better-known correspondents with access to larger audiences. He had established himself, however, as an important source of information for American policy makers. He had no contacts on the rarified levels at which Lamont functioned, though he might reach high-level authorities through Lamont. Nonetheless, he had ready access to middle echelon officials—access perhaps as good as Roger Greene enjoyed. But whereas Greene and Lamont were, by 1925, well-established at the top of their respective worlds, George Sokolsky still had great heights to scale. His first peak was reached from 1925 to 1928, when John V. A. MacMurray was Minister to China—and Sokolsky was his favorite correspondent.

28. Cheney to MacMurray, March 18, 1924, and Mayer to MacMurray, undated (postmarked March 17, 1925), Papers of J. V. A. MacMurray, Princeton University.

# PART 2

# Revolution and War in East Asia

# 4

# PRELUDE TO REVOLUTION

WITH the dedication of the magnificent buildings of Peking Union Medical College and the firm establishment of the Rockefeller Foundation's role in China, Roger Greene returned to the United States in 1921. For more than three years he directed the affairs of the China Medical Board from New York, with occasional trips to China. By 1920 the austere bachelor had married Kate Brown. The marriage proved a very happy one, was blessed with children—and Greene had all a man could ask of life. In 1923, writing of a Standard Oil representative at Changsha who was taking his wife back to the United States because she found China wearisome, Greene thought it "a pity that a man's work should be interrupted for such a cause"—his never was.[1] Largely as a result of his position—the requirements of the job, the prestige it offered, and the contacts it provided—Greene had the opportunity to extend his influence in at least three directions. He might shape the course of medical education in China. He could command an audience at home when he chose to speak or write on the affairs of East Asia or the policies of the American government in the area. And, his prestige reinforced by his reputation in the consular service, his views were of interest to the American government, especially to members of the Department of State responsible for policy toward China and Japan.

In 1920, the China Medical Board, with Greene concurring, defined the work of Peking Union Medical College as aiming "primarily to give a medi-

1. Roger to Kate Greene, November 15, 1923, RSG ms.

cal education comparable with that provided by the best medical schools of the United States and Europe." Its secondary aim was to "afford opportunities for research, especially with reference to problems peculiar to the Far East." Only "incidentally" would the school concern itself with extending "a popular knowledge of modern medicine and public health." Greene, other administrators, and the teaching faculty were committed to what they considered quality education. They had a vision of creating a Johns Hopkins in East Asia. But quite early in the school's existence, alternative models were suggested. Sokolsky's sometime friend, C. T. Wang, persistently called for what Greene described as the "wholesale production of lower-grade doctors." Greene resisted Wang's idea in 1923 and resisted strong pressure toward the same end from the Chinese government in the years that followed. If quantity rather than quality were stressed, he wondered "where . . . Chinese leaders would come from."[2]

But which man had a better sense of China's needs? Did Peking Union's well-trained elite have as much impact on Chinese society as would twice as many medical aides trained half as long? Greene wanted to produce not merely doctors but men who could be leaders in Chinese society—and several of the school's graduates did attain positions of prominence in Kuomintang China. But if, as Sokolsky and others were arguing at the time, they key to China's future was in the mobilization of the villages, would Peking Union graduates go to rural China? No. They, like the Kuomintang leadership, were part of an urbanized gloss on village China, a frosting that never permeated the cake and was all too easily scraped off when the peasants rose. Greene understood Chinese society at least as well as Sokolsky, but perhaps it was too easy for a man with his credentials to have faith in reform from above, to believe that the pyramid could be built upside down, on the foundation of a small elite corps.

Although Greene was too sanguine in his expectations of what a few modern doctors could do for China, infected, despite his years overseas, with both the optimism and the elitism of American progressives, there was nothing patronizing in his attitudes toward Chinese or Japanese aspirations. He did not conçeive of a modern China led by the United States—or of Japan needing the example of American moral leadership. Explaining Japanese imperialism to an American audience in January 1922, he discussed the

2. Ferguson, *CMB and PUMC*, 44; Greene to Henry Houghton, May 1, 1923, RSG ms.

anxieties caused in Japan by Western encroachments on China at the end of the century, and insisted that though Japanese aggressions were serious and dangerous to China, there was no great moral difference between Japan and the West. He suggested that American, Australian, and Canadian immigration policies were responsible for Japan's focus on expansion in China.[3] In other contexts, he consistently opposed American intervention in Chinese affairs—and efforts by Americans to decide what was best for the Chinese. Perhaps his position on both the internal affairs of China and Sino-American relations can be described best as reflecting a consensus among Westernized, liberal, Chinese intellectuals and liberal Americans in China.

The best illustration of Greene's role in the early 1920s is found in the controversy over the remission of Boxer Indemnity funds. In 1908, the American government decided to remit half of its share of the indemnity—but not outright. The Chinese were given the money only when they agreed to use it for educational purposes as stipulated. Early in 1924, Greene, in cooperation with A. L. Warnshuis, Secretary of the International Missionary Council, sought to have not only the remainder of the American share, but also payments due other powers remitted and used for educational purposes. Greene's task was to win the consent of the Department of State, most notably the Chief of the Division of Far Eastern Affairs, J. V. A. MacMurray.[4]

When Greene wrote to recommend a plan for pooling indemnities to remit to China for educational purposes, MacMurray did not have the usual "boiler-plate" response mailed out. Instead, with the respect due an esteemed former colleague, he replied at length, expressing his own skepticism about the possibility of international agreement on a coherent plan. He also indicated some doubt as to the wisdom of remitting any further indemnities to the Chinese, pointing to a "truculent and intractable spirit" that seemed to have arisen in China, a challenge to the treaty rights of foreigners. Had Americans, in their desire to be just, "given the Chinese to feel rather a scorn for our weakness than a gratitude for our generosity?" MacMurray was questioning rather than dogmatic and asked Greene to write or come to Washington for further discussion.[5]

Greene responded promptly, clearly defining the fundamental difference between his and MacMurray's conception of what American policy

3. Copy of address to Men's Club, Peterborough, New Hampshire, January 1922, RSG ms.
4. MacMurray to Greene, February 4, 1924, RSG ms.
5. MacMurray to Greene, February 4, 1924, RSG ms.

ought to be. MacMurray, consistent with the arguments he had offered since the Washington Conference—and with the assumptions on which his policies as Minister to China would be predicated—insisted on order in China. He viewed scrupulous regard for treaty rights by the Chinese as a prerequisite to giving the Chinese the assistance they desired, whether revision of the treaty system or remission of indemnities. Greene argued for giving aid to China as soon as possible. He did not anticipate a major change in the Chinese political situation in the near future. If the United States waited, China would want for help when it was most needed. On most issues, MacMurray's position prevailed. China did not get even the relief promised at the Washington Conference, and while France more than the United States was responsible for obstructing agreements reached at the Conference, the United States awaited order prior to supporting China. Greene tried to explain the problems of a society in transition, of new ideas, values, and institutions, stressing the need to train a modern leadership and the need for money for their education, but the lesson was lost on MacMurray and his staff. Within the Far Eastern Division there was more interest in international cooperation to deny funds to the Chinese until they behaved properly—to avoid competition for Chinese favor.[6]

Warnshuis read Greene's reply to MacMurray with approval and proposed to move immediately to enlist Senator Henry Cabot Lodge's support in the Senate for congressional action to remit the indemnity to China. But this was not Greene's style. First, he advised Warnshuis to consult with MacMurray, to work with the Department of State, to avoid a confrontation unless it was necessary, to do nothing to embarrass or irritate key members of the department—to work within the system. Throughout the year, Greene corresponded with and visited with MacMurray, trying to persuade him, keeping him informed of his own views and of those of missionary leaders. In addition, Greene testified in Congressional hearings on the remission question and mustered support from Japanese scholars and the Japanese Foreign Office—always keeping MacMurray informed.[7]

The Chinese government had no doubt that Greene was on its side. In

6. Greene to MacMurray, February 9, 1924, and undated memorandum initialled "P." (probably Willys Peck), MacMurray Papers.

7. Warnshuis to Greene, February 14, 1924; Greene to Warnshuis, February 15, 1924; Greene to MacMurray, May 13, 1924; MacMurray to Greene, May 31, 1924; Greene to MacMurray, October 27, 1924; MacMurray to Greene, November 25, 1924; Representative Stephen G. Porter to Greene, March 27, 1924, RSG ms.

September 1924, when the President of China named a board to oversee the remainder of the indemnity fund, he included five Americans, most notably John Dewey and Roger Greene. But the President of the United States still had control of the money and neither Minister Jacob Gould Schurman nor MacMurray thought the time had come to give it back to the Chinese. The Chinese Minister to the United States, Alfred Sze, with whom Greene had worked in Harbin in 1910, turned to Greene to counteract Schurman's influence with Coolidge. Sze kept Greene informed of all of his own efforts, sending copies of correspondence with American authorities. The Chinese Legation paid Greene's expenses to Washington when he lobbied on behalf of remission, but Greene proved to be an unusual lobbyist. He returned the legation's money, insisting that his efforts related to his own work.[8]

Ultimately Greene won MacMurray's approval for remission of the funds, to be distributed by the Board named by the President of China, the executive committee of which had only one American, Roger Greene. Unhappily, Coolidge delayed action until after the May 30th Incident in Shanghai, until after the revolution was in full swing in China and the initial impact of the move was minimal. Indeed it is possible, even probable, that Coolidge signed the executive order releasing the indemnity funds in July 1925 only because antiforeign demonstrations had already exploded in China and he hoped to pacify Chinese opinion, to soften Chinese hostility toward the United States.[9]

While the indemnity question was still pending, the *New York Times* carried a report that the American chargé and representatives of the other powers at Peking had notified the Chinese government that naval fighting would not be tolerated in the vicinity of Shanghai. To Greene such interference in Chinese internal affairs was unwarranted, and he returned to a theme he had developed in his days as a diplomat, to ideas emerging from his experience with the revolution of 1911. He wrote to MacMurray to urge that the United States avoid pressing the Chinese on the issue, insisting that China could never have a strong government if the powers persisted in interfering in civil strife. Greene explained that at Hankow in 1911 "all we asked was due notice of intended bombardment so those non-combatants that wished might return to places of safety." Though he had opposed the

8. Memorandum of conversation with Sze, September 20, 1924, RSG ms.

9. Memorandum by MacMurray for Kellogg and Grew, June 1925, MacMurray Papers; Copy of Executive Order, July 16, 1925, RSG ms.

desire of other consular officials to warn the Chinese away from the concessions, the Department had not rebuked him. Now again, endangered foreigners could be withdrawn and property losses compensated by standard claims practices: "I hope therefore that the Powers will stand aside and let the Chinese settle the question for themselves."[10]

On the matter of policy towards China during this civil war, MacMurray had very strong opinions of his own, related to his conviction that the Chinese were responsible for the less than millennial effects of the Consortium and Washington Conference agreements—a set of diplomatic efforts in which he had been one of the principal architects. But he listened to Greene, continued to respect Greene, even as their views came increasingly into conflict. Few other Americans had comparable access to so central a figure in the shaping of American East Asian policy.

In 1925, on the eve of the May 30th Incident, Greene's potential for influencing the American response to the Chinese revolution increased enormously. First, MacMurray was appointed Minister to China and Greene expressed delight and relief "in view of the desire in certain quarters for a table thumping or big-stick wielding type." The differences in their approaches were not yet apparent and each man saw the other as thoughtful and sound. Greene was especially pleased to see a career diplomat going to China to cope with the "present delicate situation." MacMurray's recent talks with him in New York had confirmed his confidence in MacMurray's judgment. And in the event MacMurray faltered, Greene would be close by in Peking, as the Rockefeller Foundation chose this time to send him to China as Resident Director of the China Medical Board. Finally, assuring Greene of direct access to Washington, his former protégé, Nelson T. Johnson, was appointed MacMurray's successor as Chief of the Far Eastern Division of the Department of State. Johnson expressed regret that he was returning to the United States just as Greene departed for Peking, but he was "glad in that it means I shall have a correspondent in Peking in whose judgment I have great trust." Insecure about replacing the greatly admired, learned MacMurray, uneasy as he was forced increasingly to question MacMurray's judgment, it was reassuring to Johnson to have a trusted friend providing alternative analyses. Meanwhile the tensions mounted in China.[11]

10. Greene to MacMurray, September 4, 1924, MacMurray Papers.

11. Greene to MacMurray, April 12, 1925, MacMurray Papers; Johnson to Greene, May 9, 1925, RSG ms.

With the formation of the Consortium and the subsequent agreements reached at the Washington Conference, Great Britain, France, Japan, and the United States were committed to cooperation among themselves in assisting with the modernization of China. The Consortium bankers were to provide the Chinese government with the funds it needed to build railroads and other major productive enterprises. But in the six years that followed the Washington Conference, China suffered from almost constant civil strife, first as the warlords struggled among themselves and then as Chiang Kai-shek led the Nationalists north to subdue the warlords. Provincial militarists prevented tax revenues from reaching Peking, and the military factions that controlled the capital devoured such funds as reached the national treasury. Against this setting, no amount of prompting by the British and American governments could induce the Consortium to assist China's economic development. No loans were granted. The British, in fact, frequently referred to the Consortium as a financial "blockade," designed to prevent the Chinese government from obtaining funds it would presumably misuse.

Similarly, American businessmen eager to develop or expand their interests in China failed to obtain needed capital. They did not lack support from the American government, within which the Departments of Commerce and State competed to build up American economic interests in China. But American entrepreneurs in China, like the Chinese government, found the Consortium an obstacle.

The core of the problem was the divergence between the interests of the Department of State and those of Thomas Lamont and his fellow bankers. The Department wanted the Consortium to provide capital for China's development, to help in the creation of a strong modern China in which American interests would thrive. For the bankers, the remote promise of China could not compete with the more immediate promise of Japan. American capital that might have been made available to China was lent instead to the Japanese—with some of it, by indirect means, by being "laundered" or simply by freeing other capital, facilitating the expansion of Japanese interests on the Asian mainland. And because the Japanese were competing with the Chinese for American capital, they could use their position in the Consortium to discourage loans to China. The American Group, led by Lamont, accepted this process. In short, one of the two competitors for capital worked in collusion with the potential lender to deny capital to the other. However permissible among businessmen pursuing profit, it was not consistent with the ends of public policy. Conditions in China, however, left the Department of State no means for changing the direction of the flow of capital—and Lamont proved to be remarkably skillful in leading the Department to believe that he shared its views, but he was held back by partners less interested in helping China.

After completing the Consortium negotiations, Lamont chose the occasion of a dinner given in his honor by Japanese bankers to lecture his hosts on the virtues of peaceful expansion. He conceded to the Japanese the right to expand and to prosper, to send their growing population to the Asian mainland, while condemning the "Prussian" policies Japanese militarists were pursuing in China, Korea, and Siberia. He described the widespread hatred of Japan among Chinese and Koreans and warned of the growing apprehensions of Americans. The Japanese, he contended, were wasting money, alienating the world, jeopardizing any chance to get needed capital from the United States. He offered them a simple choice: "do the right thing by China" and Americans would invest in Japan—or try to seize China or Siberia and "get Germany's fate." Lamont's conception of the new order was apparent. Japan would be assured of a dominant role in the economic development of the Asian mainland, assisted by American capital, provided arrangements with the Chinese, Koreans, and Russians were worked out on a businesslike basis, with no semblance of the atavistic militarism her Consortium partners had just destroyed in Europe. As partners the bankers of the four Consortium countries would avoid the arbitrary exclusion of each other's nationals from economic opportunities and also avoid competition that might lead to expensive and unpredictable military solutions. The alternative was a threat to withhold capital and cut off important Japanese markets in the United States, especially for silk.[12]

To the American Group in New York he cabled, through State Department channels, a similar analysis of a Japanese political system in which bankers described as "liberals" vied with a military "super Government" for power. He warned that the Japanese would be "difficult" partners: "Banking group here will make every effort to play fair but they cannot control General Staff nor Intelligence Department." He fully expected the Japanese military to continue bribing Chinese officials into offering valuable concessions. But, "unless the powers continue to give her a free hand in

12. Undated notes, 185–15, TWL ms.

China and Siberia,'' the Japanese would gradually ''learn table manners from western groups.'' In a line meant for the Department of State, and perhaps European foreign offices as well, Lamont contended that ''Japan's present economic necessities and semi-panic conditions will prove powerful factors against the Japanese Militarists.'' But Western bankers could not keep Japan in line ''unless American British and French Governments become united towards Japan in her attitude toward Asia as they have proved united in consortium negotiations.'' Again, his message was clear. The bankers were prepared to construct the new order, but they would require cooperation among the three Western governments to keep the Japanese military from interfering with the Japanese bankers.[13]

Upon returning to the United States, Lamont took his analysis to the American people—to that part of the public interested in East Asian affairs or international finance. As he explained to Norman Davis, Undersecretary of State, the plan for East Asia, for helping China in particular, would not work ''unless we have the active cooperation of the American people, that is to say, of investors.'' To this end, Lamont spoke and wrote frequently, clearing his statements and articles with the Department. He told Davis that he saw himself free to say things the Department could not—to condemn Japanese militarism while making clear to Americans that an alternative leadership existed in Japan. Lamont insisted that it was no act of friendship ''to pussyfoot'' with the Japanese, as he contended that a rival banker, Frank Vanderlip, was doing—and in the process ''he is strengthening the militarists in Japan rather than the liberals who are the only hope of Japan.''[14]

When writing to his powerful Japanese acquaintances, Lamont expressed his confidence that the commercial interests of Japan and the United

13. Lamont to American Group, via Department of State, May 14, 1920, SD 893.51/2829.

14. Lamont to Davis, July 7, 1920, SD 893.51/2871. *New York Times:* June 16, 1920, p. 18; July 11, 1920, II, pp. 1–2; July 15, 1920, p. 21 (address to Council on Foreign Relations); December 10, 1920, p. 13 (address to Academy of Political Science); June 25, 1921, p. 13 (address to Japan Society); December 5, 1921, p. 26. Lamont, ''Putting China on Her Feet,'' *Forum,* LXIV (July 1920), 90–94; Lamont, ''Banking Consortium for China as a Power for Peace,'' *New York Times,* August 8, 1920, VII, p. 2; Lamont, ''The Economic Situation in the Orient,'' *Proceedings of the Academy of Political Science,* IX (February 1921) 68–75; Lamont, ''The Chinese Consortium and American Trade Relations,'' *Annals,* CXIV (March 1921), 87–93; Jesse Lynch Williams, ''How T. W. Lamont Got the Consortium Framed,'' *World's Work,* XLI (March 1921), 452–64; see also Lamont to Herbert Croly, March 25, 1921, 185–4, TWL ms.

States were identical and developed the theme that political differences had to be reconciled to permit the development of financial relations. In 1920, the Japanese were very much interested in obtaining American capital for the South Manchuria Railroad, but political considerations as well as a shortage of investment capital for export had deterred Lamont. As he explained to Inoue, the Shantung controversy was still "an open sore" then and there was apprehension about Japanese intentions in South Manchuria. An attempt to sell bonds of the SMR in the United States would have been very unpopular. But the Consortium agreement had marked an important change of course by Japan, and removal of the threat of imminent collision between Japan and the United States. The Washington Conference of 1921–22 seemed to be the consummation of the promise of Lamont's earlier efforts, of the promise of peaceful cooperation in East Asia. Agreement on limiting economic rivalry had been followed by political and military agreements and now the Consortium partners, Great Britain, France, Japan, and the United States, could look forward to the peaceful expansion of their interests in China.[15]

For Lamont, however, the improvement of relations with Japan brought forth its own fruit—loans to Japan. He believed that his own public statements had improved American attitudes toward Japan, explaining modestly "that any partner of our house coming back from the Far East, necessarily—quite aside from his own personality—speaks with a certain amount of weight, just because of his firm associations." But he still wanted to stay away from financing the SMR, probably because the State Department would not approve loans for use in third countries "where the use of such American credit would tend to prejudice or circumscribe the opportunities for American enterprise." With specific regard to the SMR, the State Department viewed it as an instrument for the development and control of a Japanese sphere in Manchuria—for the exclusion of American competition. Lamont thought it best that the first financial operation that an American banking house conducted for Japan "be something more purely Japanese, rather than intimately relating to the mainland of Asia." After the horrendous earthquake of 1923, still warmer feelings for the Japanese developed in the United States, and the House of Morgan floated a $150,000,000 loan for the Japanese government. Other smaller loans followed, but none for direct use on the Asian mainland.[16]

15. Lamont to Inoue, March 20, 1922, 186–14, TWL ms.
16. *Ibid;* Leland Harrison to Milton E. Ailes, June 15, 1923, SD 893.51/4325.

In his May 1920 report to the American Group, composed to be read by officials of the Department of State, Lamont professed to be optimistic about China as a field for 'nvestment. He referred ritualistically to the country's immense natural resources, and to its people, whom he found industrious, honest "(outside the official class)," and peace-loving. But the government was corrupt and inefficient, unworthy of any direct assistance such as the administrative loan it wanted. He also noted opposition to the loan while civil strife continued in China, recognizing that some Chinese viewed a loan to the Peking regime as support for one among many factions vying for control of China. Despite the chaos, despite the corruption, Lamont nonetheless considered the Consortium to be under a moral obligation to conclude an emergency loan to keep the Chinese government functioning—*until* the Chinese refused to reconsider their repudiation of the German-issue Hukuang bonds. If, despite its desperate need for money and its corrupt nature, the Chinese government would not yield on the Hukuang question, Lamont was prepared to wait for it to fall and to do business with its successor. It might take a few years, but the bankers were not eager to underwrite loans to China. They could wait and the Consortium might function by undertaking loans for certain "specific constructive purposes like the Hukuang railway system," taking great care to retain for the banks "effective control to avoid wasteful expenditure."[17]

Given the unwillingness, perhaps inability, of a weak Chinese government to confront nationalist opposition to greater imperialist controls over Chinese enterprises—especially on the Hukuang railway, which had been a focus for the nationalist revolution of 1911—Lamont was stipulating conditions that precluded the possibility of business between the Consortium and the Chinese government. Added to the fact that the Consortium would not underwrite new Hukuang bonds until the Chinese had satisfied them on the old, Lamont's facade of optimism does not conceal the American Group's lack of interest in doing business with China in 1920. The State Department accepted this situation because no alternative sources of capital could be found. In addition, a consortium that did not loan money to China was nonetheless a consortium that prevented the Japanese from using loans to gain exclusive privileges in China. The opportunities for Americans were kept open—and the Chinese would have to wait.

The Department of State tried to remove the obstacle of the Hukuang

17. SD 893.51/2829.

question by seeking to enlist other Consortium governments to press the Chinese and, after the Washington Conference, by trying to get Lamont to put the issue aside. Both tactics failed. The Department and the American Group never came to terms on the Hukuang issue and, in 1924, when a Chinese regime tried to appease the bankers, new obstacles arose. Lamont wanted the Chinese to pay off their obligations out of current revenues, prior to any advance, while the Chinese asked for a loan out of which they would pay off the Hukuang coupons. The American Group announced that it would consider an advance as a "last resort" if the Chinese would secure the Hukuang bonds "in full on the salt revenues"—and so it went, with no money for China.[18]

Chinese supporters of Sun Yat-sen, or opponents of the generals who dominated the Peking regime in general, did not protest against the Consortium policy. Overseas Chinese groups all over the United States and Mexico cabled Washington in opposition to any loans. A most interesting pattern began to emerge. Chinese nationalists feared the Consortium as an obstacle to the achievement of their hopes for an independent modern China. The Department of State saw the Consortium as essential to the development of an independent modern China. The American Group, unable to derive profit from supporting the Department's policy, denied the Peking government money it needed to operate—a "benign neglect" that prevented the stabilization of the Chinese government and helped clear the way for the Kuomintang revolution of the late 1920s.[19]

When the Harding administration came to Washington, Lamont and the American Group hastened to establish their position with the new leadership. Although Lamont had split openly with the Republican Party because it had hedged on the League of Nations in the campaign of 1920, as a partner in J. P. Morgan and Company, he had no difficulty gaining admission to the highest of government circles. Even before Charles Evans Hughes was named Secretary of State, he and Lamont, both pro-League New York Republicans, had discussed problems of foreign policy to be

18. J. P. Morgan and Company to Norman Davis, June 22, 1920, and Davis to Lamont, June 23, 1920, SD 893.51/2852; Memorandum of conversation between Lamont and Simpson of J. P. Morgan and Company and Fred Dearing, H. D. Marshall, and Nelson Johnson of the FE Division, February 9, 1922, SD 893.51/3796; American Group to Secretary of State, January 16, 1925, SD 893.51/4753.

19. Crane to Secretary of State, October 25, 1920, SD 893.51/3021. See also SD 893.51/3088, 3090, 3092, 3100, 3101, 3107, 3118, 3122 for examples of Chinese protests.

faced by the incoming administration, especially those relating to financial matters. Throughout Hughes's tenure in the Department of State, Lamont was in frequent contact with him, through letters and visits, discussing a wide variety of affairs—of which those pertaining to East Asia were but a small fraction.

On March 1, just before Hughes took office, Lamont congratulated him on his appointment and reviewed the history of the Consortium. He described it as Republican Party policy designed to demonstrate "America's traditional friendliness" toward China and to carry out on a cooperative basis a plan to help with the modernization of China. He reminded Hughes of Wilson's original repudiation of the policy and of his subsequent reversal and decision to resurrect the Consortium. Several days later Lamont approached Secretary of State Charles Evans Hughes on behalf of the American Group, taking the same tack that had infuriated Wilson and MacMurray in 1913: the Group existed at great expense to itself because the Department of State believed its participation in the Consortium "would conduce to the upbuilding of general American interests in the Far East."[20]

Lamont left no doubt that the American Group was unwilling to extend any loans to China, but would continue in operation as a patriotic duty if the administration so desired. But Hughes quickly learned that Lamont's patriotism did not extend to assisting American enterprises deemed worthy by the Department of State. The examples of the Pacific Development Corporation and the Federal Telegraph Company illustrate the Consortium's role in thwarting the development of American economic interests in China.

In November 1919, the Pacific Development Corporation (PDC), an American firm seeking to exploit opportunities to expand American trade and investments in China, lent $5.5 million to the Chinese government, receiving an option to increase the loan to $20 million. The Department of State, determined to implement the cooperative loan policy inherent in the Consortium agreement, refused to sanction the loan. Although it had been made *prior* to the conclusion of the Consortium arrangements, the loan could easily complicate relations with the British and the Japanese and the Department was fretful. Though the government lacked the authority to block the transaction, the corporation leaders chose not to risk the wrath of the State Department and offered the existing loan and option to the Consor-

20. Lamont to Hughes, March 11, 1921, *FRUS, 1921,* 360.

tium. Lamont, for the American Group, expressed an interest in the arrangement and took an option on the PDC loan while arranging a direct $5 million loan to the PDC. The financial legerdemain that followed is not clear, but in July 1920, John Foster Dulles of the New York law firm of Sullivan and Cromwell, representing the PDC, complained that the American Group was behaving unreasonably toward his client. Months passed without the American Group announcing a decision, and in November the Chinese government defaulted on its servicing of the loan. Three months after that, the American Group announced that it would *not* pick up the option offered by the PDC. The PDC was left with $5.5 million of Chinese promissory notes on which the Chinese had already begun to default—and a $5 million debt to the American Group which would offer no assistance in selling the Chinese securities.[21]

In May 1921, the directors of the PDC succeeded in getting Herbert Hoover, Secretary of Commerce, to ask Hughes to help. Hoover described the PDC's inability to unload its Chinese securities and the adverse effect its financial difficulties were having on the firm's merchandising capacity, on its ability to expand American trade with China. MacMurray, to whom Hughes referred the matter for advice, conceded that the "American Group has rather ungenerously taken its pound of flesh." Because of the prevailing view that the American Group enjoyed the special favor of the government, the PDC could not get financial assistance elsewhere. No other banks would touch a matter connected with Chinese finance. But more important to MacMurray was the need to resist pressure from the Commerce Department. Bureaucratic rivalry rather than the merits of the case determined the decision against the PDC in this round. Subsequently, after Herbert White, vice-president of the PDC, humbled himself in an interview with Hughes, the Secretary of State agreed to help.[22]

Clearly the PDC was not a shoestring operation. It could employ the most prestigious law firm in the country, get the Secretary of Commerce—and the Secretary of Agriculture—to intercede on its behalf, and obtain an audience with the imperious Charles Evans Hughes. And Hughes wrote to

21. Tenney to Secretary of State, forwarding telegram from E. B. Bruce to Pacific Development Corporation, April 27, 1920, SD 893.51/2800; Dulles to Norman Davis, July 1, 1920, SD 893.51/2860; American Group to Secretary of State, February 18, 1921, SD 893.51/3271.

22. Hoover to Hughes, May 28, 1921, and MacMurray for Hughes, June 8, 1921, SD 893.51/3826; Memorandum by MacMurray of conversation between White and Hughes, June 9, 1921, SD 893.51/3457.

Lamont on behalf of the PDC, warning that there would be problems if it appeared that the PDC was forced into liquidation by the American Group. But Lamont could not be moved. He denied that the American Group had obstructed the PDC's efforts to unload the Chinese notes, insisting that the corporation's problems were due to mismanagement and had been alleviated rather than aggravated by the efforts of the American Group. Lest Hughes try to apply further pressure, Lamont insisted that the American Group existed as a public service and contended that profits for the foreseeable future would be trifling compared to the outlay and trouble already taken. The message was obvious: abandon the PDC or risk the withdrawal of the American Group. When the PDC tried to arrange alternative financing, Lamont had the State Department notify White "that as the American Group were your creditors you should consult with them with regard to arranging your financing." Lamont never released the vise in which he held the PDC and, ultimately, the corporation was forced into bankruptcy.[23]

At approximately the same time, another American firm, the Federal Telegraph Company (FTC) negotiated an important contract to develop a wireless telegraph system in China. Immediately two problems arose. First, the governments of Denmark, Great Britain, and Japan protested against the FTC agreement on the grounds that their nationals had prior contracts, violated by the FTC arrangements. The American government, however, saw the case as a test of the concept of equal opportunity for American investments and rejected the protests, successfully countering British and Japanese pressure on the Peking regime with American pressure. The State Department considered the contract to be fair, the firm reputable, and the opportunity "of vital interest to American business in the Orient."[24]

But the FTC also had to float a $4 million loan for the Chinese government to finance construction of the telegraph system—and with this problem the Department of State was initially less helpful. Before approving FTC efforts to obtain financing, the Department asked the American Group to determine whether the loan was properly Consortium business. On its part, the American Group refused to make a decision until the FTC's title was clear—

23. Hughes to Lamont, June 13, 1921, SD 893.51/3457a; Lamont to Hughes, June 17, 1921, SD 893.51/3497; Dearing to White (copy to Lamont), November 9, 1921, SD 893.51/3641c; *New York Times,* October 24, 1924, p. 28.

24. Harry W. Kirwin, "The Federal Telegraph Company: A Testing of the Open Door," *Pacific Historical Review,* 22 (1953), 271–86; Norman Davis to Lamont, February 23, 1921, SD 893.74/77a.

until foreign protests had been withdrawn. At the same time the American Group assumed that the State Department was obligated to withhold support for FTC efforts to obtain financing elsewhere. As a result, the FTC was hamstrung, unable to obtain funds or begin work.[25]

In February 1921, Norman Davis, Undersecretary of State in the lame-duck Wilson administration, begged Lamont to give the FTC support. He warned that the Department would otherwise consider itself free to give full approval to the project and let the FTC find financing elsewhere. Lamont promised to do what he could but he did hope that the Department would be careful not to let the FTC do anything to the detriment of China's credit, "as could very easily be the case," and prevent the Consortium from ever doing anything. Lamont left no doubt that he considered the pittance involved unworthy of the risk. Two weeks later, the American Group refused to undertake the FTC proposition. Lamont sent word that he thought the plan worthwhile, hoped it would succeed, but that it was too small to handle. Before the FTC looked for other financing, however, the American Group was obliged to offer the proposal to the other national groups—including the British and Japanese whose governments were attempting to void the FTC contract.[26]

The president of the FTC was outraged by Lamont's tactics, but Lamont went to Washington and won his point. The proposal was sent on to the British, French, and Japanese Groups for their consideration. To the other Groups, Lamont wrote that the American market "cannot now absorb such unsecured bonds." To him, the affair seemed an excellent opportunity for demonstrating good faith to his consortium partners—an exchange of unwanted opportunities. As he anticipated, the other groups were not interested in financing the American firm's contract.[27]

In April, the FTC complained to Secretary Hughes that the phrase used by the American Group—that the American market could not absorb unsecured bonds—"has been used publicly to injure Federal." If the FTC failed to carry out its project, it would be because of "the American Group

25. *Ibid.*

26. Davis to Lamont, February 23, 1921, SD 893.74/77a; Lamont to Davis, February 24, 1921, SD 893.74/78; J. P. Morgan and Company for American Group to Secretary of State, March 7, 1921, SD 893.74/87.

27. R. P. Sherwin to American Group, March 9, 1921, SD 893.74/92; Lamont to Henry Fletcher and American Group to FTC, March 11, 1921, SD 893.74/97; American Group to Secretary of State, March 28, 1921, SD 893.74/102.

giving adverse British and Japanese interests weapons with which to menace and injure this American project.'' The Federal Telegraph Company never was able to find financing and it was indeed clear that Lamont's handling of the proposal made it appear unworthy, a poor risk. An American enterprise, strongly supported by the American government, failed.[28]

The Pacific Development Corporation and Federal Telegraph Company cases indicate the way in which the Consortium failed to further one end of the American government: the expansion of American economic interests in China. Lamont and the American Group bankers were concerned with only one set of American economic interests—their own. In these two cases, the American Group's opportunities for profit were minimal and Lamont sacrificed the interests of both American firms to the principle of international cooperation. The State Department could hardly fault him when he reminded all and sundry of the Department's desire to place loans to the Chinese government beyond the scope of great power competition. The two cases illustrate that for Lamont, Anglo-American cooperation was a higher priority than the interests of China—or the development of American business in China. And to underscore this point, Lamont constantly kept Sir Charles Addis of the British Group informed, to the point of sending him copies of anti-British memoranda prepared by F. W. Stevens, the American Group's representative in China. Addis would then send these to the British Foreign Office as evidence of Lamont's good faith—and the Foreign Office would forward them on to the British Legation in China, to help the Legation undermine Stevens.[29]

Twice during the early years of the Consortium's existence, the ability of Lamont and his colleagues to avoid lending money to the Chinese was tested. In both instances, the American, British, French, and Japanese Ministers to China and the Peking representatives of all four banking groups recommended that the loans be granted. In both instances the diplomats and group representatives argued that the Consortium could not afford to reject Chinese overtures. But in neither instance could Lamont be moved, supporting or being supported by Addis or the Japanese government in his opposition to taking up the Chinese business.

28. FTC to Secretary of State, April 19, 1921, SD 893.74/121; Kirwin, ''Federal Telegraph Company . . .''

29. See for example text of speech by Lamont, May 20, 1921, 185–5, TWL ms, and FO 405/234/167.

Early in January 1922, while the Washington Conference was still in session, the Chinese government approached the consortium representatives and their respective legations with a request for a loan of $96 million. The loan would be secured initially by the surplus on salt taxes and then by the customs surtax which Chinese authorities had learned would be a part of the Washington agreements. The Chinese proposal also involved the first formal recognition by the Chinese of the existence of the Consortium.

The American Group informed the Department of its unwillingness to participate in the loan on the grounds that it was for administrative purposes and lacked provisions for adequate supervision. The certain opposition of the Canton regime to any loan was also noted, but the refusal was not categorical. If the Department and the other groups wanted the loan, the American Group would reconsider. When Lamont called to estimate the mood of the State Department, he found H. D. Marshall of the Far East Division unwilling to press him. But a few days later, Marshall let it be known that "the government is accused of lending its support to a monopoly which not only is failing to help trade with China but is in effect throttling it." Addis, too, was under pressure from his government, but the day was saved by the collapse of the Chinese government before the month ended. No one can know if the promise of such a loan could have saved the regime—it seems unlikely—but it is clear that in its desperation it had turned to the Consortium. And it is evident that the American Group, sustained in its attitude by the views of Sir Charles Addis—and not the Japanese government—blocked the loan.[30]

In the weeks and months that followed the Department of State reviewed the workings of the Consortium, first internally and then with Lamont. The Consortium had lent no money to China; it had accomplished nothing positive. The idea that it had been valuable because its existence stopped indiscriminate Japanese loans was reiterated but, for the first time, countered with the thought that Japan's shortage of capital would have brought an end to such loans even *without* the Consortium. The Department recognized that the bankers in the American Group were not enthusiastic about business opportunities in China—that they had delegated leadership to

30. Alston to Curzon, January 2, 1922, FO 405/238/3; Schurman to Secretary of State, January 3, 1922, SD 893.51/3668; American Group to Secretary of State, January 11, 1922, SD 893.51/3682; Memorandum by Marshall of telephone conversation with Lamont, January 12, 1922, SD 893.51/3718; Sir N. Stabb to Wellesley, January 4, 1922, FO 405/238/4.

Lamont, who alone appeared to retain some interest in the Consortium scheme. But Lamont constantly emphasized that the American Group existed merely to carry out the wishes of the Department—a position which, though true, had dangerous implications of future Department responsibilities. The State Department was also unhappy about Lamont's apparent deference to Addis, which was considered an abandonment of the position of leadership staked out when the United States introduced the proposal for the new Consortium. Finally, there was regret within the Department that it had approved the Consortium resolution to the effect that full payment of the German issue of the Hukuang loan was prerequisite to the successful floating of future loans. Preparing Hughes for a scheduled meeting with Lamont, Marshall called for a retreat to the earlier position of asking for payment only to bona fide holders who invested prior to Chinese intervention in the World War.[31]

When Lamont came to Washington, Hughes could not see him, but Assistant Secretary of State Fred Dearing, Marshall, and Nelson Johnson met with him. They found him adamant on the Hukuang question, unwilling to accept any responsibility for the failure of companies like the Pacific Development Corporation or the Federal Telegraph Company to obtain financing, and skeptical of anyone doing business in China before the Hukuang matter was "satisfactorily adjusted." When Johnson mentioned that American business in China would not develop until it had banking institutions there comparable to Addis' operation, Lamont left no doubt that he considered the British position beyond the reach of American competitors. In response to indications of dissatisfaction with the role of the American Group, Lamont reminded Department functionaries that the bankers of the American Group had "little or no active interest in China finance and were following along merely to be good fellows and because they were urged to do so." A month later, Lamont responded to Hughes directly with an implicit threat of withdrawal from the Consortium unless the Department urged the American Group to continue. Members of the group were growing restive, irritated by expenses incurred and wondering "whether it is wise to continue indefinitely the organization of the Consortium in view of the apparent unwillingness of the Chinese to utilize its services." He warned that the membership as a whole had little interest in China, far less than those like

31. Memorandum by Marshall for Hughes, "New Consortium for Loans to China," undated (probably January 1922), SD 893.51/3731.

himself who had been active in the formation of the Consortium. He personally favored continuing the participation of the American Group: what was Mr. Hughes's pleasure?[32]

Lamont's threat of withdrawal had its desired effect. Hughes called him to Washington while MacMurray warned Hughes that it would be "a calamity" if the American Group withdrew from the Consortium. He argued against giving the American Group further cause to feel that it acted at the behest of the Department, but urged Hughes to impress upon Lamont that withdrawal would "retard American trade in China for perhaps as much as a generation—just when our country must be assuring itself of the opportunity for commercial expansion in the remaining underdeveloped markets of the world." After surveying the previous decade of American entreprenurial ineffectualness in China, of opportunity after opportunity won by American diplomats and wasted by American businessmen, MacMurray expressed his hope that the new Consortium would provide still another, perhaps the greatest opportunity for the expansion of American economic interests in China. Surely Lamont and his colleagues had understood there would be no quick profits, that they were building for the future "and assuring for themselves as well as for American commerce and industry the opportunity of participation in the inevitable growth of China as a market for our goods and a field for our enterprise." MacMurray insisted that without such willingness by the bankers to forego immediate profit, there was no justification for the "peculiar degree" of government support granted to the American Group. This support, constituting a "political responsibility," was warranted only by considerations of national interest in the development of the Chinese field." He realized that Hughes could not coerce the bankers into continuing a business they considered unprofitable, but they should realize their "moral responsibility."[33]

The Consortium was more to MacMurray, however, than the instrument for American economic expansion in China. It was the foundation of the Pacific settlement reached at the Washington Conference. British support had been essential to American success at weaning Japan and France away from particularistic and exclusive policies of spheres and special interests. The British had given that support primarily because the existence of

32. Memorandum of conversation and covering letter by Johnson, February 9, 1922, SD 893.51/3976; Lamont to Hughes, March 24, 1922, SD 893.51/3716.

33. Memorandum by MacMurray for Hughes, April 3, 1922, SD 893.51/3777.

the Consortium assured them that cooperation would replace international rivalry. The Consortium, MacMurray maintained, had become "an integral part of the international political situation which we congratulate ourselves upon in the Far East." Should the United States disassociate itself from the Consortium, the entire settlement would thus be threatened.[34]

Hughes had no difficulty conveying MacMurray's sense of urgency to Lamont and Lamont duly reported the Secretary's concern to the members of the American Group. But in addition to summarizing the reasons Hughes gave him for continuing the American Group's participation in the Consortium, Lamont declared that the organization "was largely in the nature of a public service." Prior to sending off the letter, Lamont sent a copy to Hughes for approval—and MacMurray jumped on that phrase. Appreciative of Lamont's willingness to sound the Department's call throughout the land, MacMurray was nonetheless constantly annoyed by the implication that the American Group existed for the purpose of obliging the Department: "One cannot blame the bankers for assuming to be self-sacrificing patriots, but it seems to me we should put aside the implication that they are merely doing a favor in return for which an obligation on the part of the Government can be inferred." Drafting a letter that Hughes sent under his own name, MacMurray stressed the degree of self-interest involved in the banker's participation in the American Group and asked Lamont to make this point more explicitly to his colleagues.[35]

Lamont and the Department of State continued to be watchful of the snares each set for the other, but the upper hand was clearly Lamont's. Appeals to national interest might oblige the American Group to remain in existence, but the government could not make such an appeal without incurring an obligation to the bankers. And Lamont could be receptive, ostensibly providing great service to his country merely by maintaining the existence of the American Group on paper—without extending any loans. From Peking, the British Minister wrote to Lord Curzon to explain Addis's lack of enthusiasm for the loan opportunity—an explanation of perhaps equal value for understanding Lamont's position. In addition to the political uncertainties of China in 1923, and the fact that the Chinese were offering less reliable secu-

34. *Ibid.*

35. Lamont to American Group (draft) undated, 185–8, TWL ms; Lamont to Hughes with enclosure, April 7, 1922, MacMurray for Hughes, April 11, 1922, and Hughes to Lamont, April 13, 1922, SD 893.51/3788.

rity for loans than a decade earlier, the enlargement of membership forced upon their respective groups by the American and British governments meant that Addis' bank had a smaller share of the business than in 1913, meaning a smaller profit and less incentive.[36]

In May, the process began anew, triggered by a cable from the American Minister. Schurman reported that he and his British, French, and Japanese colleagues thought that the existing Chinese government provided a reasonable prospect for stability and that an offer of financial assistance might bring the desired results. The four ministers urged assistance immediately. Hughes indicated his pleasure to Schurman, then turned to the American Group and received the standard response: No. Conditions in China were not yet such as to create confidence in the minds of American investors and, of course, the Chinese would have to pay on existing defaults first. There would have to be orderly government and reestablished credit. Then there might be further loans. The Department pressed for a month, but the response from the American Group never changed.[37]

In the course of the summer Lamont apparently worried about the possibility of having irritated Hughes. He sent him a personal letter explaining his position and attempting to redistribute responsibility for the Consortium's failure to agree to Chinese loan proposals. This time he insisted that warlord armies were the "root of all evil" and their disbandment a prerequisite to economic or political stability. He called upon the American government to take the lead in demanding the elimination of these forces. But he separated such a step from financial assistance, insisting that "temporary advances for administrative purposes are only harmful half measures tending directly to the continuance of the fundamental evil." Despite his stand, Lamont did not want the American Group to be blamed, assuring Hughes that all of the groups had reacted negatively toward the proposed loan. Hughes sent a copy of Lamont's letter off to Schurman.[38]

When Schurman responded, despite the appropriate niceties of a letter intended for Lamont's eyes, he was sharply critical of the American Group. Schurman praised Lamont's analysis, his recognition of the problem of

36. Alston to Curzon, April 11, 1922, FO 405/238/37.

37. Schurman to Hughes, May 24, 1922, Hughes to Schurman, May 24, 1922 and June 17, 1922, SD 893.00/4374. See also J. P. Morgan and Company to Secretary of State, June 13, 1922, SD 893.51/3864.

38. Lamont to Hughes, August 9, 1922, SD 893.51/3938.

warlord armies, but rejected Lamont's insistence on disbandment as China's first priority. Reunification would have to come first, followed by financial rehabilitation before the Chinese government could tackle the problem of excess armies. Schurman noted that he and the ministers of the other Consortium powers were recommending a small advance again, optimistic about the prospects for reunification. He analyzed Lamont's standard response as a declaration that the "American Group will not furnish money but gilt-edged bonds which purchasers will take off their hands as investments." He remarked, disparagingly, that "when the bonds of the Chinese government are gilt-edged, the Consortium will not be needed to float them."[39]

Schurman also took exception to Lamont's claim that all of the national groups viewed Chinese business in the same way, arguing that the American Group alone regarded Chinese financial affairs solely "from the banking and investment point of view." The British, he contended, and also the French and Japanese "(when politics does not modify their action)" considered the relation of loans to other business in China, and the value of such loans to their manufacturers and traders and to existing business connections and institutions. American businessmen in China shared this analysis, according to Schurman, and felt that they suffered as a result of the American Group's approach. As anticipated, Hughes forwarded a copy of the letter to Lamont.[40]

Not only the four ministers, but the group representatives in Peking once again endorsed the Chinese loan proposal, cabling their respective principals: "We cannot too strongly urge that another failure to respond to Chinese offer to arrive at a business deal with us will be construed by them as proof that Consortium does not wish to do business." But again, the American Group repeated its formulas: first disbandment of troops and provision for payment of the German issue of the Hukuang loan. This time, however, conditions in China impressed both the Foreign office in London and the State Department in Washington as being particularly promising—the restoration of Li Yüan-hung in Peking, a reassembling of parliament, and not least the flight of Sun Yat-sen from Canton after his defeat by Ch'en Chiung-ming. When the French government seemed reluctant, Curzon moved to put pressure on France to support a loan. To his emissary in Paris he wrote of Addis and Lamont blocking a loan earlier in the year and insist-

39. Schurman to Hughes, October 3, 1922, SD 893.51/4049. 40. *Ibid.*

ing on sympathetic consideration for the Chinese request at this time. Curzon also noted that Adolf Joffe was in Peking. He did not want to leave the Chinese so desperate that they could turn nowhere but to the Bolsheviks. "Finally," he argued, "it is obviously desirable that the Consortium should commence active operations as soon as possible, since the longer it remains inactive the greater is the danger that the policy of cooperation for which it stands will in the end be wrecked." The actions of independent British financiers were already creating problems.[41]

On October 19, the Japanese Embassy in Washington notified the State Department that Japan objected to the proposed loans on two grounds. First, the loan would constitute interference in China's internal affairs—aid to the faction momentarily in control of Peking. Second, the Japanese insisted that any loans to facilitate refunding of China's external debts include the debts of the Ministry of Communications, i.e. the notorious Nishihara loans that epitomized the kind of financial dealings the Consortium was designed to preclude. But when MacMurray spoke to Lamont, the banker brushed the Japanese position aside, expressing confidence that the Japanese Group could carry its government along if the loan project could be worked out as a feasible business undertaking. He was much more concerned about the "Crisp loan," a loan to the Chinese government by a British firm outside the Consortium, and by the Department's failure to obtain the British government's disapproval.[42]

Officially, the government of the United States disagreed with the Japanese government, insisting that the Peking regime was the sole government of China and expressing support for the loan if properly safeguarded. To Hughes, MacMurray expressed the view that the terms stipulated by the American, British, and French Groups were unobjectionable, the occasion very favorable. Concerned about the objections of the Japanese government, MacMurray asked Hughes to intercede to support the British argument that a loan would not constitute an intervention contrary to the principles of the Washington Conference. Otherwise, he warned, the Chinese government would be forced to deal with independent British and Belgian interests. He

41. American Group to Secretary of State, October 10, 1922, SD 893.51/3996 and October 18, 1922, SD 893.51/4011; Curzon to Lord Hardinge (Paris), October 20, 1922, FO 405/239/10.

42. Memorandum from Japanese Embassy, October 19, 1922, and memorandum by MacMurray of conversation with Lamont, October 27, 1922, SD 893.51/4019; American Group to Secretary of State, October 27, 1922, SD 893.51/4024.

feared "a reversion to the old system of international competition and intrigue." MacMurray indicated his suspicion that elements in Japan anxious to keep China weak were behind Japanese objections to the loan and insisted that the Japanese position was untenable, that the Chinese government of Li Yüan-hung was the most promising regime since 1917.[43]

But MacMurray had one crucial reservation. Before taking a positive stand in opposition to Japan, it was "absolutely essential that for the security of our own position we should make sure of the readiness of the American Group to take up and go through with the business seriously and loyally." Accepting the sincerity of Lamont's professed interest in China, he saw little support for him among other American bankers. MacMurray feared that the American Group might embarrass the government by refusing to participate in the loan or by some less direct form of obstruction. By November 1922, MacMurray saw the American Group rather than Japan as the primary obstacle to the fulfillment of his hopes for the Consortium.[44]

Gradually, a united American, British, and French front was created to press the Japanese government to withdraw its objections to loan negotiations. The Japanese agreed to reconsider, fussed about details, while the American Group stalled and Addis informed the British Foreign Office that he considered Japanese objections "weighty," the time not quite ripe. Before the end of the year, the Foreign Office and the Department of State surrendered—not to the Japanese, but to the indifference of their own national banking groups.[45]

In February 1923, Victor Wellesley, MacMurray's counterpart in the British Foreign Office, travelled to Washington to discuss the Consortium and the details of a special conference necessitated by agreements reached at the Washington Conference to adjust China's tariff. Wellesley found MacMurray in agreement with his contention that the point had been reached beyond which the Consortium's policy of "masterly inactivity" could not be stretched without risking failure. Wellesley considered the Japanese recep-

43. Department of State for Japanese Embassy, November 23, 1922, SD 893.51/4019; MacMurray memorandum for Hughes, November 17, 1922, SD 893.51/4085½.

44. SD 893.51/4085½.

45. Eliot to Curzon, November 7, 1922, FO 405/239/16 (see also FO 405/239/18, 19); Memorandum by MacMurray of conversation with Counselor of British Embassy, November 10, 1922, SD 893.51/4053; Addis to Wellesley, November 15, 1922, FO 405/239/17; Geddes to Curzon, enclosing Hughes to Geddes, November 24, 1922, FO 405/239/23. See also Akira Iriye, *After Imperialism* (Cambridge, Massachusetts, 1965), 30–32.

tive, but worried about the apathy of the American Group. MacMurray arranged for him to meet with Lamont, his partners, and the American Group in New York—and the experience confirmed Wellesley's fears. He found Lamont's partners unmoved and unmovable, Lamont himself less responsive than he had hoped. Speaking to the managing committee of the American Group he found his audience impassive—apathetic and indifferent. To Curzon he reported that Lamont's influence was waning, "in fact, he has lost his grip." Wellesley's private inquiries convinced him that Lamont's colleagues considered him too idealistic about China, too strongly pro-British, and too much under the influence of Addis.[46]

Under these grim auspices, the Chinese government put forth another proposal for refunding its debts and obtaining an advance from the Consortium. Li Yüan-hung's government had existed for almost a year, but its financial difficulties were undermining its chances for survival. Without a loan its days were obviously numbered. Again the Consortium representatives in Peking, supported by their respective ministers, commended the Chinese proposal. Again Addis and Lamont objected and killed the proposal. On this occasion, however, Addis had been favorably inclined—until he talked with Lamont. To MacMurray it seemed clear that Lamont was responsible for Addis's rejection of the opportunity—although the British Foreign Office was itself opposed to advances to the Chinese Government at this time. In June, a military coup drove Li Yüan-hung from Peking and the prospects for Consortium action became more remote than ever.[47]

For the next two years, until the violence subsequent to the May 30th Incident radically changed the context, preventing anyone from seriously considering loans to China, Lamont and Addis, with at least the public support of their governments, sang in praise of the success of the Consortium's negative effort. They had stopped "entirely the wasteful external borrowing indulged in so long by the Chinese government." In addition, the Consortium had "a wholesome effect on the relations of the powers in China." Despite dissatisfaction with the inactivity of the Consortium, both governments were anxious to have it remain in existence. For the United States and Great Britain, the Consortium appeared to have assisted in checking the expansion of Japan's economic hold over China. For the British, continued

46. Wellesley to Curzon, February 26, 1923, FO 405/242/12.

47. Schurman to Secretary of State, April 28, 1923, SD 893.51/4272; Addis to Foreign Office, April 30, 1923, FO 405/242/30; American Group to Secretary of State, May 11, 1923, SD 893.51/4293; MacMurray memorandum for Hughes, "Present Status of Chinese Loan Proposals," May 19, 1923, SD 893.51/4321.

Anglo-American cooperation in East Asia was itself a valuable end. And the Japanese indicated no dissatisfaction with the Consortium. Indeed, when continuation of its operations was discussed by the Consortium council in July 1924, the Japanese representative opposed the idea that an individual group had a right to withdraw. He supported a renewal resolution only when assured that its purpose was to "secure renewal of the agreement in perpetuity." France, the fourth party to the Consortium agreement, appeared to its partners to be apathetic, unreliable, and forever bargaining for some trivial advantage—but supportive of the others when the agreement was renewed.[48]

Although the Consortium continued to exist on into World War II, there was never again serious consideration of a loan agreement between it and any Chinese regime. Apart from the very important place the Consortium shared with the Washington Conference agreements as a symbol of Great Power cooperation in China, its value as an instrument of American policy was doubtful. In the early 1920s, the expansion of Japanese control over China's territory and resources, of Japanese influence over Chinese political affairs, *was* checked, but the role of the Consortium is at least questionable. Did the Japanese have the will or the resources to expand further? Hara, at least, was more concerned with preserving Japan's holdings in Manchuria than with reserving options for further expansion—and the Consortium agreement was the best way to protect existing interests from the potential threat of American competition. In joining the Consortium the Japanese surrendered the freedom to maximize their position on the Asian mainland, but they yielded none of their imperial holdings in Manchuria. Certainly Addis and Lamont never doubted that the compromise, which Lamont worked out to gain Japanese adherence to the Consortium agreement, recognized Japan's special interests in Manchuria in exchange for a cooperative policy elsewhere in China.[49]

48. Lamont to Hughes, July 17, 1923, SD 500 A4E1/42; Lamont to Roland Morris, January 15, 1924, 131–12, TWL ms; MacMurray to Morris, January 17, 1924, MacMurray Papers; Addis, "Memorandum on the China Consortium," September 3, 1924, FO 405/246/11; Addis to Waterlaw, with enclosure, July 18, 1924, FO 405/246/6; Memorandum by Wellesley, March 1, 1925, FO 405/247/30. See also Joan Hoff Wilson, *American Business and Foreign Policy, 1920–1933* (Lexington, Kentucky, 1971), 203–4.

49. The British Group negotiated a large railway loan in 1937 but the Chinese would not permit the British to share it with their Consortium partners. See below, Chapter Eight. On the Consortium and Japan's special interests, see also *New York Times*, editorial, July 14, 1920, p. 8; memorandum by E. H. Carr, April 4, 1922, FO 405/238/35; and Consul General, Mukden, to Minister, Peking, August 4, 1922, FO 405/239/6.

For MacMurray, checking Japanese expansion was the means of preserving opportunities for the expansion of American interests in China. Most obvious among these were economic interests: the growth of American trade and investment in China. But Sino-American trade remained static during the 1920s and the increase in American investments in China was not impressive. As illustrated by the cases of the Pacific Development Corporation and the Federal Telegraph Company the Consortium hindered rather than helped the development of American economic interests in China—and this was the image of the Consortium that prevailed in the Department of Commerce.[50]

Finally, did the Consortium help China? Clearly the American government—most especially MacMurray, the principal architect of American policy toward China—was dissatisfied with the refusal of the Consortium to loan money to the Chinese, particularly during the year of Li Yüan-hung's resumption of the presidency. But the American government was wrong to urge the bankers to offer loans to serve American policy ends. Loans for political purposes were not the proper function of the bankers and, if made, obligated the government to a degree of support to the bankers that it could not give properly. Lamont alone showed vision when he advised Wilson to have the American government give direct financial assistance to China.

Beyond the question of the propriety of dollar diplomacy, there is reason to doubt that the loans would have helped China—except on the rigid terms put forth by Lamont. Too often in the 1920s loans to developing countries were provided for unproductive purposes and sometimes for outright graft. Interest rates were high and there was no coherent program for increasing agricultural or industrial efficiency. Loans to underdeveloped countries in advance of technical and managerial competence were wasteful and disadvantageous to the borrowing country. There was still another danger that one of MacMurray's aides recognized in 1924. Mahlon Perkins argued that the powers recognized the "so-called" government of China in order to preserve foreign rights—extraterritoriality, customs control, loans—that had been forced upon China. If there was a need to continue the practice, it was surely stupid to add to the foreign privileges that government was supposed to protect. He was apprehensive about any proposal to use the Peking regime "for the further economic penetration of China by foreign interests,

50. Wilson, *American Business,* 203–7.

even with the very virtuous Anglo-Saxon purpose of developing China for China's good."[51]

Perhaps the historian can be allowed to imagine a situation in which the Consortium, responding to the urgings of the American and British governments, lent a large sum to the Peking regime. Presumably the governments involved would be obligated to protect this loan. Under such circumstances, might the great powers have responded differently as the Kuomintang, with Bolshevik support, marched north to destroy a regime bolstered by foreign loans? Would the loans have committed the powers to a moribund regime? Hindsight suggests that the failure of the Consortium to lend money to any of the Chinese governments of the early 1920s was a most felicitous failure. Thomas Lamont and his colleagues, acting in their own interests, with minimal regard for the interests of the Chinese, nonetheless performed in a manner consistent with the national interest of China—and of the United States.

51. Memorandum by Perkins for MacMurray, June 19, 1924, SD 893.51/4628.

# 5

# THE NATIONALIST REVOLUTION

At the Washington Conference, the representatives of the great powers had been annoyed by the assertiveness of the Chinese delegates—by the apparent inability of the Chinese to know and remain in their place. The British and Americans, at least, had assembled with the intention of doing good for the Chinese, of checking Japanese expansion in China and of allowing the Chinese to solve their internal affairs free from foreign interferences—almost as though China were a sovereign country. But from the opening session onward, the Chinese made demands that were considered in poor taste and their activities at the conference were compared invidiously with those of the Japanese. The Americans, British, and Japanese, concerned primarily with stabilizing relations among themselves in East Asia, had been generous in extending an invitation to the Chinese, and were not eager to give the Chinese anything more than was necessary to please each other. Awareness of China's national aspirations existed, but China's disunity and consequent weakness precluded any sense of urgency in discussions aimed at coming to terms with Chinese demands. The era of the Washington Conference was still a time for generous gestures. It was not yet time to take Chinese nationalism seriously.

In China the months that followed the Conference justified the cavalier treatment accorded the Chinese in Washington. The warlords continued to war while Sun Yat-sen continued to plot, and from the outside all that could be seen was chaos and misery—continued instability without progress toward a unified, modern nation state. Then in June 1922 there was a sign of hope: the restoration of Li Yüan-hung to the Presidency and the resurrection of the parliament. Sun was desperate, driven out of Canton and forced to find asylum in Shanghai. The warlords appeared quiescent, their armies in check. The diplomats in Peking were impressed favorably by the potential of Li's regime, but the bankers in New York and London were not. Financial support essential to the unification, reconstruction, and modernization of China could not be found. Sun plotted in Shanghai, with Soviet agents as well as with potential Chinese allies, and the warlords grew restive. New coalitions emerged, new fighting erupted, and by June 1923 Li Yüan-hung was deposed again and chaos was the order of the day in China.

But if on the surface China seemed to have regressed, the reality was very different when Sun returned to Canton in 1923. With Soviet help his Kuomintang was reorganized along the lines of the Soviet Communist Party. Sun's aide, Chiang Kai-shek, went to Moscow to study the Red Army, and the Comintern sent Michael Borodin to Canton to teach Sun how to politicize and mobilize the masses. The Kuomintang was being rejuvenated for a new revolutionary effort. Sun's dream was of a great military expedition, marching north from Canton to unify China by force. Allied with the infant Chinese Communist Party, Sun struggled throughout 1924 and early 1925 to solidify his base in the south while mustering nationwide support for his crusade against the warlords and foreign oppression.

In March 1925, Sun died. On May 30th, before the matter of succession was resolved, an incident arising out of a strike against Japanese textile mills in Shanghai led to a spontaneous explosion of anti-imperialist sentiment that quickly spread throughout China. To Borodin's agitators, the May 30th Incident was a great gift. They were able to turn much of the ensuing antiforeignism into support for the Kuomintang and its program. Almost a year passed, however, before the struggle for power within the Kuomintang was resolved in favor of Chinag Kai-shek and before the southern provinces were sufficiently under control to permit the march northward.

Sokolsky had watched developments within the Kuomintang closely and understood them at least as well as any Westerner in China. In February 1925 he examined the strike at the Japanese cotton mills and predicted that the labor dispute would be settled easily—unless there were political complications. At that point he found "no bolshevist element" involved in the strike, but warned that the communists would doubtless use the opportunity to propagandize. When Sun died, Sokolsky fretted over the control the left wing of the Kuomintang was able to exert over the Party. While many Western observers simply assumed the Kuomintang had been bolshevized, Sokolsky saw a struggle taking place between one group highly receptive to Soviet influence and another group more directly in line with the student movement in which he had participated in 1919. After the May Thirtieth Movement was underway, he was sympathetic to its main outlines, referring to the unrest as a struggle between military feudalism and an awakening mass consciousness. He continued to worry, however, about the Bolsheviks profiting, about Russians working in "devious channels." Again and again he insisted that the Soviet Union was China's real enemy and warned that the Chinese were being deceived by the Kuomintang Left—"a Russian agency." All of these points were repeated in an article reprinted in the United States: the Bolsheviks were *not* responsible for the May 30th Incident, but were capitalizing on the ensuing disorder; the Soviet Union was China's enemy but unfortunately student leaders were blinded to Soviet imperialism.[1]

In an unsigned editorial for the *North China Daily News,* Sokolsky called for other elements within the Kuomintang to save China from the "enemies within," to drop the Left's emphasis on foreign oppression and deal with the Chinese who were responsible for China's ills. His appeal was to the "White Kuomintang," a faction allegedly led by his old friend T'ang Shao-i. Here perhaps was the quintessential treaty port response to the nationalist revolution: China was a mess and a revolution could help—but only if it swept away the Chinese villains responsible for corruption and chaos, bringing order in which foreign businessmen could thrive.[2]

The American Consul General in Shanghai, Edwin Cunningham, sent several of Sokolsky's analyses back to Washington. In December 1925 he reminded his superiors of Sokolsky's "peculiar facilities" for understanding the early days of the student movement. Cunningham advised that "his statement in regard thereto should be accepted without reservation"—and

1. *Japan Advertiser,* February 18, 1925; (unsigned) *North China Daily News,* March 21, 1925; *Japan Advertiser,* May 20 and June 15, 1925; *North China Daily News,* June 19, 1925, GES ms. "How the Shanghai Trouble Started," *Living Age,* CCCXXVI (August 8, 1925), 304–8.

2. *North China Daily News,* July 14, 1925, GES ms.

"without reservation" was underscored in Washington. In February 1926, forwarding another article, he referred to Sokolsky as "a rising young American political writer" but sent the article primarily as an indication of T'ang Shao-i's thought: "Mr. Sokolsky is in close touch with Mr. Tong Shao-yi and his articles sometimes reflect the opinions of the ex-premier."[3]

By December 1925, Sokolsky was becoming optimistic about freeing the Kuomintang from Bolshevik influences. He concluded that the students who were rallying to the Kuomintang banner were not attracted to any Bolshevik teachings other than that of the need for revolution, for fundamental change. He reported student resentment of charges they were Bolshevik agents and found that despite some ties to Soviet Russia the students were first of all Chinese patriots. Sokolsky insisted that the May Thirtieth Movement reflected this patriotic surge and that foreign emphasis on Russian provocation indicated blindness to the new mood in China. The revolution was imminent, he warned, and either the military would suppress the masses or the students would triumph over feudalism. But to those who feared the revolution he held out the comfort that "national unity and personal liberty are the ideals, not Bolshevism or Socialism." In mid-February, he was arguing that Chinese leaders did not take the Bolshevik movement in China seriously, that Russia's impact had been negligible. He insisted that the Canton regime was moving away from its ties to the Russians, that it was "childish" to call the Kuomintang either left-wing or Bolshevik.[4]

On the surface it seemed clear that Sokolsky was wrong, the victim of wishful thinking. Elements of the Kuomintang Right had been leaving the Party since the summer of 1925, and in January 1926 the leaders of the Right were expelled. Allied with the Communists, receiving Soviet support, the Left, led by Wang Ching-wei and Chiang Kai-shek, seemed firmly in control. Suddenly, in March, Chiang seized power in Canton, arresting Communists and depriving them of all positions of military authority—and Sokolsky looked like a prophet.

The compromise that Borodin then engineered—whereby the Russians continued their aid, promised support for the launching of the Northern Expedition and reined in the Chinese Communists in return for Chiang restoring most of his Soviet advisors to their posts and checking the Right's

3. Cunningham to Secretary of State, enclosures, December 22, 1925, SD 893.00/6977 and February 5, 1926, SD 893.00/7154.

4. *North China Daily News*, December 22, 1925, and February 18, 1926, GES ms.

eagerness for a purge—did not satisfy Sokolsky. He argued that the Kuomintang would have to crush the power of the Communists or be crushed itself—and he was confident that the power of the Communists was waning. But when the compromise emerged in May, Sokolsky described it as a Communist victory. He claimed that Chiang had retreated from the implications of anti-Communist resolutions he had introduced at the meeting of the Kuomintang Central Executive Committee, and blamed the retreat on Chiang's need to secure his rear while he moved his forces north against Wu P'ei-fu. He referred also to Chiang's need to retain the services of T. V. Soong—the latter allegedly prepared to withdraw his services as financial administrator if Chiang forced a showdown with the Communists. In particular, Chiang's dissolution of two right-wing groups upset Sokolsky, who concluded that "the elimination of the conservative forces from Canton cannot be received with anything but alarm even by the admirers of Canton's efforts in the direction of modern Government."[5]

American diplomats in China continued to be favorably impressed with Sokolsky's work—with his ability to obtain inside information about Kuomintang politics and with his analyses. Cunningham continued to forward his articles in the *North China Daily News* to Washington. Commenting on one series, the consul-general at Canton, Douglas Jenkins, contended it was "the most complete and trustworthy account that has been written in regard to the situation in Canton." Jenkins advised Minister J. V. A. MacMurray that Sokolsky had done his work "extremely well," noting the virtues of the Canton regime, recognizing the danger of communism, and making a point "which I fear I have not been able sufficiently to impress upon the Legation,—that Americans and American interests are not enjoying any particular advantages in comparison with other nationalities . . . that we cannot be expected to be regarded as friends of the so-called nationalist government until we abandon our 'unequal treaties.' "[6]

Jenkins also contrasted Sokolsky with Lewis Gannett, an editor of Oswald Garrison Villard's *Nation* who was visiting China—a contrast that became increasingly important to MacMurray. To the Legation, Gannett's enthusiastic sympathy for the nationalist movement, coupled with criticism of American and more specifically MacMurray's policies, was an embarrass-

5. *North China Daily News,* April 22 and June 10, 1926, GES ms.
6. Jenkins to Legation, May 13, 1926, SD 893.00/7493.

ment and an irritation. Moreover, the adverse publicity that the *Nation* provided might well stir the peace movement, anti-imperialists, and the American public generally, hampering the diplomat's ability to use or threaten to use force to protect the treaty rights of Americans in China. To MacMurray, still more was at stake. He perceived a threat to the entire Pacific treaty system, to the cooperative order he had labored to build since the closing years of Woodrow Wilson's presidency. MacMurray wanted support desperately and he found it in George Sokolsky.

The Taku Incident of March 1926 provided Sokolsky with an excellent opportunity to assume the role that so endeared him to MacMurray. The Boxer Protocol of 1901 had guaranteed the victorious powers access to the sea from Peking to prevent a repeat of the Boxers' success in isolating the foreign legations in 1900. Taku was the seaward end of the escape route and in 1926, a melee among the Northern warlords led to the closing of the Peiho and a mining of the channel. MacMurray chose to use this violation of the Protocol to teach the Chinese a lesson about the need to observe their treaty obligations—a lesson he hoped would make all Chinese parties more amenable to reason and an orderly revision of the treaty system. To this end he rallied the other legations and, with a blank check from Acting Secretary of State Joseph Grew and an indifferent President Coolidge, mustered a naval demonstration against the Chinese government. Hostilities were averted, as MacMurray anticipated, by the immediate compliance of the Peking government with the demands of the legations. Cooperative action in defense of treaty rights worked.[7]

Other Americans in Peking, led by Roger Greene, opposed MacMurray's action and his apparent reversion to gunboat diplomacy. Failing to move MacMurray, they appealed to Washington. In response to the naval demonstration and the capitulation of their government, several thousand Peking students demonstrated—and were fired upon by Chinese government troops, suffering over a hundred casualties. Estimates of those killed ranged from 17 to 40. With the help of missionary organizations and Greene's parent organization, the Rockefeller Foundation, the American government and press were alerted. Gannett also filed despatches attacking MacMurray's gunboat diplomacy, blaming him for the demonstration, accusing him of

7. Dorothy Borg, *American Policy and the Chinese Revolution* (New York, 1947), 140, footnote 58; Waldo H. Heinrichs, *American Ambassador* (Boston, 1966), 112–13.

committing the United States to the support of British and Japanese imperialism. President Coolidge was infuriated by newspaper reports that suggested a new aggressive American policy. Secretary of State Kellogg, returning to Washington after a bout with the flu, accused Grew of having declared war on China in his absence. MacMurray was notified that the United States would *not* use force in defense of treaty rights unless necessary to protect American lives.[8]

As MacMurray licked his wounds, puzzled by the lack of support from Washington and the opposition from former friends in China, Sokolsky defended him, specifically against Gannett's charges. He insisted that MacMurray was not defending British and Japanese imperialism but rather American life and property in Peking. Slapping at Gannett, Sokolsky remarked that MacMurray's concerns might be of little importance to a "tourist" but were of tremendous importance to "the American who spends his life in China." Turning to the demonstration, he insisted that it had been planned by the Soviet Embassy in Peking, that most universities had refused to participate, and that the demonstrators had deliberately provoked the guards into firing.[9]

In addition to his efforts to swing the Kuomintang to the Right and his support of the American Minister's approach to the defense of the treaty system, Sokolsky was active in promulgating the Japanese government's line on Chinese affairs, generally in unsigned articles in the *Far Eastern Review,* but also openly, in the *Japan Advertiser.* For the *Japan Advertiser,* an American-owned, Tokyo-based paper, Sokolsky called attention to Japan's new policy toward China, toward Shidehara's efforts since the Washington Conference to bring Japan forward as China's champion. Sokolsky claimed that the Chinese realized that the Japanese government sought to create a lasting friendship with China. In a comparable article, he claimed that the American government was anxious for friendship with Japan, citing a new judicial action leaving Americans in Dairen, a Japanese "leased" territory in Manchuria, to the mercies of Japanese jurisdiction. The articles for George Bronson Rea's *Far Eastern Review* were quite different in tone: shrill attacks on Soviet imperialism and American jingoism—the threats to Japanese interests on the Asian mainland. Not only was Sokolsky becoming

8. MacMurray to Secretary of State, enclosures, April 6, 1926, SD 893.00/7378; Sokolsky, *North China Daily News,* June 21, 1926, GES ms; Heinrichs, *American Ambassador,* 113–14.

9. *North China Daily News,* June 21, 1926, GES ms.

the American Minister at Peking's favorite journalist; he was also becoming the Japanese foreign minister's favorite English language commentator.[10]

Meanwhile, back on Wall Street, Thomas Lamont had become aware of the gravity of the situation in China. Unlike Sokolsky, Lamont had access to the secretary of state, and through him might easily reach the President. Addis, fearing another Boxer type antiforeign uprising, cabled his hope that Lamont was pressing the Department of State for cooperation among the powers toward restoration of order in China. In reply, Lamont indicated that he was deferring to the Department, feeling no competence to recommend policy—and forwarded copies of both cables to Kellogg. An acquaintance travelling in China on a Lamont letter of introduction reported on the intense nationalism of the Chinese, on communist influence, on the problems of businessmen, but argued against intervention. Lamont forwarded copies of the letter to the Department of State and to his sometime friend, Oswald Garrison Villard.[11]

Villard had been very close to Lamont's older brother and his affection for the elder Lamont had carried over to the younger—until Thomas moved to Wall Street. Bankers were not among Villard's favorite people and Villard was confident that had Thomas' brother lived he would not have approved of the association with J. P. Morgan and Company. With Villard's *Nation* crusading against international bankers who allegedly led the United States to war to preserve their investments and loans, tensions in the Villard-Lamont relationship were inevitable. In June 1925, *The Nation* published an article contending that the State Department was under pressure from international bankers "bewailing the obtuseness of the Chinese in declining Western inventions and in refusing to pay interest on the Six Power and other loans; they are demanding that Washington act by means of troops, a naval blockade or demonstration, or the summary execution of somebody or other." Lamont called Villard to deny the charge and asked for his sources. Villard would not identify his source, other than to claim he was highly placed in the American government. Lamont immediately reported all this to the secretary of state, indicating his skepticism, but suggesting that Kellogg check around the Department. Concluding his letter to Kellogg, he declared

10. *Japan Advertiser*, February 18 and March 15, 1925; see (unsigned) "Recrudescence of Jingoism," *Far Eastern Review* (March 1925). GES ms.

11. Lamont to Kellogg, enclosures, June 26, 1925, SD 893.00/6364; Stephan Duggan to Lamont, June 4, 1925, Lamont to Villard and to Frank Polk, July 3, 1925, 183–21, TWL ms.

that the American Group, "following the lead of the Department of State," had incurred large expenses "for the assistance of China" but had "never advocated measures of force in China." He objected to having its attitude perverted in the public press.[12]

Later in the month, Lamont reached the President. First he cabled Addis with his own view of the situation in China: "In recent years there seems to have been great growth of nationalistic feeling which probably has been aggravated by Soviet propaganda but which is still fundamental and must be reckoned with." But Lamont would have none of the kind of foolishness Villard attributed to bankers. Forcible intervention, he insisted, would be neither practical nor wise. Instead Lamont argued for carrying out the commitments made at Washington to revise the treaty system, for reexamining extraterritoriality and other foreign treaty rights. Addis replied several days later, calling for the immediate fulfillment of the Washington Conference promise to convene special conferences on tariff and extraterritoriality questions. Lamont notified Addis that the managing committee of the American Group agreed with him, but would make no formal statement because of the absence of consensus among the member banks. He then forwarded copies of these cables to Kellogg. On July 16, Kellogg wrote to Lamont indicating his agreement with Addis—and reporting that he had shown the correspondence to the President. Independently, Kellogg and his staff had reached the same conclusion as had Addis and Lamont and the cables between the bankers may have been useful in reassuring the President of the wisdom of the policy. On July 23, Kellogg notified the Washington Conference signatories of his readiness to appoint delegates to a special tariff conference and to send a commission to China to examine the question of extraterritoriality.[13]

In this first phase of the nationalist revolution, Lamont exhibited two concerns. Reflecting the dominant milieu in the United States, he opposed the use of force in China and hoped treaty revision would stem the tide of antiforeignism there. Reflecting his firm's interests in China, slight as they were, he was anxious for the tariff conference to succeed, and for the Chinese to be free to impose higher tariffs, to greatly increase their revenues, and to pay off their debts to American investors.

12. Lamont to Kellogg, July 3, 1925, SD 893.51/4827.

13. Lamont to Kellogg, enclosures, July 8, 1925, and Kellogg to Lamont, July 16, 1925, SD 893.51/4828; Borg, *American Policy and the Chinese Revolution,* 60–61.

When Bishop Logan Roots of the National Christian Council of China worried about American policy, Lamont was in a position to assure him that within the Coolidge Administration "measures of force are not being and will not be considered." In October, Lamont assembled bankers from the United States, Great Britain, Japan, and France—and Nelson Johnson from the Department of State—to hear Addis speak on the impossibility of using force or trying to bluff the Chinese. Clearly the international bankers had lined up behind a negotiated settlement with Chinese nationalism.[14]

After Addis spoke, Johnson and Lamont talked for a while about prospects for the success of the forthcoming tariff conference. Johnson was pessimistic, but Lamont promised to send the Department data the Consortium had compiled on China's financial condition and appeared optimistic. A few days later, Lamont outlined the American Group's position on the conference for the benefit of the American representatives to it. Most striking was the abandonment of his habitual emphasis on cooperation with the other Consortium nations, especially Great Britain. On this occasion, when it appeared likely that the Chinese might be able to obtain funds through a surtax on the existing tariff schedule, the cooperative policy broke down as the American Group gave priority to its particularistic interests. The program Lamont outlined was designed to give the Chinese more money than contemplated by the other powers, a surtax larger than the 2½ percent usually mentioned, but would tie this surplus to the refunding of the foreign debt. The program also revealed Lamont's indifference to the problems of American businessmen whose market in China might be constricted by higher tariffs. The American Group did not even approximate the concern demonstrated by Addis for the plight of British traders. Addis insisted that any increase in the surtax above 2½ percent be tied to the elimination of internal Chinese transit taxes (*likin*), but the American Group manifested no interest in the *likin* question. At the tariff conference, the position of the American government indicated less interest in debt refunding and more desire to facilitate trade than Lamont advocated. Like Lamont, however, his government lowered the priority it had attached earlier to cooperating with the British and Japanese. But while the delegates debated at Peking, civil war raged around them and Lamont shifted his attention to more important matters.[15]

14. Lamont to Bishop Roots, September 15, 1925, 183–21, TWL ms; Memorandum by Johnson, October 21, 1925, SD 893.00/6692.

15. SD 893.00/6692; Lamont to Johnson, October 27, 1925, SD 893.51/4855.

On the eve of his return to China in the spring of 1925, Roger Greene had written to congratulate J. V. A. MacMurray on his appointment as American Minister to China. He was relieved to know that the legation would be in the hands of a man who knew China and whose judgment he trusted. He also thought that MacMurray's "thorough understanding" with the State Department would be a valuable asset. An able, experienced career diplomat seemed the perfect choice. But in the next few years, the relationship between the two men soured, MacMurray's understanding with the Department evaporated, and American policy came closer to reflecting Greene's views than those of the American Minister.[16]

Shortly after his arrival in China, Greene analyzed conditions in China following the May 30th Incident for his wife, for George E. Vincent, President of the Rockefeller Foundation and Chairman of the Board of Trustees of the China Medical Board—and for Nelson T. Johnson, Chief, Division of Far Eastern Affairs, Department of State. For his wife, whom he wanted desperately to join him, he offered an optimistic appraisal of the safety of foreigners in Peking, having travelled without problems. But Shanghai, scene of the incident, was quite another matter. There, "the uncompromising attitude of foreign businessmen" toward the national aspirations of the Chinese, and "their tactless method" in contacts with the Chinese, kept the situation tense. The difference in ambience between Shanghai, where aggressive businessmen clawed for advantage, and Greene's Peking, serene capital, city of diplomats and scholars, is worth noting—both for the reality of the difference and for the divergent perceptions of Chinese nationalism by the American communities in the two cities.[17]

For Vincent, Greene outlined two conditions he considered fundamental to an understanding of the apparent chaos of the May Thirtieth Movement: the oppressive policies of foreign powers and the disorganization of the Chinese government. He discussed the corruption and inefficiency of the latter, and he described the agitation of the Soviet government as exaggerated but not to be ignored. Responsibility for the current antiforeign movement he placed on foreigners, especially businessmen. He professed surprise that Chinese Communist agitators had not been more successful, considering the provocation foreigners had given. Referring to the agitation, including that by noncommunist, conservative nationalists, he expressed anxiety be-

16. Greene to MacMurray, April 12, 1925, MacMurray Papers.

17. Roger to Kate B. Greene, June 12, 1925, RSG ms.

cause "with so many undesirable and criminally short-sighted Americans and Europeans living in Chinese communities thus excited, an explosive mixture is being compounded." Some of these foreigners, "especially businessmen in the open ports, advocate strong-arm methods and even regret that more of the mob was not killed [in the May 30th Incident] as a means of preventing worse trouble in the future." Fortunately others, including missionaries, had expressed regret over the incident and sympathy for Chinese aspirations, apparently having some effect "in preventing an undiscriminating hostility to all foreigners." The contempt for traders, the invidious comparisons between them and missionaries, between them and people of culture in the host country—these were attitudes that evidenced themselves in Greene's days in the consular service. They reflected values as well as an experience alien to a man like Sokolsky. Sokolsky extolled and spoke for the merchant prince, founder of middle-class democracy, but Greene, rooted as he was in the New England aristocracy and its traditions of service, had no sympathy for such men.[18]

Greene's letter to Nelson Johnson constituted a report from a professional diplomat in the field to his counterpart back home. He began with a personnel recommendation: Willys Peck was "growing"; thanks to contact with Lucius Porter of Harvard-Yenching, Peck's viewpoint was broadening and he had shown real understanding of the Chinese viewpoint; the time had come to allow him greater responsibility. Analyzing the May Thirtieth Movement, Greene asked Johnson to keep in mind that "apart from fundamental restlessness of educated Chinese at the position of inferiority which they now occupy in relation to foreigners in China," most Chinese did not know that the incident on May 30 had been triggered by a mob moving against a police station—and those who had heard the truth "refuse to believe it." Concluding with a policy recommendation, he called for the removal of the Legation guard and of the troops stationed at Tientsin. Greene submitted a detailed memorandum to the military attaché, working through appropriate channels, but provided Johnson with a summary of his argument. He did not anticipate a mob attack on the Legations such as was experienced during the Boxer rebellion and even if the Legation or the routes to the sea were attacked by an organized force, neither the Legation guard nor the Tientsin troops were adequate to provide protection. Moreover, in the

18. Greene to Vincent, June 19, 1925 (with reference to events occurring June 25), RSG ms.

existing atmosphere of intense nationalist fervor, "the display of a foreign body of troops is irritating and tends to create precisely the danger which it is intended to guard against."[19]

The split between Greene and his missionary-educator colleagues on the one hand and American businessmen in China on the other became readily apparent as the two groups responded to a speech by Senator Borah calling for an end to extraterritoriality and the avoidance of conflict with China. Whereas the Chamber of Commerce in China deprecated Borah's position, complaining that he was contributing support to Bolshevik efforts to produce chaos, Greene and over 300 other American citizens in North China joined in a cable and letter endorsing Borah's stand. The letter to Borah, *apparently* drafted by Greene, described the May Thirtieth Movement as "a justifiable protest against existing treaties no longer acceptable to a self-respecting nation," and agreed that an end to extraterritoriality and assurance of nonintervention would allay Chinese fears and promote Sino-American friendship. Greene and his cosigners argued that "American enterprise in China, particularly business and missionary enterprise, is fundamentally dependent upon the friendship and goodwill of the Chinese people." They argued that military intervention on behalf of foreign enterprise would destroy missionary work. They preferred to have their work rest upon a foundation of friendship "rather than upon unwelcome treaties or armed force." In June of 1925—and in the months and years that followed—it was the analysis of Greene and others like him, their recommendations, to which the Department of State responded—despite the opposition of the American Chamber of Commerce in China and of the American Minister.[20]

Although intensely sympathetic to the national aspirations of the Chinese, Greene never plunged into their cause to become one of them. He was too much the outsider, too much the mugwump committed to his personal vision of truth and justice, to throw himself completely into the cause. He wanted treaty revision but as the tariff conference progressed in Peking and Chinese intellectuals demanded immediate tariff autonomy, he concluded that however valuable symbolically, a return of tariff control to the Chinese in the fall of 1925 would not be in their interest. The added revenue "would fall into the hands, not of the Chinese people, not even of the Central Gov-

19. Greene to Johnson, June 19, 1925, RSG ms.
20. Greene, et al. to Borah, June 22, 1925, RSG ms.

ernment, which can represent the people better than any other organization now existing, but into the hands of the military governors throughout the country whose hold on their power would be greatly strengthened.''[21]

Greene also tried to separate himself from men whose sympathy for the Chinese he shared but whom he saw as true believers, unreliable reporters who perhaps did more harm than good. Such was the light in which he saw J. Leighton Stuart, one of the most prominent American missionary educators. In September 1925, a widely publicized conference on China had been held at Johns Hopkins University and Stuart, President of Yenching University, gave perhaps the most important speech. Generally, he argued along lines Greene could easily endorse, but Stuart also referred to the superior courtesy of the Chinese people, and this Greene could not accept. His allies were not allowed the privilege of overstatement. They could not risk appearing to be mere sentimentalists. ''The group which Dr. Stuart represents,'' Greene complained, ''is a bit wild in its statements about the Chinese.'' Indeed, he argued Chinese arrogance and discourtesy were important reasons for starting Sino-Western relations off on the wrong footing. Stuart's declaration, that if the circumstances in the May 30th Incident had been reversed the Chinese would have offered prompt apology, Greene considered absurd. In a rare declaration of favor with his countrymen, he contended that Americans were much more ready than Chinese to make apologies. Certainly Roger Greene did not want to be accused of supporting Chinese aspirations out of any uncritical Sinophilism.[22]

But Greene's real quarrel was not with imperfect friends like Leighton Stuart. It was, rather, with the American Minister, J. V. A. MacMurray. The decisive moment was provided by the Taku Incident of March 1926, when MacMurray chose to threaten the Chinese with the use of naval power if the channel between Peking and Tientsin were not opened immediately. First, Greene attempted to dissuade MacMurray from taking any action. Failing to convince MacMurray, he cabled George Vincent, insisting that action was unnecessary and ''likely to cause trouble more serious than present inconvenience besides improper interference in internal conflict.'' In response to Greene's plaintive ''can you do anything in the matter?,'' Vincent sent a telegram to Kellogg—the President of the Rockefeller Founda-

21. Roger to Jerome Greene, October 14, 1925, RSG ms.
22. Greene to Margery Eggleston, January 23, 1926, RSG ms.

tion to the Secretary of State—repeating Greene's cable, indicating confidence in Greene's judgment, and calling Kellogg's attention to Greene's experience in China.[23]

As Kellogg raged in Washington, MacMurray and Greene retained a civil relationship. The day after the naval demonstration and ultimatum, Greene led a delegation of Americans resident in Peking to a meeting with MacMurray. After MacMurray confirmed the role of the United States, Greene protested American policy and asked MacMurray to telegraph Washington for a reconsideration. He argued that MacMurray did not understand the sentiments of the American people, upon whose will American foreign policy rested. Supported by occasional remarks by Leighton Stuart, Greene cited diplomatic precedents for his argument and challenged MacMurray's interpretation of the Boxer Protocol. When the gist of this discussion was leaked to the press, Greene apologized to MacMurray, but restated his position angrily. He insisted that the United States had taken a position of leadership "in making a threat of force over a comparatively petty matter in which our vital interests are not seriously affected." He was most upset by MacMurray viewing the incident as a "heaven-sent opportunity." MacMurray responded politely, assuring Greene that he did not hold him responsible for the leak and indicating regret that his position should be "so strongly contested by one for whose good judgment and honesty of thought I have so great a respect." When Greene and his supporters were attacked by a journalist for their "cowardly and contemptible" effort to disassociate themselves from American policy, MacMurray wrote a scolding letter to the journalist. For the moment the affair was closed. When the students demonstrated and were fired upon in Peking, Greene sent evidence to MacMurray that may have provided the substance for Sokolsky's claim that the demonstrators deliberately provoked the troops.[24]

A few weeks later, as Peking grew calm again, Greene wrote a sixteen-page letter to Johnson discussing the Taku incident, MacMurray's attitude generally, and his own thoughts for a satisfactory American policy. He indicated surprise that he and MacMurray should be on different sides. He had concluded from MacMurray's speeches in New York in 1925 that "he was

23. Vincent to Kellogg, March 17, 1926, SD 893.00/7191.

24. Greene to MacMurray, March 18, 1926, and MacMurray to Greene, March 19, 1926, RSG ms; MacMurray to Secretary of State, enclosures, April 6, 1926, SD 893.00/7378, and March 25, 1926, SD 893.00/7354.

fully convinced that threats of force could no longer serve any useful purpose in China." The British had learned from their experiences in Canton and even the Japanese seemed more sensitive than MacMurray. As he had years before as a diplomatist, Greene again insisted that "unless issues of great importance are at stake," intervention in a domestic conflict was unwarranted. He left no doubt that he considered the conditions to which MacMurray had responded to be a trivial infringement of treaty rights. Still he expressed sympathy for MacMurray, who received constant complaints of Chinese violations of American rights, not only under the unequal treaties but also from victims of Chinese failures to meet normal obligations, of failures of the Chinese government to pay its just debts. Greene thought it "no wonder that he loses patience and considers that it is time to be firm whenever we can if all treaty obligations, good or bad alike, are not to be disregarded. I should probably feel much as he does, if I were in his place without my experience of recent years." But it was essential to realize, he argued, that there was no point in demanding of a government that which it could not do. It was useless to lose patience.[25]

Greene also suggested that there was a side to Chinese life which diplomats did not see: improvement in trade relations, in education, in the development of professions. He insisted that despite apparent chaos, modernization was continuing—and was visible to missionaries and educators in their daily work, explaining in part the difference between their attitudes and those of businessmen and diplomats. Greene concluded that the Department would do well to create the post of "cultural attaché" to provide the Minister with essential information on cultural and intellectual developments which, in China, he considered of greater import than the information usually obtained by military attachés. There was something, he thought, to be learned from the Bolsheviks, who "have people who keep in touch with the educational and labor world, two elements of the greatest importance in China at the present time." Not only did Greene provide Johnson and Kellogg with analyses supportive of their policies—and the knowledge that their policy had powerful supporters in the Rockefeller Foundation—he also provided a blueprint for cultural affairs officers, including details for recruiting and financing, that the Department implemented during World War II.

By the end of the summer, MacMurray had had ample time to mull

25. Greene to Johnson, April 7, 1926, RSG ms.

over the missionary response to his policy. He sent the secretary of state an eighteen-page analysis of why missionaries sincerely but wrongly sided with the Chinese nationalists against the American government. Reiterating his view that concessions to the Chinese would be regarded as weakness, leading to further demands, he noted that the missionaries trusted neither his opinions nor the validity of his sources—and singled out Roger Greene as "a salient example." He reminded the Secretary that Greene had once been "a most efficient consular officer of the United States." Nonetheless, when protesting against the so-called "Taku Ultimatim," Greene had doubted the ability of the government to keep itself as well informed about events and motives in China as did purely private agencies. If Greene could "so readily forget the great aggregate of time and painstaking effort he spent personally in keeping this Legation informed of political and economic happenings, the facility with which many missionaries discredit the information available to the agencies of our Government is little to be wondered at."[26]

Increasingly after the Taku Incident, MacMurray realized that his attitude toward the Chinese nationalists, his insistence on the Chinese meeting their treaty obligations before considering concessions, was not shared by his superiors in Washington. He was aware that Greene and the missionaries whose spokesman he had become were striking a more responsive chord in the State Department, in Congress, and among the American people. Frustrated, he could only remind the Department of his superior apparatus for analyzing events in China and hope that he could divert Johnson and Kellogg from the disastrous course of appeasement they had chosen. As the missionaries, educators, and liberal journalists opposed him, he turned increasingly to the business community and journalists like Sokolsky for support—and these he found in Shanghai, not Peking.

In the fall and winter of 1926–27, Nationalist forces drove the warlord armies out of the Yangtze valley. In March, a Communist-led uprising in Shanghai facilitated Chiang Kai-shek's capture of the city. A few days later, Nationalist forces occupied Nanking. Although Shanghai had been taken without serious incident, Nationalist soldiers in Nanking attacked foreigners and foreign property, including the American, British, and Japanese consulates. Among those murdered before gunboats came to the rescue was the

26. MacMurray to Secretary of State, September 10, 1926, SD 893.00/7767.

American vice-president of the University of Nanking. As the powers attempted to comprehend the meaning of the Nanking outrages, and to obtain satisfaction, it was becoming increasingly apparent that a great power struggle had erupted within the Kuomintang. Suddenly, in April, Chiang ordered the arrest and massacre of several hundred Communists and labor leaders in Shanghai. And all this occurred while the Left-Kuomintang operated its own government in Wuhan.

The bewilderment in foreign capitals was not eased by rumors of conflict between the Kuomintang Left and the Chinese Communists and Soviet advisors working with the Left at Wuhan. In July, the Wuhan faction of the Kuomintang turned on its Communist allies and the White Terror swept China. Communists and radicals were massacred wherever Wuhan- or Nanking-directed Kuomintang forces could catch them. Borodin and other Soviet advisors fled from China. But even this purge did not lead to unification of the Kuomintang. Chiang Kai-shek went into retirement in August, followed shortly thereafter by his principal rival, Wang Ching-wei. In November another Kuomintang regime emerged in Canton. Factionalism tore the Kuomintang apart as the various contenders for leadership refused to subordinate ambition to party unity. At this moment the Comintern ordered an uprising, the ill-fated Canton Commune. Amidst the disorder, Chiang came forward again and by January 1928 he had resumed leadership of the party.

For American diplomats trying to sort out the incredible events of 1927, Sokolsky's knowledge of the inner workings of the Kuomintang, surpassed by Borodin alone among foreigners, was of tremendous help. Sokolsky not only wrote articles analyzing Kuomintang politics and predicting events, he also reported directly to Cunningham, the American consul-general at Shanghai, to John Magruder, an American military attaché in China, and to MacMurray. It is also possible that he reported to Baron Shidehara, the Japanese Foreign Minister, who frequently praised him to the British Ambassador to Japan. In addition, he provided Lamont with a long analysis, followed by a series of articles in Lamont's *New York Evening Post*.

As the battlelines formed in the Yangtze in 1926 and Chiang's men faced an array of warlord armies outnumbering them 5 to 1, Sokolsky predicted that Chiang would win easily—that confronted by Chiang's "trained, idealistic" troops the warlords would be helpless. He contended that the masses welcomed Kuomintang troops and that even conservative bankers, fearful of Bolshevism, felt secure with "the sterner, more orderly rule of the KMT [Kuomintang]." Sokolsky insisted that the Kuomintang alone had a program of national reconstruction, that its ties to Communism were merely a "business arrangement" and that Chiang was no more a Communist than Chang Tso-lin. This analysis was not only accurate but also contained the same assumptions upon which Shidehara based his policy during the Northern Expedition.[27]

Sokolsky understood the role of the Chinese Communists and Comintern advisors in the Chinese revolution and he was hostile to their presence; but he was not blinded to the genuineness of the issues they exploited. He argued again and again in opposition to foreigners who wanted to believe that unrest was solely the work of Bolshevik agitators. One series of articles on labor unrest in the Wuhan area gained the attention of the *People's Tribune,* an English-language organ of the Kuomintang Left, and was offered as recommended reading for imperialists everywhere. Sokolsky was praised for recognizing the immense power of the Kuomintang, for attributing the Kuomintang victory in the Yangtze valley to "agitational activities" rather than fighting, and for brushing aside charges that the Kuomintang movement was Russian-inspired.[28]

In what may have been a bid to extend his contacts in the Kuomintang further left, Sokolsky praised Borodin as the most brilliant personality in the Kuomintang and praised the work of the Chinese Communists as well as that of the Kuomintang. Against their skillful agitation, he predicted Chinese "feudalism" could not stand. He explained Russian success with the KMT as based on "direct and generous aid" denied to the movement by the United States and Great Britain. But he insisted that the Kuomintang did not desire to establish a Communist state in Russia "and it is unbelievable that Mr. Borodin has any such intentions." Sokolsky contended the Russians were trying to bank goodwill in China in the event of difficulties with Britain or Japan, but warned the Russians that success would make the Nationalists less agreeable. He added: "As long as the Kuomintang are in South China, they meet Russia at no point where there can be a clash of national interest, but the day the Kuomintang reaches North China they will face an imperialist Russia with an imperialist position in Mongolia and Manchuria."

27. *Transpacific,* October 9, 1926, GES ms; Iriye, *After Imperialism,* 119–21, 130–33.
28. *People's Tribune* (Hankow), December 21, 1926, GES ms.

Sokolsky assumed the KMT and Russians would part and advised the powers to remain neutral in the interim, ultimately withdrawing recognition from Peking.[29]

In January 1927, Sokolsky wrote a lengthy analysis of the Chinese political situation for Lamont. After identifying various factions within the KMT, he focused on KMT relations with the Russians, noting mounting concern among KMT leaders, predicting a split. He suggested that the Russians were aware that the Nationalists would attempt to be rid of them upon completion of the Northern Expedition and were fomenting trouble in an effort to prevent stability. He was convinced that the Chinese Communists were trying to embarrass the Nationalist regime and predicted "sinister disturbances" that would lead to a breach between the KMT and CCP. Sokolsky's analysis proved to be accurate, as were his predictions, but Shidehara seemed more impressed with his views than was MacMurray.[30]

Although American officials in China respected Sokolsky's ability to obtain and interpret information, they were uneasy about his involvement in Chinese politics. They were aware of his tendency to blur the lines between objective reporting and "puffing" the faction or individual with whom he was allied at a given moment. MacMurray, Cunningham, and Magruder solicited information and all would have agreed with Magruder's assessment that Sokolsky was "the best informed newspaperman in China as to the Yangtze Valley situation." They would also have agreed with Magruder's caveat about Sokolsky's political ambitions and ties, in 1927, to the Right wing of the Kuomintang. They might also have noticed the favorable treatment he accorded T. V. Soong, even while Soong was in Wuhan working with Borodin. The pattern of Sokolsky's involvements in Chinese politics from 1919 to 1927 suggests that he aspired to Borodin's role: to be the leading adviser to a modern Chinese ruler like Soong—and he came very close to achieving precisely that goal, closer than Soong did to ruling.[31]

As the tensions within the KMT-CCP coalition heightened in March 1927, Sokolsky's analyses showed a peculiar but revealing ambivalence. He saw and reported various moves being made by Borodin and Chiang Kai-

29. *Japan Advertiser,* December 30, 1926, GES ms.

30. Sokolsky to Lamont, January 17, 1927, enclosure, 183–22, TWL ms; Sir J. Tilley to Sir Austen Chamberlain, February 14, 1927: "Mr. Sokolsky's name has been mentioned more than once as having been quoted to me by Baron Shidehara who recognizes him as an authority on Chinese affairs." FO 405/252b/425.

31. Magruder, "American Journalists in China," April 26, 1927, RG 165, 10639–176(58).

shek against each other's influence. He claimed that Chiang had long known that the Communists would try to destroy him and that he had no alternative but to destroy them first. Sokolsky was hostile to Russian influence, to what he feared would be Russian efforts to manipulate Chinese nationalism. Nevertheless, he admired Borodin's success at organizing a mass movement and he favored the westernization Borodin's ultimate triumph would bring. A victory by Chiang would eliminate Russian influence but it would be the victory of Chinese militarists who, though influenced by revolutionary ideals, "have not been able to divorce themselves from the average Chinese military man's conception of the state as something which belongs to him if he can hold it with soldiers." Would a China ruled by Chiang and his military clique be much different than China under the control of the warlords? Would there be the same impulse toward modernization that Borodin might have provided? Would there be a role for George Sokolsky?[32]

The day after Chiang's attack on the Communists in Shanghai, MacMurray advised the secretary of state that according to Sokolsky T. V. Soong would assume leadership of the fight against the Chinese Communists. Chiang had determined that he needed civilian assistance and Soong's ability to raise money had made him the obvious choice. Soong would be dictator, sharing power with Chiang and either Wang Ching-wei or T'an Yen-k'ai.[33]

Sokolsky was pleased by the Kuomintang's purge of the Communists and of Russian influence. His satisfaction was contingent, however, on the ability of American-educated T. V. Soong to contain the military and to turn the Chinese revolution into something approximating the American revolution. Soong recognized the need to retain the support of the middle class, to create a middle class democracy. But it quickly became apparent that Soong could not control Chiang and, of at least equal importance, that the elimination of Russian advisors and Chinese Communists did not make the Kuomintang any less antiforeign. For a few weeks, Sokolsky's writings offered advice to the Kuomintang leadership, and reflected disappointment, but by May he had become intensely critical of Chiang and his "Ningpo clique." By July he had dubbed Chiang the "Ningpo Napoleon."[34]

32. *Transpacific*, March 19, 1927, *North China Daily News*, March 23 and 25, 1927, *Japan Advertiser*, April 6, 1927, GES ms.

33. MacMurray to Secretary of State, April 13, 1927, SD 893.00/8662.

34. *Japan Advertiser*, April 21, May 18, July 14 and 22, 1927, *North China Daily News*, April 20 and July 9 (unsigned editorial), 1927, GES ms; MacMurray to Secretary of State, enclosure, May 25, 1927, SD 893.00/9152.

Sokolsky's attacks on Chiang reflected both his values and his ties to Soong—the man whose values were closest to his own. Chiang was hardly better than an old fashioned warlord, concerned with personal power, making deals with other warlords like Yen Hsi-shan, pretending that men like Yen had been won over to the ideals of the revolution. Chiang's armies continued to harass foreigners, destroy foreign property, just like the Communists. Borodin was gone but antiforeign placards were raised throughout territory controlled by the Nationalists. As Soong's influence declined, Sokolsky condemned Chiang's financial policies. He railed against the predominance of the military, of the Ningpo clique over the Canton clique, and warned Chiang that a "certain high-minded" member of his government might abandon him, destroy his prestige, leave him a mere warlord unpopular with the masses. In August, success seemed imminent as Chiang went into retirement. Sokolsky was not above claiming credit for the event, writing on August 20, 1927, of his earlier articles: ". . . Perhaps not altogether without some premonition of what was about to occur, certain changes were suggested which have now actually taken place. . . ." Cunningham sent six of Sokolsky's August articles to the secretary of state, noting that Sokolsky was "in very close personal touch with C. C. Wu, T. V. Soong and other leaders in the Nationalist movement in China."[35]

Sokolsky's initial exultation over Chiang's departure was short-lived. Within a month he was fretting about both continued Communist influence within the Kuomintang and the rising ambitions of various generals nominally loyal to the party. He saw that it might be necessary to bring Chiang back to eliminate these problems, though it would be regrettable "because his career has been such as not to inspire confidence in his political acumen or integrity." But Cunningham for one did not accept Sokolsky's analysis. The American consul-general at Shanghai could not comprehend Sokolsky's distinction between Communists and those sympathetic to their views and was convinced that Chiang was finished, "a back number."[36]

In November 1927, Sokolsky suddenly discovered a new Chiang, "rather easy-going and kindly, product of Borodin's worst judgment." This Chiang, presumably bereft of his napoleonic ambitions, was marrying So-

35. *Japan Advertiser,* June 8 and July 22, 1927, *North China Daily News,* July 18 and 19, August 4, 6, 9, 11, 13, and 20, 1927, GES ms; Cunningham to Secretary of State, enclosures, August 20, 1927, SD 893.00/9437.

36. *North China Daily News,* September 6, 1927, GES ms; Cunningham to Secretary of State, enclosure, September 14, 1927, SD 893.00/9512.

kolsky's friend, Mei-ling Soong, T.V.'s sister. Sokolsky's wife was arranging the wedding and Sokolsky himself was strutting in the pose of successful matchmaker. As Chiang made his peace with the Soong family and patched up relations with other Kuomintang leaders, Sokolsky's future as a member of the court looked brilliant.[37]

From his inside position as friend of several western-educated Kuomintang leaders, Sokolsky kept Cunningham, Magruder, and MacMurray informed. Cunningham sent several dozen Sokolsky articles to MacMurray and to Washington, generally praising the insights. To all three men—and to other American officials—Sokolsky sent confidential reports. As Chiang returned to power in January 1928, MacMurray informed Willys Peck in Washington of Sokolsky's value to the Legation. He found Sokolsky "particularly helpful because he is . . . sufficiently a part of their councils to know pretty well what is going on, while sufficiently aloof to be substantially free from particular bias in his views." MacMurray considered Sokolsky "entirely honest in his desire to be helpful to us in understanding what is going on in 'Nationalist' circles."[38]

One complaint Sokolsky voiced several times in 1926 and 1927 was that American missionary circles had too much influence over American policy toward China, causing the Department of State to be insufficiently supportive of MacMurray. Sharing the attitude of many of these missionaries, Roger Greene worked with them in China and enhanced their efforts through his contacts in the Department of State and by testifying before Congress.

In the fall of 1926, Greene returned to the New York office of the China Medical Board and from that base disseminated his views as widely as possible among interested groups in the United States. He was in particular demand as a speaker before major church organizations, such as the Foreign Missions Conference and the Federal Council of Churches. In December he had a long visit with Nelson Johnson at the Department of State and spoke also with Drysdale, who was heading the Military Intelligence Division for the Far East, and Joseph Grew. He found them all cordial, with Grew "almost apologetic" about his responsibility for approving naval action at Taku and Drysdale endorsing Greene's view that the action had been

37. Sokolsky to Magruder, November 26, 1927 (copy), MacMurray Papers.

38. MacMurray to Peck, January 11, 1928, MacMurray Papers.

unwise. From Johnson he gained the impression that the Department was prepared to yield nearly everything the Chinese wanted as soon as a reasonably responsible government was established.[39]

In January, Stephen Porter, Chairman of the House Committee on Foreign Affairs, was persuaded by A. L. Warnshuis of the International Missionary Council to introduce a resolution calling for renegotiation of the so-called "unequal treaties" with China. Warnshuis wanted the removal of restrictions on Chinese sovereignty and a redefinition of relations between China and the United States that would allow China the status of an equal. In the ensuing hearings before Porter's Committee, Greene, identified as former Consul General of the United States in China and Director of the China Medical Board of the Rockefeller Foundation, testified on behalf of the resolution. He argued that articulate Chinese were almost unanimous in seeking tariff autonomy and an end of extraterritoriality. An attempt to retain these special privileges, he contended, would require the use of force "on an inconceivably large scale." While warning that yielding before compelled to do so would not likely end antiforeign agitation in China, Greene predicted a salutary effect in the long run. A *Literary Digest* analysis of editorial opinion found "emphatic press approval" for the ideas inherent in the resolution.[40]

After debate in the House, the Porter Resolution was passed overwhelmingly on February 21, 1927. In Peking the affair was noted with irritation by MacMurray, who perceived an ignorant Congress and an uninformed public pressing the Department toward a posture of weakness. Reviewing the published hearings, he growled about the "tedium of the cocksure idealism which Grover Clark [editor of the *Peking Leader*] and Roger Greene had the opportunity to get printed at government expense." But it was clear that Greene and his friends had taken the initiative, that they were supported by the press, by the interested public in the United States, and by Congress—and that the Department of State was not far behind.[41]

Early in April, after the Nanking incident, Greene worried about demands by the American Chamber of Commerce, Shanghai, for firm action. He sent a telegram to Grew calling instead for the evacuation of American

39. Greene to Houghton, December 30, 1926, RSG ms.
40. Borg, *American Policy and the Chinese Revolution,* 242–44, 256–57.
41. MacMurray to Peck, March 11, 1927, MacMurray Papers.

citizens from the danger zones. Greene warned that if the Chamber of Commerce recommendation was followed it would involve greater expense to the government and greater loss to commercial and other interests. Grew replied that all Americans willing to withdraw were in the process of being evacuated. The Department was well aware that the public would not support the use of force on behalf of business interests in China. A few weeks later a letter from Greene arguing for the surrender of special privileges in China was published in the *New York Times.* At the end of the month, enroute to Peking, Greene wrote to commend Grew for the Department's patience in handling the Nanking incident. He also advised Grew that in the event of trouble in North China, the Rockefeller Foundation preferred to withdraw its people rather than ask for the use of force to protect them.[42]

Shortly after his return to Peking, Greene received a dramatic cable from Madame Sun Yat-sen, addressing him as the "Head foremost Medical Organization in China," asking him to send desperately needed nurses to tend the wounded in the Wuhan area. The Kuomintang Left, still allied with Borodin, still the center of antiforeign, anticapitalist agitation in China, had turned to the Rockefeller Foundation for help. For about a week Greene hurried about, gaining assurances from Kuomintang officials, approval from the American Consul at Hankow, and recruiting doctors and nurses. Despite obstruction by the acting British consul-general in Shanghai, Greene had nine doctors and sixteen nurses on the way eleven days after Madame Sun sent her cable. Two days later he followed, accompanied by a second group. Now it was Greene's turn to be singled out by the *People's Tribune.* On June 22, 1927, an editorial praised Greene and his staff who, in contrast to foreigners of the Shanghai mentality, "have closed their eyes to petty political and racial considerations, because their eyes have been filled with the greater inner vision of human helpfulness which over-rides narrow racial and political prejudices."[43]

Reporting his experiences to Nelson Johnson, who was still Chief of the Division of Far Eastern Affairs, Greene claimed to have won some good will, perhaps to have stimulated better feeling toward the United States, and

42. Greene to Grew, April 4, 1927, SD 393.11/538; *New York Times,* May 3, 1927, VII, p. 12; Greene to Grew, April 27, 1927, SD 893.00/8874.

43. Madame Sun to Greene, May 30, 1927, Greene to British Minister, June 11, 1927, to Bishop Roots, June 10, 1927, RSG ms; *New York Times,* June 17, 1927, p. 10; *People's Tribune,* June 22, 1927, Greene to Francis W. Peabody, July 7, 1927, RSG ms.

to have lessened the sense of separation between the Chinese and non-Russian foreigners. To Johnson and to another friend he expressed doubt that the Kuomintang Left was headed by Communists. He warned against the rigidity of American consular officials and naval officers who he feared would drive the Chinese into the arms of the Russians. Greene obviously enjoyed his contacts with the young Kuomintang leaders, in particular Eugene Chen, Quo Tai-chi, C. C. Wu, and T. V. Soong. He probably preferred them, despite their inexperience and revolutionary pretensions, to Chiang, whose "harshness in dealing with the labor leaders and all so-called communists, many of whom are not communists at all, makes many good people suspicious of him." A few weeks after Greene returned to Peking, the Kuomintang Left attacked its Communist allies, both Russian and Chinese. His analysis of the Wuhan leadership had been validated, but in the American Legation, his sympathy for the Nationalists won for him reference as "that swine, Roger Greene."[44]

Greene's acceptance of the Nationalist revolution, despite his instinctive preference for order, rested upon the acceptance at an intellectual level of disorder as a necessary part of the process of tearing down the old China to build a new society. In his convocation address to Peking Union Medical College in September 1927, he explained to his audience that they were witnessing the crumbling of an old social and political order, and that they had to endure all the painful readjustments in thought and behavior inherent in basic social and political change. He conceded that not all men would agree on the desirability of the transformation China was enduring, but argued that contact with the rest of the world left the Chinese no choice but to modernize. In the usual fashion of convocation or commencement speakers he spoke of the enormity of the task ahead, of the vast numbers of leaders to be trained, of the techniques to be mastered. He saw signs of progress, however. Despite the unrest there had been an increase in trade, in the number of schools, in the number of competent men, in the growth of public spirit among Chinese leaders. He noted rising aspirations among the masses and called for encouragement of these expectations. At Peking Union Medical College Greene and the China Medical Board would make their contribution, hastening the spread of modern medicine and public health systems.[45]

44. Greene to Johnson, June 30, 1927, RSG ms; Ferdinand Mayer to MacMurray, August 16, 1927, MacMurray Papers.

45. Text of Convocation Address, September 18, 1927, RSG ms.

Despite his empathy for Chinese nationalism, Greene's resistance to turning the administration of the medical school over to the Chinese is useful for taking the measure of the man. In May, just before he responded to Madame Sun's plea, he reported growing sentiment within and without Peking Union for a Chinese Director or Vice Director. There were pressures from the existing Chinese government and greater pressures anticipated when the Kuomintang reached Peking. And there were undoubted advantages to having a Chinese executive. He would bring the college into closer relation with the community and could more easily handle problems of status among the Chinese staff. But Greene expressed concern that the choice would be limited to individuals not easily spared from very important positions they already held, presumably within the college. In subsequent correspondence, he found other reasons for holding back, suggesting that the China Medical Board wait for the Kuomintang to come and then negotiate. As an interim measure the school's trustees in New York created the post of Vice Director and it was filled by Dr. F. C. Yen "in the hope that a Chinese in this position might meet anticipated Chinese educational regulations." During the summer, Dr. Henry S. Houghton submitted his resignation as Director and pressure from New York for a Chinese Director mounted. Greene conceded the value of such a step, but suggested that the staff might not be ready for it, resulting in a loss of confidence, perhaps the resignation of several key people. He saw several alternatives as wiser in the short run. Eventually, the Committee of Professors responsible for recommending candidates for the posts unanimously recommended Dr. Liu Jui-heng as Vice Director and Roger Greene as Acting Director—a post which he held until 1934.[46]

Greene's opposition to the naming of a Chinese Director of Peking Union Medical College cannot be explained in terms of insensitivity to Chinese nationalism. On the other hand, the shifting basis of his opposition suggests the possibility that he was being less direct, less candid than usual. It is at least conceivable that he wanted the position for himself, but could not bring himself to ask for it. Certainly such behaviour would fit with the pattern of his entry and advancement through the Consular Service and in the employ of the Rockefeller Foundation. Others had to recognize that he was the only man for the job. There could be no "advertisements for my-

46. Greene to Richard Pearce, May 28, May 31, and July 23, 1927, RSG ms; Ferguson, *CMB and PUMC,* 61.

self.'' There are, however, other less egocentric possibilities. Some of the Western staff might well have been unwilling to serve under a Chinese Director, or Chinese willing to accept status inferior to an American doctor might not have been willing to see one of their peers elevated. Greene was unquestionably concerned with the quality of instruction offered and was undoubtedly sincere in his fear that catering to nationalism might lead to an unnecessary sacrifice in quality. In addition, he was aware that the New York office was anxious to turn the whole school over to Chinese as a means of drastically reducing the budget. Western doctors and administrators were too expensive and Chinese doctors were on the same pay scale. Once the staff was composed entirely of Chinese, the trustees intended to introduce a pay scale more in line with Chinese standards. Greene expressed himself as ''heartily in favor of this principle'' but argued for waiting until Chinese were available of equal competence with the foreigners the school was able to recruit. By 1927, Peking Union had two Chinese department heads, selected on the basis of quality rather than nationality, and Greene wanted to maintain the same standards. Were the cries of ''quality'' and ''standards'' merely smoke screens, rationalizations for opposition to change—or were they the sensible arguments of a man who would not be stampeded in his efforts to provide China with the best medical education possible? The answer is not clear, but the long term support Greene received from Chinese doctors, intellectuals, and officials suggests that they accepted his arguments as sound. In January 1928, he formally became acting Director of Peking Union Medical College, and concurrently Vice President of the Rockefeller Foundation in China.[47]

47. Greene to Pearce, November 5, 1927, RSG ms.

6

# "MAKING IT" IN EAST ASIA

THOMAS LAMONT's advice to the Department of State for coping with the Northern expedition would have pleased Roger Greene rather than the American Chamber of Commerce in Shanghai. In November 1926, he forwarded excerpts from a letter by Addis in which the latter brushed aside claims of Bolshevik influence over the Kuomintang as "arrant exaggeration" and suggested recognition of the Kuomintang as the de facto government of China. In January 1927, Lamont spoke with Nelson Johnson and expressed pleasure at learning that Johnson supported the Porter resolution. Lamont professed to believe that the special privileges of the treaty system were an anachronism best disposed of by meeting the Chinese half way, in hope of garnering some good will in this fashion. Perhaps out of dissatisfaction with British or Japanese maneuvers at the tariff conference of 1925, Lamont recommended independent American action if cooperation proved an impediment to accommodation with the Chinese. Johnson reported that Lamont favored treating the Chinese with the "utmost liberality."[1]

But Lamont had other interests that took precedence over his approval of China's national aspirations. In March 1927, he reported and received approval of the purchase by J. P. Morgan and other banks of approximately $20 million in Tokyo Municipal bonds, to be offered for public subscription. In September, Lamont was off for Tokyo at the invitation of the Japanese

1. J. P. Morgan and Company to Secretary of State, November 4, 1926, enclosure, SD 893.00/7808; Memorandum of Conversation between Lamont and Johnson, January 12, 1927, SD 711.93/113.

government: a morning with the Emperor, lunch with the premier, engagement after engagement with Japan's top industrialists and government officials. Enroute he stopped in St. Paul to chat with Secretary of State Frank Kellogg and to be briefed on the condition of Japanese-American relations. Kellogg reported that the Japanese had been wonderfully cooperative in China and at the Geneva Naval Disarmament Conference—more so than the British. A few days later Lamont notified Ogden Mills, Undersecretary of the Treasury, of the reasons for his trip, but was surprisingly vague. Perhaps the Japanese wanted outside advice on financial problems, or to bring Morgan and Company up to date. But in a few days the purpose of Lamont's invitation was clear. On October 4, Lamont cabled Morgan that his friend Inoue had asked on behalf of the Japanese government that Morgan issue $30 million worth of South Manchuria Railway bonds.[2]

The SMR had first tried to borrow money from American bankers in 1923. The Department of State, recognizing the SMR as the principal instrument of Japanese expansion in Manchuria, opposed the transaction successfully. The SMR was forced to obtain funds from the Japanese government—funds available in part as a consequence of an American loan, for other purposes, to the Oriental Development Company, another instrument of the Japanese government. Early in 1927 the SMR, backed by a guarantee of the Japanese government, attempted once more to raise money in the United States. At a cabinet meeting in March, President Coolidge expressed a willingness to countenance any loans sought by the Japanese government in its own name. He feared, however, that approval of a loan to the SMR would imply American acceptance of Japan's claim to a special position in Manchuria. There the matter rested until Lamont, who had already conceded to Japan a special position in Manchuria, travelled to Tokyo.[3]

Morgan responded favorably to Lamont's cable, explained how the SMR bonds would be handled, and added in passing: "We must in due

2. J. P. Morgan and Company to Secretary of State, March 19, 1927, SD 894.51T572/–; *New York Times,* September 17, 1927, p. 24; Memorandum of conversation between Lamont and Kellogg, September 19, 1927, 189–8, TWL ms; Lamont to Mills, September 24, 1927, 189–9, to J. P. Morgan and Company, October 4, 1927, 189–28, TWL ms.

3. Herbert Feis, *Diplomacy of the Dollar, 1919–1932* (New York, 1966), 35–36; Cho Yukio refers to an effort in 1922 involving Lamont, blocked by the Japanese government. See his "An Inquiry into the Problems of Importing American Capital into Manchuria," in Borg and Okamoto, *Pearl Harbor as History,* 383; Memorandum by Arthur N. Young, March 19, 1927, Johnson to Young, March 21, 1927, and Leland Harrison to Young, March 25, 1927, SD 893.51/5027.

course, consult United States Government." Lamont and Morgan knew the American government was opposed to direct loans to the SMR, but Lamont advised Morgan that Kellogg had assured him of the Department of State's approval of any loan requests that came up while he was in Tokyo. Convinced of the profitability of the proposed business and of the value of positive economic cooperation with Japan, Lamont was determined to see the American government reverse its policy.[4]

When the Department of State began to receive rumors of Lamont's activities, the Office of the Economic Advisor reminded Nelson Johnson and Kellogg of the Department's previous opposition to loans to the SMR. Kellogg declared that if the matter came up, the Department would continue its opposition. But Lamont, upon returning to the United States, pressed the Department, trying to present it with a fait accompli. He informed Undersecretary Robert Olds that it had never occurred to him, when negotiating with the Japanese, to mention the possible intervention of the Department of State—certainly not after his conversation with Kellogg in St. Paul. The SMR, he insisted, was a "superb property" and Manchuria the only stable area in all China. He argued that the Japanese were a stabilizing force in Chinese affairs and that their development of Manchuria was an advantage to the Chinese. He explained that the Japanese had abandoned the use of force on the Asian mainland, were trying to get along with the Chinese, "and the cardinal feature of their policy is friendship and cooperation with America." Lamont contended that the Japanese government needed American help and that the opportunity existed to provide such help on a basis favorable for American investors. Concluding his argument, he suggested that a strong Chinese government would not object to an American loan to the SMR because the Japanese "have developed the country in an economic way to extraordinary advantage for the Chinese themselves." Lamont left these thoughts with Olds, promising to call in a few days to ascertain the Department's view.[5]

The earlier decision made by Hughes and MacMurray to oppose loans to the SMR was based on the presumption that the expansion of Japanese

4. Morgan to Lamont, October 5, 1927, and Lamont to Morgan, October 6, 1927, 189–28, TWL ms.

5. Young to Johnson, October 5, 1927, SD 893.51/5050; Young to Johnson and Kellogg, Johnson to Young, November 1, 1927, SD 894.51/So8/–; Lamont to Olds, November 11, 1927, 189–30, TWL ms.

economic interests in Manchuria was disadvantageous to the development of American interests there. In 1927, a new concern emerged. Mayer, at the American Legation in Peking, cabled warnings that both Chang Tso-lin and the Kuomintang had been alerted to Lamont's negotiations in Tokyo. They had indicated that an American loan to the SMR would be considered a departure from the traditionally friendly policies of the United States. Kellogg feared the Chinese would likely infer that the United States was supporting Japanese policy in Manchuria. Given the care with which the Coolidge administration was treating the new China, Kellogg doubted the advisability of a change in American policy. But Lamont's maneuver troubled him. How would the Japanese respond if the Department refused to permit the loan? Lamont had succeeded in trapping the American government. It was forced to choose between alienating the Chinese or Japanese governments. Japanese power and the strong economic ties between the United States and Japan seemed to dictate a decision in Lamont's favor: a decision for continued cooperation with Lamont's banking friends who appeared to have wrested control of their nation away from the Japanese military. But first Kellogg wanted more data.[6]

From Tokyo, Ambassador Charles MacVeagh warned that refusal to sanction the loan would be viewed by the Japanese as American distrust of their intentions in Manchuria, as lack of faith in Japan's repeated pledges to respect Chinese sovereignty. If disappointed the Japanese might have to turn to the Soviet Union for financial assistance! MacVeagh wanted the loan to be allowed as a means of convincing the Japanese of the American desire to help them. He argued against reliance on precedent or concern over Chinese attitudes, insisting that the excellent relations that had existed between the United States and Japan since the Washington Conference required a new official attitude toward loans to the SMR.[7]

More surprising was support for the loan from Mayer in Peking. He argued first that on ethical grounds the United States could not oppose Japanese plans in Manchuria "in view of measures we have taken in our correspondingly vital zone—the Caribbean." Pragmatically he contended that there was no alternative to creditor control for serving American interests or protecting Chinese interests in Manchuria. Mayer concluded: "All consider-

6. Mayer to Secretary of State, November 19, 1927, SD 894.51/So8/1 and 893.51/5027; Kellogg to American Ambassador, Tokyo, November 19, 1927, SD 894.51/So8/1a.

7. MacVeagh to Kellogg, November 21, 1927, SD 894.51/So8/2.

ations therefore appear to point to the expediency of some form of indirect financial participation with Japan in Manchuria should she wish it and should our financial interests be so inclined."[8]

High level support for the loan also emerged in the Department, centering around Undersecretary Olds—formerly Kellogg's law partner. Olds had initially suggested to Lamont that the Japanese government itself borrow the money and use it for the SMR. Certainly this approach was implicit in the cabinet's earlier endorsement of loans to the Japanese government when it sustained the policy of opposing loans to the SMR. But the Japanese government wanted more than money. As the Kuomintang pressed northward toward Manchuria, the Japanese government wanted to link the United States to the SMR when the inevitable conflict with the Chinese came. To Olds, Lamont's office replied that the Japanese government insisted, "we think wisely," that each government enterprise stand on its own and finance itself as far as possible. Olds was apparently satisfied and a few days later rejected the idea of trying to get the Japanese government to ask for a direct loan. He argued that previous reasons for objecting to loans no longer applied. The Japanese had not been discriminating against American interests and Manchuria was not a competitive field for the investment of American capital. Olds conceded the fact that the SMR was central to Japanese exploitation of Manchuria but contended that the United States could not avoid taking sides in the Sino-Japanese controversy over control of the region. And if the United States had to choose sides, Olds considered it "far less serious to refrain from objection than deliberately to interpose it and defeat the transaction." It would be best to treat the matter as routine and allow Lamont to underwrite the loan to the SMR.[9]

Lamont's soundings, especially his talks with Olds, left him optimistic, but he continued to orchestrate his moves carefully to ensure success. Reporting his activities to Inoue, head of the Bank of Japan, he asked to be sent a cable to the effect that "Japanese Government has asked you to give assurances that there will be no discrimination against Americans or interference." Once he received such a cable he believed the State Department would approve the loan. A few days later Inoue sent the desired message, which Lamont dutifully passed on to the Department—without indicating he

8. Mayer to Secretary of State, November 22, 1927, SD 894.51/So8/4.

9. Arthur Anderson to Olds, November 19, 1927, SD 894.51/So8/49; Memorandum by Olds, November 21, 1927, SD 894.51/So8/50.

had solicited it. At the same time, Lamont had a member of his staff prepare a memorandum on the history of the SMR and of Japanese rights in Manchuria. The document was so utterly sympathetic to the Japanese position as to omit any indication that Manchuria was Chinese territory, control of which had been seized under duress, or even that the Chinese might have a vital interest in regaining control. Copies of the report were sent to Olds and to key opinion leaders like Walter Lippmann, Herbert Croly, and James MacDonald of the Foreign Policy Association.[10]

On November 22, 1927, the Chinese Minister, Alfred Sao-ke Sze, advised Nelson Johnson that he was under instructions to enquire about reports that Lamont had met with Kellogg to discuss the SMR loan. He warned Johnson of concern in China over Japanese policy in Manchuria as evidenced by the activities of the SMR. Johnson informed Sze that the Department had not reached a decision, but also contended that the railway had a right to borrow money wherever it could. Despite his personal sympathies for China's national aspirations, Johnson had put the Chinese on notice of a pending shift in American policy.[11]

In the next few weeks Chinese protests, from both the Peking and Koumintang regimes, mounted. Stories hostile to the SMR loan appeared in the American press, and American officials in China warned against approval of the loan. To Frank Lee, representing the Kuomintang regime, Johnson insisted that the loan "could not possibly be interpreted as indicating that the policy of the United States in China had been in any respect altered." Lee replied that the Chinese "most positively" would regard a loan to the SMR as American support for Japanese policy in Manchuria. He warned that the issue would be exploited by factions favoring closer relations with the Soviet Union and hoped that American bankers would save their money to help China with development projects.[12]

In Peking Mayer shifted to opposition to the loan when he learned it was to be made directly to the SMR. He warned that the reaction in China would be serious and might include a boycott of American goods and an anti-American campaign. Reflecting both his and MacMurray's distaste for

10. Lamont to Inoue, November 23, 1927, 189–30, TWL ms; Inoue to Lamont (copy), November 29, 1927, SD 894.51/So8/51.

11. Memorandum of conversation between Sze and Johnson, November 22, 1927, SD 894.51/So8/6.

12. Memorandum of conversation between Lee and Johnson, November 30, 1927, SD 894.51/So8/27.

what they considered Washington's weakness in face of Chinese pressures, Mayer did add that courting Chinese good will had done little for American interests. He implied strongly that the SMR loan, if combined with a "resolute independent policy of self-interest," with determination to brook no disregard of our rights, might be preferable. But if Kellogg and Johnson were not returning to gunboat diplomacy in China and if the United States continued in its determination to appease the Kuomintang, Mayer would not advise going ahead with the loan. Admiral Mark Bristol, Commander in Chief of the Asiatic Fleet, was infinitely more supportive of administration policy and he warned Kellogg that a loan to the SMR would jeopardize the success of that policy. It would make the protection of American interests more difficult and create a situation in China that would offset any good will gained in Japan.[13]

Faced with pressures against the loan the primary concern of the Department seemed to be self-protection. Publicly Kellogg insisted that the whole affair was a private matter between the SMR and the bankers, of little concern to the government. To the Legation he noted that Lamont had not submitted a concrete proposal to the Department. In a meeting with the Japanese Ambassador, Matsudaira Tsuneo, on December 1, Kellogg and Johnson took the same position. No proposal had been received from Lamont and the Department viewed the question "as being purely financial and in no way connected with matters of policy in the Far East." American policy, Johnson instructed the Ambassador, "was made in Washington and not dictated by bankers or shippers of steel." Having claimed the right to pass on foreign loans, the Department now sought desperately to escape from the dilemma of choosing between the Chinese and the Japanese.[14]

Lamont had little choice but to respond to the Department's needs by withholding temporarily a formal request for approval of the loan. On the day Matsudaira met with Kellogg and Johnson, Lamont informed Inoue that a high official of the Department had advised him of the nature of the protests it was receiving. The Department still did not object to the loan, but

13. Mayer to Secretary of State, November 25, 1927, SD 894.51/So8/8; Bristol via Mayer to Kellogg, December 3, 1927, SD 894.51/So8/16.

14. Kellogg to Legation, Peking, December 3, 1927, SD 894.51/So8/18a; Memorandum of conversation between Matsudaira, Kellogg, and Johnson, December 1, 1927, SD 894.51/So8/17.

was uneasy and Lamont thought it best to be tactful, to allow the storm to clear. To Matsudaira he explained less candidly that the Department had no objection to the loan, but an unfavorable press gave him "a poor market for the operation itself." Ambassador MacVeagh learned of Lamont's decision through the Japanese and reported evidence that important Japanese leaders were disturbed by the Department yielding to Chinese pressures. Kellogg explained that the bankers and not the Department had made the decision and the bankers rather than the Department would provide information. For MacVeagh's purposes, Kellogg reported that the bankers had advised him informally that unfavorable publicity had affected the market adversely "and that in view of this and the doubtful wisdom of underwriting a financial transaction which is so evidently involved in Far Eastern politics, the bankers have decided to defer any consideration of the loan at this time."[15]

The Department and Lamont continued to receive protests against the proposed loan from private groups and individuals friendly to China or hostile to Japanese imperialism—generally involving people prominent in the peace movement and a variety of other progressive causes but including Standard Oil of New York. Lamont decided, therefore, to intensify his campaign to educate the American public to the virtues of the new Japan. In December, while presiding over a dinner held by the American Council of the Institute of Pacific Relations, he assured his audience that Japan had no imperialistic designs upon China. To Julia Ellsworth Ford, a socially prominent activist who had organized an open protest letter to Lamont and had written several letters to his wife, he insisted that he was "as fond of the Chinese as you are." But, he contended, they had shown no capacity for organized government and were fussing over the SMR loan to attract sympathy for themselves. He assured her that the Tanaka regime in Japan was talking of a positive policy in China for domestic purposes only. Tanaka, like Shidehara, favored conciliation of China. "Our Chinese friends" were the obstacle to improved Sino-Japanese relations. If they "would stop yelling and sit down and discuss business, they could clear up any outstanding railway problems in Manchuria without much difficulty." In January, before

15. Lamont to Inoue, January 9, 1928, repeating Lamont to Inoue, December 1, 1927, 189–33, and Lamont to Matsudaira, December 9, 1927, 189–32, TWL ms; MacVeagh to Secretary of State, December 9, 1927, and Kellogg to MacVeagh, December 10, 1927, SD 894.51/So8/20.

the Japan Society, he spoke of the growing liberalism of Japan and of Japan's need for American capital.[16]

Again and again Lamont stressed the changes in Japan's policy toward China since 1920. The sword had been put aside and all Japanese statesmen favored conciliation. Japanese leaders realized the importance of Chinese markets and were aware that the use of force against the Chinese would hurt sales. They also realized that force no longer had a place in the world. He insisted that no one surpassed him in sympathy for Chinese national aspirations, but China was a mess and there were no signs that the Chinese had developed a capacity for satisfactory political or economic organization. The thrust of Lamont's campaign was clear: Japan was not a threat. Japan rather than China should be the recipient of American development capital. He was preparing the market for the SMR loan and he received editorial support from the *New York Times*.[17]

Early in January, Ambassador MacVeagh reported that Inoue understood, from his communications with Lamont, that as soon as the loan question was dropped by the press in the United States, Morgan would issue the loan overnight without publicity. A few days later Lamont wrote to Inoue to explain his recent cables and to recommend a new strategy. He admitted that the storm of protests against the loan had exceeded expectation and was not dying out as rapidly as he anticipated. Rather than simply try again, Lamont proposed waiting a little longer, then starting with a loan to the SMR for refunding purposes only. Lamont could then announce this was merely a loan to enable to SMR to meet its upcoming obligations rather than one that would enable the railway to expand its operations. He advised Inoue to curb SMR officials who were making provocative statements about Manchuria being separate from China, and to have all publicity about the SMR stress its cooperation with Chinese authorities. Further reports about Chinese immigration into Manchuria, "their contentment and prosperity and their desire to have the Japanese continue economic development," Lamont thought

16. See for example Henry F. Ward, American Committee for Justice to China, to Kellogg, December 15, 1927, SD 894.51/So8/28, and Dorothy Detzer, Women's International League for Peace and Freedom, to Lamont, January 24, 1928, 189–33, TWL ms; Lamont remarks at dinner of Institute of Pacific Relations, December 13, 1927, 186–26, Lamont to Ford, January 4, 1928, 189–33, Lamont remarks at dinner of Japan Society, January 5, 1928, 150–7, TWL ms.

17. *New York Times,* January 4, 1928, p. 7, and editorials October 20 and December 29, 1927. See also Lamont to Inoue, June 1, 1928, explaining his success with *Times* editorial board, 186–28, TWL ms.

"would coincide with the facts and would be helpful." For the long run, Lamont suggested that the Japanese government create a holding company, including in its assets the Japanese government's investment in the SMR. He explained the technical convenience of the plan and enclosed a memorandum on how to implement it. Lamont was most explicit in his reasoning. This form of borrowing would not only be convenient, but "what we have in mind is to avoid in this market the name of the South Manchuria Railway." Reference to the SMR would raise violent opposition for years to come and there was no reason for provoking it and "incidentally causing the Department of State embarrassment."[18]

A few days later he explained to Sir Kengo Mori, Financial Commissioner of the Japanese Government, that Chinese protests had not been taken seriously, but he could not ignore criticism from within the United States. He mentioned that not only church groups and peace societies and "liberal clubs," but also American business interests, fearing a Chinese boycott, had protested. Even these protests might not have stopped him, he implied, had the State Department not crumbled before the onslaught. Clearly, Lamont wanted the SMR business—and wanted it badly enough to plot stratagems to enable the Japanese government to outmaneuver those elements in American society and in the American government who did not want to support Japanese expansion in Manchuria.[19]

Winter passed, spring came—and in April, Lamont returned to the Department of State with a proposition for a $20 million loan to the SMR. He explained that this loan was solely for the purpose of refunding two domestic Japanese loans and that it did not involve any extensions or new constructions in Manchuria. Kellogg cabled MacMurray in Peking, advised him that the Department could not object to what appeared to be a normal refunding operation, and asked for his views. MacMurray warned that the new guise of the loan would not prevent a loud Chinese outcry, but doubted whether the clamor would have any lasting effect. He thought the loan should be approved. The scenario was proceeding just as Lamont predicted, but he had not reckoned with the Japanese army.[20]

18. MacVeagh to Secretary of State, January 4, 1928, SD 894.51/So8/44; Lamont to Inoue, January 9, 1928, 189–33.

19. Lamont to Kengo Mori, January 14, 1928, 188–29, TWL ms.

20. Memorandum of Lamont meeting with Olds, April 18, 1928, SD 894.51/So8/60; Kellogg to MacMurray, April 19, 1928, SD 894.51/So8/58a; MacMurray to Secretary of State, April 24, 1928, SD 894.51/So8/59.

As Lamont paused during the winter of 1927–28, waiting for the American public to forget about the SMR loan, Chiang Kai-shek returned to Nanking and control over the armies of the Kuomintang. Old wounds were healed with the Kwangsi clique, bringing the able Pai Ch'ung-hsi and Li Tsung-jen back to his side. Two of the most powerful northern warlords, Yen Hsi-shan and Feng Yü-hsiang, joined the fold. As Lamont concluded that the moment was opportune to submit his prettified SMR proposal, Chiang's forces were marching north once again to depose the Peking regime and to unify China under the Kuomintang.

Chiang and Tanaka were both anxious to avoid a clash between Chinese and Japanese forces. But on April 18, the very day Lamont chose to see Undersecretary Olds about the SMR loan, Tanaka ordered an expedition of 5,000 Japanese soldiers to Shantung for the express purpose of defending Japanese nationals there. Despite efforts by the Kuomintang to avoid provoking Japanese forces and Tanaka's continued hopes for good relations with Chiang, fighting broke out between Chinese and Japanese forces at Tsinan on May 3—the result of unauthorized action by the Japanese general on the spot. A few days later the Japanese attacked in force and drove the Chinese from the city. Not only were hopes for a Sino-Japanese rapprochement shattered, but the events indicated that Thomas Lamont was something less than a prophet. In a few days of fighting the Japanese military blotted out Lamont's assurances that the sword had been sheathed forever; that the Japanese would not again use force in China. He had picked a singularly inopportune moment to attempt to float a loan for the SMR. When Chiang cabled President Coolidge to ask his attitude toward the Japanese attack, the American government was noncommittal—but it could not authorize a loan to the SMR. Anxious as he was for the business, even Thomas Lamont was forced to surrender for the moment.

The Tsinan incident did not stop Lamont's efforts to win public support for a more sympathetic view of Japan and Japan's needs. In August, however, the Far Eastern Division of the Department of State prepared a systematic study of the SMR's operations and of Lamont's activities and decided firmly against *any* direct loan to the SMR. The study concluded that Lamont and friends should be dissuaded from presenting the proposal to the Department formally. If they persisted, the Department should decline to apply the "no objection" formula. In addition to a clearly stated disinclination to be associated with a railway operation that performed "practically all the functions of a colonial administration," the document revealed considerable irritation with Lamont's tactics: "The circumstances under which the project has been developed, the manner in which it is urged, and the refusal of its sponsors to give any heed to the suggestion that it may cause the American Government immediate and/or future embarrassment give ground for suspicion."[21]

From the field, American diplomats in Manchuria discounted the significance of SMR appeals for foreign investment, contending that only the SMR would benefit, that it was merely an attempt to tie the United States to Japanese policy in Manchuria while expanding the railway's operations. It was just another variation on the theme of "foreign money and Japanese brains." The Japanese desire to link the United States to the SMR was frustrated, but the need of the Japanese government for foreign capital to expand its empire was not. In September 1928, the Oriental Development Company floated another loan in the United States. Of perhaps greater significance—and certainly of greater satisfaction to Thomas Lamont—was a $50 million loan to the Japanese government underwritten in May 1930 by a group of American bankers headed by J. P. Morgan and Company, fiscal agents for the Government of Japan.[22]

Lamont wanted approval of the SMR loan primarily and obviously because it promised profits for his company. But Lamont was also convinced by his contacts with Japanese statesmen and businessmen that the new Japan run by his liberal capitalist counterparts had foresaken militarism and was operating by the rules of a postimperialist world order: that the Japanese would not use force in China; that Japanese and Americans could and should cooperate in the economic development of China and Japan; and that a Japanese-American partnership was in the best interests of China, Japan, and the United States. Until the Tsinan incident, his case seemed convincing, even to the top echelons of the Department of State. Certainly Olds was convinced and Kellogg appeared ready to reverse the Department's policy in November 1927. Only strident public opposition in the United States stopped the loan from being approved at that time. One question remains: how did the press find out? How did word of the loan leak out to the interested public?

There seems to be little doubt that the Chinese themselves stirred up

21. Memorandum by Joseph Ballantine for FE Division, August 31, 1928, SD 893.77/2640½.

22. American Consul, Dairen, to Secretary of State, September 29, 1928, SD 894.51/So8/62, and Consul General, Mukden, to Secretary of State, October 12, 1928, SD 894.51/So8/64; Feis, *Diplomacy of the Dollar*, 38.

some of the opposition by alerting friends of China to rumors of the transaction. But Lamont's explanations refer to two other sources. Writing to Inoue, he suggested that outspoken remarks by the director of the SMR had led to adverse publicity. In December 1928, defending his position in a letter to Oswald Garrison Villard, Lamont claimed that he and the Department and the Japanese had decided to drop the project as inopportune and then—*afterward*—some minor functionary in the Department of State leaked the story of the loan proposal to the press. Although the letter to Villard was filled with statements of questionable accuracy, Lamont's reference to a leak does suggest the possibility that the loan was prevented by one bureaucrat unwilling to accept the consensus being built within the Department toward approval of the loan. The episode suggests that the American failure to support the Japanese program in Manchuria was not based on a rational calculation of American interests or on opposition by the American government to Japanese operations. It was rather a *political* response to domestic opposition reflecting vestigial mistrust of Japan and perhaps stimulated initially as a result of bureaucratic politics within the Department of State.[23]

In the aftermath of the Tsinan incident, Japanese army officers arranged for the assassination of Chang Tso-lin. With Chang's death, the Peking regime ceased to exist and the Kuomintang was clearly the defacto ruler of China. Whatever that party's failings, the field was all but uncontested and the American government hastened to come to terms with it. Kellogg instructed a reluctant MacMurray to negotiate a new tariff treaty granting tariff autonomy to China and providing for a mutual guarantee of most-favored-nation treatment. On October 10, 1928, "Double Ten," Chiang Kai-shek proclaimed the existence of the National Government of China, under the "tutelage" of the Kuomintang.

One important step prerequisite to an American rapprochement with Kuomintang China had been settlement of the Nanking incident of 1927. After Chiang resumed power early in 1928, symbolizing a temporary resolution of factional disputes within the Kuomintang, progress toward a settlement proved possible. When MacMurray travelled to Shanghai in February, Huang Fu, Minister for Foreign Affairs, invited him to Nanking to negoti-

23. Lamont to Inoue, January 9, 1928, 189–33, to Villard, December 10, 1928, 186–30, TWL ms. Arthur N. Young, who left the State Department to work for the Chinese government in 1929, was the most likely source of a leak.

ate. Advised by Sokolsky not to go to Nanking, MacMurray declined and succeeded in having the Chinese agree to preliminary negotiations at Shanghai. Sokolsky shared his insights into Kuomintang politics, telling MacMurray whom to see and whom not to see, warning against continued antiforeignism, and predicting inaccurately the ascendency of his friend T. V. Soong over Chiang Kai-shek. Sokolsky was afraid that Chiang would swing too far to the right, driving most of the Kuomintang back into the arms of the Communists. Sokolsky's analysis was based on assumptions that the Kuomintang center was in control, with the Right out of the country and the Left discredited. Nonetheless he worried about the military and about the ability of a man like Soong to contain Chiang—and he worried about the continued strength of the Communists. His estimates, as they appeared in a three part series in the *North China Daily News,* were forwarded to Peking and to Washington with the endorsement of the American consul-general in Shanghai.[24]

In March, MacMurray and the Chinese settled the Nanking issue, with MacMurray receiving congratulations from Roger Greene, among many others. As Greene wrote to Nelson Johnson, he was delighted to be able to commend MacMurray after their sharp differences in 1926. MacMurray in turn sent his thanks to Sokolsky: "I realize it was not easy for you to play the game fairly with all concerned while I was in Shanghai. But, to the best of my knowledge and belief, you did it. You were at any rate of great assistance to me, and I want you to realize that I appreciate and am most grateful for it." To MacMurray, Sokolsky had demonstrated his value as a broker between the Kuomintang leaders he served and the American government to which he presumably pledged his allegiance. For the remainder of MacMurray's tenure in Peking, Sokolsky was privileged to report to him directly.[25]

In the spring of 1928, Sokolsky forwarded a remarkably prescient analysis of China's future by a recently released Soviet military advisor. The Russian predicted that the Kuomintang would fail to serve the people and that its reactionary tendencies would drive even elements that were not radical into the arms of the Communists. He considered a Communist revolution inevitable—to originate with the Chinese peasants. In an aside, Sokolsky

24. Memorandum of meeting with Sokolsky, February 25, 1928, MacMurray Papers; Consul General, Shanghai, to Secretary of State, February 29, 1928, enclosure, SD 893.00/9866.

25. Greene to MacMurray, April 4, 1928, MacMurray Papers; Greene to Johnson, May 17, 1928, RSG ms; MacMurray to Sokolsky, April 9, 1928, MacMurray Papers.

noted that he was sheltering Quo Tai-chi, sometime Minister of Foreign Affairs, whose arrest had been ordered. A few days later he warned MacMurray about the Sino-Japanese troubles at Tsinan and of troubles between Chiang and Feng Yü-hsiang. MacMurray immediately cabled the report to the secretary of state. In June, Sokolsky wrote disparagingly of the Nanking government, insisting that the unification of China under Chiang Kai-shek was at best nominal. He also claimed credit for driving Huang Fu out of public life by insisting that the Nanking settlement was a great diplomatic victory for MacMurray—an argument not likely to alienate MacMurray. MacMurray liked Sokolsky's analysis and jumped on a chance remark about C. T. Wang to try to get more information. Sokolsky obliged by inviting Wang, then Foreign Minister, and other dignitaries, both Chinese and American, to his home for dinner and reporting Wang's remarks back to MacMurray.[26]

At the same time that Sokolsky was placing the benefits of his contacts with Kuomintang leaders at the service of the American government, he used his pen for other purposes. In an unsigned analysis of the Tsinan incident published in the *Far Eastern Review,* he defended Japanese actions. He blamed the troubles on the failure of Nationalist authorities to protect the lives and property of foreigners in the cities they marched through. His articles in the *North China Daily News* were used to criticize Chiang and his coterie while "puffing" T. V. Soong. All of Sokolsky's activities can be reconciled, not simply as self-serving, but as adhering to a specific pattern. Sokolsky was using the American Minister, as he used his writings, to discredit Chinese leaders with whom he lacked *kuan-hsi*—a special personal and beneficial relationship—while enhancing the career of T. V. Soong. Soong, of all the Chinese with whom Sokolsky had been allied, came closest to his ideal of the western merchant prince—and he worked hard to make Soong appear not only indispensable to the Chinese, but an ascending star to all concerned. Even Sokolsky's criticism of Chinese handling of relations with Japan could be fit into this pattern as Soong emerged as the man who would negotiate a settlement with the Japanese—and Sokolsky emerged as the middleman between Soong and the Japanese Foreign Minister.[27]

26. MacMurray to Secretary of State, forwarding Sokolsky to MacMurray, April 23, 1928, SD 893.00/9897, and April 30, 1928, SD 893.00/9905; Sokolsky to MacMurray, June 15, 1928, and MacMurray to Sokolsky, July 9, 1928, MacMurray Papers; Consul General, Shanghai, to Secretary of State, enclosing memorandum by Sokolsky, SD 893.48/202.

27. "Tsinan," *Far Eastern Review,* May 1928, *North China Daily News,* May 29 and July 7, 1928, GES ms.

Although Greene was in many ways the antithesis of all Sokolsky stood for, especially the meddling in Chinese politics, he too was impressed most favorably by T. V. Soong. Greene found that he had readier access to the leadership of Kuomintang China than he had to the leaders of the old regime. Several key figures were old Harvard friends, and Kung and Soong were friendly. In June 1928 he was more optimistic than Sokolsky about the future of China, noting that "all of these returned students now have much more political and business experience than they had at the time of the revolution [1911]." Never had China had so able a finance ministry as it now had under Soong. And Greene, too, could serve as a go-between, bringing Kung and MacMurray together when the Chinese official felt he had been slighted by the American Minister.[28]

On July 25th, MacMurray and Soong signed the treaty which, in effect, granted the Chinese tariff autonomy and constituted the first major breach of the treaty system. Greene was delighted, congratulated MacMurray, and notified Nelson Johnson of the pleasure expressed by his Chinese friends. But Greene was puzzled by reports that the United States was considering "recognizing" the Nationalist government. Why was that necessary? What more formal act of recognition could there be than the signing of a treaty between two governments? This, ultimately, was the position taken by Secretary of State Kellogg and the Chinese government, with no indication that Greene's view provided anything more than reassurance.[29]

Immediately after MacMurray and Soong signed the tariff treaty, C. T. Wang tried to both upstage Soong and further undermine the treaty system. Without noting the signing of the treaty or the fact that Kellogg's offer to negotiate was limited to the tariff question, Wang informed MacMurray that he was sending a representative to negotiate with him, presumably on matters like extraterritoriality. MacMurray finessed this move by advising Wang that "since the time at which it may be presumed your note was written" the tariff treaty had been signed and that this act concluded the negotiations Kellogg had in mind. Kellogg reprimanded MacMurray for responding without first consulting Washington, but Sokolsky was gleeful. MacMurray had outfoxed Wang and Soong alone bore the laurels.[30]

28. Greene to Richard Pearce, June 22, 1928, RSG ms; Greene to MacMurray, July 25 and MacMurray to Greene, July 26, 1928, MacMurray Papers.

29. Greene to MacMurray, undated, MacMurray Papers; Greene to Johnson, August 4, 1928, RSG ms.

30. Borg, *American Policy and the Chinese Revolution,* 402–3; Sokolsky to MacMurray, August 15, 1928, MacMurray Papers.

Sokolsky also continued his critical analysis of Chiang and the Nanking regime, claiming that conditions in China were the worst he had experienced in his ten years in the country—a degree of pessimism that even MacMurray could not endorse. Contemptuously, he wrote of Chiang "using all his highly developed Ningpo mentality to keep control," managing "thus far to prevent anyone from sending him to Fenghua to raise peaches." Predicting that Feng Yü-hsiang would likely come out on top, Sokolsky ridiculed Chiang's plans to use generals to administer the government.[31]

By October Greene's estimate of Chiang and the Nanking regime was surprisingly close to that of Sokolsky. With Nelson Johnson he agreed that the irresolution of the Chinese government was incomprehensible. He concluded that Chiang would be a disappointment as an administrator. Perhaps his ability had been overestimated at the time of the Northern Expedition—"probably more credit was due to his Russian advisors than we supposed." But Greene did not retreat from his insistence that further steps be taken toward placing relations with China upon a basis of equality. He wanted foreign troops and ships removed from China—an end to interference in Chinese affairs to protect foreign interests. He also wanted greater civility in Sino-American relations: diplomatic representation at Nanking rather than correspondence between the Legation at Peking and the Chinese government untold miles away. *And* he wanted American diplomats who could be courteous, imaginative, and positive, perhaps like Admiral Bristol as opposed to Cunningham and MacMurray.[32]

As Americans grew impatient, Chiang's government began the incredible task of attempting to unify and to modernize China. The treasury was empty and the regime lacked adequate sources of income. With the exception of the United States, the powers still controlled the tariff, limiting that potential source of revenue, and countless obstacles blocked the collection of internal taxes. China's credit was nonexistent and neither past defaults nor the regime's revolutionary nationalism were likely to attract foreign capital. Chiang had little more to work with than his brother-in-law, T. V. Soong, but Soong had George Sokolsky.

If Soong was to play the role Sokolsky had cast for him, if he was to emerge as the leader of a new progressive China, he would have to find

31. Sokolsky to MacMurray, August 15, 1928, and MacMurray to Sokolsky, October 1, 1928, MacMurray Papers.

32. Greene to Johnson, September 26 and October 15, 1928, RSG ms.

money somewhere. And if Sokolsky was to be the key member of the court, the time had come to play fairy godfather, to lead Soong to the sources. One tack he tried was toward Thomas Lamont. In October 1928 he informed Lamont of his relationship to Soong and explained their efforts to settle China's debts. Lamont's reply could not have warmed any hearts in China. He warned that there was nothing that could be done until China reestablished its credit by paying off old defaults. Until then Chinese representatives in the United States would find individual American bankers sympathetic, but unwilling to issue any loans.[33]

Sokolsky's primary course was steered toward the Japanese. Returning from Tokyo a few days before writing to Lamont, he advised MacMurray that the Japanese wanted to ease tensions with the Chinese. They were ready to come to terms with the Chinese on all issues except those relating to Manchuria. He had talked with Japanese Prime Minister Tanaka and came away convinced that the Japanese would yield their tariff and extraterritorial privileges in China proper. After returning to China Sokolsky acted as liaison between Soong and the Japanese Consul General in Hankow, Yada Shichitaro, attempting to eliminate obstacles to agreement on tariff autonomy for China. The Japanese were determined to reach an agreement on debt consolidation, to obtain from the new Chinese government a commitment to pay unsecured loans, i.e. the Nishihara loans of 1917–18. According to the reports from Sokolsky to the American government, Soong was willing to set aside part of the income from the increased tariff to pay unsecured debts. He feared, however, that such an accommodation with the Japanese would be used by his enemies in China to undermine his position. Though Sokolsky despaired, railing occasionally at C. T. Wang or Chiang Kai-shek, Soong and Yada persevered and a formal agreement was reached early in 1929.[34]

A peripheral issue, the status of Manchuria, provided an opportunity for Sokolsky to show good faith with his Japanese contacts. In his reports to MacMurray, correspondence with Lamont, and *signed* articles in the *North China Daily News,* he stressed Japanese fears of Soviet pressures against Manchuria. Because of these fears the Japanese could not allow a weak

33. Sokolsky to Lamont, October 18, 1928, and Lamont to Sokolsky, January 24, 1929, 183–27, TWL ms.

34. Sokolsky to MacMurray, October 12, 1928, MacMurray Papers; MacMurray to Secretary of State, October 25, 1928, SD 893.51/5092; Sokolsky to MacMurray, November 6, 1928, MacMurray Papers; Iriye, *After Imperialism,* 246–48.

China to control Manchuria. There could be no discussion of a limitation of Japanese rights there. Japan might be even more liberal than the other powers in reaching an accommodation over affairs in China proper, but "for the retention of her treaty rights in Manchuria, Japan will fight." To MacMurray and Cunningham he reported Japanese interest in American capital in Manchuria, and the absence of any desire to monopolize economic opportunities there. In a letter to Lamont he enclosed an eleven-page memorandum calling for turning Manchuria into an autonomous region—a proposal that seemed to come from an agent of the SMR rather than from a confidant of T. V. Soong. Lamont, however, was skeptical. Let the Chinese and Japanese work out their differences over Manchuria. He knew the Japanese were ready to do so. Autonomy for Manchuria would have to wait a few years.[35]

In the last weeks of 1928 and early months of 1929, Sokolsky continued to write articles critical of the Kuomintang leadership. Generally, he accused the party of being undemocratic and devoid of ideas and talent. He claimed it had moved too far to the right since driving out the Communists. In an article published December 21, 1928, Sokolsky argued that only the Communists were working among the masses and that they alone had the foresight to shift their emphasis from intellectuals and laborers to the peasantry. The peasants were ready for a radical revolution. They were the weakest link, but the Kuomintang did nothing to strengthen that link, relying instead on censorship to block the spread of communism. In April, 1929, Sokolsky wrote a series of four articles analyzing the Kuomintang's Third Party Congress. He had been friendlier to C. T. Wang since Wang had approved his work in bringing about the tariff agreement with Japan, so Wang and Soong were praised for their leadership. Even Chiang was linked with Soong and Wang and praised for holding the government together. The main target of Sokolsky's criticism was Ch'en Kuo-fu and his family, whom he charged with controlling the party, blocking cooperation with Feng Yü-hsiang and Chinese capitalists, and blocking a stand for civil rights at the Congress. About two weeks later, Sokolsky found himself under a concerted attack in the press and threatened with deportation.[36]

35. *North China Daily News*, October 17, 1928, GES ms; Sokolsky to MacMurray, October 12, 1928, MacMurray Papers; Cunningham to Secretary of State, October 17, 1928, SD 793.94 Manchuria/43; Sokolsky to Lamont, enclosures, November 10, 1928, and Lamont to Sokolsky, January 24, 1929, 183–27, TWL ms.

36. *North China Daily News*, November 29 and 30, December 1 and 21, 1928, April 5, 8, 9, and 10, 1929, GES ms; Consul General, Shanghai, to Secretary of State, April 23, 1929, SD 893.711/37.

Suddenly, the good life of George Sokolsky, bon vivant, confidant of the mighty, broker of power, verged on collapse. The attack on the Ch'en brothers, who dominated the party apparatus, proved to be fatal to Sokolsky's aspirations. The Ch'en faction, the "C. C. clique," was highly conservative, considerably to the right of Soong and the middle-class democracy Sokolsky envisioned for China—and it was intensely nationalistic, brooking no interference from foreign dabblers in Chinese politics. In a letter to Cunningham, Sokolsky attributed the deportation efforts to Ch'en Li-fu. He reported that Ch'en objected to his influence with Soong and other ministers, considered him pro-Japanese and pro-British, blamed him for the result of the tariff negotiations with Japan, and accused him of trying to undermine the government with his articles in the *North China Daily News.* And, of course, Ch'en was not far from the mark.[37]

Other enemies quickly surfaced. Thomas F. Millard and John B. Powell, American journalists highly sympathetic to the Kuomintang government, not above presuming to advise the Chinese themselves, assailed Sokolsky in English language publications in China and in despatches published in newspapers like the *New York Times* and *New York Tribune.* Millard was critical of the editorial policy of the *North China Daily News* and of Sokolsky's work with the *Far Eastern Review,* which he described fairly as "a Japanese organ." He also associated Sokolsky with the American Chamber of Commerce and the resistance to Chinese efforts to regain complete sovereignty. Powell's *China Weekly Review* acknowledged Sokolsky's contribution during the May Fourth Movement, but explained that Chinese animosity toward him "is due largely to the fact that in recent years he has lent himself to various foreign propagandas which have had the effect of neutralizing his previous sympathetic attitude toward the Chinese." Perhaps to discredit Sokolsky with the Western community in China, one critic made snide reference to him as "our Jewish friend."[38]

Sokolsky was profoundly shaken by the attacks. In letters to Lamont and MacMurray he flailed out at Millard and Powell and revealed his paternalistic, even imperialistic attitudes toward the Chinese people. He wrote bitterly of Millard and Powell trying to "spoil my business, to make it im-

37. Sokolsky to Cunningham, April 22, 1929, SD 893.711/37.

38. Millard despatch to *New York Tribune,* dated April 19, 1929, GES ms; Consul General, Shanghai, to Secretary of State, April 29, 1929, enclosing "KMT Action Against Mr. Sokolsky and the North China Daily News," in *China Weekly Review,* April 27, 1929, and *China Critic,* April 25, 1929, SD 893.711/38.

possible for me to act as intermediary, to cut out my millions of commissions and squeeze"—to drive him home. He inferred that they were being subsidized by the Chinese government. Depressed, he complained that the Chinese always abandoned old friends and advisors. Would the Americans that came to help China after him learn "that China is different from all other states, that here memory is fleeting and gratitude like the breeze over the Whangpoo?" He had thought he might "play a small part in assisting China to find the sinews of reconstruction," but his hopes for himself and for China—perhaps indistinguishable—had been crushed. He could, however, still be generous in his moment of tribulation: "I cannot hate the Chinese for anything they do, for were they not, at times, childish, immature, hysterical—were they full-grown and well-organized, we should all be facing an imperialistic menace such as mankind has not yet known." For his childish, immature, and hysterical Chinese friends, he prescribed the colonialist remedy of firmness: "The Chinese must learn that they cannot always be coddled children."[39]

Sokolsky was not deported, partly because the Kuomintang decided not to focus on him but to attempt to arrange for the deportation of several foreign correspondents hostile to the regime. In addition, Soong was able to work behind the scenes in his behalf. The broadening of the attack to include other journalists became an attempt to silence critics rather than to remove an allegedly corrupt propagandist, and it diluted the case against Sokolsky. The affair eventually quieted down without an official request for Sokolsky's expulsion, but he remained depressed, cut off from important contacts for several months. Although he retained the confidence of American, British, and Japanese diplomats, his ability to work with Chinese leaders had been limited severely. Whatever else he might become, Sokolsky would not be another Borodin.[40]

A letter from Powell to MacMurray suggested what Sokolsky *had* become by 1929. Powell knew that Sokolsky, MacMurray, and Cunningham were friends, but decided to be blunt. First, denying Sokolsky's charge that the *China Weekly Review* was subsidized by the Nanking government, Powell noted Sokolsky's statements that he, Sokolsky, received a salary from

39. Sokolsky to MacMurray, April 25, 1929, MacMurray Papers; Sokolsky to Lamont, April 20, 1929, 183–29, TWL ms.

40. MacMurray to Secretary of State, April 30, 1929, SD 811.91293/146; MacMurray to Sokolsky, July 13, 1929, MacMurray Papers.

the American legation for writing confidential reports on Chinese affairs. He claimed that Sokolsky was receiving money from Chinese officials who feared him because of his influence with MacMurray and Cunningham—and offered to provide the names of the Chinese officials Sokolsky was in effect blackmailing. Reviewing Sokolsky's finances while in China, Powell alleged he had received retainers first from the Chinese, then from foreign interests like the British-American Tobacco Company and the Japanese Cotton Mill Owners Association. Kuomintang authorities had reported that the deportation effort "was due solely to Mr. Sokolsky's blackmailing activities with Chinese officialdom. In other words he was threatening certain officials with exposure in the *North China Daily News* or in confidential reports to the American officials unless the Chinese officials 'came across.' " Powell added that Sokolsky was showing the Chinese letters from prominent American diplomats to demonstrate his own great importance, implying that MacMurray's correspondence was being used thusly—which probably accounts for the fact that MacMurray did not answer Sokolsky's letters during the crisis, waiting until July to send a note of consolation.[41]

The truth of Powell's allegations *cannot* be demonstrated "without a shadow of a doubt." But Sokolsky unquestionably was involved in the activities of the businessmen and officials of at least three countries—and there is no reason to suspect him of *donating* his time and effort to these various and sometimes antithetical causes. MacMurray, who had earlier advised Stanley K. Hornbeck, Chief of the Bureau of Far Eastern Affairs, that Sokolsky was trustworthy and often very helpful, sent a copy of Powell's letter back to the Department of State.[42]

But Powell had been critical of MacMurray and critical of American policy prior to the accommodation with China. Sokolsky's friends in the American Legation appeared to be a little more cautious in their dealings with him, but continued to have a high regard for him. In October 1929, the American military attaché, Major John Magruder, reported that despite the campaign to intimidate Sokolsky, which he attributed to Chiang Kai-shek, Sokolsky remained beyond compare as an analyst of Chinese affairs. Reports from Sokolsky continued to reach Washington via the consul-general in Shanghai and the American minister in Peking. In June, 1930, the

41. Powell to MacMurray, May 17, 1929, MacMurray Papers.

42. See MacMurray to Hornbeck, November 15, 1928, Papers of Stanley K. Hornbeck, Hoover Institution.

British Ambassador to Japan informed London that Baron Shidehara, again Minister of Foreign Affairs, cited Sokolsky as his source of information for the internal affairs of China. Shidehara praised Sokolsky as one of the few men able to predict the outcome of military affairs in China and explained his close ties with Soong to the British. And Miles Lampson, the able and knowledgeable British minister to China, cited Sokolsky as his source when analyzing the communist movement in China for his superiors in the summer of 1930. Most of all, T. V. still needed him—and in June 1930, Sokolsky set off for New York, via Tokyo, to try to turn his relationship with Thomas Lamont into financial assistance for China.[43]

Lamont and the New York bankers were not interested in loans to China and had been most direct on this point from the inception of the Nationalist government. But the bankers were not above offering the Chinese a bit of gratuitous advice. In Feburary 1930, Lamont warned the Chinese not to demonetize silver and detailed the solution to Chinese financial difficulties: "First of all you must put your own house in order." Balance your budget and when you have a slight surplus income "you can then take up the matter of your credit abroad." After a favorable comment on Soong, he warned of the need to seek "the friendly counsel" of foreign debt holders—and of the importance of paying off old debts, including interest. Continued difficulty managing China's silver reserves led to Chinese consideration of a duty on silver, and prompted a cable to Soong and letter from Lamont opposing the step. By this time, however, Sokolsky was in New York—and Lamont proved surprisingly susceptible to his stroking. A very pleased Lamont reported to his partners that Sokolsky "tells me that as a matter of fact our cable advising against the proposed step arrived just in time to strengthen the Minister to the point of being able to defeat the project, and he is consequently very grateful." But Lamont did not respond to Sokolsky's expression of Soong's gratitude in a Chinese way. He continued to oppose loans to China and to argue in favor of closer ties to Japan.[44]

43. Major John Magruder, Military Attaché, to Assistant Chief of Staff, G-2, "Mr. Sokolsky and the Present Situation," October 26, 1929, RG 165, 265-I-388; see for example, MacMurray to Secretary of State, November 26, 1929, SD 893.50A/8, and Legation to Secretary of State, repeating Shanghai telegram, December 8, 1929, SD 893.00/10666; Tilly to A. Henderson, June 27, 1930, FO 405/266/24; Lampson to Henderson, August 3, 1930, FO 405/267/17; Sokolsky transcript (1956), Oral History, Columbia.

44. J. P. Morgan and Company to Acting Secretary of State, February 7, 1930, enclosing Lamont to Jun Ke Choy, SD 893.51/5226; Memorandum for R. C. Leffingwell and Partners from Lamont, July 11, 1930, 184–2, TWL ms.

While in the United States, Sokolsky spoke on Chinese affairs at the Williamstown Institute of Politics—an address favorable to the Nationalist government that received coverage in the New York papers. The *New York Herald Tribune* published an editorial discussing his talk with favorable references to his analysis. An opportunity to contribute to the *New York Times* arose, arranged by Lester Markel, a *Times* editor Sokolsky had known at Columbia. George Sokolsky was not quite ready to return to the land of his birth. He wanted to try once more to ride to glory with T. V. But the contacts necessary for a comfortable homecoming had been established.[45]

By November 1930, Sokolsky was back in operation in China, but there were snags. He claimed to have returned with a plan which would enable the Chinese to get all the money they wanted in the United States, but Soong seemed to be plagued with political enemies and kept him at a distance. The factional flow had changed enough for Sokolsky to be uneasy, no longer sure who was friend and who was foe. He told the American minister, now Nelson Johnson, that he was tired of the whole business and would go home if Soong did not make use of his plan. In February he reported that Soong was sending him back to the United States to explore another possibility for financial assistance, trying to extradite China from the difficulties caused by American silver purchases. He seemed buoyant, explaining to Johnson that he had been in line for appointment as Financial Advisor, but had been blocked by Madame Kung, the center of power in the Soong family. Now, however, he was back in her good graces and off to New York and Washington. But it was all over for George Sokolsky. Soong had other willing advisors, more reputable in the world of high finance, and in 1931, as in 1917, he embarked on a long journey only to discover at the other end that he had been cut off from his means of support.[46]

From talks with Hornbeck in Washington, May 1, 1931, it appeared that Sokolsky's plan involved a debt consolidation and currency reform loan to be granted by the Consortium banks. Apparently he had benefited from a

45. *New York Times,* August 3, p. 2 and August 26, 1930, p. 11; *New York Herald Tribune* editorial, August 27, 1930, GES ms; "China's Warrior President Outwits His Foes By Speed," *New York Times,* June 28, 1930, IX, p. 3, and "The Key to Struggling China: A Drama of Three Zones," *New York Times,* November 30, 1930, X, p. 3.

46. Mahlon Perkins to Secretary of State, December 9, 1930, enclosing memorandum of Sokolsky-Johnson conversation, November 24, 1930, SD 893.51 SILVER/19; Perkins to Secretary of State, March 5, 1931, enclosing memorandum of Sokolsky-Johnson conversation February 26, 1931, SD 893.51 SILVER/48; Perkins to Secretary of State, March 12, 1931, SD 893.00/11396.

rumor in Shanghai that he was secretly employed by J. P. Morgan and Company and perhaps had so persuaded some Chinese officials—while he represented Soong to Lamont. He claimed to have found the Japanese responsive, prepared to scale down Chinese debts. While he waited for Lamont to return from Europe, however, he received a cable from Nanking advising him that Sir Arthur Salter, formerly of the League of Nations, would be authorized to speak to the American financiers. In an oral history interview twenty-five years later, Sokolsky's story was similar, but the culprit was Ludwig Rajchmann, a "communist agent" representing the League of Nations. Sokolsky argued that the breakdown of the arrangements he had devised led to a war with China that the Japanese had hoped to avoid; that the Japanese liberals had needed at least a token settlement to restrain the military in 1931. But Sokolsky personally did not fare too badly at the time. He wrote on Chinese and Japanese affairs for the *New York Times,* and the outbreak of hostilities in Manchuria in September created a demand for men with his knowledge, guaranteeing him considerable exposure.[47]

As Sokolsky scurried back and forth across the Pacific, serving men of great power in Nanking, Tokyo, and New York, Roger Greene worked rather more quietly in his mission to help China. Like all friends of China he was disturbed by the continued fighting among the militarists from 1929 to 1931. In particular he continued to be disappointed by Chiang's leadership, but these were affairs at a level at which he could not function. Instead, he focused his attention on problems of famine relief in 1929, and public health in 1930. Influential Americans like James Shotwell and Nelson Rockefeller visited with him when in Peking and wrote afterward for his opinion on various affairs of China. Chinese intellectuals, specifically western-educated Chinese intellectuals, sought and received his advice on matters of bureaucratic politics, on dealings with private and public American organizations. It was a useful, sensible, establishmentarian life, especially when compared with the garment-center type machinations of Sokolsky. With his protégé, Nelson Johnson, now Minister to China, Greene was cautiously optimistic about the future of China. In January 1931 he wrote that despite all the government's shortcomings, "if peace can be preserved for a year or two, as seems likely," the Chinese government would be strengthened to the point

47. Memorandum of conversation between Sokolsky and Hornbeck, May 1, 1931, SD 893.00/11443; Sokolsky transcript (1956), Oral History, Columbia.

where it could even stand the loss of Chiang and Soong. Similarly, in March, Johnson modified his own pessimism and contended that "given five years of peace and reasonable crops" the chances of the Nationalist government surviving were "pretty good." But what passed for peace in China lasted hardly more than five months.[48]

48. Greene to Johnson, March 19, 1929, SD 893.48L/121; Memorandum of conversation between Greene and Johnson, April 13, 1929, Papers of Nelson T. Johnson, Library of Congress; Greene to Nathaniel Peffer, March 25, 1930, to J. Heng Liu, November 26, 1930, to Manley O. Hudson, January 21, 1931, RSG ms; Johnson to William Castle, March 25, 1931, Johnson Papers, and SD 893.00/11642.

7

# CHINA AND JAPAN AT WAR

DESPITE the consensus in Japan on the absolute necessity of Japanese hegemony over Manchuria, the Kwantung Army grew restive as the authority of the Nanking government spread through the region. Powerful elements within the Japanese Army came to doubt the resolve of the politicians in Tokyo. On the evening of September 18, 1931, the Army began the action it considered essential to securing its fief. Setting off an explosion on the South Manchuria Railway in order to allege Chinese provocation, Japanese troops executed carefully planned operations, capturing Mukden within hours and preparing the military conquest of Manchuria. Shidehara might yet dream of a peaceful solution to frictions with China, but the Japanese Army was no longer willing to leave vital matters of national security in the hands of civilians.

When the Kwantung Army struck, George Sokolsky was in the United States, finding a limited market for unfulfilled Borodins. Lamont had not responded favorably to his schemes for settling China's financial problems and America in the depression was not an easy place in which to build a new life. He wrote a few articles explaining China for the readers of the Sunday *New York Times,* participated in a few panel discussions and hoped something would turn up that would enable him to go back to China to live out his dream of becoming the power behind the throne. The call from China never came, but the explosion on the SMR focused the attention of the

American public on East Asia and created a demand for men who could explain Chinese and Japanese affairs. There was certainly no one else in the United States who had been so deeply involved in Chinese politics, had enjoyed recent discussions with Japanese leaders, and had the ability to provide the kind of background and color stories that an American audience needed. As a result, Sokolsky was called upon to write dozens of articles for the *New York Times* in the year that followed the Mukden Incident. East Asia became a popular subject on the lecture tour and Sokolsky made the rounds, talking about the same kinds of things he wrote about for the *Times* magazine section. If the work was less exciting than brokering power between Nanking and Tokyo, with an occasional visit to Wall Street, there was still considerable prestige—an identity a man could live with.

Sokolsky's initial articles on the crisis provided historical background with particular reference to the development of Russian and Japanese interests in Manchuria. He constantly stressed the Japanese view of these Chinese provinces as their "first line of defense," detailing the strategic and economic interests Japan had developed in the area. He explained the conflict in terms of Chinese determination to exercise complete sovereignty over Manchuria and Japanese determination to protect their interests there. As of 1931 the relationship between these two countries in Manchuria was unsatisfactory, requiring a new arrangement if there was to be stability in northeast Asia—but the Chinese and Japanese would have to settle the problem *alone,* by negotiation or warfare. Sokolsky claimed that the people of China and Japan were not antagonistic, but had become involved in this crisis because politicians in both countries were exploiting relatively minor incidents for domestic political advantage. On the Japanese side he explicitly distinguished between Shidehara and Japanese businessmen, who were anxious to avoid friction with China, and their opponents of the Seiyukai and the military, who were demanding that the Chinese be reminded of the need to respond to Japan with respect. Sokolsky predicted that economically, culturally, politically, and racially, the future of Manchuria would be Chinese. He stressed Chinese profit from Japanese and Russian investment in Manchuria, but included a vague and perhaps ominous reference to Manchuria developing along Chinese lines but not in the same way as China proper.[1]

Sokolsky's analysis did not reflect official Japanese propaganda—as did

1. *New York Times,* September 27, 1931, V, p. 7 and IX, p. 3.

the despatches being received in the United States from correspondents in Tokyo. It was also markedly different from the impassioned condemnations of Japanese aggression and imperialism Hallett Abend was filing from China. Sokolsky made no effort to discuss the issue in moral terms, expressed no shock at Japan's use of force or violation of treaty obligations. Indeed, he indicated some sympathy for Shidehara's efforts to protect Japanese interests in Manchuria. His friend Thomas Lamont was willing to go much further. Writing to Walter Lippmann, Lamont blamed everything on the Chinese. He argued that they violated their treaty obligations by building railroads to compete with the SMR—using money they owed the Japanese in the process. "In other words," Lamont contended, "China has conducted the most lawless and aggravating course possible." To a banker, failure to pay debts and the building of competing railways seemed a worse offense than that committed by the Kwantung Army. And Lamont assured his Japanese friends of his support, even advising Inoue in affairs of the press. A staunch supporter of the League of Nations, Lamont nonetheless refused in early November to sign a letter endorsing American cooperation with the League during the Manchurian crisis, claiming that the League was biased in favor of China.[2]

Sokolsky, also, was dissatisfied by the League's involvement in the Manchurian dispute. He insisted that League intervention injected considerations of "face," preventing the Chinese and Japanese governments from localizing the conflict, weakening the Japanese moderates. He prepared a formula for ending the crisis by means of two Sino-Japanese Commissions, one to oversee the evacuation of Japanese troops and the other to study the cause of frictions in Manchuria. To Lamont he explained that his plan required the sponsorship of a major American figure, but Lamont held back. Instead he wrote to Hamilton Fish Armstrong, editor of *Foreign Affairs,* noting Sokolsky's good work for the *New York Times,* referring to his inside knowledge of Chinese and Japanese affairs, and recommending that Armstrong have Sokolsky write an article for him. Armstrong replied immediately—and negatively—expressing great mistrust of Sokolsky: "I don't know his present affiliations, but it is common knowledge that in the past he

2. See Ernest R. May, "U.S. Press Coverage of Japan, 1931–1941," in Borg and Okamoto, *Pearl Harbor as History,* 515–17; Lamont to Lippmann, October 1, 1931 (copy to S. Sonoda, Yokohama Specie Bank), 187–10, Lamont to Raymond Fosdick et al., November 9, 1931, 29–17, TWL ms.

has had many and very diverse irons in the fire.'' He noted that Japanese sources were also urging *Foreign Affairs* to obtain Sokolsky's services. Lamont signed off more guardedly than in his initial endorsement of Sokolsky: ''I don't hold any brief for him and he is not my child. He is an amusing and interesting character. I think he is somewhat of a realist, and apt to see both sides of the question.''[3]

Although Armstrong claimed that the *Times* had been distressed by the ''pro-Japanese'' character of Sokolsky's writings, his appearances in that newspaper increased. In November, he published ten articles, with essays in the magazine section four out of five Sundays. In December his byline appeared thirteen times and his analyses continued with great frequency as long as East Asia stayed in the headlines. In his magazine section articles he explained the Chinese use of the boycott, described student activism in China, analyzed the role of the emperor in Japan, and discussed the difference between the Chinese and Japanese peoples. When the Japanese began to flirt with the idea of establishing an ''autonomous'' state in Manchuria, Sokolsky introduced Henry P'u-yi to the American public. In an article on the Soongs, ''The First Family of China,'' he kept the door open for a return to China by praising them all, describing T. V. as a man ''generally regarded as the most competent administrative official that China has produced since Marquis Tseng Kuo-fan.''[4]

Sokolsky's analyses of the situation in Manchuria were thoughtful and balanced. To a generation of foreign policy specialists weaned on the ''realism'' of Hans Morgenthau and George Kennan, his amoral approach to the Sino-American conflict would not be shocking. He saw two sides to the issue of Japanese interests in Manchuria and to the dispute over the validity of Japanese treaty rights there. Although not outraged by the use of force to accomplish Japanese ends, he recognized the fact that the Japanese military was operating independently of Shidehara's control and he sympathized openly with Shidehara. More clearly than most he realized that the Japanese people had rallied behind the military and hoped that Saionji, last of the genro, could induce the emperor to support the civilians. Sokolsky under-

3. Sokolsky note and memorandum for Lamont, undated, 187–6, Lamont to Armstrong, November 16, Armstrong to Lamont, November 17, and Lamont to Armstrong, November 18, 1931, 184–5, TWL ms.

4. *New York Times*, November 8, 1931, V, p. 5, December 6, 1931, V, p. 3, January 3, 1932, V, p. 6, November 29, 1931, V, p. 5, November 15, 1931, V, p. 8.

stood that Shidehara did not differ from the Japanese military in his determination to defend Japanese interests in Manchuria or in his hopes for Japanese hegemony over East Asia. He did have illusions, however, about Shidehara's ability, with or without the help of the emperor, to deny the army its choice of means toward these nationally shared ends.[5]

Sokolsky also understood that Chiang Kai-shek and T. V. Soong, had they been spared the pressure of student activists, would have deferred a confrontation with Japan. First, they wanted to deal with internal enemies, to consolidate their hold on China proper. When the students drove Chiang from power in October, Sokolsky feared the worst: Communists behind the demonstrations, Chiang gone for good, China's best chance for unity destroyed. Once again, he underestimated Chiang's resiliency and tactical skills.[6]

Sokolsky was particularly critical of the role played by the League of Nations in the fall of 1931. Some of his irritation may have stemmed from personal pique—a belief that the interference of League officials had wrecked his own plans for China's financial reconstruction. Nonetheless, his argument was consistent with both his realism and his idea that China and Japan had to work things out between themselves. He contended that the appointment of a commission to study the situation in Manchuria was useless by December. The League had acted too slowly and the Japanese had already accomplished their ends. The League resolution of December 10 said nothing about the withdrawal of Japanese troops and would be viewed by the Chinese people as a betrayal. Friendless, the Chinese would turn increasingly toward the Communists. His public skepticism about the League apparently did not go unanswered. A month later he was complaining to MacMurray about being attacked by advocates of the League, and threatening to have his adversaries investigated by a Senate committee.[7]

Sokolsky also wrote of the American stake in Manchuria, which he restricted to trade and investment. Conceding that Manchuria might someday become an important market, he offered statistics to indicate the minimal importance of the region to the United States in 1931. Like Roger Greene many years before, he wrote of the need for American representatives in

5. *Ibid.* November 15, 1931, IX, p. 1, November 16, p. 2.

6. *Ibid.*, December 12, p. 10, December 16, p. 16.

7. *Ibid.*, December 11, 1931, p. 6; Sokolsky to MacMurray, January 21, 1932, MacMurray Papers.

China to stimulate trade. Like some of the earlier advocates of dollar diplomacy, he suggested that low American investments in Manchuria might be responsible for low trade levels. Without establishing the point explicitly, Sokolsky indicated that there was little reason for Americans to be terribly concerned about who controlled Manchuria.[8]

On January 7, 1932, Secretary of State Henry Stimson, unable to take action to undo Japanese aggression and unwilling to acquiesce silently as the Japanese conquered Manchuria and disregarded their obligations under the League covenant and the Kellogg-Briand treaty, chose to try moral diplomacy. Unlike Sokolsky, Stimson had an image of a new world order in which moral sanctions, appeals to world public opinion, might keep the peace. Analysis of press opinion by the *Literary Digest* and of public opinion by Stanley Hornbeck suggested that the American people were convinced that Japan had violated treaties of importance to them and would respond favorably to an effort to call Japan to account.[9] And so Stimson informed the Chinese and Japanese governments that the United States would recognize no impairment of its treaty rights, including those relating to the sovereignty, independence, or territorial and administrative integrity of China. Furthermore, the United States would not recognize any situation resulting from resort to war, from violations of the Kellogg Pact.

To this note, later known as the Stimson or Hoover-Stimson Doctrine, Sokolsky responded initially with great praise. It was neither a warning nor a remonstrance but rather a full and frank statement of American policy. The United States was acting independently, not participating in "a world attempt to spank Japan." Stimson had not attempted to judge Japan's conduct but concentrated instead on the sole concern of the United States: the Open Door in Manchuria, infractions of which would not be tolerated. Sokolsky thought Stimson's tone, friendly to both countries, was perfect. He found not a single word at which the Japanese could take offense. The United States was offering China and Japan a chance to end the military phase of the conflict, to find a way out—and Sokolsky believed that Japan's economic condition was such that it could not flout American opinion. He concluded that in the past American statesmen had misunderstood the psychol-

8. *New York Times,* December 23, 1931, p. 13, December 27, III, p. 1.

9. *Literary Digest,* CXI, October 10, 1931, p. 11, October 24, p. 5, October 31, p. 3. See also CXII, January 23, 1932, p. 5 for evidence of approval of Stimson note; Hornbeck memorandum, December 6, 1931, SD 793.94/4314.

ogy of the Japanese people, outraging them by giving orders, but "Mr. Stimson does not make that mistake. He is not ordering Japan to do anything."[10]

When the Japanese reply came, Sokolsky had to admit he had not anticipated its stiff tone. The argument that infractions of the Open Door were the fault of the Chinese he thought "not altogether fair, nor must it be allowed to stand."[11] The note created problems for Sokolsky. It was one thing to defend Japanese arrogance when it was directed against the Chinese, but quite another matter when it was directed against his own country. Patriotism might dictate a rebuke to Japan; so might fear of losing one's audience—or one's opportunity to write. Obviously Japan's economic condition had not made the Japanese as conciliatory as he anticipated. Sokolsky might have been less sanguine had he been in closer touch with the operations of his friend Lamont.

Three days after Stimson sent his note to Tokyo and Nanking, J. P. Morgan and Company arranged with the Japanese government to permit it to delay payments due that month, January 1932. At least some of the financial pressure on the Japanese government was thus eased before the Japanese replied to Stimson. When the Department of State moved to prevent Japan from obtaining funds in the United States it was too late. *After* the brusque Japanese response, Stimson approved a memorandum noting that Japan's need for money was a potential American weapon and declaring that the Department would encourage no loans until Japan behaved satisfactorily in Manchuria. Undersecretary of State William R. Castle called Lamont, who, with less than complete candor, assured him that he had received no requests for loans from the Japanese government and that there was no chance of a loan being granted if requested. Lamont gave no indication of disapproving of Japanese actions in Manchuria. Instead he based his position on the fact that Japan had gone off the gold standard, was suffering from declining trade, and was, therefore, no longer good security.[12]

On the day that Castle called Lamont, the Japanese Navy attacked Shanghai. The Chinese had begun boycotting Japanese goods over incidents in Manchuria even before September 18, 1931, but the actions of the Kwantung Army had intensified the boycott and increased Chinese abuse of

10. *New York Times*, January 8, 1932, p. 2. 11. *Ibid.*, January 17, 1932, p. 27.

12. "J. P. Morgan's Financial Assistance to Japan," January 14, 1932, SD 894.51/332; Wilson, *American Business*, 233–34; Hornbeck memorandum, January 19, 1932, SD 793.94/3607; memorandum of conversation between Castle and Lamont, January 29, 1932, SD 894.51/325.

Japanese nationals, most notably in Shanghai. The Japanese admiral on station demanded that Chinese authorities put an end to the disturbances in Shanghai and, dissatisfied with their response, landed marines in the city. When Chinese troops there disobeyed orders and resisted the Japanese, full-scale fighting erupted. In the city with the largest international settlement in China, Japanese planes bombed Chinese troops and civilians. Off-shore Japanese ships bombarded Chinese positions—and public opinion in the United States and much of the rest of the world turned sharply against Japan. Apologists for the attack on Shanghai were rare and elements of the American peace movement attempted to organize a nationwide boycott of Japanese goods.

Both Lamont and Sokolsky were embarrassed by Japanese actions at Shanghai and refused to condone them. Both tried to distinguish between defensible Japanese policy toward Manchuria and inexcusable, stupid acts in Shanghai. Sensitive to the rapid crystalization of anti-Japanese sentiment even within the Japan-American Society, Lamont arranged to cancel the Society's scheduled dinner with the Japanese Ambassador. To his friends at the Yokohama Specie Bank branch in New York, he sent word that confidence in Japan had been greatly undermined and it would be almost impossible for Japan to borrow abroad. A few days later came the greatest shock of all: a cable announcing the assassination of Inoue, his closest, most respected, and most powerful Japanese friend. When Lamont had argued throughout the 1920s and even after the Mukden incident that Japan had changed, that it was not the imperialistic and militaristic Japan of the 21 Demands but a new liberal Japan, he had based his assumption on the power of friends like Inoue and Dan Takuma of Mitsui to control the Japanese government and to contain the Japanese military. Now Inoue was dead and four weeks later the assassins murdered Dan.[13]

Lamont's confidence in the new Japan suffered one shattering blow after another, and he was willing to cooperate with Hoover and Stimson. He obtained information about Japanese finances for Stimson. In response to a telephone call from Hoover, Lamont sent a warning to Finance Minister Takahashi Korekiyo, whose concern over the implied threat of financial pressure may have facilitated Japan's decision to terminate the Shanghai af-

13. Memorandum of conversation between Castle and Lamont, February 1, 1932, SD 811.43 Japan-America Society/1; *Diary of Kido Koichi* (International Military Tribunal translation), 14; Sonoda to Lamont, February 9, 1932, 187–13, TWL ms; Heinrichs, *American Ambassador,* 412, footnote 19; Lamont to Sonoda, March 7, and Sonoda to Lamont, March 9, 1932, 188–22, TWL ms (copies to Stimson, SD 793.94/4953).

fair. He sent letters to his surviving friends in Japan, warning them of the hostile turn of American opinion, urging upon them the importance of a rapid resolution of the situation in Shanghai. He sent copies of these letters to Stimson, along with copies of the replies. To Takahashi's defense of Japanese actions he replied that "so far as the general so-called Western public is concerned, nothing will ever convince it that the Japanese military and naval forces at Shanghai have acted with prudence and restraint." He had lost his friends, Japan had lost the leaders upon whom he had counted, and the good will he had worked for years to build for Japan had been dissipated. He warned the Japanese government that it would have to show that "aggression of the Shanghai type is not to be repeated."[14]

Despite his concern over the course of events in Tokyo and Shanghai, Lamont refused to support a campaign to organize an economic boycott against Japan. Explaining his position to President A. Lawrence Lowell of Harvard, Lamont not only spoke to the issues but also revealed his conception of the proper way to use influence. With the Japanese he had considered himself best suited to appeal privately, as a friend. That role would be compromised if he publicly endorsed a boycott. But he also saw the boycott as a form of pressure on the American government and he advised Lowell that he was opposed to pressing the government to take specific steps. Rather than stimulating a public campaign that might embarrass concerned officials, he preferred to work with them privately. Lamont was the private man, manipulating behind the scenes, most reluctant to arouse the people and involve them in the process of making policy decisions. *He* had access to the powerful—and [illegible] would be well. For his partners he left a memorandum explaining that Stimson had been "rather restive and resentful" of Lowell's boycott campaign, but had not felt free to take it up with Lowell himself. Lamont had volunteered to attempt to bring Lowell into line and Stimson had called him to express approval of his letter. In a second memorandum he noted that "with the approval of the Department of State" he had explained to the Japanese Finance Minister the effect on Americans of recent Japanese policy. Clearly, Lamont had been of considerable service to his government during the Shanghai incident.[15]

14. Lamont to Stimson, March 18, 1932, SD 894.51/331¾; Lamont to Takahashi, March 30, 1932, 188–22, and to Kengo Mori, April 8, 1932, 188–31, TWL ms.

15. Lamont to Lowell, March 10, 1932, and memoranda dated April 15, 1932, 188–22, TWL ms.

Sokolsky responded to events at Shanghai with articles on treaty port life. As the crisis developed he predicted accurately that Chinese officials would yield to Japanese demands, but would be unable to suppress the boycott. Two days before the shooting started he reported that Japanese businessmen in Shanghai were angrily insisting that the boycott was an act of war not to be tolerated. He thought Japanese pressures on Shanghai authorities and the Nanking government were senseless and misplaced. The boycott was a popular response to the Kwantung Army's operations in Manchuria, not to any order of Chinese authorities. When the Japanese attacked, he seemed most disturbed by the Chinese inability to respond, condemning Kuomintang factionalism, decrying the lack of unity. But when the Chinese did fight back at Shanghai, he thought them mistaken. To readers of the *Times* Sunday magazine he explained the fighting in terms of "face." The Chinese boycott and abuse of Japanese had constituted an unacceptable loss of face to the Japanese. Similarly the Chinese were forced to respond to the Japanese attack on Shanghai. Now the Japanese could not admit that their navy had been wrong. To him it seemed obvious that the Japanese wanted a way out of the mess at Shanghai, but they needed a face-saving device.[16]

But as the fighting in Shanghai continued and the Japanese-created regime in Manchuria declared its independence of China, Stimson worried less about Japan's "face," less about strengthening the moderates in Tokyo. Instead he wrote a public letter to William Borah, Chairman of the Senate Foreign Relations Committee, expressing the hope that the world would endorse his nonrecognition policy. He reaffirmed the American commitment to the principles of the Nine Power Treaty, insisting that China had the right to modernize in her own way, free from foreign interference. And he warned Japan that if it ignored the Nine Power Treaty, it would undermine the entire treaty structure of 1922, freeing the United States to build up its fleet and to fortify its Pacific possessions.

Sokolsky realized that the United States would not recognize an autonomous Manchuria, but argued that nonrecognition would make no difference. Eventually, if the United States hoped to trade in Manchuria, it would have to come to terms with the Japanese. By March 1932, after Manchukuo came into being as an "independent state," Sokolsky's remarks

16. *New York Times*, January 25, 1932, p. 4, January 27, p. 10, January 31, III, p. 8, February 7, V, p. 7, February 14, V, p. 3.

in his lectures around New York state, in Chicago, and in Louisville were increasingly critical of American policy. He contended that the only American interest in China was in trade, that the territorial integrity of China was not important to the United States. He warned his audiences against jeopardizing the tremendous economic stake the United States had in Japan in both trade and investments. Stressing the need for a "realistic" policy he urged his audiences to forget about the League of Nations, to forget about the Kellogg-Briand pact, and to think in terms of "hard cash." He insisted that the United States could not settle the Sino-Japanese dispute and had best stay out of it. Japan could not subdue China and the Chinese could not drive the Japanese out of Manchuria. One other theme that had appeared often during his days with the Japanese-supported *Far Eastern Review* crept in: Japanese control of Manchuria was preferable to Russian. At least the Japanese would not spread communism. For much of the year he lectured several times a week hitting at these themes and discussing less controversial Asian subjects before foreign affairs, business, and women's groups, civic organizations, Jewish groups, library clubs—whoever would pay the fee.[17]

In April, a few weeks before the Japanese finally extricated themselves from Shanghai, an American employed by the SMR as a propagandist named Sokolsky as one of a handful of writers who "have been remarkably staunch and have shown great eagerness to obtain the facts from the Japanese side." In July, his friend MacMurray expressed disappointment in Sokolsky's attitude toward China, reporting that he had become "slightly anti-Chinese and pro-Japanese." The official reporting the conversation to Washington indicated that MacMurray had given no explanation for Sokolsky's change, but in the margin of the report someone at State, possibly Hornbeck, pencilled in "easy." Recollections of Sokolsky's ability to work for many masters allowed suspicion that he might be working for the Japanese, but arguments and analyses similar to his were also offered then and since by men less suspect.[18]

During the summer of 1932, when most Americans had ceased to be concerned about events in East Asia, Sokolsky spent two weeks at the Williamstown Institute of Politics, participating in round table discussions of

17. *Ibid.*, February 28, 1932, IX, p. 1; clippings from lectures, March 1932, GES ms.

18. C. Van H. Engert, Legation, to Stimson, April 17, 1932, enclosing memorandum by Henry W. Kinney, SD 793.94/5257; Legation to Secretary of State, July 22, 1932, SD 861.5017 Living Conditions/495.

the crisis in Manchuria and the role of the various countries involved. At approximately the same time, his book-length study of East Asian affairs, *Tinder Box of Asia,* was published. The book, written earlier, prefaced in May 1932, was largely a collage of the articles he had been publishing in the *New York Times,* but it was more clearly critical of Stimson's policies and more willing to defend Japanese actions. He decried the American habit of coddling China and argued that China had been weakened by the assumption that the United States would always save her from her own mistakes. At Williamstown he argued that Japan had acted in Manchuria to avert war with Russia—that the Japanese could not wait until the strategic balance in the area had shifted against them. At one point he teamed with two Japanese participants to oppose the argument that Japan had violated her obligations under the League, Kellogg, and Nine Power pacts. Sokolsky insisted that the new world order of which people in the peace movement spoke did not yet exist; that there was no guarantee that peace and justice would prevail throughout the world, no assurance that the peace system would work, no assurance that Japan would have access to food and other vital raw materials. In the real world Japan had to face the possibility of being destroyed by China and Russia, had to act before it was too late.[19]

In a radio broadcast late in August, Sokolsky argued that the real menace to world peace in the Manchurian situation was Western interference. Stimson and the League of Nations were responsible for expanding the quarrel which could be settled only through direct negotiations between China and Japan. He insisted that there was a basis for negotiations; that the two countries needed each other; that a weakened Japan would leave China open to Western predators. Whether Sokolsky was working for the Japanese or not, it would have been difficult for him to have been more understanding of their cause. Certainly by the end of August 1932 he had formulated rationalizations reminiscent of the views of the Japanese Army rather than those of Shidehara at the time of the Mukden incident.[20]

Despite Sokolsky's apologies for Japan, he continued to have occasional opportunities to write for the *New York Times* as long as the Manchurian problem remained newsworthy—until Japan left the League of Nations in March 1933. He continued on lecture tour and was able to publish

19. *Tinder Box of Asia* (New York, 1932); *New York Times,* August 14, 1932, p. 5, August 21, p. 11, and August 23, p. 8.

20. *New York Times,* August 29, p. 4.

articles in a wide range of respectable periodicals including the *Atlantic Monthly, Asia, Christian Century,* and *Commonweal.* When he spoke in New York City or on major out-of-town programs, the *New York Times* reported his views. Via lectures, radio broadcasts, his writings and newspaper coverage of some of his activities, Sokolsky was able to present his analyses to the interested public and to achieve recognition as an authority on the affairs of East Asia. Although *Tinder Box of Asia* received mixed reviews, it was praised by some liberal friends of China like T. A. Bisson in the *New Republic* and Lewis Gannett in the *Nation*—with Gannett declaring that "George Sokolsky probably knows more Chinese more intimately than any other foreigner in China."[21]

In September 1932, almost a year after the Mukden Incident, Sokolsky wrote a long article for the *Times* in anticipation of the Lytton Report. He noted Japanese claims that their action in Manchuria was consistent with their obligations to the League and to the Kellogg and Nine Power Pacts. Without indicating that he had endorsed those claims, he reported almost universal disbelief of the Japanese position. Without effort to defend Japanese policy, he indicated that it was clear that Manchukuo would be a Japanese puppet; that the Japanese claims to be doing nothing more than the United States was doing in Cuba were not true. But he warned that even if the Lytton Report was unfavorable to the Japanese, they could not withdraw from Manchuria. On the contrary, considerations of face might well force Japanese withdrawal from the League. Sokolsky also realized that presentation of the report, presumably unfavorable to Japan, would present a dilemma for the League and for both the United States and the Soviet Union. Could the League accept the report and then do nothing? Stimson had indicated that the American and Japanese positions were irreconcilable—what would the United States do?[22]

When the report was presented to the League early in October, Sokolsky liked it. Speaking at a League of Nations Association luncheon, he praised the Commission's understanding of the complexity of the issues and saw the report as a sound basis for negotiations between China and Japan.

21. See "The American Monkey Wrench," *Atlantic Monthly,* CL (December 1932), 739–48; "What Matters in Missions," *Christian Century* L (January 11, 1933) 52–54; "Let's Change Our Foreign Policy," *Asia* XXXIII (March 1933), 175–77; "Catholic Missions in China," *Commonweal* XVII (March 22, 1933), 573–74; *New Republic* LXXI (August 10, 1932), 348; *Nation,* CXXXV (August 24, 1932), 174.

22. *New York Times,* September 11, 1932, VIII, p. 1.

Once again he stressed the importance of avoiding Western interference, blaming the Stimson Doctrine, American pressures, for Japan's decision to recognize Manchukuo. Copies of this speech were distributed by the League of Nations Association. Similar speeches by Sokolsky at the School of Public and International Affairs, Princeton, and at the Town Hall Club of New York, were duly reported in the *Times*.[23]

Lamont, of course, worked more directly, writing to Stimson the day after the Lytton Report was unveiled. Gently but clearly he presented the message Sokolsky was shouting from the rooftops: "I feel quite clearly that this is an excellent time for all of us to lie pretty low in regard to public statements so far as Japan's attitude is concerned." He feared that the Japanese people had become hostile to the West, including America. Thus any Japanese political leader who appeared responsive to the United States risked his life. But Lamont informed Stimson that the situation was not hopeless, that he liked the Lytton Report. Now he hoped the League would simply refer the report to the Chinese and Japanese as a basis for negotiations—and *not* act itself. On the same day Lamont wrote to Philip Nash, Director of the League of Nations Association, warning him to be discreet in the pronouncements of the organization, to stay out of high politics. Nash was reminded of the interest of Mr. and Mrs. Lamont in the work of his organization, of "how cordially we have supported it"—an implicit threat to withdraw support if Nash did not follow the advice to use "prudent discretion."[24]

Stimson replied immediately to assure Lamont that he intended to offer no public comment on the Lytton Report, which he found supportive of his position. He agreed that Japan should not be irritated, but also believed the Japanese were capable of bluffing other nations into inaction. World opinion would still require leadership and would have to remain set against the Japanese if there was ever to be a setback to Japan's military leaders. The Secretary of State was defensive, but accepted Lamont's advice.[25]

At the same time Lamont contacted Japanese friends, praising the Lytton Report and expressing the "fervent hope that your Government will wholeheartedly take advantage of it." Copies of these letters and the replies

23. *Ibid.*, October 14, 1932, p. 6, November 15, p. 5, and December 14.

24. Lamont to Stimson, October 4, 1932, enclosing Lamont to Nash, SD 793. 94 Commission/494½.

25. Stimson to Lamont, October 4, 1932, SD 793.94 Commission/499½.

were sent to Stimson. Lamont also attempted to convince Stimson that world public opinion need not be rallied, that it was irrelevant because the Japanese people were responding only to their military leaders. Change had to be brought about from within Japan. Lamont also forwarded to Stimson as his own a proposal by Sokolsky that the League Assembly, when accepting the Lytton Report, also resolve that China and Japan undertake negotiations, with the report as a basis. Lamont-Sokolsky argued that it was important for both China and Japan to realize that the world expected them to settle between themselves.[26]

In February 1933 the League of Nations adopted the Lytton Report. In March the Japanese formally withdrew from membership in the League. Fighting continued as the Japanese pushed on to Inner Mongolia. To Matsuoka Yosuke, who had defended Japan at the League meeting, Lamont sent warning that it would take a long time for the American people to forget the Shanghai affair, "especially when the Japanese Army continues apparently to do everything within its power to keep the Shanghai memory alive." To Saito Hiroshi, a Japanese diplomat, Lamont also expressed concern that continued operations by the Japanese Army would not allow American opinion toward Japan to soften. With Inoue and Dan dead, his other Japanese friends muffled, and "semi-barbarous" Japan dominant again, Lamont's sympathy for Japan was eroding.[27]

Sokolsky came to terms with Japanese policy perhaps more readily than Lamont. In an informal debate with Drew Pearson in March, Sokolsky contended that he did not anticipate a war with Japan. He brushed aside Japan's rejection of the League as nothing more than the United States had done first. He insisted that the morality of affairs in Asia was irrelevant to the United States; that American policy should be based on "utility" rather than morality; that American investments in and trade with Japan were too important to be thrown away over unstable moral issues. The choice, Sokolsky argued, was between building a navy that would permit the United States to punish offenders or to send agents over to improve trade and make money. Obviously there was no point to passing resolutions of disapproval or calling for nonrecognition of reality. Stimson had allowed himself to be used by Eu-

26. Lamont to K. Horinouchi, October 4, 1932, and Horinouchi to Lamont, October 8, 1932, 187–17, Sokolsky to Lamont, October 5, 1932, 131–8, Lamont to Stimson, October 11, 1932, 209–25, TWL ms.

27. Lamont to Matsuoka, April 24, 1933, to Saito, May 18, 1933, 187–21, TWL ms.

ropeans who wanted to have the United States punish Japan. Settlement between China and Japan had been prevented by European nations less concerned with the peoples of those countries than with a test of the League Covenant.[28]

Sokolsky's views worried Stanley Hornbeck at the State Department. In April, Sokolsky met with the attorney general of the new Roosevelt administration, and Hornbeck sent a warning to Secretary of State Cordell Hull to prepare Hull for anything Sokolsky brought forth. He described Sokolsky as "very well informed with regard to forces and events in the Far East. He is less well informed with regard to the underlying forces and facts of American foreign policy as a whole. He is *clever* as a writer and speaker." Hornbeck described Sokolsky's mind as more Oriental than Occidental, noted that he had previously served Chinese officials informally, and warned Hull that some people believed him to be a Japanese agent at present.[29]

Throughout the crises in Manchuria and Shanghai, Roger Greene was in Peking administering the medical school, chatting with Nelson Johnson, and involving himself in public health and cultural problems. When the League secretariat sought an American to serve on the Lytton Commission, both Roger and his brother Jerome were among those nominated to Hornbeck—who chose to recommend MacMurray. Toward the end of 1931 Nathaniel Peffer, an authority on East Asian affairs, wrote to Greene bemoaning the state of affairs. He remembered an earlier time when Greene alone had kept his perspective while Peffer and others "had lost our heads about Japanese aggressions in China." Peffer professed to have "lost a good deal of anti-Japanese feeling I had then," but he was unable to condone Japanese actions in Manchuria. Greene agreed: "Personally, I am quite disgusted with the way in which the Japanese have behaved. Aside from my dislike of such imperialistic policies in general, the lack of straightforwardness on the part of the Japanese is intolerable."[30]

Greene was nevertheless satisfied with his work and felt no compulsion to direct the course of American policy. In December 1932 he did stop and write a letter to his old friend and colleague on the Harvard *Crimson*, Franklin Roosevelt. He discussed some of the problems of East Asia, but his

28. *New York Times*, March 26, 1933, II, p. 1.

29. Memorandum with tag dated April 12, 1933, Hornbeck Papers.

30. Memorandum by Hornbeck, December 16, 1931, SD 793.94 Commission/7½; Peffer to Greene, November 24, 1931, and Greene to Peffer, December 17, 1931, RSG ms.

primary concern was with advising the president-elect to retain Nelson Johnson and Joseph Grew as his representatives to China and Japan. He praised Grew and especially Johnson before going on to remark that despite his upbringing in Japan and friendly feeling for the Japanese people, he believed Japan to be "wholly in the wrong in her present course." He advised Roosevelt that many Japanese, including diplomats, were shaken by the actions of the military, but thought that the Japanese people, subject to systematic propaganda, were unaware of much of what was happening. Roosevelt replied warmly, remarking that he had just run into another *Crimson* buddy and had enjoyed a long talk about Roger Greene and the old days. He invited Greene to come by when he returned to the United States.[31]

As the crisis reached its denouement in the early months of 1933, Greene was temperate in his criticism of Japan. He was prepared to admit that Chinese maladministration in Manchuria justified some though not all of Japan's complaints. He remained aware that the position of the Western powers was not morally superior to that of Japan. In China, there was not much to choose from between the current Japanese imperialism and "past activities of other powers, the fruits of which are still being enjoyed." If Japan was to be restrained, all the powers should surrender those of their interests in conflict with Chinese sovereignty. As for the United States, it had little to give up in China and a declaration of its willingness to sacrifice such interests would carry little weight. "Where we come in," he wrote, "is in the Western Hemisphere. There . . . we should have to give up things comparable to what we expect Japan and European powers to give up in China." Greene's analysis was certainly not far removed from that of the Japanese—or Sokolsky—who argued that Japan was only seeking the hegemony in East Asia that the United States claimed for itself in the Western Hemisphere.[32]

Wondering how the Japanese might have been stopped, Greene struggled with the idea of economic sanctions. Early in February he argued that a boycott against Japan would arouse such passions among the Japanese, lead to such provocative actions on their part against European and American interests in East Asia, that it would lead to war. He warned against using a boycott unless the boycotting powers were willing to fight. He had expressed doubt previously that American interests in the Western Pacific were sufficient to justify conflict with Japan even if the Japanese moved against

31. Greene to Roosevelt, December 9, 1932, and Roosevelt to Greene, January 5, 1933, RSG ms.

32. Greene to Peffer, January 23, 1933, to J. A. K. van Hasselt, February 20, 1933, RSG ms.

an independent Philippines. In March, however, he disagreed with his brother Jerome's argument that "economic measures are hardly to be distinguished from war and require similar justification." Lecturing his brother on the differences, Roger maintained that "the operation of economic measures is so gradual that steps can be taken to lessen their immediate harmful effects, while there is also time for the parties to reconsider their policies before any irremedial damage is done." As though he were comparing the British blacklist to the German submarine in 1917, he argued that warlike measures, on the other hand, "such as those which Japan is using, have resulted in the death or wounding of from ten to twenty thousand Japanese and Chinese soldiers in the near neighborhood of Peiping in the last few days, and no compromises can restore those individuals in their previous condition." For Jerome's benefit he went further, wondering if coercion by the League would mean war. Perhaps "if the British, American, and French fleets had moved to the Far East immediately after the September, 1931 incident," the Japanese might have backed off.[33]

In June, however, Greene seemed much closer to the position Sokolsky had argued consistently. He admitted that "I have felt that the League of Nations and the United States, in making so much of their League organization for peace and of the Kellogg-Briand Pact, have really made China's case much worse." Had it not been for the publicity given the peace machinery and the advice given by League experts to the Chinese, they probably would have come to an arrangement with the Japanese immediately. Instead, China turned to the League, "with consequently disastrous results."[34]

By the summer of 1933, it was difficult for anyone to have a kind word for the League's handling of the Manchurian crisis—or for the verbal interventions of Henry Stimson. If the issue was a test case for the world's peace machinery, the test had ended in failure—and China had lost all semblance of control over a vast and valuable territory. Lamont, Sokolsky, and Greene had all come to conclude that China could not have fared worse had she bargained for herself in September 1931.

For the next few years, the Japanese Army slowly penetrated the Great Wall, extending Japanese control over North China. In the United States the

33. Greene to E. C. Carter, February 2, 1933 (copy), and Greene to Johnson, January 2, 1933, Johnson Papers; Roger to Jerome Greene, March 15, 1933, RSG ms.

34. Greene to Payson Treat, June 14, 1933, RSG ms.

administration of Franklin Roosevelt appeared to lose interest in East Asia, determined only to avoid conflict with Japan as it tried desperately to bring about economic recovery at home. These were also the years in which Sokolsky's Chinese wife died, and he surrendered his dream of returning to China. Instead, he built a new life for himself in the country of his birth. For Roger Greene the years were probably more traumatic as the life he had settled into in China, the identity he enjoyed so much, were wrested away from him. He, too, had to find a place for himself in America. Even for Lamont, one of the most secure men in the world, the early days of the New Deal were not easy as the bankers came under attack for their misdeeds at home and for their alleged manipulation of foreign policy.

After the spring of 1933, Sokolsky found himself in little demand as a writer on East Asian affairs. He published a color piece on the city of Peking in the *New York Times* in June, and a revised edition of *Tinder Box of Asia* appeared in July, along with an article in *Annals*. He published only one more article on Asian affairs in 1933 and only one in each of the following two years. He tried to branch out in international affairs, covering the London Economic Conference in the summer of 1933, perhaps also hoping to play an advisory role to the Chinese Mission. But, despite letters of introduction from Hornbeck to American diplomats in Europe, he published only one sterile interview with Hull. Early in the fall his wife was seriously ill and, short of funds, Sokolsky had to appeal to Lamont, who guaranteed a bank loan. A few days later, Rosalind Phang Sokolsky was dead.[35]

A letter from Sokolsky to Hornbeck, written less than a week after his wife died, made no reference to his loss. Hornbeck had berated him for repeated references to friction between Chiang Kai-shek and T. V. Soong, apparently believing that Sokolsky's line hurt Chinese chances of obtaining financial assistance in the United States. Sokolsky replied that his statements were not based on partiality to any Chinese faction but on American interests. He insisted that it was to no one's advantage for additional American money to be lost in China.[36]

Soong had stopped in the United States en route to the London Confer-

35. *New York Times,* June 4, 1933, VI, p. 4 and July 19, p. 15; Hornbeck to Counselor, American Embassy, Rome, and others, June 17, 1933, Hornbeck Papers; *New York Times,* August 3, 1933, p. 9; Lamont to President, Bankers Trust Company, October 4, 1933, 131–8, TWL ms; *New York Times,* October 7, 1933, p. 15.

36. Sokolsky to Hornbeck, October 12, 1933, Hornbeck Papers.

ence, and had seen Hornbeck, Lamont, and Roosevelt. All were agreed that Lamont had to be won over before China could hope to obtain a loan in the United States—and Lamont remained wedded to the Consortium and Japanese participation. But if Sokolsky saw Soong, either in New York or in London, no invitation to return to China was forthcoming. In his correspondence with Hornbeck he became increasingly bitter about his own situation, about being caught in the cross-currents of Chinese politics. Vengefully he insisted that the United States could not back Soong's financial plans because he would then use his success to fight Chiang. The United States would be trapped as Japan was when it backed the Anfu clique and lost. His understanding, he admitted, derived from his own experience, and as a result, "when I should be in China doing a grand job of reconstruction, I am here in the United States lecturing to women. . . . The trouble is that the men or groups that you support in China disappear before your eyes and the foreigner is left holding the bag." He begged Hornbeck not to ask him to have faith "in the men who quarrel in Nanking amongst themselves and who sell their country and their friends. . . ." Whatever the cause, the good life in China seemed firmly out of reach, and in January 1934, on a lecture tour again, grinding out a living, he described himself to Lamont as the "proverbial Jewish peddler, this time of words and ideas." It was not an image he liked or intended to live with, but it was almost all he had in 1934.[37]

The one article on East Asian affairs that Sokolsky published in 1934 contained an interesting analysis of Soviet-Japanese tensions over the Chinese Eastern Railway. He wrote off the war scare as propaganda by means of which the Japanese military justified larger appropriation demands, arguing correctly that the Russians would rather sell than fight. He whipped Stimson and the League of Nations once more for allegedly strengthening the hands of the Japanese military, and suggested that American recognition of the Soviet Union had also helped the Japanese Army by providing a semblance of reality to their fears of a Soviet-American alliance.[38]

In 1935, Sokolsky created a bit of a stir with an article entitled "Why

37. Memorandum of conversation between Maxwell Hamilton et al. and Stanley Reed (Reconstruction Finance Corporation), May 25, 1933, SD 893.48/729; Memorandum of conversation between Hornbeck and Soong, August 8, 1933, SD 711.93/302; Sokolsky to Hornbeck, undated, Hornbeck Papers; Sokolsky to Lamont, January 9, 1934, 131–8, TWL ms.

38. "The Russo-Japanese War Myth," *American Mercury,* XXXII (May 1934), 80–86.

Fight Japan?'' Sokolsky's thesis was that there was no economic basis for conflict between Japan and the United States, no substantive issues to divide them. He warned the United States not to intensify Japanese fears, presumably via Stimsonian threats, and asked the Japanese to abandon nineteenth-century imperialism and militarism. He felt the Japanese could afford to play by Wilsonian rules now that they controlled Manchuria. Other than implicit acceptance of Japan's hegemony over Manchuria, the article did not seem notably pro-Japanese. The *New York Times* preview indicated Sokolsky's concern over anti-Japanese sentiment in the United States and repeated his argument that short of the failure of the New Deal, the United States would have no reason to compete with Japan, no reason to go to war. But in China, the English-language, Chinese-owned and edited *China Critic* published an editorial attacking Sokolsky and the attack was reprinted in the *China Weekly Review*. The editorial referred to Sokolsky's days with the *Far Eastern Review* and tried to establish guilt through his association with George Bronson Rea who, by 1935, was employed by the Japanese as Manchukuo's unofficial representative in Washington. The writer was indignant about Sokolsky's failure to indicate that Japan's government was under military control, and to indict Japan for sabre-rattling. He had always been, or so it was alleged, unusually understanding toward the Japanese.[39]

In the years that followed Sokolsky wrote occasionally on Asian affairs and frequently referred to his years in China, but by 1935 he was well on his way to acquiring a new identity. For ''Why Fight Japan?'' *Current History* had identified him as a student and observer of *American* life who for many years had been a Far Eastern correspondent of various American papers. The Sokolsky who served many causes in China had already faded away and in his place was emerging the self-styled apostle of capitalism and Jeffersonian democracy—enemy of the New Deal. Increasingly he lectured and wrote on domestic subjects, as an ex-radical who understood the evils of radicalism and appreciated the values of the American way. And he found it profitable. As Hornbeck had said in another context, he was a clever writer and speaker. Business groups and patriotic societies enjoyed him as he attacked social security, the labor movement, and Roosevelt's alleged efforts to set up a dictatorship. By 1936 he was writing a weekly column for the *Herald Tribune* and receiving retainers from the National Association of Manufac-

39. *Current History*, XLI (February 1935), 513–20; *New York Times*, January 20, 1935, II, p. 2; ''Sokolsky on 'Why Fight Japan?' '' *China Weekly Review*, March 16, 1935, GES ms.

turers and the American Iron and Steel Institute. He had remarried and begun a new family—a new life in America.[40]

Roger Greene's personal crisis was less related to affairs of state than to circumstances revealing of his character and style. In all his work, from the years with the consular service through those with the China Medical Board, he had shown a tendency to force those with whom he worked to demonstrate their confidence in him. He had twice threatened resignation from the consular service and had been begged to stay. In 1930 he had resigned from the Harvard-Yenching Board of Trustees when the Institute took an action against his advice. Once again, he was begged to withdraw his resignation and the authorities at Harvard promised to reorganize their operations to suit his taste. But his luck had run out. In the early 1930s tension began to build between Greene as acting director of Peking Union Medical College and his superiors in New York, both at the China Medical Board and the Rockefeller Foundation. Part of the problem stemmed from normal pulling and hauling over budgets, grimmer in the depression years than before. Part of the problem centered around the poor relationship that had developed between Greene and John D. Rockefeller, III. Greene was contemptuous of Rockefeller's involvement in China Medical Board activities and would do nothing to appease the young man's sense of his own importance. But there was also a serious difference between Greene and the elder Rockefeller about the religious atmosphere at the medical school, about the future of the Department of Religion.[41]

In 1916, when John D. Rockefeller, Jr. established Peking Union Medical College, he acquired the facilities of a British missionary medical school and declared his intention to retain its religious atmosphere. The Department of Religion served to fulfil that pledge. Greene, however, had come to believe that the effort to instill Christianity in medical and nursing students was an anachronism in modern China. As Chinese nationalism grew more intense in the 1920s and 1930s, students and faculty both objected to the Department of Religion. Greene, under budgetary pressure, viewed religious training as the most expendable element in the curriculum. As always he fought tenaciously for his beliefs but, for the first time in his career, he suf-

40. *New York Times,* December 20, 1935, March 12, March 17, April 23, and May 12, 1937; *New Republic,* XCIII(December 29, 1937), 211; *New York Times,* July 22, 1938, p. 8.

41. Greene to Dean Wallace B. Donham, Harvard, December 24, 1930, RSG ms; Ferguson, *CMB and PUMC,* 70–101.

fered the shattering experience of losing a major confrontation. To be right was not sufficient when opposing the Rockefellers, both father and son, over the direction of an organization whose existence depended upon their philanthropy.[42]

In March 1933, the Director of the Division of Medical Education for the Foundation, Alan Gregg, wrote from New York to try to give Greene a sense of how he appeared to the people at the home office—at the China Medical Board and at the Rockefeller Foundation. Greene had asked for a frank appraisal and Gregg appears to have responded. Greene had "given the impression of a man with reserved bearing, an intensity of feeling, a sense of personal responsibility for the PUMC, and conspicuous singleness of purpose." Some people suspected "coldness . . . intolerance . . . delusions as to your own importance . . . ruthlessness." He insisted that Greene's value was appreciated and that the New York offices had confidence in him, but warned that "just as you have made this confidence in you, so you can diminish it: in the degree that you insist it be absolute you subtract from its completeness." To many that met Greene he seemed the archetypal New Englander: austere, righteous, and rigid. He was highly principled and uncompromising. As Gregg concluded, he was "not easy to deal with"—he was not the model organization man.[43]

Gregg's letter did not help. Greene's troubles mounted through 1933 and 1934. When he returned to New York in mid-1934, he was asked to resign. But the decision to rid themselves of Greene had been made by the Rockefellers, the heads of the Foundation, and the China Medical Board, without consulting anyone closely connected to him. When his resignation was announced it created an uproar at Peking Union Medical College and among prominent Chinese and American educators in China. The Rockefeller Foundation was apparently unprepared for the intensity of the protest and for a few months Greene dared to hope that the decision might be reversed. He formulated conditions under which he might stay and asked his brother to prepare a campaign on his behalf. The Chinese Minister to the United States, Greene's old friend Alfred Sao-ke Sze, personally went to New York to protest against Greene's resignation, arguing that Greene was important "to the future of North China as a symbol of American interests

42. Ferguson, *CMB and PUMC,* 89–101.

43. Gregg to Greene, March 20, 1933, RSG ms; See also L. C. Goodrich transcript, Oral History Collection, Columbia University.

and confidence in the political stability of that region." But Gregg and Jerome Greene convinced him that the end had come—that the mounting pressure might force the Rockefellers to yield, but they would not change their minds about Greene. To stay on would be detrimental to the College, the China Medical Board, and everyone involved. Roger Greene had to go in order to bring the episode to an end—and he was devastated.[44]

If only to show the depths from which he would later rise, it is worth seeing where Greene found himself at 2:00 A.M. on the morning of February 9, 1935. With no prospects for other employment, with his illusions of being able to rise taller from this resignation destroyed, he wrote to George E. Vincent, President of the China Medical Board and the man he held responsible: "I had always felt that you were my friend; you had been a guest in my house for a considerable time. . . . In the fifties, at a time when to most men old age begins to seem rather near, when I had at last found a place in which I could take full satisfaction in my work, and was apparently giving satisfaction to those most intimately associated with me, you seem to be acting with those who are trying to displace me. I feel that leaving this post at my time of life and in the present state of the world, is like the ending of my active life. And I am as a man who has been suddenly shot by a trusted friend." After recounting his contributions to the college, the suffering, the sacrifices, and the successes, he asked: "How can you have done this to me . . . I do not know whether there is any work left for me in life."[45] And in June 1935 he officially departed from his beloved Peking Union Medical College.

Greene had too much strength to be broken, however, even by the loss of much of what constituted his identity at the age of 54. The hard core of his personality remained, and within a few months he had concluded that he had done what had to be done. Trouble with the Rockefellers could have been avoided only if he had "boot-licked and pussyfooted" like two of his associates, "who might as well be dead as far as their independent personalities are concerned." It was time for building a new life and he wrote, with obvious difficulty, to Nelson Johnson and Joseph Grew, to express interest in a high-ranking position in the Department of State. To Hornbeck he wrote a long, thoughtful letter on reaching an accommodation with Japan—which

44. Ferguson, *CMB and PUMC*, 102–9; Roger to Jerome Greene, November 8, 1934, and Gregg to Greene, November 10, 1934, RSG ms.

45. Greene to Vincent, February 9, 1935, RSG ms.

may have been related to his interest in a post at State. Hornbeck responded seriously to Greene's ideas, but a job opportunity never developed.[46]

For the next few years Greene was unemployed, living off a generous pension from the Rockefeller Foundation and perhaps some savings, and remaining involved in both philanthropic and political affairs. His connections with the China Foundation—an educational organization overseeing the use of remitted Boxer Indemnity funds—enabled him to travel back to China and the focus of his interests never left East Asia. Unlike Sokolsky, he could not become a student of American affairs. From his earliest years growing up in Japan he had been conscious of being an alien. This childhood sense of being outside of the community combined with lack of association with other Americans left him feeling even more isolated when he returned to the United States—and in 1935 he wrote, "that feeling has never entirely passed."[47]

Greene continued his conversations and correspondence with Chinese cabinet officers and diplomats, with American officials, especially Johnson but Hornbeck also, and scholars like Leighton Stuart and Frederick Field. These men and the media occasionally asked for his opinions on a wide range of matters relating to China, to American-East Asian relations, and to world affairs generally. He was eager to discuss medical education in China and particularly to defend Peking Union Medical College against charges of being elitist, unrelated to Chinese realities. He understood China's need for an enormous quantity of doctors, but insisted that large numbers of schools for something like present-day paramedical training would still require well-educated teachers. He insisted that the college had done more than any other institution "to bring the benefits of modern public health and medical practice to the people at large." Denying that its graduates were materialistic, he noted how few worked in the cities and pointed to the Tinghsien experiment, where some of them were making "the most original contribution" to rural health work in China.[48]

46. Roger to Kate Greene, March 24, 1936, RSG ms; Greene to Johnson, October 10, 1934, Johnson Papers; Grew to Greene, October 29, 1934, Greene to Hornbeck, December 12, 1935, and Hornbeck to Greene, December 14, 1935, RSG ms.

47. Greene to Johnson, February 21, 1936, and to Mrs. Harry B. Price, January 30, 1935, RSG ms.

48. Greene to Wang Shih-chieh, August 4, 1935, to Y. T. Tsur, September 8, 1936, to Nelson Johnson, April 13, 1936, to Leighton Stuart, October 5, 1935, to Frederick Field, July 24, 1936, RSG ms; Greene to Johnson, February 21 and June 10, 1936, Johnson Papers; "Report of Acting Director for the Year 1934–1935," (PUMC) RSG ms.

Greene was highly optimistic about China's progress generally in the mid-1930s. Recommending the withdrawal of the American Legation guard and an end of extraterritoriality, he argued that Chinese law had developed to the point where Americans received better treatment in Chinese courts than in Russian or South American. His estimation of Chiang Kai-shek became much more favorable and he thought Chiang was doing a good job of pacifying Kiangsi and Szechuan—that Chiang had developed a genuine concern for his country and his people. He saw promising signs of government-supported flood control and rural reconstruction projects. But China needed peace, order, for all these healthy developments to continue and Greene could not approve of student demonstrations demanding confrontation with Japan. He accepted his friend Hu Shih's contention that Chiang was right to suppress anti-Japanese activities because China was not yet strong enough to fight. More time was needed to build a modern nation. Asked to join a group of prominent Americans including John Dewey and Albert Einstein in protest against the arrest of anti-Japanese demonstrators in China, Greene refused.[49]

The crisis over Manchuria obviously had a profound effect on Greene's thinking about international politics. The basic problem seemed to be to find a way to contain Japan without involving the United States in a war. Greene unquestionably favored American cooperation with the League of Nations, arguing that there was no other way to prevent wars. He did not like the neutrality legislation that Congress passed in 1935, favoring plans that gave Roosevelt discretion to use economic sanctions against an aggressor. He reasoned that in most cases "a thoroughgoing economic boycott should be sufficient to stop the war without any collision except between the offender and the nearest states and the aggressor would have little chance of success." But he also had a realistic sense of public attitudes in the United States, of the unwillingness of the American people to accept any responsibility for maintenance of the peace of East Asia. He preferred, under these circumstances, to have American statesmen sit back quietly. Like Lamont and Sokolsky he concluded that protests not backed by force had no moral effect, serving only to irritate the Japanese, perhaps worsening the situation.

49. Diary of William Phillips, November 14, 1933, Papers of William Phillips, Houghton Library, Harvard University; Greene to Embree, May 25, 1934, to Kate Greene, May 12, 1936 and May 22, 1936, to Alan Gregg, June 25, 1936, to Y. T. Tsur, September 8, 1936, to Professor William H. Kilpatrick, January 4, 1937, RSG ms.

Unlike Lamont and Sokolsky, Greene thought that the League and the United States should have been willing to use economic sanctions in 1931, but he also considered it basically healthy for the Chinese to realize that they had to rely on themselves. Similarly, he believed the loss of Manchuria might prove salutary, as it had increased national solidarity in China and left Chiang with a more manageable area to govern.[50]

Greene hoped the United States would find quiet ways to help China and to improve relations with Japan. He wanted to see an end to the privileges of the unequal treaties in China, continued efforts to repair the damage American silver policy had done to the Chinese economy, encouragement of Japanese exports to the United States, and an end of discrimination against Chinese and Japanese in American immigration policy. He hoped the American government would make a long-range effort to educate its people to join the rest of the world in submitting *all* disputes to judicial adjustment and to assist in enforcing these decisions by economic and political means. In 1936, however, he thought that if war broke out in East Asia the United States would have to remain neutral because of the political impossibility of joining in a League program of sanctions—"Which I should consider highly desirable if they were politically feasible." Early in 1937, the *Literary Digest* asked a number of congressmen, Henry Stimson, and Roger Greene about a reported Anglo-American understanding in the Pacific. Greene spoke emphatically in favor of such an understanding as a force for peace, warning that "isolated, we move inevitably toward a choice between intolerable humiliation and war."[51]

Much as he would have preferred to be in Peking or Washington, Greene was still finding a meaningful existence working out of his home in Worcester, Massachusetts. He was by no means a forgotten man. Among men to whom the affairs of East Asia were of constant importance, Greene's reputation was undiminished, his opinions still sought and respected. But he was restless, anxious to answer a call, be more active, be in the main stream. The years of semiretirement brought little satisfaction.

By contrast, Thomas Lamont suffered some indignities as the President railed against economic royalists and congressmen blamed J. P. Morgan and Company for the depression and American involvement in the World War,

50. Greene to Johnson, February 21, 1936, Johnson Papers; Greene to Field, July 24, 1936, to Leighton Stuart, October 8, 1935, to Hornbeck, December 12, 1935, RSG ms.

51. Greene to Field, July 24, 1936, RSG ms; *Literary Digest,* CXXV (February 19, 1937), 2.

but he continued to represent the country's most distinguished banking firm, continued to wield great power, continued to receive solicitations from the Department of State. His primary interest in East Asia during the mid-1930s was the Consortium. He wanted to be rid of it. The American Group was convinced that there was no money to be made out of China and that continuation of the organization was not worth the bother or the expense. After the Banking Act of 1933 prohibited banks of deposit from underwriting or offering securities, Lamont explained to Hornbeck that his own firm and most members of the American Group could no longer participate in loan operations even if they were to become feasible on a business basis. But for years Hornbeck hemmed him in, keeping the Consortium alive, at least on paper.[52]

Within the Consortium, the British Group had been unhappy about a loan to purchase American cotton and wheat extended by the Reconstruction Finance Corporation to the Chinese government in 1933. Addis noted that he had not anticipated competition from any of the *governments* sponsoring the Consortium agreement. While the RFC loan did not violate the agreement, he feared that the Chinese would be diverting income from the reconstruction and development projects the Consortium had been formed to finance. But friction did not develop among the banking groups. Lamont and representatives of the Japanese and French groups agreed that Chinese revenues might better have been directed toward repayment of defaulted loans, but all reluctantly accepted the American claim that the loan was humanitarian in intent.[53]

The wellspring of mutual affection and esteem with which Addis and Lamont regarded each other dried quickly in 1936 when Addis obtained more advantageous terms for British bondholders than the Chinese were willing to offer their American creditors. Lamont angrily threatened to withdraw the American Group from the Consortium, but the threat alone sufficed to move the Department of State to support him with representations to the British government. Addis not only outmaneuvered Lamont on this occasion but followed up by negotiating a large loan for railway construction with the Chinese government. Instead of sharing it with the other groups, Addis next

52. Lamont to Johnson, June 20, 1934, 184–10, TWL ms; Lamont to Hornbeck, October 11, 1934, SD 893.51/5931.

53. Addis to Orde with enclosure, June 9, 1933, FO 405/272/244; J. P. Morgan and Company for American Group to Secretary of State, June 16, 1933, SD 893.48/750.

tried to rescind the Consortium resolution providing that the Chinese would be free to make purchases with loan proceeds on the open market. He insisted that the British government would not permit the loan without provision that the proceeds be spent entirely in Great Britain. Before Lamont or the Department of State could obtain satisfaction on this demand, clearly contrary to the spirit and letter of the Consortium agreement, the British indicated that, reluctant as they were to break up the Consortium, they wanted the business which the Chinese were willing to give to them but *not* to their partners. The British government quickly indicated that it supported the British Group. Sir Alexander Cadogan, Under Secretary of State for Foreign Affairs, called in the counsellor of the American Embassy to explain that Chinese insistence on doing business with the British alone, combined with British law requiring foreign loans to be expended in Great Britain, forced the British government to conclude that the Consortium agreement should be dissolved. Cadogan contended that the Consortium had become an obstacle to the reconstruction of China. An alternative was needed that would permit members liberty of action while somehow finding a way to maintain the desired cooperation among the powers and China.[54]

While the British Foreign Office resolved to withdraw from the Consortium, Addis and Lamont toyed with ideas for a revised Consortium. Lamont was interested in having the American Group transferred to "associate membership," presumably with less responsibility, financial and otherwise. But Hornbeck and Secretary Cordell Hull apparently were resigned to accepting dissolution, providing it was clearly understood by the British that the United States valued the agreement and that Great Britain accepted responsibility for destroying it. Conceivably the reply to Cadogan, defending the Consortium and complaining about inconsistencies in the British position, was intended to embarrass the British into backing off from the proposed dissolution. President Roosevelt intervened, however, to prevent the State Department draft from being sent. He struck out the paragraphs defending the Consortium and complaining about the British, and indicated his willingness to accept Cadogan's argument. Cadogan and Eden were gratified by

54. Lamont to Hornbeck, March 20, 1936, SD 893.51/6125; Hornbeck to Lamont, April 13, 1936, SD 893.51/6131; Hornbeck memorandum of conversation with Lamont, December 29, 1936, SD 893.51/6274; Hornbeck memorandum of conversation with Mitchell of J. P. Morgan and Company, February 2, 1937, SD 893.51/6286; Atherton (London) to Secretary of State, February 10, 1937, SD 893.51/6296. See also Eden to Knatchbull-Hugessen (Peking), February 23, 1937, FO 405/276/14.

the American reply, but remained concerned about the American attitude and were fearful of having irritated Washington.[55]

With no regrets, Lamont headed for London to work on formal dissolution in March 1937. When the President of U.S. Steel wrote to him of the need for an organization to finance the export of material and equipment for Chinese railroads, Lamont agreed, but returned to his earlier formula: ". . . unless our Government steps in I don't see the answer. How about the Export-Import Bank?" Early in May, Lamont reported that Addis wanted to continue cooperation, but agreed with his government's position on dissolution of the Consortium. Lamont and Addis were exploring the possibility of a new, "loosely-knit" group to try to continue cooperation, but they would keep the Consortium's executive council in existence until the governments involved completed their discussions of dissolution. When the council met, it agreed to waive the provisions that prevented the British Group from undertaking the loan independently. To the British Foreign Office Addis reported that he dared to go no further because "a general resolution in favor of dissolution by mutual consent would have been lost." Lamont's report to the Department of State indicated that he had pressed for dissolution and had overcome the opposition of the Japanese representative. The next step was for the governments concerned to agree to dissolution.[56]

Lamont returned to the United States and in June advised Hornbeck that the British Foreign Office assumed that the United States approved dissolution of the Consortium on the condition that an arrangement be worked out to keep alive "the Consortium principle." Hornbeck replied that there had been no condition to American approval of the British request. Blandly he declared that the agreement had been worked out among the banking groups—not the governments—and it was for the bankers to dissolve on whatever terms they wished. The United States merely joined the Foreign Office in hoping that the principle might be kept alive. Further efforts by Hornbeck to worry the British over their responsibility for the demise of the Consortium were blocked by Sumner Welles in July 1937. Lamont looked

55. SD 893.51/6286; Hornbeck memorandum of conversation with Lamont, February 16, 1937, SD 893.51/6303; Hull to Roosevelt, March 2, 1937, SD 893.51/6307; Roosevelt memorandum for Hull, March 11, 1937, SD 893.51/6329; Bingham to Secretary of State, March 15, 1937, SD 893.51/6330; Eden to Knatchbull-Hugessen, April 26, 1937, FO/405/276/35.

56. Lamont to Hornbeck, enclosing George C. Scott to Lamont, March 19, 1937, SD 893.77/3068; Lamont to Hornbeck, May 5, 1937, SD 893.51/6367; Addis to Orde with enclosure, May 10, 1937, FO 405/276/46.

forward to the end of "a perfectly anomalous and amorphous creature"—but he had to wait eight more years. By July 1937 the Japanese army was engaged in full-scale hostilities in China and Hornbeck was able to prevail.[57]

Despite the submerged tensions over the Consortium, or perhaps to strengthen his position with the Department of State, Lamont maintained an extensive correspondence with Hornbeck on other affairs of mutual interest. Japanese and Chinese leaders were forever paying court and Lamont frequently sent memoranda of his conversations or copies of his correspondence to Hornbeck who passed some items on to Hull. Lamont wrote occasionally to Nelson Johnson in Peiping and once to Joseph Grew in Tokyo—to express outrage at Prince Konoe's indiscreet report of Lamont's confidential remarks to him.[58]

To his Japanese contacts Lamont urged prudence, advising them not to close the door in China to American trade, not to push the United States into a naval race, not to mistake the peaceful attitude of the United States for a willingness to brook any affront the Japanese military might care to offer. He also indicated that he did not believe the United States would be willing to undertake China's defense. To other Americans he continued to stress his pre-1931 contentions that American interests in East Asia were best served by cooperation with Japan. To Johnson he wrote that he would be sorry to see China controlled by Japan, but if the Chinese could not protect themselves from exploitation or aggression, they could not expect anyone else to come to their rescue. "Certainly," he added, "America is not going to court trouble by any quixotic attempt to checkmate Japan in Asia."[59]

Within the Department of State, Roger Greene's optimism about China's progress was not shared in 1936. Americans stationed in China were troubled by Chiang's attempt to arrogate dictatorial powers and by the apparent lack of social conscience or constructive programs among his closest

57. Hornbeck memorandum of conversation with Lamont, June 29, 1937, Welles to Hull, and Welles to Hornbeck, July 17, 1937, SD 893.51/6414; Lamont to Hornbeck, July 23, 1937, SD 893.51/6428.

58. See for example Lamont to Hornbeck, October 15, 1934, 187–2, and to Grew, September 28, 1934, 187–28, TWL ms.

59. Lamont to Hornbeck, October 15, 1934, 187–2, to Fuksi Eigo, September 13, 1935, 187–32, Memorandum by Martin Egan for Lamont's use at Council on Foreign Relations Round Table, October 31, 1935, 145–2, TWL ms; George Blakeslee to Hornbeck, December 4, 1935, Hornbeck Papers; Lamont to Johnson, May 19, 1936, Johnson Papers.

associates. They were appalled by the continued disunity among Chinese politicians and the continued Kuomintang-Communist struggle—while the Japanese tightened their control over north China. After the Sian incident, however, when Chiang was arrested and freed after agreeing to rapprochement with the Communists in a united front against Japan, there was a great surge of national unity in China—and men like Hornbeck and Johnson became less skeptical about China's future.

In July 1937, the Chinese and Japanese governments allowed an incident at the Marco Polo Bridge to develop into a major confrontation and the second Sino-Japanese War began in earnest. Although these events were remote from what had become his primary concerns, Sokolsky was moved from time to time to comment on them. He found Chiang useful as a club with which to beat Roosevelt. Just before the election of 1936, explaining why he was voting for Alf Landon, he wrote: "I saw Chiang Kai-shek rise to power establishing a people's government—and no man ever forged the shackles of a personal despotism more swiftly and fiercely upon any people." In a review article for the *New York Times,* published later that month, he criticized the Chinese for doing nothing to save themselves, for indulging in selfish civil wars while hoping some outside agency would rescue them from Japan. But only a few weeks later, when Chiang was taken prisoner at Sian, Sokolsky was fulsome in his praise of Chiang's ability, judgment, and "his capacity to use every instrument of power to the advantage of his country." Chiang, he contended, had done as good a job as could be done, making more progress in ten years than China had made in the previous century. Similarly, in an article on the Soongs published early in 1937, Sokolsky praised Chiang as a great patriot and downgraded his old friend T. V. to the status of one who "might have been" great had it not been for his jealousy of Chiang. However else his new image of Chiang can be explained, it was clear that Sokolsky had given up on the Soong connection.[60]

When full-scale fighting began in July, Sokolsky professed to be unmoved. Fighting in Asia no longer involved him emotionally: "the only fight that stirs my blood is the fight over the Supreme Court." He hoped the Chinese would be able to hold Peiping, but if they weren't willing to die for it, "then it means very little indeed and the Japanese might as well have it."

60. *New York Herald Tribune,* November 2 and December 21, 1936, GES ms; *New York Times,* November 29, 1936, IV, p. 9; "The Soongs of China," *Atlantic Monthly,* CLIX (February 1937) 185–88.

In August Sokolsky explained that Chiang had always tried, wisely, to avoid direct clashes with the Japanese but the people of China would no longer tolerate nonresistance to Japanese aggression. And there would be no outside help for him. The Russians were trapped by the anti-Comintern pact, and the United States went in for "model letter writing" but never acted. "Chiang must go it alone."[61]

When Roosevelt gave his "quarantine speech," Sokolsky insisted that the Japanese would not be frightened off. Expansion on the continent of Asia was essential to the development of Japan and the Japanese "prefer to take their chances with the devil to remain a first-rate power." In December, he suggested that Japanese control over Manchuria and China was the only way to stop Soviet expansion and echoed Japanese concern over Chiang's ties to the Chinese Communists after Sian. Now that Sokolsky was a spokesman for American capitalism, the ambivalence of his earlier attitude toward the Chinese Communists vanished and the men he had described in 1932 as the "best elements in the nationalist movement" were now the scourge of China. But his central message to the American people was that the war in Asia was nothing for them to be concerned about.[62]

In terms of material benefits to the United States, trade and investment, Roger Greene did not dissent from Sokolsky's analysis. In an address in mid-July 1937, he conceded that the Japanese occupation of large parts of China would not necessarily injure American trade interests. Indeed, the extension of Japanese influence in China, by hastening the process of modernization, might lead to an increase in American exports there. But Greene did not share Sokolsky's values. Unlike Sokolsky's conception of "realism," Greene's views were remarkably similar to those pronounced by Henry Stimson during the Manchurian crisis. Despite the absence of immediate economic benefits, he thought it worth stopping Japanese aggression for the "cause of peace," to avoid a long period of disorder ruinous to both China and Japan and ultimately to American trade with both. As he was wont to do whenever he had an audience he asked for an end to special privileges in China, equality of treatment for all foreigners in the United States, fairer trade and immigration opportunities for the Japanese. He warned that the

61. *New York Herald Tribune,* August 2 and 16, 1937, GES ms.

62. *Ibid.,* October 18 and December 6, 1937; "Communism Under Four Flags," *New Outlook,* CLXI (November 1932), 27–31; *New York Herald Tribune,* December 27, 1937, GES ms.

Chinese would soon be troubled by the same kinds of issues that had vexed Japanese-American relations—and that only more pressing problems had left the Americans immune from Chinese hostility.[63]

In August Greene went to Washington to spend a day with Hornbeck and his subordinates in the Division of Far Eastern Affairs. He indicated his availability for emergency service during the crisis, but the Department did not take advantage of his offer. For the next few months, Greene's primary outlet for his views was his correspondence with friends and scholars, supplemented by an occasional speech. He brooded about the unwillingness of the American people or their government to act, not only in Asia but in Europe. He hoped that Americans would get over their false sense of being secure from foreign aggression—that the instinct of self-preservation would lead the United States to cooperate in "all international measures for bringing about a reign of law instead of a reign of force." He argued that the American people could not consider themselves truly peaceful so long as they would not even join the World Court.[64]

When Philip Jaffe, editor of *Amerasia,* asked authorities on East Asia for their attitudes and advice, Greene, despairing of American participation in the Court or the League, recommended that the United States declare its neutrality. He hoped, however, that the neutrality laws would be modified to give the president more discretion. He also argued for the inclusion of oil at the top of the list of items to be proscribed. But Greene ruled out unilateral American intervention. The Japanese did not have to be told what Americans thought of their activities in China. The American people were opposed to the use of force—and he had no desire, in any event, to give any impetus to militarism in the United States. Given American attitudes, cooperation with the League was the best that could be hoped for. To Derk Bodde, a young Sinologist, he insisted that the issues at stake in China were as important to Americans and Europeans as to the Chinese. Greene did not believe in fighting for commercial opportunities in China, but he contended that "the principle of pacific settlement of international disputes is worth fighting for." By the end of the year he was arguing against letting the Germans, Italians, and Japanese bluff the United States. It was better to risk a showdown now than to have to fight a big war alone later, when the predator na-

63. Address at Institute of Public Affairs, University of Virginia, July 17, 1937, text, RSG ms.

64. Roger to Kate Greene, August 26, 1937, to Chester N. Frazier and to John R. Ware, September 9, 1937 RSG ms.

tions would have turned their attention to Latin America. Without question, Greene had emerged as an outspoken advocate of collective security, distinguishable from the leaders of the collective security wing of the American peace movement only by his deep concern for China.[65]

Lamont watched the hostilities for two months, then began to write to high-ranking Japanese officials and powerful businessmen, indicating his displeasure with events in China. To an old acquaintance, now Ambassador to the United States, Saito Hiroshi, Lamont indicated his distress, warning that "Japan certainly is gaining no new friends." To the consul-general in New York Lamont detailed his friendship for Japan, his sympathy for her position in Manchuria, but insisted that "recent developments are quite a different matter, and I think that the worst thing a friend of Japan can do is to minimize the feeling in America in regard to them." He warned that Americans were "shocked and distressed beyond measure at the manner in which the Japanese military have conducted their operations in and around Shanghai." Lamont insisted that Americans put no stock in Japanese apologies for their actions and that the results would be unhappy for the people of Japan. In a letter to Kadano Chokyuro, copied for Ambassador Saito, he complained of "the cruel and horrifying bombings which the Japanese high command has been guilty of permitting." The bombings troubled Lamont deeply and he wrote several letters deploring them, responding angrily to Japanese who tried to defend their government's policies.[66]

In October, Lamont followed Roosevelt's quarantine speech with a major foreign policy address of his own—carried on page one of all the New York and Chicago newspapers, widely circulated among the elite in the United States and Great Britain, reported in newspapers all over the eastern half of the country. His topic was "Is the European World Moving Towards or Away From General War?" He answered "away," hoping that British and French appeasement might "possess the seeds of final and peaceful composition." About five percent of the speech was devoted to the situation in East Asia and he argued *against* economic sanctions, against a joint Anglo-American embargo on the sale of oil to Japan. He contended that economic sanctions were a form of warfare, and that they never worked unless supported by a blockade. If not successful they were simply irritants uniting

65. Greene to Philip Jaffe, September 13, 1937; to Bodde, November 13, 1937; to Alan Gregg, November 12, 1937; to Capt. and Mrs. C. C. Brown, December 17, 1937, RSG ms.

66. Lamont to Saito, September 7, 1937, to K. Wagasugi, September 17, 1937; and to Kadano, September 24, 1937, 188–4, to Araki, September 27, 1937, 188–5, to Shibusawa Masao, December 1, 1937, 188–6, TWL ms.

the people against whom they were applied. If they did work, economic sanctions constituted a cruel form of warfare against noncombatants. American interests in Asia he deemed inconsiderable—and seemed to suggest that responsibility for Asia would fall upon Great Britain. Joseph Grew, for one, thought Lamont might be arguing to allow Britain to protect her own interests and hoped doubtfully that Lamont and Morgan might be moving toward his own Anglophobia. More likely, Lamont's intent was to suggest that sanctions would provoke Japan, that Great Britain would have to bear the brunt of Japan's anger—and that the British already had their hands full in Europe.[67]

Despite his opposition to sanctions, perhaps wise given the discrepancy between the military preparedness of Japan and the United States in 1937, Lamont had unquestionably ceased to be tolerant of Japanese expansion into China. When Mrs. John D. Rockefeller, Jr. wrote to ask him if it was true he was still lending money to the Japanese, he denied the charge emphatically. He assured her that he knew of "no one who is lending money to the Japanese Government now and of no one who has been doing so for a long time past." For Lamont the love affair with Japan was over. Sadly, he expressed his sorrow that "the Liberal element in Japan has been so completely blanketed by the militarists carrying on their outrageous aggression." What remained was not the Japan Thomas Lamont had defended since 1920 but rather the Japan he had been so sure his friends had buried.[68]

Sokolsky, Greene, and Lamont each recognized their country's unwillingness to become involved in the tragic fighting in East Asia. Sokolsky and Lamont, their lives and work leading them to stress concrete, material interests, were saddened by the atrocities, by reports of human misery, but saw no reason for their own country to become involved. Greene came out of a different tradition, despising the market place and its material values, ever ready to fight for a principle he perceived to be at stake. And, though he like Sokolsky had returned involuntarily to the land of his birth, Greene never really completed the transition, never surrendered the identity that had been formed in East Asia. Greene was a genuine internationalist, readily able to transcend the exclusive interests of his own country for a more abstract conception of world peace—even if it meant fighting to maintain that vision of peace.

67. Text of speech, October 22, 1937, clippings, 144–8, TWL ms; Grew Diary, October 14 (?), 1937, Grew Papers.
68. Lamont to Mrs. Rockefeller, December 30, 1937, 188–6, TWL ms.

# 8

# THE UNITED STATES AND THE PACIFIC WAR

IN China the Japanese went on bombing cities, blockaded the coast, sank the U.S.S. *Panay,* took Shanghai, Nanking, Canton, and Hankow. On and on they pressed, with European and American protests to no avail. In Europe, too, the situation grew grimmer as Nazi Germany annexed Austria and moved toward Czechoslovakia. Thomas Lamont and George Sokolsky did not like what they saw happening in the rest of the world but they continued to define realism as acquiescence in German and Japanese aggression.

Writing to Nelson Johnson, who had become Ambassador to China when the legation was raised to embassy status in 1937, Lamont reported overwhelming American sympathy with China and his own disillusionment with Japan. Whatever the basis of his earlier friendship with Japanese liberal leaders, however defensible the Manchurian operations might have been, he deemed Japan's present aggression to be totally without justification. No longer able to listen to his remaining friends in Japan, he called upon the Lord to sink the Japanese islands and to strike the entire Japanese army with one bolt of lightning. But if the Lord would not act, neither should the United States. Lamont noted the existence of a boycott movement among "so-called liberal groups," but indicated that neither he nor Secretary of State Hull approved of private means of warfare. Lamont thought a boycott—he probably meant an embargo as well—would be silly: ineffective against Japan and a source of problems for American manufacturers and labor. In late December 1938, during an exchange with Walter Lippmann, Lamont explained that he, too, had a "human longing for China to win." But he continued his opposition to loans or other assistance to China on the grounds that neither the United States nor Great Britain would support China to the bitter end. The ultimate results would be demoralizing, presumably to the Chinese. Assuming that the United States did not have enough at stake in East Asia to sustain a long term effort there, Lamont argued that it was best not to begin.[1]

Sokolsky, plagued by the revelations of Senate investigators that he received retainers from the National Association of Manufacturers and the American Iron and Steel Institute as he metamorphosed into a "one-man intellectual front for conservative capital," still found time to muse about world affairs. His position on the war in Asia was clear. The United States must not intervene, must not become engaged in a conflict with Japan. He liked the calm way in which Roosevelt handled the *Panay* affair. But on two matters Sokolsky took stands not entirely consistent with his desire to avoid trouble with Japan. After the Japanese sank the *Panay,* he argued *against* evacuating Americans from China, against elimination of the American military presence. Not only did he extol the work of American missionaries there and warn that the withdrawal of American forces would be viewed as cowardice, as a green light for the fascists, but Sokolsky of all people called upon Americans to transcend materialism! He insisted it was important to have "a sense of right" and that this sense of right required retention of American forces and American missionaries in China. Despite Sokolsky's plea, a *Fortune* poll in April 1938 (three months after he wrote) suggested a marked public preference for the withdrawal of all Americans in China in the face of Japanese attacks.

The second issue on which Sokolsky was willing to risk Japan's wrath was in the realm of relief activities in China's behalf. He supported the efforts of a missionary friend, George Fitch, to obtain assistance for Chinese sufferers. The United States, he argued, owed China a great debt for encouraging China to take costly stands without providing the support implicit in the encouragement. Sokolsky called for aid to China by charitable contributions through missionaries—not through political organizations. His column

1. Lamont to Johnson, February 26, 1938, 184–14, to Lippmann, December 29, 1938, 105–3, TWL ms.

was reprinted and distributed by the Board of Foreign Missions and by the United Lutheran Church in America.[2]

When Lamont and Sokolsky viewed European affairs there was a similar response to the appeasement of Hitler. In July 1938, Lamont contended that Chamberlain's approach was sound "when he says that he does not relish having three wars on his hands at the same time, one in Spain, one in Czechoslovakia, one in the Far East." He insisted that Chamberlain's critics had no constructive solution to offer as an alternative. When the terms of the Munich agreement reached him, Lamont congratulated Roosevelt for his part, and told Hull that he thought Chamberlain had done the best job possible. He thought that the agreement provided a "chance to work gradually for a broader peace settlement in Europe and in the world generally." Sokolsky went still further, greeting the work at Munich as an "act of moral grandeur unequalled in our time."[3]

Roger Greene's thoughts were running in very different channels throughout 1938. He was troubled by what he saw as a world movement toward the use of force and aggression to accomplish national ends. To him there seemed a clear link between events in Asia and those in Europe, between Japan's successes and Hitler's ambitions. Similarly, he believed that if China could somehow exhaust Japan, the effect on Germany would be beneficial. Hitler would be more cautious if Russia did not have to worry over her eastern flank and Britain's problems with Germany might be eased. The question was how to enable China to surmount the Japanese onslaught.[4]

Like Sokolsky, Greene favored relief to China and worked actively to stimulate American contributions through the Red Cross and a variety of other agencies. In these endeavors he tried to work closely with Hornbeck, keeping Hornbeck informed of his activities, asking for advice on how to approach Roosevelt, how to be useful to the Department of State. To his many other contacts he would then explain Hornbeck's views and recommend steps to have Hornbeck better informed on certain points. He wrote letters to the *New York Times,* gave speeches, participated in radio broad-

2. *New York Times,* July 22, 1938, p. 8; *Time,* 32, (August 1, 1938), 22; *New York Herald Tribune,* January 3 and May 2, 1938, GES ms; *Fortune* poll from Hadley Cantril (ed.) *Public Opinion, 1935–1946* (Princeton, 1951), 1074.

3. Lamont to Johnson, July 1, 1938, 184–15, to Hull, October 4, 1938, 209–29 TWL ms.; *New York Herald Tribune,* October 10, 1938, GES ms.

4. Roger to Jerome Greene, January 4, 1938, RSG ms.

casts, and received coverage by the *Times* when he returned in June 1938 from a visit to China.[5]

But relief efforts did not satisfy Greene and his mind returned to the idea of economic sanctions. While in China in the spring of 1938, he heard a long-time acquaintance, Edmund Stinnes, argue that Japan was the weakest link in the ring of aggressive nations, all of whom could be brought down by supporting China. The key to the Stinnes proposal was an embargo on oil, metal, and cotton shipments to Japan and a boycott of Japanese teas and silk. Greene thought the plan quite convincing but for the "determined isolationism" of the American people. He thought it would be cheaper for the United States to finance China's struggle "against the Fascist powers as represented by Japan" than to fight either Japan or Germany and Italy itself. He believed, or so he told his wife, "that if the United States had sufficient resolution to adopt this plan, and immediately to supply to China the credits which she will soon be needing badly, we should soon be freed from the necessity of expanding our navy and thereby make an enormous saving." Enroute back to the United States he stopped in Tokyo to discuss the idea with Grew, who was skeptical of public support but encouraged Greene to explore it further.[6]

After Greene returned, he discussed with friends the possibility of assisting China with credits, hampering Japan with an embargo on oil, iron, steel, and cotton. He offered the plan in public speeches and took it up with Hornbeck, others at State, and friends in military intelligence. Hornbeck and friends at the Treasury Department led him to believe that "up to the highest quarters there is a desire to help China if it can be done without stirring up too much internal criticism of our government." Hornbeck in particular wanted to act and Roosevelt agreed to see Greene in August. He was told by "Washington friends" that they could not take the initiative. They wanted him to mobilize public support first. Greene had few illusions about his ability to influence policy, but hoped to interest Roosevelt in taking some steps to educate the people—and hoped to contribute to the "cumulative effect."[7]

5. Greene to Editor, *New York Times*, published January 21 and March 7, 1938; Greene to E. C. Lobenstine, March 16, 1938, RSG ms; *New York Times*, June 15, 1938, p. 2 and July 8, 1938 p. 8.

6. Roger to Kate Greene, May 22, 1938, RSG ms.

7. Greene to Alan Gregg, June 10, 1938; to Hornbeck, June 20; from Hornbeck, July 7; to Kate Greene, July 7; to Julean Arnold and to J. B. Chevalier (American Asiatic Association), July 22; and to Robert Lim, July 26, RSG ms.

In June 1938, Frank and Harry Price, two missionaries and sons of a famous missionary to China, met with some friends and created an organization that was called the American Committee for Non-Participation in Japanese Aggression. The Committee, usually referred to as the Price Committee, was designed to conduct a campaign to stop American "assistance" to Japan. Financial support was soon forthcoming from the Chinese government. There is no evidence to prove that the formation of the organization was inspired by Chinese authorities but given the relationship between the two and the fact that one of the founders, Earl Leaf, was employed as a propagandist for the Chinese government, this possibility cannot be ignored. In July, Greene joined the national board.[8]

Greene began his active participation on the Price Committee by urging that money received from Chinese officials be returned, warning that the organization might otherwise be viewed as the instrument of foreign propagandists and its influence greatly reduced. Harry Price, directing the committee as executive secretary, never seemed to share Greene's concern. When he received a letter from the Department of State enclosing a copy of regulations for the registration of agents of foreign principals, however, he chose to follow Greene's advice.[9]

Although the Committee was closely associated with the collective security wing of the peace movement, led by Clark Eichelberger, the founders carefully and deliberately avoided involvement in the kinds of issues that divided both the peace movement and the American people generally. Seeking the broadest possible support, they did not refer to the League, disarmament, the World Court, or collective security in their program. They asked only that the United States cease "cooperating" with Japan in its war with China—cease serving as Japan's "partner." They hoped that pacifists as well as advocates of collective security might be drawn to a movement to

8. Donald J. Friedman, *The Road from Isolation: The Campaign of the American Committee for Non-Participation in Japanese Aggression* (Cambridge, Massachusetts, 1968), 1–5; see also Helen M. Loomis to H. Price, June 28, 1938, Price to Loomis, August 10, 1938, Greene to Price, August 17 and September 7, 1938, Price to P. C. Chang, September 15, 1938, and Earl Leaf to Price, March 27, 1939, Files of the American Committee for Non-Participation in Japanese Aggression (hereafter Price Committee Papers), Littauer Center, Harvard University.

9. Greene to Price, August 17 and September 7, 1938, Price to Chang, September 15, 1938, Price Committee Papers; memorandum by Joseph C. Greene, SD 894.24/728. In May 1941 Greene was still arranging to return money the Chinese Ambassador had contributed through his American nurse. See Roger to Kate Greene, May 3 and May 19, 1941, RSG ms.

embargo the sale of war supplies to an aggressor, saying "we will not underwrite Japan's cruel war."[10]

Public opinion polls and letters received at the Department of State, the White House, and on Capitol Hill all suggest that Price, Greene, and their associates were betting on a sure thing. Americans who cared at all about the outcome of the Sino-Japanese War were almost unanimously sympathetic to China. A poll published early in June 1938 indicated that 84% of the American people wanted the United States to stop selling war materials to Japan—although 63% wanted to stop sales to China as well. In the same month, the Department of State received 1,396 telegrams, postcards, and letters—several enclosing petitions—favoring an embargo on war materials to Japan. In July, *before* the Price Committee's campaign was underway, the volume of mail demanding an embargo more than doubled. Congressional pleas for help from the Department of State indicated that people were demanding that their congressmen act to stop the flow of supplies to Japan. Mobilizing public support for the Price Committee's program would prove easy relative to the task of translating the people's will into government action.[11]

On August 1, 1938, the Committee began its campaign by mailing 22,000 copies of a booklet entitled "America's Share in Japan's War Guilt." The addressees included every congressman, selected officials of the Department of State, and key people in a variety of academic, civic, and church organizations. The booklet contained materials selected to label Japan as an aggressor, demonstrate the importance of the American sale of war supplies to Japan, and indicate widespread support for economic sanctions among congressmen, church leaders, union members, and youth groups. In the foreword were stressed not only China's suffering but the problems that helping to build the Japanese war machine posed for the United States.[12]

A few weeks after the Committee's initial offering had been circulated, Greene advised Price to change strategy. He suggested that appeals be signed by people less closely identified with China, and that they be directed

10. Friedman, *Road from Isolation,* 1–27, *passim.*

11. Cantril, *Public Opinion,* 1156; Memorandum from Office of Arms and Munitions Control, Department of State, to Division of Far Eastern Affairs, August 5, 1938, SD 894.24/288.

12. Friedman, *Road from Isolation,* 7–8; for copies, see SD 894.24/326.

toward more than humanitarian instincts. He also wanted to avoid the appearance of seeking to bring pressure to bear on the authorities. Greene explained that the question at issue concerned the interests of people in the United States and that for such a discussion, "we might well be considered prejudiced by our Chinese connections." Fearing that too many Americans had become insensitive to humanitarian appeals, he asked that they stress the argument that the defense of China would benefit the whole world by discouraging future aggression. He wanted to contend that "American self-interest is concerned, for an independent China means a better balance of power in the Pacific with consequently less need for expanding our own armaments." Finally, Greene asked that the Committee releases imply that its object was to make Roosevelt, the Department of State, and Congress aware of public opinion. For him, the difference between applying pressure and creating awareness was more than semantic. Greene's style was to work within the system, to cooperate with the authorities, to avoid the appearance of attacking from without.[13]

Greene's focus on American rather than Chinese ends and his tendency to view problems in a global rather than Asian setting created occasional friction within the Committee, most notably with Geraldine (Mrs. George) Fitch but sometimes with Harry Price as well. In October, Price wrote expressing fear that Greene's idea of seeking arbitration of the Sino-Japanese War would result in China being betrayed, as Czechoslovakia had been a few days earlier at Munich. Greene urged Price not to be "unduly anxious about the possibility of injustice to China," and mentioned that he had seen Roosevelt, who was "surprisingly well informed about the Far Eastern situation and keenly interested in it." In December, when Greene accepted the chairmanship of the Price Committee, he expressed the desire to work with and be guided by the Department of State. He thought it particularly important for the Committee to retain its good relationship with Hornbeck. Mrs. Fitch and a few others sought to condemn American policy and to fight the American government on behalf of the Chinese—with funds supplied by the latter. As a result, Price sometimes found himself in a crossfire between Greene and a "China first" group. Though he was sometimes lax and accepted suspect financial contributions, Price realized the wisdom

13. Greene to Price, August 26, 1938, RSG ms.

of Greene's course, especially if establishment figures like Henry Stimson were to play a role in the organization's campaign.[14]

Greene was very gratified by his talk with Roosevelt, who "seemed frankly eager to help China." Most of their discussion was about methods of helping and Greene stressed transportation development in southwest China, presenting Roosevelt with a memorandum on the subject. Roosevelt, indicating his sensitivity to public fears of becoming involved in a war, thought Greene's proposal valuable. Several days later he sent it on to Hull with instructions to read and return it. The whole day in Washington was enormously satisfying as Greene heard approval of his efforts from Hu Shih, now Chinese Ambassador, and Hornbeck. Another Chinese friend, K. P. Chen, was in Washington trying to get credits with which to buy trucks and Greene thought "my missionary work at the Treasury last time and with F.D.R. this time may be very much to the point." When, a few weeks later, the Chinese succeeded in getting the desired credits, Greene was lauded by friends who assumed his influence had carried the day. Modestly, he explained that there was no way to measure the effect of his remarks on Roosevelt. He noted that there were good friends of China in the Treasury as well as in the State Department and "those favorable elements, together with the confidence that our people in Washington have in Hu Shih and K. P. Chen . . . were undoubtedly the controlling factors." But having had an agreeable meeting with Roosevelt, Greene wrote to him from time to time and was assured by Felix Frankfurter that his work had Roosevelt's support.[15]

In December, Stimson and Greene accepted the position of Honorary Chairman and Chairman respectively, and discussions with Hornbeck helped to give the Committee direction. It would not work for specific legislation but would seek instead to increase public and congressional opposition to the sale of war materials to Japan. Price and Greene found the administration friendly to their objectives—as well it should have been. Early in January

14. Price to Greene, October 11, 1938, Greene to Price, October 18, 1938 and December 21, 1938, Mrs. Fitch to Price, December 15, 1939 and January 5, 1940, Price to Mrs. Fitch, December 30, 1939, Price Committee Papers; Friedman, *Road From Isolation,* 19.

15. Roger to Kate Greene, October 12, 1938, RSG ms; Roosevelt memorandum for Hull, October 14, 1938, enclosure, Papers of Franklin D. Roosevelt, PSF, China 1938, Box 19, Franklin D. Roosevelt Library; Greene, to Roosevelt, November 4, 1938, to Derk Bodde, December 28, to Price, December 30, RSG ms.

1939, the Gallup pollsters reported that by a margin of 48 to 32 percent, Americans had responded negatively to the question: "Would you favor changing our neutrality so as to give more aid to China but no aid to Japan?" Any organization that served to neutralize opposition to the idea of discriminating against aggressors might help Roosevelt to obtain the discretionary power he sought. At a minimum, by adding new sounds to the voice of the people, the Price Committee's campaign would leave the administration free to do—or not to do—as it pleased. For Hornbeck in particular it provided public support for a stiffening of American policy toward Japan, a course for which he was the principal advocate within the Department of State.[16]

In January 1939, a few days before the *New York Times* announced the organization of the American Committee for Non-Participation in Japanese Aggression, headed by Stimson, Greene, and Harry Price, Thomas Lamont launched another drive to rid himself of the burden of participation in the Consortium. At a meeting he requested with Hornbeck he explained that several members of the American Group had already withdrawn or were in the process of doing so, and that J. P. Morgan and Company did not want to carry on alone—especially without any chance of profit. Hornbeck contended that the time was inopportune, comparing the situation to the timing of the withdrawal of American troops from North China. Lamont was skeptical, pointing to past Chinese opposition to the Consortium, but Hornbeck claimed that dissolution or the withdrawal of the American Group would be viewed with regret by the Chinese and gratification by the Japanese. Lamont remained dubious, insisting that the Japanese *wanted* the Consortium kept alive, would *regret* dissolution. He ended the discussion by warning Hornbeck that the expense of continued membership was "more than we can afford to pay" and that the American Group might have to withdraw despite the attitude of the State Department.[17]

From London came support for Hornbeck's argument. British bankers were reported by the American Embassy to be resentful of the American Group's threat to withdraw. They considered the moment inopportune, of benefit to Japan and harmful to British and American interests. British

16. Price to Hornbeck, December 12, 1938, SD 894.24/604; *New York Times*, January 19, 1939, p. 3; Cantril, *Public Opinion*, 1156.

17. Hornbeck memorandum of conversation with Lamont, January 13, 1939, SD 893.51/6807.

bankers, including Addis, were reported to be irritated because the American Group was fussing over a trifling sum—one member's share of a £750 annual fee. On the basis of the cable from London, Hornbeck rallied support for his position within the Department and pressed Lamont. Hornbeck quickly deduced that if the British would waive or reduce the American Group's fee and he added "a little official urging on our part," the American Group could be stilled and the Consortium continued in existence. Sumner Welles, Undersecretary of State, authorized Hornbeck to do the "official urging" and Lamont responded as anticipated. He was agreeable if the fee required of the American Group could be reduced.[18]

Early in February, the British government officially declared that conditions in China necessitated postponement of its 1937 effort to dissolve the Consortium. The emphasis in the aide memoire was on Anglo-American cooperation and on the desirability of keeping the American Group bound by the Consortium agreement until all groups were released. The American reply indicated that the American Group had changed its position on withdrawal, desiring only administrative adjustments. The American government saw no need to discuss dissolution. Hornbeck had won his point—although it took ten months, until December 1939, for Hornbeck to generate enough pressure at the top levels of the British government and banking world to bring about the fee reduction that was Lamont's price for keeping the American Group in existence.[19]

But in 1939, events in Europe, the growing likelihood of war there, captured the attention of Americans concerned with foreign policy issues. Roosevelt worked anxiously to have the neutrality laws revised to allow for the shipment of arms on a cash basis, in the buyer's vessels, to belligerents. Had he succeeded, arms and munitions could have been sold to the European democracies but, still lacking authority to discriminate against aggres-

18. Johnson (London) to Secretary of State, January 19, 1939, SD 893.51/6780; Hornbeck memorandum of conversation with Lamont, January 20, 1939, SD 893.51/6808; Hornbeck memorandum of conversation with Arthur Anderson, January 21, 1939, SD 893.51/6809; Hornbeck memorandum of conversation with Lamont, January 23, 1939, SD 893.51/6810.

19. British Aid Memoire, February 10, 1939, and American Aid Memoire, February 16, 1939, SD 893.51/6829; Hornbeck memorandum of conversation with V. A. L. Mallet, Counselor of British Embassy, August 2, 1939, SD 893.51/6982; British Aid Memoire, August 21, 1939, and American Aid Memoire, August 29, 1939, SD 893.51/6983; Hornbeck memorandum of conversation with Lamont, December 22, 1939, SD 893.51/7206 and December 27, 1939, SD 893.51/7027; Lamont to Hornbeck with enclosures, December 27, 1939, SD 893.51/7029; Johnson (London) to Hornbeck, December 20, 1939, and Hull to Johnson, December 29, 1939, SD 893.51/7017.

sors, Roosevelt would be able to do nothing against Japan—or for China. The administration was unwilling to jeopardize its European policy by openly admitting that it would put aid to the victims of aggression ahead of neutrality.

The Price Committee opposed the bill ultimately introduced by Senator Key Pittman which not only repealed the arms embargo but also required the neutrality laws to be applied to undeclared wars. Price wrote to Pittman, Hull, and Sumner Welles to spell out the difficulties Pittman's proposal created in the Far East. He noted that the cash-and-carry stipulation presented no obstacle to Japan, but China, dependent upon credit and other nations' carriers, would be affected adversely. Unlike those whose ultimate concern was collective security or those concerned primarily with the war in Europe, China's friends could not be comforted by compromises that aided Britain and France against Hitler without commensurate support for China.[20]

Sokolsky, a Jew, had no sympathy for Nazi Germany. Unable to find American interests at stake in a European war, however, he wanted no part of aiding European nations at the expense of America's strength. Lamont, on the other hand, convinced that events in Europe *were* important to the United States, tried unsuccessfully to get Herbert Hoover to support Roosevelt's efforts against "the dictators." When Hoover chose instead to stress the importance of keeping the United States out of the next war, Lamont professed to agree, but argued that the neutrality legislation should be repealed if the dictators started a war. Perhaps, he thought, it would be better to change the law *before* a war began. Roosevelt had asked Hitler and Mussolini for assurances they did not plan war against European and Near Eastern nations and Lamont, though he opposed the scolding of dictators generally, thought Roosevelt's tactic useful.[21]

Greene was in China again during the spring of 1939, and again stopped off to see Joe Grew in Tokyo on the way home. This time the visit was less pleasant, as Grew expressed disapproval of the activities of the American Committee for Non-Participation in Japanese Aggression. Greene attributed Grew's position to Eugene Dooman, his deputy, whom he considered "a dangerous adviser for a man like Grew, who though a fine character

20. Price to Hull and to Welles, April 4, 1939, with copy of earlier letter to Pittman, SD 811.04418/375.

21. "America's Town Meeting of the Air," *New York Times*, March 10, 1939, p. 13; Lamont to Hoover, February 10 and May 18, 1939, 98–23, TWL ms.

is, after all, rather mediocre intellectually.'' Grew's diary entry was equally unflattering to Greene, whom he described as looking like ''a cadaverous undertaker.'' Grew noted that Greene was working with the ''Stimson anti-aggression committee and we radically disagreed as to the wisdom of that committee's activities.''[22]

But Greene, Price, and their followers continued their efforts to have economic sanctions imposed on Japan. The Committee worked with Hornbeck and various members of Congress to have bills introduced in both the House and Senate. Despite intensive lobbying and indications in the polls of strong public support, these efforts were unsuccessful. In the late spring and early summer, the imminence of war in Europe overshadowed concern for China and the friends of China had difficulty obtaining a hearing. Greene wrote twice to Roosevelt, reporting his own efforts, indicating his understanding of the president's need to be cautious, and asking for help with Congressional Democrats. Roosevelt's replies were cordial—''Dear Roger''—polite, and perfunctory. Concerned by Hull's temporizing, Price spoke to him on July 25.[23]

Then suddenly, on July 26, the administration served the required six months' notice of intent to abrogate the Treaty of Commerce and Navigation between the United States and Japan. Often cited as an obstacle to economic sanctions, as of January 26, 1940, the treaty could no longer be used as an excuse. Most scholars are agreed that the administration chose to terminate the treaty because of congressional pressures and public support for an embargo on the scale of war supplies to Japan. Afraid that such sharp measures might lead to a crisis with Japan at a time when the European situation appeared ominous, Hull chose termination of the treaty as the safest way to encourage the Chinese government and relieve the pressures generated by the Price Committee and other friends of China. Denunciation of the treaty,

22. Roger to Kate Greene, May 3, 1939. This letter also contains the sole reference to contacts between Greene and Sokolsky. RSG ms; Diary of Joseph C. Grew, May 5, 1939, Grew Papers.

23. Robert A. Divine, *The Illusion of Neutrality* (Chicago, 1962), 245; Friedman, *Road from Isolation*, 31–32; undated memorandum, probably July 1939, Papers of Harriet Welling, University of Chicago; Gallup polls published in June 1939 indicated 66% of respondents favored boycott against Japanese goods and 72% favored an embargo on the sale of war materials to Japan. George H. Gallup, *The Gallup Poll: Public Opinion, 1935–1971* (New York, 1972), I, 159–60; Greene to Roosevelt, May 10, 1939, and Roosevelt to Greene, May 27, 1939, RSG ms; Greene to Roosevelt, July 21, 1939, and Roosevelt to Greene, SD 893.24/695; Price to William Allen White, September 15, 1939, enclosing minutes of meeting August 30, 1939, Box 224, Papers of William Allen White, Library of Congress.

notes from Roosevelt and his secretary, and a letter declaring that Greene's introduction was responsible for Roosevelt's willingness to see a caller led Greene to consider the possibility "that perhaps I do have some influence with the President."[24]

Shortly after the administration took this step, apparently in the direction sought by the Price Committee, Greene suggested that the organization merge with Clark Eichelberger's American Union for Concerted Peace Efforts. He feared that the Price Committee's program would collide with efforts to revise the neutrality legislation. Greene personally believed that if the administration wanted to be cautious, it should carry out the embargo against Japan first, but there was always the danger that it would opt for Pittman's cash-and-carry plan. To forestall this possibility, with the attendant frustration of their hopes of helping China, he suggested that they work with Eichelberger to give Roosevelt what he really wanted: approval for discriminating against aggressors.[25]

In response to Greene, Price indicated the narrower concern of many members of the committee. Opposing the merger, he informed Greene of a general unwillingness to dilute the focus on the Far East. Earlier Mrs. Fitch had argued that the Pittman bill approached the problem backwards in that it failed to recognize that "the Far East is the crux of the whole world situation." Price, never so extreme, conceded that neutrality revision and the embargo against Japan were complementary, but he was unwilling to risk the success of the latter to work for the former. He found the quest for neutrality revision full of complications, ethnic and political, which the clear-cut issue of nonparticipation in Japanese aggression did not possess. Price feared that the Committee would lose the support of people who were not prepared to urge revision of the neutrality legislation, and he reminded Greene that their work was not yet done, that no sanctions had been imposed upon Japan. For the moment, the merger idea had to be dropped.[26]

For those whose principal interest in world affairs focused on China, there was indeed reason for concern. Eichelberger had consistently favored

24. Herbert Feis, *Road to Pearl Harbor* (Princeton, 1950), 21–23; Robert A. Divine, *The Reluctant Belligerent* (New York, 1965), 80–81; Roger to Kate Greene, July 28, 1939, RSG ms.

25. Greene to Price, August 5, 1939, Price Committee files.

26. Price to Greene, August 15, 1939, and testimony of Geraldine Fitch before the House Committee on Foreign Affairs, July 19, 1939, Price Committee files.

sanctions against Japan. But he would never sacrifice to a "China first" appeal his larger program for revision of the neutrality legislation and sanctions against all aggressors. By the summer of 1939, of the major private groups attempting to influence American foreign policy, only the Price Committee concentrated on the war in East Asia—and many of its most active members, like Greene, were increasingly distracted by the threat of war in Europe.

On the eve of Hitler's invasion of Poland, approximately a year after Price and Greene had begun their efforts, the polls indicated overwhelming popular support for an embargo on the sale of war materials to Japan. The influence of the Price Committee on the public was apparent in letters to Washington demanding "nonparticipation in Japanese aggression," enclosing Committee leaflets or parts of pamphlets, and referring to Dr. Walter Judd, the Committee's most effective speaker. But the only actions by the administration for which Price and Greene might take credit were a small loan to China and the notice given Japan of the intent of the United States to terminate the commercial treaty. By the summer of 1939, however, American opinion had been brought to the point where economic sanctions against Japan were possible—had the administration desired to impose them.

The coming of the war in Europe reaffirmed Roosevelt's conviction that the neutrality law had to be revised to enable Great Britain and France to purchase military supplies in the United States. Although he remained cautious, even devious, insisting that his aim was a return to traditional American neutrality rather than admitting that he wanted to aid Hitler's enemies, Roosevelt openly called for repeal of the arms embargo. There was loud, immediate and substantial opposition to neutrality revision and Roosevelt sought help from Eichelberger. Eichelberger formed a new committee, succeeded in getting William Allen White to head it, and received important assistance from Stimson, Al Smith, Henry R. Luce, and Frederick C. McKee in the campaign to win public support for repeal. Although the proposed changes to the law did not alter American policy toward China or Japan, all of these men, except Smith, were involved with the Price Committee.[27]

Price himself was not easily persuaded to suspend efforts to obtain an embargo against Japan. But Greene, apparently supported by Stimson, re-

27. Divine, *Illusion of Neutrality,* 303–5.

mained adamant in his view that the campaign would have to be reined in until the neutrality law was revised. Meanwhile Greene tried unsuccessfully to win Grew over to the embargo program, questioning his earlier estimate of the danger of war. Similarly, Eichelberger endeavored to keep the war in the public consciousness. Price was forced to go along with these preparations for a *future* campaign. On October 30 he made a virtue of necessity, informing Pittman that "we have purposely refrained from pressing the Far Eastern issue during the present special session."[28]

Once the neutrality law was revised, Greene, Price, and Stimson wasted little time before returning to action. Two days after Roosevelt signed the new law, Greene wrote to congratulate White for his work on behalf of revision and to enlist his aid in the forthcoming campaign for an embargo against Japan. Five days after the law was signed, Stimson hosted a luncheon at which Greene and Price were to work out a legislative program with Pittman. Characteristically, Pittman missed the meeting but a telegram sent in his name requested that the group advise him on the course he was to follow. Price prepared a synopsis of the talks, participated in by Edward C. Carter of the Institute of Pacific Relations, the executive secretary of the Federal Council of Churches, Henry Luce and several other businessmen, as well as the Committee stalwarts. In brief it was decided that the Committee would keep its program separate from neutrality revision. Following Pittman's advice, it would concentrate on a legislative program to be passed at the end of January 1940, when the commercial treaty between Japan and the United States would lapse.[29]

A week after the Pittman-less meeting was held, Thomas Lamont delivered a major address on the war in Europe and America's role in it. An audience of about a thousand people, including leading economists, educators, businessmen, and financiers heard him declare that the United States should keep out of the war in Europe, but encourage the sale of war supplies to Great Britain and France. Sensitive to charges that businessmen sought war for profit, he insisted he and businessmen generally feared war and were

28. Price to Maxwell Hamilton, September 15, 1939, SD 894.24/715; Greene to Stimson, September 18, to Price, September 23, to Grew, September 13, 1939, Price Committee files; Price to Pittman, October 30, 1939, Files of the Senate Foreign Relations Committee (SFRC) 76A-F9 (Japanese Aggression), National Archives.

29. Greene to White, November 6, 1939, Box 226, White Papers; memorandum, November 9, 1939, Pittman to Stimson, November 9, 1939, Stimson to Pittman, November 9, 1939, SFRC 76A-F9 (Japanese Aggression).

most anxious to stay out. A hopeful Lamont predicted a British and French victory and called for a postwar United States of Europe, a great free trade region comparable to the United States. The *New York Times* gave the speech front page coverage.[30]

For Lamont, war in Europe was clearly of a different magnitude than war in Asia. He wanted the United States to keep out of both wars, but the indifference he exhibited toward the outcome of the Sino-Japanese war was not evident in his discussion of the war in Europe. In part this may have reflected the fact that his firm's business in Asia was with the all-conquering Japanese, unthreatened by the course of events while England and France were more important to J. P. Morgan and Company than Hitler's Germany. But Lamont was also loyal to a vision of the Atlantic community, nucleus of a liberal capitalist world order, that went beyond business profit—although whether it could have been sustained had it been detrimental to his business interests is certainly a legitimate question.

Sokolsky persisted in arguing that American interests would be served best by staying out of either war, but focused more attention on Asia than did Lamont. His columns on the Sino-Japanese War seem to have been written for the Japanese rather than for the American public and called upon the Japanese to sever their ties to Hitler and Mussolini. Joining the Berlin-Rome axis had been "a stupid move" and he argued that the Japanese were better off allied with Great Britain. On the eve of the war in Europe he returned to that theme and warned the Japanese that they were wrong to assume that because Americans did not want war that they would not fight. The United States would not fight to keep the "open door" open in China—"the 'open door' in China brings practically no revenue to this country"—but the American people would not long tolerate the starvation of civilians and the mistreatment of women and children. And in particular, Americans would not likely tolerate attacks on "whites" in China. The Nazi-Soviet nonaggression pact served his argument well. The Japanese had been betrayed by the Germans, outsmarted by Stalin. Now they had no choice but to find a way to restore good relations with Great Britain and the United States. As a Jew who hated the Soviet Union, Sokolsky found another form of solace in the Nazi-Soviet pact. Now Hitler and Stalin were together and he called upon the United States to use its economic power against them.[31]

30. *New York Times*, November 16, 1939, p. 1.

31. *New York Herald Tribune*, May 15, July 10, September 11, 1939, GES ms.

Several weeks later, sharing the platform with Herbert Hoover, who expressed agreement with him, Sokolsky left no doubt that he was not countenancing acts of war: "If we go into this war, shackles will be formed which will enslave the peoples of America. Whether our sympathies are with Great Britain, Poland, or Czechoslovakia, our obligations are to America." And in November, expressing opposition to the decision to abrogate the Japanese-American commercial treaty, he argued that only the use of force would drive Japan out of China—"and Americans don't want war anywhere." Explicitly, Sokolsky called for a policy of weaning the Japanese away from the Axis powers.[32]

Although Greene was a little discouraged by "the depressing lack of initiative" in the Department of State, and anticipated little support for the Price Committee's embargo proposals, in January 1940 he opened an office in Washington to facilitate the Committee's lobbying efforts. At best he thought the administration would offer some direct aid to China or some form of import controls. The optimism with which members of the organization had looked to the end of the commercial treaty was evaporating quickly. Despite strong indications of public support, by mid-January it was apparent there would be no sanctions against Japan. Thwarting Greene's efforts were Roosevelt, Hull, and the Department of State. The administration had concluded that the danger of a conflict with Japan resulting from the imposition of sanctions was too great to risk, given the war in Europe. As a result, pressures mounted within the Committee for a break with the administration.[33]

Price called for immediate action, contending that the public had long indicated support for a more aggressive anti-Japanese policy, and Pittman was prepared to work for an embargo. He argued that if the Committee continued its campaign, putting pressure on the administration, they might at least be able to get legislation authorizing the president to impose sanctions on Japan. Unable to grasp Roosevelt's evaluation of the relative importance of the European and Asian wars, Price professed himself unable to understand why the courage shown by the administration in the fight for neutrality

32. *New York Times*, October 26, 1939, p. 12; *New York Herald Tribune*, November 27, 1939, GES ms.

33. Greene to Price, December 18, 1939, RSG ms. Advised that some Congressmen wanted to forbid the sale of gasoline and other war materials to Japan while others feared trouble with Japan, 75% of the respondents to a Gallup poll in January 1940 favored forbidding such sales. Cantril, *Public Opinion*, 1159.

revision was not demonstrated on the embargo issue, where public support was overwhelming. Greene was relatively sanguine at the outset, convinced that Roosevelt and Hull would make no concessions to Japan. Within the administration he found support for a program of gradual pressure by tariff manipulation and direct financial aid to China, but he soon came to fear that Hull would not push either of these measures. Ultimately he agreed with Price. The Committee had to go ahead with its campaign in the hope that the pressure it generated for an embargo would be used by the administration to help China in other ways. In February, Hull sent word to Greene that further credits would be made available to China and these were forthcoming in April. Once again the administration charted its own course, this time disregarding a Gallup poll indicating that the public opposed such credits.[34]

Price and Greene continued to press for stiffer action against Japan, with Price especially worried that a spring offensive in Europe would divert public attention from Asia. In the midst of the German blitzkrieg, Price was able to speak with Hull for 45 minutes. Hull praised the Committee for its efforts and accomplishments but Price was not put off by flattery. He warned Hull that despite his desire to continue a constructive relationship with the administration, there were pressures which he could not resist unless effective action were taken against Japan. Hull indicated his fear that embargo bills, if voted upon, might fail and the problem be further complicated by election year politics. Price concluded that Hull would block any attempt to obtain mandatory embargo legislation but would like to have the authority to impose economic sanctions—if it could be obtained without the administration having to face warmongering charges. But, as Greene understood, disgusted as they were with the administration, there was nowhere else they could turn.[35]

During the month Greene was in Washington, lobbying for an embargo, Lamont was still writing to Japanese friends expressing disapproval of Japanese actions. In April he spoke at Harvard and the *New York Times* quoted him as saying that Britain and France were fighting to maintain American-style "liberty of thought and freedom of action." But on both

34. Price to Greene, January 20, 1940, and Greene to Evans Carlson, January 28, 1940, Price Committee files; Roger to Kate Greene, February 8, 1940, RSG ms; 52% opposed and 34% favored credits to China in February 1940. Cantril, *Public Opinion*, 1102.

35. Price to Greene, February 19, 1940, to Stimson, April 25, 1940, Price Committee files; Roger to Kate Greene, April 12, 1940, RSG ms.

fronts, Lamont remained cautious about American involvement, almost certainly a defensive response to tirades about bankers wanting war. Despite his obvious support of Hitler's enemies in Europe, at Harvard he said "America can and must keep out of the armed conflict in Europe." Asked by a friend to see Price, Lamont refused, declaring that he did not favor economic warfare against Japan—"unless our own government decides that that is the policy to pursue."[36]

In May, German forces invaded Belgium, Holland, and France, and Price's fear of public loss of interest in East Asia was realized. Ironically, the Nazi onslaught also resulted in the National Defense Act, one section of which authorized the president to prohibit the export of materials necessary for the defense of the United States—authority that could be used to embargo the sale of war supplies to Japan. Although this section had been inserted at the request of the army, Price and Greene may have played a part in its formulation and acceptance by Congress and the administration. Almost from the moment news reached the United States of the invasion of the Low Countries, they had campaigned for export restrictions as a means of conserving critical resources. This new tack, stressing national defense rather than discrimination against aggressors and treaty violations, interested Pittman, Hull, and Hornbeck. Unable to see Roosevelt, Greene tried to persuade him with letters. Approximately a month after Greene suggested that Roosevelt obtain legislation "that would enable the President to withhold from export any basic war materials and equipment as a means of conserving our own national resources," the National Defense Act, with the support of the administration, was passed by both houses of Congress. On June 17, 1940, Price and Greene informed their supporters that "our legislative hurdle is passed." Exhilarated, Greene told his wife "I get a lot more credit for it [the embargo] than I deserve, though perhaps the stroke at the end was a contribution of my own."[37]

Greene and Price soon concluded that coercion of Japan was forthcoming and that their energies might be used elsewhere. Greene returned to his suggestion of a merger with Eichelberger's American Union in May, a few days after the Germans swept into France. Price held back until a talk with

36. Lamont to Count Kabayama Aisuke, February 14, 1940, 188–10, to Go Toshi, May 10, 1940, 188–11, TWL ms; *New York Times,* April 20, 1940, p. 5; Lamont to James Shotwell, March 19, 1940, 130–4, TWL ms.

37. Friedman, *Road from Isolation,* 33–36; Greene to Roosevelt, May 17, 1940, SD 894.24/952 and May 20, 1940, SD 894.24/944; Price to Maxwell Hamilton, June 19, 1940, SD 894.24/960; Roger to Kate Greene, June 1, 1940, RSG ms.

Stimson in June stimulated his interest in working with an organization dealing with broader issues of foreign policy. Greene, who had joined the Committee to Defend America by Aiding the Allies, continued to press Price, contending that more could be accomplished by working for action in Asia within a general rather than a regional organization. He became especially insistent late in the summer, arguing that the country faced urgent questions outside the Far East and that it would be difficult for the Committee to raise funds for another campaign. Disagreements over liquidation kept the American Committee for Non-Participation in Japanese Aggression in existence until February 1941, but it had ceased to be of significance by July 1940.[38]

Coercion of Japan was indeed forthcoming, but not without a little more help from Greene—and not on the scale for which Greene and Price had hoped. In July, after Stimson had joined the cabinet, he sent for Greene, explaining that Sumner Welles, Undersecretary of State, was obstructing proposals to restrict oil and scrap iron sales. Stimson asked Greene to launch another effort and a few days later Roosevelt agreed to add aviation gasoline and high grade scrap iron to the list of articles for which export licenses were required. Licenses were then denied to Japan. This was a far more limited version of the embargo than that advocated by the Price Committee, but it was an important step—the first meaningful victory for those who demanded economic pressure against Japan. Again Greene thought "I can take a share of the credit for this since I have been working on it lately and perhaps, through Mr. Stimson, rather effectively."[39]

These were heady times for Greene as he moved among the wielders of power in Washington. He dined with Ben Cohen, Harold Ickes, and Robert Patterson, as well as with Stimson and his friends at State. Worried about Mrs. Roosevelt's views on Asian affairs, he went to lecture her on the subject. Troubled by her talk with Greene, she asked Sumner Welles for information on assistance Japan was getting from the United States. Welles asked Hornbeck to prepare a memorandum for Mrs. Roosevelt—and Hornbeck called Greene to the Department to help draft it. Things could be done and he was doing them.[40]

38. Greene to Price, May 7 and 15, June 16, 1940, Price to Greene, June 15, 1940, Greene to Price, August 22, 1940, Price Committee files; Friedman, *Road from Isolation,* 75–81.

39. Feis, *Road to Pearl Harbor,* 88–94; Henry L. Stimson Diaries, XXX, 26 (microfilm from Yale University); Roger to Kate Greene, July 22 and 25, 1940, RSG ms.

40. Roger to Kate Greene, September 3 and 25, 1940, RSG ms.

The desire for a complete embargo on war supplies was not fulfilled, however, during the years of the Price Committee's existence. Japan continued to buy huge quantities of American oil until after the freezing of Japanese assets in July 1941. Greene was intensely disappointed, but not entirely surprised. Recognizing the administration's preoccupation with the crisis in Europe, he hoped through his work with the Committee to Defend America by Aiding the Allies (White Committee) to alert authorities to the necessity of countering aggression across the Pacific as well. In August 1940 he believed the European and Asian problems were about to merge and hoped that if Britain could be sustained, it would be easier to get "the necessary action taken for China."[41]

Within the Committee to Defend America by Aiding the Allies there was, however, little inclination to include China among the "Allies." The committee had been organized by the ubiquitous Eichelberger in May 1940 in response to the blitzkrieg. That summer, with William Allen White as chairman, it focused its campaign entirely on aid to Great Britain as the "first and vital duty" of the United States. On those occasions when the Japanese were mentioned in Committee literature, their activities were conjured up as further justification for rushing aid to Britain. Indifference to China in particular and Asia in general persisted even after the success of the Committee's campaign to obtain old American destroyers for the British navy (the destroyer-bases deal). On September 8, Greene was invited to attend a meeting of the executive committee, at which he was asked to continue his study of the situation in the Far East. The following day he appeared at a meeting of the advisory committee, only to have the problems of China and Japan brushed aside again. An outline of policy for that date declared that the subject of the Pacific "is now too complicated for much attention by this committee . . . it would distract attention from the need of rushing all material to Britain instantly."[42]

Later in the month Greene was allowed to send out a newsletter calling for an American initiative in East Asia in which he focused his argument on the relevance of the situation there to Britain's position. This was the surest way, and perhaps at this time the only way, to interest the White Committee

41. Greene to Price, August 22, 1940, Price Committee files.

42. Walter Johnson, *The Battle Against Isolation* (Chicago, 1944) is a history of the White Committee; Minutes of the Executive Committee, September 8, 1940, notes on Advisory Committee Meeting, September 9, 1940, Files of the Committee to Defend America by Aiding the Allies (White Committee), Princeton University.

leadership in anti-Japanese activities. For Greene to win support for further sanctions against Japan or assistance to China, he had to demonstrate a relationship between the European and Asian wars. He had to convince men whose attention was focused on Great Britain's battle for survival that Japan too threatened Britain, that China too was fighting America's battle. It was, of course, the Japanese who made the fulfillment of Greene's task possible when, on September 27, they signed the Tripartite Pact.[43]

For Americans, including the leaders of the White Committee, the Japanese decision to ally with Nazi Germany suggested that the outcome of the Sino-Japanese War really mattered, that the war in Europe and the war in Asia had become one war. The White Committee reported that "it would now seem that China is unmistakably an ally," worthy of support. But White did not want to see an American commitment to East Asia that might reduce aid to Great Britain. Eichelberger, though he declared "Britain and China in the Pacific, with Britain in the Atlantic" the front lines of America's defense, added that "the key to our entire future is the survival of Great Britain." There could be no change in the policy of all aid to Great Britain as quickly as possible. China, the other "ally," should be given as much assistance as possible "without lessening the tempo of our aid to Britain."[44]

Greene was encouraged, however, when Eichelberger, to supplement assistance to China which might well be nonexistent, called for a complete embargo on all products needed for Japan's war machine. Undeterred by the continued focus on Britain he prepared a memorandum, "How a Strong American Policy in the Far East Could Help Britain," and persuaded the Committee to circulate it. The memorandum was accompanied, however, by a disclaimer: "not all of the views expressed herein represent the official policy of the Committee to Defend America by Aiding the Allies." This was obviously a less than complete vote of confidence, especially in view of Greene's deliberate appeal to the Europe-oriented. It was, of course, indicative of the difficulty of obtaining serious consideration for the problems of the Pacific.[45]

43. Greene to Roosevelt, September 18, 1940, enclosure, Price Committee files.

44. Eichelberger to White, October 1, 1940, enclosing draft response to Tripartite agreement, CDAAA boxes, White Papers; Johnson, *Battle Against Isolation,* 133; White to Livingston Hartley, October 11, 1940, Box 243, White Papers; Eichelberger to Chapter Chairmen, October 15, 1940, White Committee files.

45. William Allen White News Service, October 28, 1940, White Committee files; Daily Report of National Office, October 28, 1940, CDAAA boxes, White Papers.

In his analysis Greene contended that Britain had shown that it could stave off invasion, thus postponing the threat to the United States from across the Atlantic "so long as Britain can continue to get men and supplies from other parts of the empire and from neutral states." Unfortunately the Suez Canal, lifeline of the British Empire, was now being threatened. Reinforcements for British troops in the area would have to come from Australia, New Zealand, and Canada through the Indian Ocean. But if Japan were left unchecked in Southeast Asia, the dominions would need these forces for home defense and Japan could cut off the flow of supplies from India. If Japan were checked, however, there would be no problem. And Japan could be checked by economic aid to China and an embargo on war materials to Japan. A boycott might even be imposed on Japanese imports into the United States. Naval "precautions" might be taken by sending part of the U.S. Navy into the western Pacific. With Britain strengthened in the Middle East, there was a possibility that Turkey and the Soviet Union would be deterred from aiding Germany. But the heart of Greene's message was that economic pressures against Japan would preserve the British position at Suez, ultimately saving Britain—and the United States.[46]

One important segment of American society did not seem to be responding to Greene's efforts. In September 1940, a *Fortune* poll of business leaders revealed that 40 percent of the respondents favored the appeasement of Japan and 35 percent favored leaving things to "nature." Fewer than 20 percent favored an embargo or threat of force. But in November Thomas Lamont came to the rescue. Called upon to preside at the annual dinner of the Academy of Political Science, Lamont decided to respond to the Tripartite Pact. After consulting with Hull and informing him that he thought that the new Axis treaty had created a new situation in which businessmen, i.e., Thomas Lamont, would support economic sanctions, he sent a draft statement to Hornbeck, who made some "minor corrections." The resulting speech sounded very much as if it had been written by Greene and modified by Eichelberger. Lamont insisted that the Tripartite Pact "definitely makes Europe and the Far East a single, great struggle. The conflict becomes truly a world war." Most important was to continue and increase aid to Great Britain, then continue and increase assistance to China. In addition the time had come for a *complete* embargo on war materials to Japan, and he con-

46. *Ibid.*

tended that American business would wholeheartedly support a government program of economic sanctions against the Japanese, including restrictions on imports.[47]

Copies of Lamont's speech were sent to leading Chinese and Japanese statesmen, as well as to American diplomats. It received front page coverage in the *New York Times* and was carried all over the United States and to Asia by the wire presses. The replies from Konoe and Matsuoka were not heartening, but Grew responded with enthusiastic approval. He was sorry to see eight years of his work swept aside, but the United States had to be firm with Japanese extremists. He warned that a firm policy would entail risks, but "a policy of laissez-faire on our part would, in my opinion, lead to future dangers of far greater magnitude."[48]

With major business support and the State Department apparently lined up behind an embargo, Greene had every reason to be optimistic. Two weeks after Lamont's speech, Greene became associate director of the White Committee, providing assurance to China's friends that the Orient would not be neglected. But still there was little progress. The government did not act and the White Committee persisted in its basic strategy of advocating aid to China only after Britain's needs were met. The administration had extended credits to the Chinese government and several new items were added to the list of materials excluded from export, but oil still flowed from the United States to Japan in enormous quantities. As Lamont explained to a friend, "Hitler is the main target, and while the Far East is a part of the same target, it is not quite so near the bull's eye. I don't believe in precipitating conflict in the Far East that might weaken our effort in aid to Britain across the Atlantic!" The State Department, he added, feared that a complete embargo would precipitate Japanese action against the Dutch East Indies and Singapore, steps which neither the United States nor Great Britain were prepared to meet. Lamont was working with the White Committee, intimate with its leaders, but he was not ready to go all the way with Roger Greene.[49]

47. *Fortune* poll in Cantril, *Public Opinion,* 961; "The Far Eastern Threat: A Friendly Caution to Japan," November 13, 1940, text and clippings, 141–4, Memorandum for Leffingwell, November 6, 1940, 141–3. See also correspondence with Hornbeck, 141–5, TWL ms.

48. *New York Times,* November 14, 1940, p. 1; Konoe to Lamont and Matsuoka to Lamont, December 27, 1940, Grew to Lamont, December 26, 1940, TWL ms.

49. Daily Report of National Office, November 23, 1940, CDAAA Boxes, White Papers; Lamont to J. Barton Leach, November 30, 1940, 141–9, TWL ms.

During the winter of 1940–41, the White Committee worked primarily to muster support for Roosevelt's lend-lease program, with continued emphasis on aid to Great Britain. In February, Greene and Admiral Harry E. Yarnell, colleagues during the active days of the Price Committee, exchanged counsels of despair: why did the United States continue to arm Japan "when every indication pointed to eventual war"? While the Lend-Lease Act was pending, the White Committee reflected the administration's caution and avoided new initiatives that might be construed as warmongering. But once the lend-lease program became law, Eichelberger gave Greene his full support. Greene's entire program for the Far East became part of the official program of the Committee. At a meeting of the national board on March 15, 1941, Eichelberger announced that the local chapters were unanimous in advocating a strong policy toward Japan. With the help of Chester Rowell, a prominent California newspaperman, Greene's statement was adopted. The committee thereby called for an increase in American naval strength in the western Pacific, more aid to China, extension of embargoes on war materials to Japan, and naval cooperation between the United States and Great Britain in the Pacific. In addition it warned of America's determination to prevent the conquest of Singapore and the Dutch East Indies. There was opposition to the clause referring to naval strength in the Pacific, but the dissenters failed to delete it. Greene later admitted that this was a technical matter beyond the concern of the Committee, but "since we cannot always depend on the administration to take far-seeing and energetic action in time, it does not seem inappropriate to interest ourselves in such details." Faith in the wisdom of the administration had ceased to be a part of Greene's intellectual baggage.[50]

At Greene's request, Livingston Hartley of the White Committee visited the Department of State and obtained confidential information indicating that the navy had already been reinforced. Through a variety of clever devices the government was preventing Japan from obtaining oil and other materials required for the Japanese war effort. Hartley liked these methods, which he believed would accomplish the ends Greene sought without arousing hostile feelings in Japan. He warned Greene not to pass this information

50. Greene to Yarnell, February 27, 1941, Yarnell to Greene, March 3, 1941, Greene to Hartley, February 26, 1941, minutes of National Policy Board meeting, March 15, 1941, and Greene to E. Guy Talbott, March 22, 1941, White Committee files; Greene to White, March 20, 1941, Box 252, White Papers.

on to his anti-Japanese friends or even to the local chapters of the White Committee because of the importance of moving quietly. Greene, however, had heard these lines before and refused to be put off with less than an end to the sale of petroleum products to Japan. For the next several months, with the assistance of Price and the approval of Eichelberger and Hornbeck, Greene criticized the Department of State and pressed for an embargo on the sale of oil. In June the executive committee issued a sharp statement demanding that the Department "immediately lay down a rule that no more licenses for export of petroleum or petroleum products to Japan shall be issued."[51]

Lamont continued to work in support of the White Committee's efforts and in April 1941 gave another widely reported speech calling for aid to Britain and China and an embargo on scrap iron and oil shipments to Japan. But Lamont liked to work closely with the administration on affairs of state in which he had no professional involvement—and he was becoming alarmed over the Committee's criticism of Roosevelt's policies. As Eichelberger moved out in advance of positions Roosevelt was prepared to take, Roosevelt called Lamont for help in reining in the Committee. When Greene's statement in early June condemned "this continued appeasement—appeasement which is strategically indefensible and morally bankrupt," Lamont was furious. He and Lewis Douglas found the Department of State unhappy about the charge, but in fact Hornbeck had been consulted and was pleased. Despite the anger of Lamont and Douglas, Eichelberger continued to support Greene.[52]

Lamont's irritation with Greene was clearly not over the substance of Greene's policy recommendations but only the tactical issue: work *with* the Department of State, work from within, never attack. Two weeks later he tackled the problem in his own way, preparing a lengthy memorandum on the Far East, copies of which he sent to Hornbeck and Walter Lippmann, among others. Discussing a wide range of issues including disposition of fleet units, economic sanctions, and the attitudes of the British, Dutch, and

51. Hartley to Greene, March 26, 1941, Greene to Hartley, March 28, 1941, Eichelberger to local chapters, April 18, 1941, Price to Greene, May 24, 1941, Minutes of the Executive Committee, June 6, 1941, press release, June 9, 1941, White Committee files.

52. "China and the Dictators," text of speech, April 28, 1941, 139–1, memorandum for Leffingwell, April 21, 1941, 147–2, TWL ms; *New York Times*, April 29, 1941, p. 11; Lamont to Roosevelt, April 8, 1941, enclosure, 21–5 and memorandum, June 11, 1941 on Greene letter, June 6, 1941, 21–16, TWL ms; Roger to Kate Greene, June 9 and 11, 1941, RSG ms.

Chinese governments, Lamont stated explicitly that he did not agree with those of his friends who would like to forget about East Asia and concentrate on cleaning up the mess across the Atlantic. He concluded that in general he would probably follow the same course the administration had chosen "yet I have a feeling that the Administration overrates somewhat the Japanese threat, and could without undue risk invoke at least gradually more severe economic measures."[53]

Although he won the battle over the White Committee's Far Eastern program, Greene increasingly became concerned over the willingness of his colleagues to appease Japan in order to concentrate their efforts across the Atlantic. He doubted that appeasement would provide security from attack by Japan should the United States become deeply involved in European affairs. The Japanese would assume they were next in line after the defeat of Germany and would not wait quietly for the United States to isolate them. Greene's apprehensions were not alleviated by letters from Hartley and Donald Blaisdell, both working out of the Committee's Washington office. With incredible gaucherie, given Greene's known views, Hartley assured him of the wisdom of the administration's gentle tactics with Japan and their effectiveness in deterring Japan in Southeast Asia. As a result of these tactics, he reported, "we will obviously be freer to carry out our policy in the Atlantic."[54]

In late July 1941, the Japanese appeared in Camranh Bay on the coast of southern Indochina. Appeasement had not deterred the Japanese advance. On the day the Japanese were sighted, Roosevelt called the Japanese ambassador's attention to "the bitter criticism that had been leveled against the administration" for allowing oil to be shipped to Japan. Two days later, July 26, the White Committee added to that criticism, responding to news of the Japanese advance in Indochina. The Committee insisted that there was no longer any reason to hope the continued flow of supplies would limit Japanese expansion. An embargo against Japan, long urged as a moral duty and an obligation to China, had now become essential to the national defense and America's security in the Pacific. Finally, the Committee urged "the immediate adoption of direct embargoes of all shipments of essential war

53. Memorandum dated June 16, 1941, 188–12, TWL ms; Hornbeck to Lamont, June 25, 1941, Hornbeck papers.

54. Greene to Yarnell, June 12, 1941, Hartley to Greene, June 19, 1941, and Blaisdell to Greene, June 19, 1941, White Committee files.

materials to Japan and a freezing of Japanese assets in the United States.'' On the same morning the order to freeze Japanese assets was signed by Roosevelt.[55]

But Greene, aware of the strength within the administration of those who opposed putting pressure on Japan, disgusted by what he considered to be a lack of courage in either Hull or Roosevelt, continued to worry. From Lauchlin Currie, a presidential assistant concerned with lend-lease for China, he learned that a complete embargo on oil would not be imposed immediately. Some licenses to use frozen funds and to export oil would continue to be granted. Indeed, on August 1, Roosevelt approved such a program. Throughout August Greene fretted and worked with Eichelberger to launch a new campaign for an oil embargo. In an article for the Committee's Washington Office Information Letter he warned that the United States might wait too long before doing anything and expressed fear ''that for the moment the influence of appeasers in Washington will prevail against really decisive action.'' In the same letter, however, Hartley bracketed Greene's article with two of his own that stressed the need to avoid war in the Pacific and insisted that ''the Atlantic remains the vital area in which America's destiny will be decided.'' The task of handling Japan at this juncture was extremely delicate and day to day planning should be left to the authorities. A week later Hartley replied indirectly to Greene's argument, conceding that ''the Chinese'' might see the oil policy of the United States as appeasement but arguing that a larger view suggested this policy was in China's interest. He explained that the liberation of China depended upon ''our victory,'' which might not have been possible had Japan been provoked into attacking Singapore in 1940.[56]

Eichelberger, however, gave constant support to Greene's position, particularly in his regular letters to the committee's various chapters. Finally, on September 2, Greene was satisfied that Japan would get no more oil and indicated a willingness to relent in his attack on the administration. He had been watching a number of Japanese oilers in west coast ports and learned that although the Department of State and the administrator for export control had approved licensing for the sale of oil, the Treasury Depart-

55. *FRUS, Japan, 1931–1941*, II, 527–28; press release, July 26, 1941, White Committee files.

56. Greene to T. L. Power, July 30, 1941, Washington Office Information Letters, No. 29 (August 1, 1941), No. 30 (August 8, 1941), White Committee files.

ment had successfully resisted the attempt to license funds. Now Greene was willing to admit the possibility that the pressure on Japan was so strong that an occasional easing might be in order.

As the summer drew to a close with intensified American pressure on Japan and continued resolve in Tokyo, the possibility of war between the two nations was apparent. In both countries, there remained men who were willing to continue to try to avert war, to accomplish their ends by other means, to work for at least a modus vivendi between Japan and the United States. Because any such agreement with Japan would likely come at China's expense, the friends of China worked furiously to stir public opposition to a settlement with Japan. The most effective campaign to prevent the administration from seeking a modus vivendi with Japan was probably the one fought by Greene, Eichelberger, and Price. They worked primarily through the White Committee but also through the journal of the League of Nations Association and in personal letters and appearances. On September 16, 1941, the White Committee prepared a new statement of policy calling for the rejection of any agreement with Japan that sacrificed American principles respecting China. Greene was pleased by the strong support for the statement, which included a tip from Washington, probably from Hornbeck, that a letter and telegram campaign to Hull and Roosevelt would be valuable. Using the statement he had already drafted, Greene sent out a special appeal under Price Committee auspices, with the organization presumably resurrected for the occasion.[57]

In November, while the Japanese ambassador, Nomura Kichisaburo, talked with Hull, Hartley and Herbert Bayard Swope attempted to dilute the White Committee's stand on China. Swope wanted all reference to China deleted from the committee's new policy statement to allow maximum opportunity for the success of the Japanese-American negotiations. By this time Greene was no longer active with the committee, having been dropped, ostensibly for financial reasons, but Eichelberger stood firm. The United States, he insisted, had to atone for supplying the materials for Japan's aggression in China. There could be no further appeasement and there was a good chance that Japan would yield if America stood firm. Despite his dedication to peace, Eichelberger took the position that if Japan would not yield, better war than appeasement. Swope and Hartley could hope for no

57. Statement of policy, September 16, 1941, Power to Greene, September 17, 1941, Greene to Power, September 19, 1941 and October 1, 1941, White Committee files.

support from Lamont, who insisted in a letter to Walter Lippmann that the Japanese were just stalling, and would not dare attack the United States. He insisted that "China cannot and must not yield. America will certainly not budge an inch. She ought not to. She ought to continue to tighten her blockade. . . ." On November 28, the White Committee demanded an end to the negotiations, charging that the talks were a stall designed to delay American action in the Pacific while Japan built more battleships and the Germans sought to regain the initiative in Europe. In the twilight hours of peace the White Committee proved unrelenting in its attitude toward Japan. On the same day, Greene learned from the Chinese ambassador, Hu Shih, that the Chinese were satisfied with American handling of the negotiations with Japan, and told his son "the danger of yielding to Japan seems past for the moment."[58]

Sokolsky, however, continued to hope that Roosevelt could find a way to avoid war with Japan. Throughout 1941, he wrote of the need to win Japan away from her European allies and praised Roosevelt's efforts to find a formula that would keep peace in the Pacific. In August, he described most Americans as neither interventionist nor isolationist, but anxious to aid Great Britain without going to war and without allying the United States with the Soviet Union. Presumably the description fit George Sokolsky as well. In September he discussed Japan's "bitter plight," Konoe's desperate need to reach some sort of accommodation with the United States before Japan was cut off from essential raw materials or found itself at war. He hoped Konoe's overture for a meeting with Roosevelt could be turned into a larger Pacific Conference including Chinese, British, and Soviet representatives. A month later, perhaps whistling in the dark, he wrote that Japanese-American relations were not as bad as they appeared to be. The Japanese people were tired of war with China and there was opposition to the militarists in the foreign office, among businessmen, and even in the navy. Conceding general American sympathy for China, he insisted few Americans wanted war with Japan.[59]

58. Hartley to Power, November 26, 1941, Swope to Power, November 25, 1941, Price to Power, November 25, 1941, Eichelberger to Chapter representatives, No. 14, November 22, 1941, White Committee files; Lamont to Lippmann, November 13, 1941, 188–13, TWL ms; Roger to Edward F. Greene, November 28, 1941, RSG ms; press release, November 28, 1941, White Committee files.

59. *New York Sun,* March 11, May 22 and 28, August 5 and 28, September 6, October 16, 1941, GES ms.

Having dedicated much of the previous eight years to opposing Roosevelt and his policies, Sokolsky found much to applaud in Roosevelt's approach to East Asia—while attacking the work of people like Roger Greene. Roosevelt "has withstood the pressure of the militant pro-Chinese as well as the attacks on his Far Eastern policy by the so-called liberals who are invariably opposed to what they call appeasement, although they are responsible for our lack of an adequate army and navy to meet the demands of their current bellicosity." As Japanese-American negotiations continued, Sokolsky explained the bargaining positions and the progress of the negotiations in his columns. He found American policy "astute." Roosevelt and Hull had found a way to aid China and to embarrass Japan without going to war. However painfully—almost certainly in the hope of sustaining Roosevelt against Greene and his friends—Sokolsky declared "we must admit that his Far Eastern diplomacy has been magnificent so far."[60]

On December 2, Sokolsky was still praising Roosevelt's diplomacy, but by then he was also worrying about Hull's preaching. Even after the attack on Pearl Harbor, Sokolsky continued to praise Roosevelt. He reported having followed the negotiations closely and told of being "astonished at the forbearance, the breadth of view of the President. He has tried hard and the Japanese who were in this country expressed their faith in him. They felt that he alone could save Japan from this horrible war." Again Sokolsky defended Roosevelt against charges of appeasement. Roosevelt's policies had allowed the Japanese to isolate themselves, to unite the American people: "Had the President pursued the policy which some Sinophiles desired, he would never have achieved this unity."[61]

With regard to the war in Europe, the difference between Sokolsky on the one hand, and Lamont and Greene on the other, narrowed significantly after the success of the Nazi blitzkrieg in the spring of 1940. Lamont and Greene were close to the leadership of the collective security movement and both immediately perceived an American stake in the outcome of the European war. Sokolsky was closer to the conservative leadership of the Republican Party, fearful that Roosevelt would use the war to consolidate his power. Sokolsky lacked the Anglophilia so prevalent in the establishment. But as a Jew, Sokolsky could not but dread the triumph of Hitler's Germany and as an American knowledgeable about world affairs and problems of na-

60. *Ibid.*, October 16, 21, 23, and 25, 1941, GES ms.
61. *Ibid.*, December 2 and 11, 1941, GES ms.

tional security, he could not but fear the worst when France fell. All aid to Britain short of war was a cry common to these three men—and most Americans—after Wendell Wilkie endorsed Roosevelt's policy in the presidential campaign of 1940. A year later, Greene, at least, was ready to intervene, but if American intervention was necessary to stop Germany, Lamont and Sokolsky were not far behind.

The conflict in East Asia elicited a very different, but predictable pattern of responses. Sokolsky insisted to the last that the United States had no stake in the outcome of the Sino-Japanese War. He was certainly willing to concede Manchuria, perhaps all of Japan's ambitions toward a New Order in East Asia, to prevent a confrontation between the United States and Japan. Lamont persisted in his opposition to economic sanctions until the signing of the Tripartite Pact in September 1940. Far more concerned with European affairs than with those of Asia, he was persuaded that the pact made one war of two and that Japan had to be weakened as a means of aiding Great Britain. But Lamont moved cautiously, working closely with administration figures—though apparently not aware of the sharp split within the Department of State between Hornbeck and men like Sumner Welles. But as spokesman for J. P. Morgan and Company, his public support for economic sanctions—especially after his early opposition and because of his known ties to Japan—provided a powerful boost for the more militant sanctionists like Roger Greene.

Greene's efforts with the Price Committee frequently were frustrated by the administration's Europe-first orientation. After the signing of the Tripartite Pact, however, he and his colleagues were able to capitalize on mounting American opposition to Germany to generate sentiment against Japan. By disassociating himself from members of the Price group who seemed more interested in China than in the United States, by his close association with Eichelberger, and by his ability to recognize the primacy of the European theater, Green won for his program the support of the influential White Committee. He was thus able to gain for the Asian theater the attention of the vastly larger audience to which that organization appealed. It is conceivable that without Greene's presence in a position of authority in the White Committee, the prevailing voices in that organization would have been those favoring concentration on the Atlantic community to the point of appeasing Japan.

In the autumn of 1941 the advocates of collective security and the friends of China joined forces in a final campaign against Japan. Greene's efforts within the White Committee prevented that organization from ignoring China's cause. The White Committee would not countenance appeasement in East Asia—nor would the American people, long sympathetic to China and conditioned by three and a half years of Price and White Committee campaigns. Polls released in October and November of 1941 revealed that overwhelming majorities favored steps to keep Japan from becoming more powerful, "even if this means risking war with Japan."[62] To the extent that public opinion dictated the American response in the negotiations with Japan, the work of the Price and White Committees—of Roger Greene—helped to determine that response.

62. Cantril, *Public Opinion,* 1076.

9

# WAR AND THE COMMUNIST TRIUMPH IN CHINA

THE attack on Pearl Harbor brought full-scale war to the American people and the subsequent declaration of war on the United States by Germany and Italy underscored the fact that America had enemies on both the Atlantic and Pacific fronts. Thomas Lamont was 71 when World War II came to his country, and two years later, with the death of J. P. Morgan, Jr., he reached the very top of the ladder: chairman of the board of J. P. Morgan and Company. Among various war-related activities he served as chairman of the Red Cross War Fund Advisory Committee and he continued to be available for consultations with the President of the United States and other public officials who sought his advice and company. Roger Greene was younger, only 60 when the United States went to war, but in poor health. He would have liked an emergency position in the higher echelons of the Department of State, but knew he had made enemies and was glad to serve as a consultant on medical affairs in China for the Department's Cultural Affairs division. George Sokolsky, in the prime of life, surrendered his radio program but his column, "These Days," was syndicated in 1941 and picked up by King Features in 1944. Ultimately readers of approximately 300 newspapers across the United States had the opportunity to share Sokolsky's thoughts.

While the war continued, Lamont urged Morgan to contribute generously to China War Relief. But he had few illusions about China. He accepted reports of a corrupt and reactionary government in Chungking as normal and warned Walter Lippmann not to expect China to be a great power after the war. He anticipated continued confusion and dissension there and apparently foresaw an extension of the chaos of the 1920s. He was angry with the Japanese, expressing to Grew a deep sense of having been betrayed, but his only sustained interest in East Asia was manifest in his efforts to get out of the Consortium. In December 1944, Lamont made another unsuccessful attempt to be rid of his responsibilities with the American Group. Hornbeck was still on the scene, still anxious to preserve the Group. Trying again a few months after the war ended, Lamont met with success. The Department of State agreed that continuing the Consortium, with or without the American Group, served no useful purpose. In May 1946, legal counsel for the Hong Kong and Shanghai Banking Corporation ruled that the Japanese had abrogated the Consortium agreement by commencing hostilities against their partners in 1941. Lamont and the Department of State accepted the ruling and the Consortium came to an end.[1]

Greene and Sokolsky devoted themselves much more closely to Asian affairs. They studied the particulars of Chinese politics, tried to get more aid for China, and brooded about the extent and justice of America's "Europe First" strategy for fighting the war. Greene was discouraged by the lack of interest in China, by the low priority aid to China received in Washington. He thought the United States could be doing more to soothe the Chinese, "to strengthen them a little." But he never doubted the wisdom of trying to "clean up Hitler first." Defending America's Europe First policy to the Chinese publicist, Lin Yu-tang, Greene even expressed doubt that it would have been good for China if he had been successful in getting an embargo against Japan in 1939. To his brother Jerome he explained, in another context, that he was not sure "that the centre of gravity has shifted from the Atlantic to the Pacific already, whatever may happen in the future."[2]

Shortly after the Japanese attack on Pearl Harbor, Sokolsky expressed

1. Lamont to Morgan, April 7, 1942, 19–5, Henry Luce to Lamont, April 26, 1944, Lamont to Luce, May 4, 1944, 184–20, Lamont to Lippmann, July 2, 1944, 105–4, to Grew, September 15, 1942, 96–19, TWL ms; Lamont to Hornbeck, December 11, 1944, Hornbeck Papers; Lamont to Secretary of State, November 19, 1945, James F. Byrnes to Lamont, January 5, 1946, Emilio G. Collado to Lamont, January 28, 1946, SD 893.516/11–1945.

2. Greene to T. L. Power, March 23, 1943, to Lin, September 15, 1943, to Jerome, April 5, 1943. RSG ms.

the fear that Americans would underestimate the Japanese because of American contempt for Orientals. But at the beginning of 1942 he endorsed the Europe First strategy. It was a difficult decision. He knew that the defeat of Germany would not cause the collapse of Japan, but he thought the situation in East Asia could wait. Hitler, he contended, wanted the United States to concentrate on Japan, but "those who are charged with the strategy of this war are not to be taken in by Hitler's desire."[3]

Then, on January 20, Sokolsky reported Chinese fears that American and British preoccupation with Europe would mean disaster for them. By the end of the month, Sokolsky was defending Americans who wanted to fight Japan first. He spent some time with Col. Robert McCormick, publisher of the *Chicago Tribune,* and reported that the people of Chicago were more hostile to Japan than to Hitler. Then he worried about the prospect of the destruction of the British Empire in Asia and concluded that "Singapore is infinitely more important to us than Smolensk." He was irritated by "American communists and their associates in Washington" who refused to see the seriousness of the situation in Asia. In his column published February 23, 1942, Sokolsky shifted completely, arguing that "not even Hitler menaces us as sharply as this explosive power of Japan." The war in Asia was "our war—directly our war. . . . Soviet Russia has thus far refused to become our ally in this war. . . . It is this Asiatic war we dare not lose. We must concentrate on it—if we are to remain a respected people among our neighbors."[4]

Fear that a victorious Japan would menace American markets, in Latin America as well as China, that the Japanese would colonize "crucial political and strategic economic areas on this continent" seemed to shake Sokolsky loose from his long argued conviction that Japanese hegemony in East Asia was of little moment to the United States. But there may have been other, more important reasons for the transformation. Conservative Republicans with whom he was closely associated, like McCormick, were identified with the Asia First movement. Attacking the administration for focusing on the wrong front was one of the few foreign policy issues that could be exploited without danger of appearing treasonous in time of war. The fact that the Soviet Union and the American Communist Party were insisting on the primacy of the European theatre served to assure men like

3. *New York Sun,* December 13, 1941, January 2, 1942, GES ms.

4. *Ibid.,* January 20 and 27, February 9 and 23, 1942, GES ms.

Sokolsky and his friends, who hated the Soviet Union and Communists, that it was best for the United States to fight in Asia. But whatever the reason, Sokolsky stressed the importance of fighting Japan throughout 1942, urging the Russians to attack Japan, to join America's second front, and demanding aid for China.[5]

Only when the Chinese had the audacity to complain to Wendell Wilkie about the inadequacy of American aid did Sokolsky respond angrily. He contended that the United States had kept them from subjugation all through the 1930s, that "we came to their aid, not they to ours." Admittedly he would prefer that the United States took the offensive against Japan, but "I must concede that Gen. Marshall and his staff officers have proved since Pearl Harbor that they know their business, that their judgment is sound, and that they are entitled to the full confidence of the American people." He insisted that Chinese and American interests were not identical and that Americans had to worry about the United States. Beware of Chinese playing their historic game "of stimulating divisions among the Western powers to the Chinese advantage."[6]

Greene and Sokolsky both were eager to use the wartime alliance with China as a means of getting rid of vestiges of the unequal treaties and the most blatant evidence of American racism. In August 1942, working with the Council on Foreign Relations and with Hornbeck, Greene pressed for the abolition of extraterritoriality in China. Hornbeck had been unresponsive when Greene argued that the practice was unnecessary in 1930, but in 1942 he was much more receptive. A few months after Greene's approach the administration signed a treaty surrendering extraterritorial rights and the Senate acquiesced. Sokolsky focused his efforts on repeal of the Chinese Exclusion Act which he called "outmoded, insulting, shameful legislation that gives the lie to every word that is being spoken as a justification for our participation in this war. It is an act worthy of Adolf Hitler and belongs with the text of 'Mein Kampf.' " And an added pleasure in working for repeal must have been the joy of attacking the AF of L leadership for opposing repeal—the joy of being able to attack the labor unions on an issue in which they were "morally wrong." Sokolsky's goal was also attained in 1943.[7]

5. *Ibid.*, February 23 and March 3, 1942. GES ms.

6. "These Days," November 5, 1942, and January 8, 1943, GES ms.

7. Greene to Hornbeck, August 13, 1942, and Hornbeck to Greene, August 26, 1942, RSG ms; "These Days," August 16, 1943, GES ms.

Affairs like the Chinese recall of Hu Shih, Ambassador to Washington, the qualifications of Clarence Gauss to be American Ambassador to China, and the relief of Stilwell were of great interest to Greene and Sokolsky. Greene corresponded with the columnist Raymond Clapper, expressing regret over the loss of Hu and the appointment of Gauss. Sokolsky contended that Chiang had erred in recalling Hu and managed a slap at his erstwhile friend and employer, T. V. Soong. Greene had acknowledged the problems of Hu trying to represent his country while Soong carried on his own diplomacy, but Sokolsky went further, writing of T. V. that "he does not possess the gracious urbanity, the breadth of culture, the unerring wisdom of Hu Shih." Greene and Sokolsky had very different views of Clarence Gauss, however. Greene thought Gauss epitomized the treaty-port mentality, a pessimist who "can rarely believe anything good of the Chinese and is not in the least interested in the best people among them." In general he considered old China hands unsuited to head the American mission and believed the Chinese anxious to have a glamorous, well-known figure. Sokolsky, however, thought old China hands the only kind of representatives to send to China in any capacity. He had no use for a "new, fresh, dumb" point of view. When Stilwell was relieved, Greene was not surprised, having warned Hornbeck that Stilwell and Chiang would probably not get on. But he doubted whether "the Angel Gabriel could handle the job of cooperating with Chiang K'ai-shek, Ho Ying-chin, etc." Sokolsky called Stilwell's relief "one of the first good breaks the Japanese have had in a long time," and thought Roosevelt and Hopkins probably responsible for undermining Stilwell.[8]

Sokolsky had never been overly concerned with consistency, but his eagerness to fault Roosevelt during the election campaign of 1944 allowed for a classic of inconsistency. All through the fall of 1941 he had praised Roosevelt for trying to avoid war with Japan. In January 1942 he quite reasonably charged that the American response of November 26, 1941 to the Japanese terms for a modus vivendi would have required the Japanese to withdraw from both China and Indo-China; that the Japanese had then faced the situation realistically, and attacked. In April he wrote that the United States had not anticipated war with Japan until 1943, that the Japanese

8. Greene to Clapper, September 7, 1942, to Lauchlin Currie, July 6, 1943, RSG ms; "These Days," September 8, 1942, and November 7, 1944, GES ms; Greene to Nelson Johnson, October 29, 1944, RSG ms.

preferred to talk "and we were appeasing them until public opinion forced the administration to adopt a stronger tone." But the column that should have astonished the long-time Sokolsky-watcher appeared on October 27, 1944. Appeasement, the effort to avoid conflict with Japan, was no longer a virtue. The Hoover administration—the last Republican administration—had been willing to act to stop Japanese aggression in 1931 and 1932, but "Mr. Roosevelt fiddled away on Far Eastern policy until most of China was in Japanese hands and the war was upon us." Roosevelt left the United States vulnerable, while selling scrap iron to the Japanese. Suddenly a leading critic of the Hoover-Stimson Doctrine announced that Hoover and Stimson were the men who knew how to handle the Japanese and Roosevelt was an appeaser who left his country unprepared for war: was a man like Roosevelt worthy of a third term as President of the United States?[9]

In the last years of the war, as plans for the postwar era began to be formulated, Greene was selected by the Council on Foreign Relations, along with Lamont, Hornbeck, Henry Luce, Tyler Dennett, John Foster Dulles, Arthur H. Dean, and a few other prominent scholars and businessmen to meet with equally prominent Chinese to chart the future of Sino-American relations. Illness prevented Greene from playing a major role with this group, at least in its early meetings. From his home in Worcester, he mused about how to end the war in East Asia and was uneasy about the demand for Japan's unconditional surrender. He wanted to allow the Japanese to decide for themselves whether they wanted an emperor, but when he learned that Grew was opposing abolition of the emperor system, he wavered. If Grew meant to perpetuate emperor worship, he was opposed. He did not hesitate to question Grew's judgment, even to imply that Grew's efforts to maintain friendly relations with Japan were ultimately responsible for Japan's disregard of American sensibilities—and thus for the war. Greene saw no need to occupy Japan, to prohibit heavy industry or shipping, arguing that deprivation of empire would be sufficient demonstration of defeat. A powerful Soviet Union and an American-supported China would suffice to check Japan in the future. He was confident that a discrediting of the military through defeat and the ending of intellectual isolation imposed on the country by the military would lead to the revival of liberalism in Japan.[10]

9. *New York Sun*, January 31 and April 9, 1942, "These Days," October 27, 1944, GES ms.

10. Walter H. Mallory to Greene, March 25, 1944, Greene to Charles C. Griffin, May 31, 1944, to Julius Pratt, July 28, 1944, RSG ms.

Sokolsky was vaguer than Greene, but on two occasions in 1945, in Feburary and in late July, he argued that the Japanese continued to fight because they did not know how to disengage themselves from the war. He contended that no country ever surrendered "unconditionally" short of complete conquest—which Greene thought was not worth the lives of tens of thousands of Americans. Sokolsky seemed heartened in February by the apparent prominence of Shigemitsu Mamoru in the Japanese cabinet, presuming this was a sign of a Japanese peace offensive. Curiously, though criticizing the Japanese for thinking in July 1945 that they still were in a position to retain the emperor system, Manchuria, Korea, and Taiwan, he apparently thought they had the means to fight on for another year before they would have "no bargaining power at all."[11]

All three men realized that the Soviet Union would likely emerge from the war second only to the United States as a world power and as a force in East Asia. In 1942 Greene contended that in Europe and in East Asia "Russia is now and is likely to continue to be more powerful than we." He warned William Allen White about deceiving the American people into underestimating Soviet power. He feared Americans would not realize that on some questions Soviet views would have to be decisive. He feared also that constant exalting of American supremacy might lead the Russians to think the United States planned to ignore or override their wishes. In April 1945, when rumors about the Far Eastern protocol of the Yalta agreement began to percolate among the friends of China, Greene decried the tendency to assume that the Russians were determined to regain control of Manchuria. He did express the hope, however, that the United States would train and equip the Chinese to drive the Japanese off the continent rather than urge the Russians to enter the war in East Asia. In general Greene recognized Soviet power, was apprehensive about how it would be exercised, and hoped that through realistic appraisals and cultural exchange programs, mutual understanding and cooperation would prove possible.[12]

For the first two years of American participation in the war Sokolsky swallowed his distaste for the Soviet Union. He was annoyed at Soviet calls for a second front in Europe and advised the Russians to bomb Osaka instead—to join America's second front. He informed his readers that he had

11. "These Days," February 23 and July 23, 1945, GES ms.

12. Greene to White, October 2, 1942, to Hu Shih, April 12, 1945, to editor of *Fortune,* April 24, 1945, to Bryan Hovde, May 30, 1945, RSG ms.

learned to despise communism in Petrograd in 1917 and had no love for Soviet Russia, but the Russians were useful allies against Nazi Germany and he would accept them. He hoped the price for cooperating with the Russians would not be too high. In 1943, when Thomas Dewey endorsed the idea of a postwar Anglo-American alliance, Sokolsky rejected it as likely to lead to conflict with the Soviet Union. He saw the American role as that of arbiter between Great Britain and the Soviet Union, the keeper of the peace. But by the end of the year, with the tide turned against Axis aggression, Sokolsky began to ease the rein on his suspicions. He did not like the fact that Roosevelt and Churchill held separate conferences at Cairo with Chiang and at Teheran with Stalin. Why didn't Stalin and Chiang meet? Their problems, he insisted, were "close and intimate." Russian attitudes toward Manchuria, Mongolia, and Turkestan might have been clarified—and there might have been a settlement of the problem of the Chinese Communist armies. In late 1944 he brooded over the threat of Soviet imperialism in East Asia, Mongolia, and Turkestan—and he contended that the Chinese Communist armies "represent the power of a foreign country."[13]

After Roosevelt, Stalin, and Churchill met at Yalta, Sokolsky's concern grew intense. In early March, less than three weeks after the meeting, he reported a campaign to discredit Chiang and the Kuomintang in the interest of Soviet imperialism and expressed fear that China had been betrayed at Yalta. He referred to the conference as an occasion when "the three members of the Holy Alliance met to redistribute territory in Europe and perhaps in Asia." In April he speculated about the possibility of a secret agreement on Manchuria and refuted the argument that there was a legitimate historical basis for the Russian claim to that territory. By May he was deeply troubled by Soviet activities in Eastern Europe and reported that "the Chinese live in terror that Soviet Russia will become our ally in the war against Japan and will use that excuse to seize Manchuria, Korea, and North China." To Sokolsky the new threat to Europe and to Asia, to the ideals for which Americans were fighting, was manifest.[14]

Surprisingly, it was Thomas Lamont, still refusing to be the stereotypical capitalist, who was most sanguine about relations with the Soviet Union. In September 1942 he wrote a long letter to the editor of the *New*

13. *New York Sun,* February 21 and March 19, 1942; "These Days," September 10, December 4 and 9, 1943, November 28, 1944, GES ms.

14. "These Days," March 2 and 6, April 19 and 23, May 11, 1945, GES ms.

*York Times*—a three-column letter preceded by the editor's 37-line identification of its author—urging whole-hearted support for the Soviet Union. He expressed regret over the "censoriousness" which led some Americans "to attack Russia because of the domestic policies of our great friend and ally." He buttressed his argument with a good deal of foolishness about Russian contributions to civilization and Russian generosity in making Alaska available to the United States, but his basic point was that the Russians were allies and the United States had to aid them against Hitler. A few months later, in his usual style, he wrote a warm letter to Soviet Ambassador Maxim Litvinov defending the American decision to invade North Africa instead of France. Russia would benefit far more from the African operation than from an unsuccessful effort against heavily fortified positions on the Atlantic coast. He also warned Litvinov that some Americans were troubled about the Russian position on the Baltic Republics, failing "to realize that America played her share back in 1919 in the separation of the Baltic provinces from Russia, and in fact in support of the counterrevolution in 1917."[15]

In May 1944 when the Russians were troubled by evidences of anti-Soviet attitudes in the United States, especially within the Catholic Church, the Soviet Ambassador came to New York in an unsuccessful effort to get Lamont to undertake a good will mission to Russia. Lamont reminded the Ambassador, now Andrei Gromyko, of his efforts toward obtaining American recognition of the Soviet Union in 1917, 1918, and finally in 1933. He then turned to the question of Poland and recommended that the Russians make as liberal a settlement as possible to help Roosevelt with the Polish vote in the coming election. He followed this talk with a letter to the Soviet consul-general in New York, explaining that the Russians could not expect private capital investments after the war—unless of course there were a postwar Soviet-American alliance. He also advised that a "humane" settlement of the Polish question was important if the Russians were to retain American good will. In December his friend and antagonist of long standing, Oswald Garrison Villard, complained to him about Soviet actions in Poland, and Lamont responded with the kind of realism he had once exhibited about Japanese imperialism in Manchuria. First, it was essential that the United States get along, coexist, with the Russians, however difficult the

15. *New York Times*, September 20, 1942, IV, p. 8; Lamont to Litvinov, November 9, 1942, 128–16, TWL ms.

task might prove. He did not like what Stalin was doing in Poland anymore than Villard did, but he professed to understand the Soviet position there—and in the Baltic states. There was not much that could be done about it in any event—and the territory had been unfairly taken away from Russia by the Brest-Litovsk and Versailles treaties. Thomas Lamont had lived seventy-odd years in an imperfect world and he had no desire for a conflict with the Soviet Union over Poland and the Baltic Republics.[16]

In the last months of the war, as the defeat of Germany and then Japan grew imminent, as the moment for the liberation of China approached, knowledgable men and women began to focus their attention on the struggle between Chiang Kai-shek and Mao Tse-tung for control over the future of China. Edward Carter of the Institute of Pacific Relations asked Lamont to write to the *New York Times* to urge that lend-lease supplies be made available to Mao's forces as well as to Chiang's. Lamont refused, claiming to be insufficiently informed. He told Carter he always checked his information with the Department of State and revealed that his earlier letters to the *Times* had been cleared with the Department.[17]

Lamont never participated in the intensely bitter debate over American policy toward China amidst the Kuomintang-Communist conflict, but he referred to the situation in China in a book written just before his death. Claiming—with a marked lack of candor—that he had long thought China to have a great future, he wrote of the disappointment of recent years, of the inability of the Chinese to establish stable government untainted by corruption, or to demonstrate an interest in democracy. He saw China's rulers in 1947 as in 1920, trying to overwhelm the opposition with force rather than seeking unity. He claimed that in 1920 Sun Yat-sen asked for $25 million to enable him to unify China by force and "now it is his younger brother-in-law, Marshal Chiang, who asks for America to equip his rabble armies to the same end, in order to crush his opponents coming down from the North, the so-called Communist armies." In his last remarks on China Lamont wrote that much as he detested communism "and the police state (which seems to be its outward and visible sign), I still believe that the Northern

16. Lamont memorandum of dinner with Gromyko, May 26, 1944, Lamont to Eugene D. Kisselev, June 20, 1944, 128–16, TWL ms; Lamont to Villard, December 7, 1944, Papers of Oswald Garrison Villard, Houghton Library, Harvard University.

17. Lamont to Carter, July 5, 1945, 36–3, TWL ms.

armies may be ranked as Chinese first and Communists second.'' He warned ''that in any event they are not to be won over merely by force of arms.'' He died in February 1948, with Mao's forces in control of north China and the Kuomintang reeling in defeat.[18]

Greene, of course, had long been aware of the Chinese Communist movement and, until the last year of his life, had studied it with considerable detachment. His review of Edgar Snow's *Red Star Over China* in February 1938 contained a clear expression of his perceptions. He was critical of the Communists because he held them responsible for starting the civil war and forcing China into hostilities with Japan before it was ready. He also considered the Communists guilty of excesses against so-called landlords and capitalists who were themselves poor people. But Greene was favorably impressed by the accomplishments of the Long March. He was also aware of the great appeal the Communists had for the poverty-stricken rural masses whose suffering a ''corrupt political administration'' had not alleviated. Drawing a parallel with earlier agrarian uprisings in China, he thought the leadership of the Chinese Communist Party distinguished by education and high ideals. ''Their primary objective,'' he agreed, was ''the improvement of the condition of the masses, which is long overdue in China.'' Although Greene wondered about the extent of Russian influence on the movement, he concluded that the Chinese Communists were ''certainly . . . no longer dependent either on Russian advice or Russian money.'' [19]

Returning from China in the spring of 1938, he reported that the Communists had modified their policies profoundly after they moved to the northwest. There was no doubt that they had muted their call for class warfare. He found the Communists and the government cooperating and thought the association useful to both sides. The government was now giving more attention to the needs of the common people and the Communists seemed to be abandoning ''their extreme position,'' more at peace with traditional Chinese individualism, accepting a society ''not more socialistic than that of many western European countries.'' In 1938 the euphoria of the united front still pervaded China—and even the Kuomintang regime, anxious to deny Japanese claims to be fighting in China to contain communism, gave credence to simplistic analyses of Mao's tactics.[20]

18. *Across World Frontiers,* 264.
19. *Worcester Telegraph,* February 13, 1938, RSG ms.
20. Press release, June 14, 1938, RSG ms.

Implicit in both the review of Snow's book and his remarks upon returning from China was Greene's own ideological stance. The Chinese people suffered terribly and the Communists were determined to help them. This was good. The Communists were men of high ideals, unlike the corrupt government administrators. Social justice and clean government were ends Greene valued highly—as did so many of his generation when they tried to clean up America during the Progressive era. But the Communists were more agreeable to Greene in 1938 because they appeared more moderate, less given to unacceptable practices, like class warfare. In a discussion of Chinese politics with Derk Bodde earlier in 1938 he had explained that "if I am prejudiced it is against violent revolutions and in favor of trying to improve an existing government instead of overthrowing it."[21] Clearly, Greene was very much a part of the American liberal tradition: reformist, gradualist, anxious to improve society—but not by violent means. But as he looked at political developments in China during the last years of his life, he saw a struggle between the Kuomintang and the Communists, *neither* of which shared his values—and he was asked to take sides.

In the early months of American participation in the war, the primary concern of the friends of China was to obtain aid to enable the Chinese to continue their resistance to Japan. As the war progressed, however, tensions between the Kuomintang and the Communists, the possibility of renewed civil war—i.e., the internal affairs of China—began to compete for their attention. One manifestation of this concern was Greene's irritation over what he believed to be excessive Communist influence in the New York office of the Institute of Pacific Relations. Specifically, he complained about Chinese Communists on the Pacific Council and the role of Frederick Field on the executive committee. Greene had been active in the IPR shortly after it was founded "to study the conditions of the Pacific peoples with a view to the improvement of their mutual relations." His brother Jerome had been chairman of the organization and Roger had been closely associated with its leadership throughout the 1930s. Members of the American Council, Field and Edward Carter, had cooperated with him in his work with the Price Committee. But Greene had been angered by Field's opposition to aid to Great Britain during the days of the Nazi-Soviet nonaggression pact and no longer trusted his objectivity. In addition, Hu Shih had told him that the Chinese members of the Pacific Council staff in New York were Communists. Read-

21. Greene to Bodde, January 6, 1938, RSG ms.

ing the work of American IPR scholars, Greene feared that they were dependent on Chinese research assistants who were politically committed; that the results were consistently distorted in favor of the Chinese Communist view of events in China.[22]

When corresponding with various IPR personnel on these questions, Greene tried to assure them that he was not a "red-baiter," that he was not opposed to occasional contributions by Chinese leftists. He simply wanted more objectivity which he thought could be obtained by hiring Chinese researchers of high academic standing, men who would be acceptable to presumably independent liberals like Hu Shih and Chiang Mon-lin. And he insisted that the Chinese did not have to be leftist to be progressive. Although he threatened at one point to discontinue his modest contributions to the IPR, he continued his support in 1943 and 1944.[23]

China's internal affairs were not settled, however, in the offices of the IPR. Tensions in China persisted and Greene and his friends tried to evaluate the situation there and to think of appropriate policies for the American government to pursue. In January 1944 he met with Nathaniel Peffer and John K. Fairbank, a young historian he had befriended in Peking, to discuss ways to prevent Chiang from setting aside American military aid for use against the Communists after the war. They did not solve the problem. Later in the year, Fairbank's father-in-law, Walter B. Cannon, a noted physiologist and one-time visiting professor at Peking Union Medical College, wrote to the Chinese Ambassador decrying the government blockade which prevented medical supplies from reaching Chinese Communist troops fighting against the Japanese. Greene expressed reservations about Cannon's letter, reporting that some Chinese friends, not supporters of the Kuomintang, thought Americans exaggerated the extent and significance of Communist guerilla activities. Greene also thought there was some justice in the Kuomintang blockading an area dominated by forces unwilling to accept government orders. He suggested that a more balanced approach would be to question the Kuomintang's judgment in handling the blockade without complete acceptance of the Communist position.[24]

Again and again Greene stressed the complexity of the situation in

22. Greene to Edgar J. Tarr, August 12, 1943, to Harriet C. Moore, August 14, 1943, RSG ms; See also John N. Thomas, *The Institute of Pacific Relations* (Seattle, 1974), 3–64.

23. Greene to Moore, August 22, 1943, to Tarr, September 17, 1943, and to Raymond Dennett, August 17, 1944, RSG ms.

24. Roger to Kate Greene, January 21, 1944, Greene to Cannon, September 19, 1944, RSG ms.

China and argued that foreigners had no right to try to impose a solution on the Chinese. To his daughter he conceded that many of the men on whom Chiang depended or to whom he was obligated were generally considered corrupt or inefficient. Similarly the Communists "seem to be unusually devoted to their ideals, honest and considerate of the common people." He was receiving conflicting reports from friends about the extent to which the Communists were fighting, with Americans claiming they fought more than Chiang's forces, but Chinese claiming stories of Communist action were exaggerated. Greene explained that he did not know the truth of the matter, but considered it inappropriate for outsiders, who would not have to live with civil war, to tell the Chinese government to trust the Communists, "who after all do not obey orders." To the editor of the *New York Times* he noted traditional American hostility to foreign interference in the affairs of the United States, but a propensity for Americans to interfere elsewhere. Noting favorable reports of the Chinese Communists and the growing demand among Americans for an end to Chinese disunity, an end of the Kuomintang blockade, and the supplying of arms to the Communists, he deplored these demands as irresponsible. Americans would not have to endure the consequences if they were wrong. Conceding that Americans had a legitimate interest in wanting a unified China to facilitate the joint effort against Japan, he argued "that interest is small compared with what the Chinese have to gain or lose in the future organization of their own country." Ostensibly taking a neutral, hands-off position, Greene was aligning himself with those opposed to supporting the Communists.[25]

Greene did not deceive himself about the effect of a "neutral" policy, of "noninterference." Writing to Ch'ien Tuan-sheng, a brilliant Chinese scholar, he acknowledged "that so long as we do anything in China we can hardly avoid helping one side or the other." Greene asked Ch'ien what he thought the United States should do, and Ch'ien recommended calling for a coalition with slight Kuomintang superiority. He hoped such a coalition would result in mutual toleration, mutual checks and allow for lend-lease supplies to be given to both armies. Ch'ien thought American opinion "bewildered by leftist propaganda on one side" and "by traditional bonds—chiefly for the missionary group—on the other." He suggested that Yenan was only half as promising as claimed by its friends and "Chung-king cer-

25. Roger to Katharine Greene (daughter), November 2, 1944, to editor, *New York Times* (not published), November 5, 1944, RSG ms.

tainly needs a great deal of transformation.'' Again the ''liberal'' solution: the truth is somewhere in between, form a coalition to achieve the mean.[26]

Gradually, but not without misgivings, Greene concluded that the liberal society he hoped to see emerge in postwar China would be realized more likely under Kuomintang rule than under the Communists. In May 1945 he told Julean Arnold, long-time American commercial attaché in China, that he was persuaded by Walter Judd's arguments in favor of Chungking, despite good things he heard about Mao's regime. But he was troubled by the fact that ''few indeed of my young friends around here agree with me,'' presumably a reference to Fairbank. To Judd, a colleague from the days of the Price Committee, he expressed his concern over the fact that so many of his liberal-minded young friends were ''naively trusting'' of the Chinese Communists. Greene claimed that they seemed to think China was composed of only two elements, the Kuomintang and the Chinese Communist Party. He insisted that they ignored the vast majority of educated Chinese who belonged to neither party. Like himself, his Chinese friends, ''practically without exception, want to see the Chinese Government become more liberal, but they definitely do *not* want to entrust the future of themselves and their children to the Communists.'' And to his son, Greene wrote with evident pleasure of Chiang Mon-lin returning to Chungking to an important position in the Executive Yuan. Though Chiang was an old Kuomintang member, Greene saw him as ''first and foremost a liberal, and perhaps for that reason was not very close to the top people lately.'' He regarded the appointment ''as another indication of a more favorable tendency in the Chungking government.''[27]

In June 1945, the *Amerasia* case created a minor scandal in Washington. The editor of a journal critical of the Kuomintang had obtained classified government documents, some of which were reports written by and given to him by John S. Service, a foreign service officer. Service had been stationed in Yenan and his analyses of the Chinese Communist movement, though generally considered accurate, compared Mao's regime favorably with Chiang's. Greene's initial reaction, to Walter Judd, was an expression of astonishment over the harshness of the State Department's attitude toward Service. He used the occasion to attack Grew, contending that the suppres-

26. Greene to Ch'ien, March 7, 1945, and Ch'ien to Greene, March 11, 1945, RSG ms.

27. Greene to Arnold, May 30, 1945, to Judd, July 1, 1945, to Edward Greene, July 2, 1945, RSG ms.

sion of information by people like Grew since 1931 was far more serious than what Service had done. Writing to Randall Gould, once the *Christian Science Monitor*'s man in China, Greene admitted that he was sympathetic in most matters with the men who favored doing business with the Communist regime in Yenan and was "outraged by the action taken against Service and others." He respected their reports of "observed facts," but questioned the validity of their arguments. To Gould and later to Nelson Johnson, Greene expressed the view that Service and others had demonstrated competence in their criticism of the Kuomintang, but were apparently putting aside their critical faculties when examining activities of the Communists. To dispose of the arguments of men like Service, he reached back to his long-standing conviction that the Chinese—or any other people—should be left to fight their civil wars to a finish. He told General Frank McCoy that if the Communists were as good as his friends claimed and the Kuomintang as bad, the Communists would win in the end without American interference—without pressure for a premature peace.[28]

In the closing months of 1945, on into 1946, it became clear that Greene was moving further toward those of his acquaintances who supported the Kuomintang. On several occasions he compared the Yalta agreement to Munich, called it an "almost treacherous secret agreement," and referred to the United States selling out the Chinese. He did not want the United States to withdraw from China, to withdraw support from the Chinese government—although he did oppose the use of American troops to fight against the Communists. In August 1946 he denied the claim, on the part of the Citizens for a Democratic Far Eastern Policy, that all Chinese liberals wanted the United States to leave China. He insisted that the United States, because it had aided Japan between 1937 and 1941, because it had betrayed the Chinese at Yalta, was too deeply involved in Chinese affairs for a complete withdrawal to be beneficial. Perhaps the most obvious evidence of the direction in which Greene was moving was the shift in his attitude toward Geraldine Fitch. When Greene and Mrs. Fitch worked together for the Price Committee and again as late as November 1945, he thought her "pretty close to being professional rather than amateur as an apologist for Chungking." He knew that her husband was employed by the Chinese government but was

28. See John S. Service, *The Amerasia Papers* (Berkeley, California, 1971), 7–52; Greene to Judd, July 1, 1945, to Gould, August 8, 1945, to Johnson, December 17, 1945, to McCoy, July 24, 1945, RSG ms.

not sure whether she was receiving Chinese money. In October 1946 his mistrust gave way to praise as he wrote to congratulate her for presenting the strongest argument he had seen against the position of Evans Carlson and other advocates of the Chinese Communists.[29]

The clearest expression of Greene's reasoning in the last months of his life came in a letter to Archibald Chien, a Chinese who had worked with him when he was in the consular service and followed him to the Peking Union Medical College. In September 1946, Chien was working with General George Marshall as he tried to prevent civil war in China. Greene wrote of being unable to forget that the Communists had broken away from the Kuomintang nineteen years before and started using force without any attempt to use peaceful means to accomplish their ends. He remembered "that to most observers in China it seemed clear enough that the people at large supported Chiang's Government and most of its policies, as witness the enthusiastic rejoicing when Chiang was released from captivity in 1936." Of perhaps greater importance, he remembered "how education, public health, transportation and various industries progressed under Chiang's Government before the Japanese attack in spite of the heavy handicap created by the Communist rising." Greene was not convinced that the Kuomintang was incapable of reform. He argued that a large part of the famine and other distress in China in 1946 was "due to the interruption of communications by the Communists, who have not hesitated to sacrifice the welfare of the common people by using such means to forward their cause." He would not have Americans fight in China, but saw "no reason why the Chinese Government should not enjoy the advantages which come from being the recognized government and having access to all the supplies and equipment that can be brought in by sea."[30]

Violence versus peaceful reform. Gradual modernization brought about by western-educated liberal intellectuals, or sudden upheaval at the hands of Marxist-Leninists. Peaceful, gradual reform under Kuomintang leadership was an empty dream in 1946, but Greene remembered how the world had looked to him from Peking. He remembered the years of working with Chinese liberals, their slow but steady progress hampered by first the Com-

29. Greene to Raymond Dennett, October 12, 1945; to Hu Shih, February 23, 1946; to Maude Russell, August 29, 1946; to Kate Greene, November 16, 1945; to Geraldine Fitch, October 15, 1946, RSG ms.

30. Greene to Ch'ien, September 5, 1946, RSG ms.

munists and then the Japanese—and he wanted those men to have another chance. They were a few grains of sand in a great desert, but that Greene had forgotten. As his Chinese liberal friends had to choose, so he had to choose. And when they chose the Kuomintang, an urban leadership rooted shallowly in the rural mass, so did he. Whether Greene would have become identified with the "China Lobby," like Judd and Fitch and others with whom he had worked, though likely, cannot be known. After years of illness, he died in March 1947.

Probably no one in the United States knew as much in the 1940s about the origin and early development of the Chinese Communists as did George Sokolsky. There were few Americans who could equal his understanding of factional politics within the Kuomintang. Sokolsky had been a major source, perhaps the principal informant on Chinese politics—certainly the most respected informant—for American military intelligence and American diplomats in China during the 1920s. With his syndicated column and later his editorials for the *New York Mirror,* he was in an extraordinary position to educate the American people about the background of the Kuomintang-Communist struggle and to provide them with valuable analyses of the events of the 1940s. He had the opportunity and he had the intelligence—but George Sokolsky worshipped strange gods.

When Sokolsky returned to the United States in the 1930s, one of the subjects upon which he wrote and lectured was communism in China. His analyses were generally straightforward and accurate. There were occasional errors on details, as when he once described Mao as French-educated, but Sokolsky unquestionably understood the nature of the Chinese Communist movement. He wrote and spoke of it sympathetically and, until the appearance of Snow's *Red Star Over China,* had probably provided the best information available to the American public. In his *Tinder Box of Asia* he had warned against the assumption that the Chinese were too conservative a people for communism and contended that China was ready for revolutionary change, more likely to be carried out by the Communists than by any other element in the country.[31]

In December 1932 Sokolsky published an article in *Asia* that analyzed the Chinese Communist movement in depth, sketched its past, and predicted

31. *New York Times,* August 10, 1932, p. 7; *Tinder Box of Asia,* 346–47.

its future. The analysis was brilliant, the predictions strikingly accurate, and the tone suggests that a slightly different turn of the wheel of fortune would have found Sokolsky in Yenan before Snow. He warned that Chiang's anti-Communist campaigns were doomed to failure, that the Communists could not be suppressed by military force, "for where does the Red Army end and the peasant population begin in those Southern provinces?" He insisted that the Chinese Communist Party had become "an indigenous Chinese movement led by Chinese intellectuals and finding its greatest strength among the dispossessed tenant-peasants and workless bandits of South China." They took root where Kuomintang tax collectors and militarists were so oppressive that "the outraged peasants gladly turn to the Communists as saviours." He attributed the successes of the Red Armies to their social and educational work among the masses, the decency of their commanders, and their kindness to the peasants—rather than to the appeal of their Marxian economic program. "The Chinese will do to Communism," he predicted, "what they have done to Christianity and to Buddhism. They will make it Chinese." And Sokolsky concluded by arguing that the Communists would grow in numbers and that no force in China could stop them.[32]

During World War II Sokolsky developed very different analyses of Chinese politics and of the nature of the Chinese Communist movement—analyses which, by 1945, were more in keeping with his role as a spokesman for conservative capital, for the conservative element in the Republican Party. There were no more derogatory references to Chiang as dictator or "Ningpo Napoleon." His problems in gaining the cooperation of the Communists were spelled out as early as December 1941, along with the arguable but reasonable contention that actions of the Chinese Communist armies depended upon the policy of the Soviet Union toward Chiang's regime. Chiang received considerable praise, in keeping with Sokolsky's advocacy of an Asia First strategy. He was conducting an "amazingly heroic defense of China." He was "the bravest and most tragic figure in this war." Evidence was found of his genius as a statesman.[33]

When criticism of Chiang's regime and worries about Kuomintang-Communist tensions began to appear in the public prints in late 1943, early 1944, Sokolsky explained some of the internal problems of China to his

32. "The Red Armies of China," *Asia,* XXXII (December 1932), 620–26.

33. *New York Sun,* December 20, 1941, March 28, May 4, and June 17, 1942, GES ms; "Asia for the Asiatics," *American Mercury,* LV (July 1942), 72–81.

readers. He seemed almost amused that his fellow Americans were discovering the weaknesses of Chiang and the Soong family. He wrote of having observed these foibles for many years, the corruption and the nepotism. He claimed that those who had earlier brushed aside critics of Chiang's regime as pro-Japanese had become the most bitter in their disappointment with its performance. Obviously, the opportunity to defend his past record was irresistible. But rather than determine whether Chiang or Mao was right, Sokolsky urged the United States to force them to cooperate. They must fight Japan, he insisted, and not each other. Sentiments like these, not notably different from those being voiced by Chou En-lai, American observers in China, or liberal commentators in China, led to an attack on Sokolsky in the vehemently pro-Kuomintang magazine, *China Monthly,* which accused him of being pro-Communist in its June 1944 issue. But except when he was pleading special causes like that of Hu Shih or settling old scores with the Ch'en brothers or T. V. Soong, Sokolsky did not give Chungking's American friends much more cause for concern.[34]

In September 1944 Sokolsky insisted that China would endure revolution and civil war after the defeat of Japan and wrote critically of Russian support for the Chinese Communists. By November he claimed that the Chinese Communists armies represented Russian power in China and implied that they were instruments of Russian imperialism. Abandoning his call for pressures to force the Kuomintang and Communists to compromise their differences, he contended that these were irreconcilable. The United States had to choose between supporting Chiang or supporting Russian policy and allowing a pro-Russian puppet to take his place. Before the year was out he was warning against the Soviet conquest of Europe and Asia, of the possibility of Stalin succeeding where Hitler failed. The British were right to try to stamp out communism in Italy and Greece. The American preference for self-determination was laudable but unworkable in practice. "In China," he charged, "we have forced Chiang Kai-shek into an armistice with Stalin's Chinese adherents." And he fretted about Russian use of local politicans "who insist that they are not dominated by Soviet Russia but by a curious confusion of Communism plus nationalism."[35]

34. "These Days," April 21, 1944, GES ms; Cited in Ross Koen, *The China Lobby in American Politics* (New York, 1973), 118.

35. "These Days," September 16, 21, and 22, November 28, and December 9, 1945, GES ms.

As Soviet influence spread in Eastern Europe and rumors of the Yalta agreement were about, Sokolsky became more strident in his warnings about Stalin and Soviet imperialism. The Chinese Communists were "the Russian puppets at Yenan." He insisted that patriotic Chinese could not distinguish between Mao, who served Soviet Russia, or Wang Ching-wei, whose puppet regime had served Japan. He expressed frequent concern for what he considered to be the likelihood of Russian attempts to occupy Chinese territory. In June he wrote of Chiang, "who with inspired brilliance and rare capacity has saved his country from conquest by Soviet Russia" and called for the United States to support him. A few days after the Japanese surrender Sokolsky complained that the Russians were taking Chinese territory. They were using the Chinese Communists as their instrument—and "these Chinese Communists are continuing to conduct a civil war and to confuse the peace of the world by their wicked, chaotic, selfish, doctrinaire rebellion." The Chinese Communists were, "in effect, mountain bandits supported by an alien Power to keep their country in turmoil and therefore weak." Despite all the understanding, even sympathy showed in the early 1930s, in August 1945 Sokolsky wrote that "not a single year has passed since May 30, 1925, that these communists have not found a reason and a means for bringing misery to their own country."[36]

Sokolsky's contention that the Chinese Communists were Russian puppets remained a standard part of his repertoire throughout the 1940s and 1950s and was generally accepted as fact by the American public. A poll in 1948 indicated that approximately 65 percent of those respondents aware of a civil war in China believed that the Chinese Communists took orders from Moscow. In December 1950, 81 percent thought that the Chinese intervened in Korea under orders from Russia. Only five percent dissented.[37] Sokolsky evidenced no difficulty in contradicting his earlier estimates of Mao and his followers—and probably would have suffered little pain had he lived long enough for public awareness of the Sino-Soviet split to have required another shift. But Sokolsky found the situation in China a weapon for his primary goal in the postwar years: the destruction of liberalism and Democratic hegemony in the United States by the discrediting of Roosevelt and the New Deal.

For Sokolsky, the communist conspiracy in the United States was al-

36. *Ibid.*, March 19, May 16, 19, 21, 22, and 23, June 8, August 20 and 31, 1945.
37. *Gallup Poll,* I, 728–29, II, 955.

ready evident in August 1945. He found the Russians behind a world-wide propaganda campaign to undermine support for Chiang. They were particularly successful in the United States, "where magazine writers and radio commentators, who generally take their 'line' from the American communists, reached the American people with their plausible but unwarranted arguments in support of the Chinese communists." As the weeks passed he wrote of the betrayal of China at Teheran and at Yalta. In November 1945, following Patrick Hurley's resignation as American Ambassador to China, Sokolsky demanded an investigation of the Department of State. He called Hurley's action "a courageous rebuke to the wicked policy of truckling to Soviet Russia." Communists and fellow-travelers in the State Department were so powerful that "appeasement is the only rule it knows." To his conservative readers the spread of communism may have been as fearsome a prospect as the spread of fascism. As Soviet hegemony in Eastern Europe became apparent and as the Chinese Communists refused to come to heel, Sokolsky pointed to alleged communists in the American government to explain the state of world affairs.[38]

Early in 1946 Sokolsky resurrected the Hoover-Stimson doctrine as a club with which to beat the Truman administration. Neglecting to mention his opposition to Stimson's policies, he called the doctrine to the attention of Secretary of State James F. Byrnes, demanding to know if it was "dead." Again and again he repeated the argument that the United States was forcing the Chinese to give to the Russians all that the Japanese wanted in Manchuria: "Manchuria, over which China and Japan fought since 1894, has now been given to Russia by the United States—that is, by Roosevelt, Truman and Byrnes . . . will the American people suffer dishonor complacently?" When the Russians withdrew their forces from Manchuria in March 1946, Sokolsky managed to argue both that the Russians were retreating in the face of the first evidence of determination *and* to condemn the weaknesses of Roosevelt and Byrnes. Presumably the "country" and not the Democratic administration had called the Soviet bluff.[39]

The skills Sokolsky had demonstrated in Shanghai in the 1920s when he wrote for the conservative British *North China Daily News* and the pro-Japanese *Far Eastern Review* while advising Chinese political leaders and

38. "These Days," August 31, October 3, November 30, 1945, GES ms.

39. *Ibid.*, February 21 and 28, March 14, 1946.

serving as an informant for the American government were demonstrated again in 1946 when he began to write unsigned editorials for the *New York Mirror*. In his regular column published July 23, 1946, he insisted that the United States pay less attention to the corruption of T. V. Soong than to the need to strengthen Chiang's government sufficiently for it to serve American purposes in China. The *Mirror,* however, was not much interested in aid for anybody, so, in August 1946 Sokolsky wrote an editorial attacking UNRRA for wasting aid by giving it to China, specifically to T. V. Soong, who withheld it from starving people. But the main thrust of his writing on China in 1946 was in support of Chiang's regime. He was critical of General George Marshall and Ambassador Leighton Stuart for implementing a weak policy that gave the Communist status they did not deserve.[40]

Sokolsky's anticommunism won for him an unusual accolade in late 1946. The NAM and the DAR had long since found him attractive, but in November 1946 an article in the staunchly anticommunist *Catholic World* listed him among Jews who were opponents of Communism. Erik v. Kuehnelt-Leddihn, author of "Do Jews Tend Toward Communism?" selected Sokolsky for special mention among Jewish columnists who could be trusted. The essential justice of the notice was apparent a year and a half later when Sokolsky joined Roy Cohn and Alfred Kohlberg to create the American Jewish League Against Communism.[41]

George Marshall became the central target for Sokolsky immediately upon becoming secretary of state. His strategic decisions during World War II were pronounced wrong and Sokolsky was unfavorably impressed by Marshall's "petulant assumption that because he failed in an impossible task in China, the United States must withdraw its support from Chiang Kai-shek." Unity in China between the Kuomintang and the Communists was neither possible nor desirable. After the Truman Doctrine was promulgated, Sokolsky argued that Marshall's course in China had been exactly the opposite of that announced by Truman. If the United States was committed to supporting free peoples resisting subjugation by armed minorities, what about the Chinese? Why send aid to Greece and not to China?[42]

As late as 1941 Sokolsky had insisted that the war in Europe and the

40. *Ibid.*, July 23, 1946; *New York Mirror,* editorial, August 15, 1946, GES ms.

41. "Do Jews Tend Toward Communism?" *Catholic World,* CLXIV (November 1946), 160–62; Joseph Keeley, *The China Lobby Man* (New Rochelle, New York, 1969), 248–51.

42. "These Days," February 22 and June 5, 1947, GES ms.

war in Asia were two separate wars, but in 1947 he insisted that what Soviet Communists did in Europe and Chinese Communists did in Asia constituted one threat: "While attention is being focused on the European situation, Soviet Russia is making marked advances in the Far East. Chinese communists, a direct arm of the Soviet international armed forces, retreated from their war capital at Yenan and entered upon a military career in Manchuria." He contended that if Marshall's mediation effort had been successful, "Soviet Russia would by now be as completely in the saddle in China as it is in Hungary." Sokolsky argued that the "Soviet imperialist movement in Asia" paralleled Soviet activities in Europe; that "to the Russians the problem is one. To us, it must be one." Again, Sokolsky found a way to criticize the administration even when its anticommunist policies in Europe might have seemed worthy of his approval. And the same kind of universalism, the demand for an Asian policy equivalent to policy toward Europe, could be used to attack the Marshall Plan. But if Marshall showed himself willing to send money to China as well, then Sokolsky was capable of arguing that Marshall should be stockpiling; instead "he wants to give Europeans and the Chinese lots of money—our money."[43]

The consistent point in Sokolsky's writings was criticism of the Democratic administration. Attack it for not giving aid to China and attack it for giving aid to China. Attack it for not standing up to the Soviet Union, and when it stands up to the Soviet Union somewhere, attack it for not standing up to the Soviet Union everywhere. Sokolsky was unquestionably anticommunist in his postdepression identity, but he used his anticommunism in the 1940s primarily as a partisan tool. Although he was associated with Kohlberg, the self-styled "Mr. China Lobby," and with Kohlberg's assault on the Department of State and the Institute of Pacific Relations, he did not share Kohlberg's commitment to Chiang. Although Sokolsky did much to give currency to Kohlberg's views, to create the milieu in which Service, John P. Davies, and others were persecuted, he could also attack the Chinese for demanding assistance from the United States or criticize the administration for giving such assistance. The affairs of China were not terribly important to Sokolsky. Although he was genuinely concerned about Soviet expansion in Europe, his ultimate concern was to prevent another four years of Democratic government.

43. *Ibid.*, June 12 and November 12, 1947, *New York Mirror*, editorial, November 25, 1947, GES ms.

In February 1948 he explained that the Far Eastern Division had been served by outstanding men like MacMurray, Johnson, Gauss and Hornbeck—and then it was taken over by "New Dealers," "smart boys," and they made a mess of everything. Stilwell, whose recall he had once bemoaned, was vain. Marshall had told Chiang to "love thine enemy." Leighton Stuart was presumably an old fool—and "that is the kind of representation we have been having in China." Only Hurley and Wedemeyer passed his inspection. Looking over relations with the Soviet Union and China in March, he found serious problems, largely the result of Roosevelt's "tragic policies." Roosevelt had told the American people that we were helping China but in reality we were doing nothing but aiding the Soviet Union to conquer China through the Chinese Communist Party. "It all adds to the record of Franklin D. Roosevelt's duplicity," wrote George Sokolsky. As the election neared, he warned of the importance of ridding the country of Truman and Marshall: "the China situation is perfect for a general war. Chiang Kai-shek is in real peril, largely because of the politics pursued by Harry Truman and George Marshall. It is possible to start a war with Soviet Russia in China, Manchuria, and Korea at a moment's notice. For that, only George Marshall is responsible. . . ."[44]

In August, Sokolsky announced that much of China's problem was monetary, a direct result of American silver policy—and he demanded to know who was responsible. Parroting Kohlberg, he produced a roster of potential villains, claiming falsely to have been critical of Lauchlin Currie, Owen Lattimore, Stilwell, Marshall, and John Carter Vincent throughout the years. Now he asked: why did the United States send paper money instead of vital war supplies over the hump? Why did the United States try to force Chiang to work with the Chinese Communists despite evidence of Soviet efforts to use the Chinese Communists to conquer China? Why was this policy continued even after the Soviet Union disclosed its aims? Sokolsky called for a Congressional investigation, but he already knew the answer to his questions. The "truth will be that somewhere in the directing line, on the high level of policy, were powerful Americans who were working to hand China over to Soviet Russia, which would have given that country, in short time, the whole of Asia, and made America subject to Russia's will."[45]

Despite election eve slurs by Sokolsky, Harry Truman was reelected

44. "These Days," February 27, March 20 and 31, and July 21, 1948, GES ms.
45. *Ibid.*, August 6, 1948.

president of the United States. Resigned, Sokolsky warned that Truman would have to face "the imminent conquest of China by Soviet Russia." His insistence on the need to aid Chiang persisted in late 1948 and early 1949, with continued criticism of Marshall and Stilwell, continued arguments of the need to take a stand in China against Soviet imperialism. In one editorial for the *Mirror* he warned that the loss of China imperilled Alaska and concluded that "we defend ourselves in China or we defend ourselves on our own soil." In another he attributed Stilwell's alleged decision to work with the Chinese Communists to "the promptings of the Communists in the State Department." In the same editorial he managed to tar T. V. Soong by labeling him the last wartime hope of the Communists in the State Department.[46]

While Chiang's cause retained some faint vestige of hope, in late 1948 Sokolsky played variations on what was later known as the "domino" theme. He warned of the danger to Southeast and then to South Asia or the Philippines or Alaska or Main Street, U.S.A., if China fell to the Soviet menace. Once Chiang fled to Taiwan, he reported that the United States had won the Cold War in Europe, but the Russians had won in Asia. With the passage of time he did not hesitate to argue that the "storehouses of natural wealth" and the "great new industries" of Asia were more important than Europe. Asian manpower would enable Russia to "overpower an effete Europe."[47]

Chiang's collapse permitted review of the causes of America's "loss" of China, and the Kohlberg, "China Lobby" line, was increasingly in evidence in Sokolsky's writings in 1949 and 1950. Roosevelt begot Teheran and Yalta. Stilwell and Marshall tried to force Chiang into a coalition with the Communists, remaining hostile to Chiang even after Marshall became less sympathetic to the Communists. A Communist cell in the Treasury Department, revealed by Elizabeth Bentley and Whittaker Chambers in testimony before the House Un-American Activities Committee, consisting of Lauchlin Currie, Sol Adler, and Harry Dexter White, among others, could not be ignored in trying to understand a monetary policy that wrecked China. Acheson showed some antagonism to Russia in Europe but pursued a

46. *Ibid.*, October 28, November 6, and December 1, 1948; *New York Mirror*, editorials, November 2 and 29, 1948, January 18, 1949, GES ms.

47. "These Days," November 11, 1948, January 26, May 4, June 1, 1949, and October 6, 1950, GES ms.

pro-Russian course in Asia—because pro-Russian, pro-Communist elements remained in control of American policy toward China. The Institute of Pacific Relations, Frederick Field, Agnes Smedley, Anna Louise Strong, and Edgar Snow joined Lattimore, Currie, Vincent, and Marshall as Sokolsky filled his columns and his *Mirror* editorials with these charges. It was a little like the old days in China, as recounted by his enemies. Cross George Sokolsky and his column would report having found you in a compromised position. Befriend him—and *your* enemies had best beware. In April 1949 he called again for a Congressional investigation of American policy toward China, 1939 to 1949. And "they might also look at the Amerasia case, at the Institute of Pacific Relations, at the American silver policy which bankrupted China, at the possession of American arms by the Asiatic Communists and how they got them, and at the retention in office and promotion of those American officials who pursued a pro-Russian policy in China." Some of these were Sokolsky's causes. Others were obviously Kohlberg's—and Sokolsky did not hesitate to credit Kohlberg as a source, though he did not devote a full column to his friend Alfred until July 1950.[48]

In April 1949 Sokolsky added Walton Butterworth to his list and took a wild shot at Ben Cohen, asking if Cohen had written the directive for Marshall's mission to China. Cohen's associate from the most glorious days of the New Deal, Tommy Corcoran, was dragged into the same column and his dealings with T. V. Soong questioned. As Alger Hiss faced Whittaker Chambers' charges and the Hiss case was exploited as symbolic of New Deal "muddle-headedness and susceptibility to treason," Sokolsky played a steady accompaniment. How explain "the treacherous stupidity" of State Department policy toward China? How explain the fact that the Department's policy toward China "has been designed to assist Soviet Russia to conquer China through an army of 'agrarian reformers' "? The blame, Sokolsky announced, belonged to American liberalism—the intellectual upbringing of Dean Acheson and Philip Jessup. In "The China Story," published in *Catholic World* in September 1949, Sokolsky focused on Hiss in a list of "New Dealers" who had made the interests of the Soviet Union the measure of American policy toward China. Including Service and Vincent among the New Dealers he castigated, Sokolsky elevated Hiss to the posi-

48. *Ibid.*, January 21, February 16, March 14, 1949; *New York Mirror*, editorials, April 19, 22, and 23, May 3 and 4, 1949; "These Days," April 21, 25, and 28, 1949, July 18, 1950, GES ms.

tion of Roosevelt's expert on Far Eastern affairs. And if the "White Paper" published by the Department of State to review its work with China failed to substantiate his charges, it was clear that "the most vital facts [were] omitted" to protect Acheson and his fellow-travelers.[49]

On October 1, 1949, Mao proclaimed the establishment of the People's Republic of China and, given the abuse the Truman administration had suffered at the hands of Sokolsky and his comrades, recognition of the new government of China was postponed. Gallup polls released in November 1949 and June 1950 indicated that a large majority of those aware of the existence of Mao's regime opposed recognition. In bold-faced type one of Sokolsky's editorials for the *Mirror* declared "Soviet China must not be recognized," but contained evidence of his fear that Great Britain would persuade the United States to ignore his advice. In keeping with the *Mirror*'s pronounced Anglophobia, Sokolsky accused Acheson of running the State Department in Great Britain's behalf. When Herbert Hoover, Senator William F. Knowland, and Senator Robert A. Taft called for the United States to commit itself to the defense of Taiwan, the administration's refusal was again blamed on the pro-British group in the Department of State. Even in his signed column, Sokolsky charged that the Department's minimizing of the strategic importance of Taiwan was "deceitful propaganda in support of the British and may, with safety, be discounted." Attacks on Acheson as being pro-British and tailoring American policy for British interests persisted alongside charges that he was pro-Soviet, running a Department that existed for Russia's benefit.[50]

Sokolsky did not think it necessary to explain charges that to some may have seemed contradictory. Any means of discrediting the "prissy dandies who preside over our affairs in the State Department" was acceptable. And when Acheson withdrew American diplomats from China because of Communist harassment, Sokolsky brayed with apparent outrage: "What we should do is to take a city—any city—Canton, Swatow, Amoy, or Shanghai, and hold it until Soviet China treats us with the respect that is our due. The American flag must not be a symbol of cowardice." So much for

49. Eric Goldman, *The Crucial Decade-And After* (New York, 1960), 105; "These Days," June 1 and 3, 1949, GES ms; "The China Story," *Catholic World*, CLXIX (September 1949), 406–11; *New York Mirror*, editorial, August 10, 1949, "These Days," January 17, 1950, GES ms.

50. Gallup Poll, II, 868–69, 915; *New York Mirror*, editorials, October 17, 1949, January 4 and 11, 1950, "These Days," January 9, 1950, GES ms.

Acheson's "gentle and carefully worded" notes. Even during the Korean War Sokolsky kept accusing Acheson of plotting to put across "the dream of his career," the recognition of the People's Republic and the seating of its representatives in the United Nations.[51]

In February 1950, Joseph McCarthy launched his career as a leader, ultimately the symbol of the anticommunist crusade Sokolsky worked so hard to stimulate in the United States. Fittingly they shared a close associate in Roy Cohn, a young man prominent in Kohlberg's American Jewish League Against Communism. As McCarthy raged against the State Department, proclaiming essentially the same charges Sokolsky had offered ad nauseam since 1945, Sokolsky wrote constantly in support of him. All of the old charges against all of the old villains were trotted out again and the *Amerasia* case linked to the Hiss trial. As if these lies were not sufficiently obscene, he wrote in March of homosexuals in the State Department, asking what part they had played in shaping American policy since Teheran. Anticommunism, Anglophobia, anti-intellectualism, now sexual aspersions—no appeal was too vile for Sokolsky. And, of course, the Congressional investigations he demanded were soon forthcoming.[52]

In November 1949 Sokolsky had argued for military preparedness, warning of the danger to Japan and Alaska if "Soviet China marches into Southern Korea below the 38th parallel." In June 1950 North Korean forces crossed that parallel, the United States intervened, and before the year was out found itself fighting against the Chinese People's Liberation Army. For Sokolsky the situation in Korea was the "inevitable result" of the United States pursuing the wrong policies in East Asia. All through the war he repeated his charges, and claimed American responses to the outbreak of war, especially the decision to protect Taiwan, were proof of the accuracy of his analyses, of the errors of the Department of State—"engineered by the Alger Hiss group." In November he summed up five years of his writings with the charge that "American boys are being killed in Korea today because of errors made by Roosevelt, Truman and the State Department in the conduct of our Far Eastern policy." And in December he brought it all

51. "These Days," January 18, 1950; *New York Mirror,* editorial, October 18, 1950, GES ms.

52. "These Days," March 16, 21, 22, 24, 27, 28, and 31, April 14 and 15, June 21, 1950, GES ms. A Gallup poll released in July, 1950, indicated that 75% of the respondents had never heard of the *Amerasia* case but another poll showed 86% were aware of McCarthy's charges against the Department of State. Gallup, *Gallup Poll,* II, 924, 911.

together, including the link between his anti-Soviet and anti-British campaigns. Listing eight "demonstrable errors" committed by American leaders since 1939, number eight read:

> The abandonment and betrayal of Chiang Kai-shek by the State Department from 1944, when he was still fighting, to this moment, when he is still offering to fight, is one of the most grievous errors in all history. It was designed originally by Soviet Russia and carried out by Russian agents in the State Department, among whom the most publicized is Alger Hiss. A vast and untruthful campaign to justify this treason was conducted by the State Department.
>
> After Soviet Russia had won a complete victory in China, Great Britain accepted the role of appeaser which the American State Department imitated. That policy produced the Korean War.[53]

Sokolsky wrote for almost twelve years after Americans and Chinese began killing each other in Korea, but he had little more to say, little more to do. Those deaths, exploited by Sokolsky and McCarthy and their friends, left a legacy of hatred and suspicion that prevented a Sino-American rapprochement until 1971. The targets of their attacks were driven from the State Department, sometimes from the country—and at least on one occasion, to death. The climate they created in America, the lies upon which it was based, contributed to a degree of human misery, especially in Asia, that surely merits them a circle in hell not far from that of Hitler and Stalin. Sokolsky wrote many columns on other subjects, even about American foreign policy, that were perfectly sensible, sometimes contradicting some of his more grotesque lies, but his epitaph must stand: his was a major contribution to the creation of McCarthyism—perhaps greater than Joe McCarthy's.

53. *Ibid.*, November 12, 1949, June 27, July 5 and 10, August 10, November 14, and December 4, 1950.

# CONCLUSION

In the aftermath of America's war in Vietnam, acceptance of the idea that a foreign policy "establishment" influences American policy has been widespread. Godfrey Hodgson, in an analysis of the American establishment, suggested that its members came from what George Orwell called the "lower upper middle class." Most of them, Hodgson thought, came from old families, but not necessarily wealthy families. The typical establishment man of the pre-World War II era of Dean Acheson and the Dulles brothers, the sons of clergymen, came from a family that "could afford to give its sons the inheritance of a superior education, but had little money to leave after that." With these antecedents the young man went on to Harvard or Yale and ultimately to a connection with the Council on Foreign Relations. From a place of eminence within American society, ideally a Wall Street law firm, he would attempt discreetly, privately, to steer the country along a course that would lead to American hegemony in world affairs, benignly exercised.[1]

Roger Greene and Thomas Lamont came from precisely the kind of families Hodgson had in mind. Had the term been in use in the United States during his life time, Lamont would have been considered the quintessential "establishment" figure. Greene, far less powerful, especially after his fall from grace with the Rockefellers, was forced to use less private means to express his opinions, was forced to attempt to manipulate public opinion.

1. Hodgson, "The Establishment," *Foreign Policy,* 10 (Spring 1973), 3–40.

George Sokolsky was also a clergyman's child, from a family of limited means that was nonetheless able to provide him with a Columbia education. But Sokolsky was a Jew, an "amusing" Jew, but still beyond the pale. Lacking a gentleman's access to the top, he never bothered to cultivate a gentleman's ethic. Struggle in the ghetto provided other lessons and Sokolsky developed few scruples in his personal quest for power. Excluded from the foreign policy establishment, he found the means to operate outside it, and to triumph over it.

Roger Greene: thoughtful, responsible, constructive, far-seeing, he was an *able* man, outstanding as a consular official, as a medical administrator, and as a lobbyist. There were, however, aspects of his personality and character that created problems for him. His contemporaries often respected him but they did not always like him. They found him austere, cold, unapproachable. Some, like Joseph Grew, thought him self-righteous—and, clearly, he was more ideological than men like Grew or Lamont, in the sense of having uncompromising views, and of placing a greater value on ideas than on being considered a good fellow. There was too much of the crusader in Greene for him to be comfortable with the establishment—or it with him. His missionary heritage, his formative years during the Progressive era, left him very much a man with a profound commitment to leave a better world than the one into which he was born.

Perhaps Greene's most attractive characteristic was his loyalty to his subordinates, his willingness to fight their battles with his own superiors, in both the Department of State and the Rockefeller Foundation. During an interview for an oral history project, Dr. John B. Grant, once a public health specialist for the Rockefeller Foundation, was told that Greene was the " 'knight in shining armor' who always came to your protection whether you knew it or not."[2] And sustained by early triumphs, Greene was a man who never hesitated to oppose his superiors when he considered them to be in error. Once too often he pressed his beliefs in the face of overwhelming power and, at the hands of the Rockefellers, sustained a crushing defeat that ended his career—and opened the way for his most important role as an opinion maker.

Growing up among the Japanese, of missionary parents who were

2. "Reminiscences of Dr. J. B. Grant" (1961), 230, Oral History Collection, Columbia.

markedly liberal in their religion, Greene never doubted that Asians were human, worthy of whatever benefits man and god had to offer Americans or Europeans. He was never "tolerant" of Asians. He admired some Chinese and Japanese and disliked others, without regard for their "Asianness." As a diplomat he despaired of his own country's unfair treatment of the Chinese, but he never became an apologist for his little Oriental brother. He never hesitated to criticize Chinese, Japanese, or American policy that displeased him. With the exception of his attitude toward Jews, most of whom he apparently found offensive—and for whose plight in Nazi Germany he demonstrated no noticeable sympathy—Greene was very much a humanitarian internationalist, a man whose desire to improve the lot of other men was not limited geographically or racially.

In China, Greene's major contribution was made through Peking Union Medical College and especially through efforts on behalf of men like Grant in the field of public health. The Medical College appears to have merited charges that it was elitist, in that it turned out too few doctors too slowly to meet China's needs. Its function can best be justified in Greene's terms: that to start at the beginning there was a need for well-trained doctors, not as practitioners, but as teachers ultimately able to generate doctors or paramedical aides in geometric progression. At the same time Greene was aware of the lack of public health facilities. According to Grant, he had the ability to carry Rockefeller Foundation efforts to the national level in China, working with Chiang's regime and exhorting his superiors in New York to support Grant's efforts, especially in municipal public health programs.

From his own government, Greene demanded justice, fair treatment for Asians generally and especially for the Chinese who labored under the vestiges of the "unequal treaties" until 1943. Having lived abroad virtually all of his life he was disturbed by the narrow nationalism of the American people amidst the crises in Europe and Asia during the 1930s. Financially secure, he did not share his countrymen's pre-eminent concern with domestic economic recovery. Aware of the meaning of poverty in Asia, he was insensitive to its less obvious manifestations in America. From 1938 to 1941 he committed all of his energies to the cause of collective security: the punishment of aggressors and the provision of aid to their victims. Best known for his work in China, he quickly emerged as a leader in the fight against Japanese aggression. But unlike many of his colleagues he was not so committed to China that he lost sight of the danger Hitler's Germany posed for the Western world. Like Clark Eichelberger and a few others within the Committee to Defend America by Aiding the Allies, Greene was a univeralist who shared Roosevelt's priorities. But he also demanded aid for the country he considered America's ally in Asia. In the closing months of his life, as he watched China rent once more by civil strife, he abandoned his lifelong insistence on nonintervention in China's revolutions and approved of aid to Chiang's government, the refuge of the Chinese liberals he thought most likely to create a modern democratic government in China.

As an opinion leader Greene generally functioned privately through access to decision-makers until he became a lobbyist in 1938. He did not make any sustained effort to influence public opinion until that time. From 1914 to 1935 his institutional ties, to the Rockefeller Foundation and its affiliated China Medical Board and Peking Union Medical College, provided him with access to American diplomats in China and to policy-makers in Washington. His position conferred status that opened doors for him when he visited Washington and brought men of power to his threshold in Peking. In addition to his position, Greene had unusually extensive personal, individual ties to key members of the Department of State's Division of Far Eastern Affairs. These derived principally from early contacts when he was a highly respected consular official working with Paul Reinsch, protecting and educating Nelson Johnson, cooperating with J. V. A. MacMurray. His years on the Harvard *Crimson* with Roosevelt and Grew opened other doors, as did the prominence of his brothers, especially of Jerome, long-time Secretary of the Harvard Corporation, sometime president of the American Asiatic Association and of the Institute of Pacific Relations. In short, Greene's access to decision-makers on matters of East Asian affairs was on both an institutional and an individual basis while he remained in the employ of the Rockefeller Foundation. While the personal relationships seem more important during these years, the importance of his status as, for example, Vice President of the Rockefeller Foundation, must not be underestimated. It can easily be appreciated by imagining what might have happened to old personal ties had Greene left the consular service to teach at a small denominational college or to become a small businessman.

Prior to 1938, Greene's major effort toward influencing American policy came during the Nationalist revolution, 1925 to 1928. His position with Peking Union Medical College, with the Rockefellers, made him an attractive leader to missionaries anxious to stave off gun-boat diplomacy. He represented the kind of secular power they may well have assumed would gain a hearing for their arguments. As a former diplomat he could be expected to understand the forms and symbols to which diplomats responded. Working with J. Leighton Stuart in Peking and with A. L. Warnshuis in New York, he was a prime witness for their cause, with both American diplomats and congressmen. He took a delegation to meet with MacMurray, spoke to MacMurray privately, corresponded with him—and went over his head with letters to Nelson Johnson and to Senator Borah and by inducing his superiors in New York to contact the secretary of state directly.

Of greatest importance was Greene's access to Johnson. Johnson and Kellogg were being subjected to conflicting pressures. MacMurray, supported by the American Chamber of Commerce, Shanghai, was calling for firmness, including a show of force where necessary. The mood of the American public as interpreted by Congress precluded the use of force. Greene and his missionary friends had helped to stir Congress with the Porter resolution and as Johnson tried to decide how to advise Kellogg, his former mentor was carefully explaining the errors in MacMurray's approach. Again, the point is not that Greene influenced Johnson's decision to act contrary to the advice of the American minister but rather that he had access to the key decision-maker at the critical moment.

After the American recognition of Kuomintang China, Greene continued to submit his opinions on Chinese affairs and on Sino-Japanese relations to Johnson, Hornbeck, Roosevelt and others. It was not until 1938, however, that he became a professional opinion-submitter—a lobbyist. Although his access to decision-makers on the basis of personal ties still existed, his access to Hornbeck, to Stimson, and to an attentive public was a function of his offices with the Committee to Defend America by Aiding the Allies and the American Committee for Non-Participation in Japanese Aggression. In the years 1938 to 1941, Greene's positions with these organizations enabled him to reach people who did not know him personally, who were responding to the organizations rather than to his reputation. Now Greene had behind him the apparatus of national organizations working to influence policy by stimulating public support for his opinions. He was also in a position to influence other opinion-makers, like Clark Eichelberger and Harry Price, to have them modify their tactics or the substance of opinions they submitted to decision-makers, congressmen, and the public.

In 1927 Greene had deviated from his preferred course of private persuasion and in the open letter to Borah and testimony before the House Committee on Foreign Affairs attempted to bring pressure to bear on the American government. His initial lobbying activities in 1938 and 1939 convinced him of the wisdom of working with the administration. Roosevelt and Hornbeck were both receptive to his opinions and eager to have him work to change the climate of opinion both in Congress and among the American people. But by 1940 he had grown skeptical of Roosevelt's willingness to impose sanctions on Japan. He continued to support Roosevelt's policies in the European war, but in collusion with Hornbeck, Stimson, and other friends in the administration, he worked to evoke public pressure to push Roosevelt to take action against Japan that the president preferred to delay.

That access to decision-makers or the public did not guarantee influence is evidenced by the fact that on numerous occasions, Greene submitted opinions that were rejected by MacMurray, Hornbeck, Grew, and Roosevelt. On other occasions, decision-makers, especially Hornbeck, used Greene in an effort to transmit their own opinions to nongovernmental opinion leaders or to segments of the public. But on the single issue of American policy toward China and Japan, in the years 1925 to 1941, no one outside the government was in a better position to exercise influence than Roger Greene.

When Roger Greene died, the *New York Times* honored him by printing his portrait with his obituary. When Thomas Lamont died, the *Times* carried the story on page one and eulogized him editorially a day later.[3] Lamont was not only one of the most powerful men of the twentieth century, he was also a man of great popularity—surely a rarity among Wall Street bankers. In addition to remarkable ability as a businessman, Lamont seems to have possessed extraordinary charm. A man who lusted for wealth and power, a man whose ends and occasionally questionable means did not always meet with the approval of friends like Oswald Garrison Villard, Lamont used his money well. He contributed most generously to his schools, Phillips Exeter and Harvard, and to world affairs organizations like the League of Nations Association, the Council on Foreign Relations, and the Foreign Policy Association. Groups like the Japan Society and the Institute of Pacific Relations received contributions, as did a host of other educational, cultural, and

3. *New York Times,* March 29, 1947, p. 15, February 3, 1948, p. 1, February 4, 1948, p. 22.

policy-oriented associations. And Lamont gave not only money but his time, participating frequently in the affairs of civic groups concerned with questions of foreign policy. With the aid of his secretary, Martin Egan, he wrote countless articles on world economic and political problems. All of these activities contributed to his image as an enlightened international banker, a diplomat on Wall Street.

Lamont was well along in life before he had any extensive contacts with Asians or turned his attention to Asian affairs. Before 1920 his overseas travel was restricted to Europe and his interests in international affairs limited to the Atlantic community. He was fifty when he first went to Japan and made his only trip to China. All together he spent about three months of his 77 years in East Asia, far more than the average American, but not enough to see Asians as real people. They remained "Chinks" and "Japs" to him throughout his life and he was never able to see the affairs of China as anything more than opera bouffe. Like Theodore Roosevelt, he had infinitely more respect for the Japanese, especially their great capitalists—until they angered him. In 1920 when the agreement he had worked out to bring Japan into the Consortium appeared to be breaking down and again in the late 1930s, he labeled the Japanese savages, a people unworthy of being treated as a civilized nation. To China Lamont made little if any contribution—unless he be credited for keeping down China's foreign debt by refusing loans during the 1920s. On the credit side, he headed the American Committee for the China Famine Relief Fund in 1920 and ran an imaginative campaign that brought in close to five million dollars.[4] From December 1940 onward he added his voice to those calling for sanctions against Japan. But throughout the 1920s and early 1930s Lamont not only acquiesced in Japanese imperialism in Manchuria, he consciously supported Japanese efforts to extend their control over China's northeastern provinces. The Chinese were suitable recipients for charity, but China was not a place in which to do business. Japan interested him much more—a good growth stock. In Japanese leaders like Inoue Junnosuke and Dan Takuma, he saw men like himself. Such a country had great potential and Lamont was instrumental in obtaining for Japan scarce capital that country needed desperately in the 1920s, especially if it was to maintain its empire on the Asian continent.

At home Lamont labored to create a more favorable image of Japan, to

4. Andrew James Nathan, *A History of the China International Famine Relief Commission* (Cambridge, Massachusetts, 1965), 6.

facilitate the sale of Japanese government bonds. He also tried to get the American government to transcend its fixation with China and to shift its support to Japan, a truly important trading partner and a secure market for American capital. When the Japanese Army conquered Manchuria in 1931 and 1932, Lamont did what he could to obtain a sympathetic hearing for Japan's position, to keep Secretary Stimson quiet, and to undermine the boycott movement led by President Lowell of Harvard. All this only a few months after Harvard had granted him an honorary LL.D., with Lowell describing Lamont as "by nature a statesman, by occupation a financier; sagacious in council on affairs that affect all nations."[5] Japanese actions at Shanghai in 1932, the assassinations of Inoue and Dan, and Japanese barbarism at Nanking in 1937, shook his faith in Japan severely. But always the pacifier, always a man who stressed "getting along," he opposed actions that would antagonize the Japanese—and incidentally threaten the value of Japanese bonds held by his firm. Only in December 1940, when the Tripartite Pact convinced him that Japan was playing Hitler's game, did Lamont announce his willingness to support economic sanctions.

Lamont's strength as an opinion leader was institutional, derived from his position as a partner in J. P. Morgan and Company from 1910 on. He was generally recognized as second only to Morgan in power within the firm from the 1920s to Morgan's death in 1943—when Lamont took the reins. But because J. P. Morgan, Jr., was a very private person, attempting to stay out of the headlines, Lamont served as his outside man, his ambassador to the rest of the world. And so it was Lamont who was covered constantly by the *New York Times*, whose every word and movement seemed newsworthy. Augmenting the power Lamont had because of great private wealth, control of other people's money, and the status conferred upon him by the mass media, was his great charm, presumably a tremendous asset in the face-to-face contacts with decision-makers assured him by his position.

Lamont had extraordinary access to decision-makers and to the media. He was consulted not merely on Asian affairs but on a wide variety of foreign and domestic problems by Presidents Wilson, Harding, Coolidge, Hoover, and Roosevelt. He advised most of their secretaries of state and treasury. Not only New York newspapers but newspapers all over the country carried reports of his major addresses. Business and general news

5. Quoted in *New York Times*, February 3, 1948, p. 1.

magazines featured his activities. At times he owned the *New York Evening Post* and the *Saturday Review of Literature,* engaging in friendly public debates with his editors. Oswald Garrison Villard and Walter Lippmann were personal friends with whom he often argued—and always placed his views. Often he, or Martin Egan in his name, wrote articles for popular or scholarly journals, explaining the world economic situation or the Consortium or bankers' attitudes on issues of war and peace. He also had access to great sources of power abroad, especially in Great Britain and, in the 1920s, Japan. The prime ministers, financial ministers and foreign ministers of these countries sought his advice and sometimes his assistance. He did not hesitate to offer recommendations on foreign policy to Japanese statesmen throughout the 1920s and 1930s. It was before Lamont that T.V. Soong had to humble himself when China looked for assistance from the United States after the Nationalist revolution. Manifestly, Lamont's access to the top levels of government decision-making at home and abroad was unsurpassed by any other private citizen anywhere. His access to the mass media at least equalled that of any other nongovernmental authority in the United States.

Lamont was much more of a public figure than the typical member of Hodgson's foreign policy establishment, but he never used his access to the media to put pressure on the American government. Generally—he claimed always—his letters to the editor of the *New York Times* or public addresses on questions of policy were cleared with the Department of State. His public warnings to Japan in 1940 and 1941 had been carefully worked out with Hornbeck to warn the Japanese, to win the approval of Americans, especially businessmen, for a program of sanctions, and to retain complete flexibility on policy for the government. His statements on the Consortium, on China's potential for American economic expansion, and on assistance to the Soviet Union, were all issued with the approval of the Department of State. Public criticism of the government was alien to his nature, to his constant concern with cooperation between business and government, among bankers of the world and nations of the world.

Lamont, the public man, preferred to influence policy privately, where his advantage in terms of access was overwhelming. But again, access was no guarantee of influence. His efforts to rid himself of the Consortium were unsuccessful until 1946. He failed to get government support for a loan to the South Manchuria Railway. His opposition to Stimson's criticism of Japan did not still the secretary of state or bring about the more sympathetic

American attitude toward Japan which he advocated. On the other hand, no one ever persuaded Lamont to lend money through the Consortium and he negotiated a large loan with the Japanese government that ultimately assisted the SMR, satisfying Lamont completely—although the Japanese government would have preferred a direct loan to the railway.

Lamont also worked with other opinion-makers, especially in organizations like the League of Nations Association and the Committee to Defend America by Aiding the Allies. He lent his name to these groups, gave financial support, and often had a say on major issues confronting them. On at least one occasion, Lamont served as a go-between, used by Roosevelt to get Eichelberger and the Committee to Defend America to ease up on the convoy question. Similarly, he tried to restrain Greene's criticism of the administration's East Asian policy while privately sending a suggestion to Roosevelt that he try to say a little more about China.

For approximately twenty-five years, Lamont was an opinion leader on a national level on a wide variety of issues. Although he concentrated his attention on world affairs, East Asia was a secondary concern for him. Nonetheless his great prominence, plus his roles with the Consortium and in loans to Japan, allowed him to appear to speak for American business on policy toward East Asia. He served as a bridge between the government and the business community on major questions pertaining to that region. The opinions he submitted to the public were rarely his own, as he had few commitments to specific ideas about policy. More often than not he served the government as a medium for governmental opinion-makers, and he served it well, except on those rare occasions when government interests conflicted with those of J. P. Morgan and Company.

George Sokolsky was at once an intriguing and a repulsive figure. He was a man of apparent charm, jovial and outgoing—a man who made friends easily. He was intelligent, he loved and patronized good music, and he could write with almost poetic sensitivity, as evidenced by the fragment of his autobiography buried among his papers at Columbia. But Sokolsky, by the mid-1920s, was a man without principles, irresponsible, loyal to no one but himself as he fought to satisfy his appetite for power and status. As a journalist in China he learned that the power to malign carried with it the power to destroy—and he used this knowledge to further his own cause, protected from angry Chinese politicians by the privileges foreigners enjoyed under the treaty system. Groping for a new identity when he returned to the United States in 1931, his opportunities to write for the *New York Times* and the *Herald-Tribune* enabled him to become a respected, honest reporter of domestic and foreign affairs. Sokolsky could not resist, however, the profitable relationship offered by powerful business orgnizations; nor did the *Times* or the *Herald Tribune* offer adequate scope for his hatreds, for his vindictiveness, for his war against the very genteel folk for whom these papers existed. Writing for Hearst was more congenial and joining forces with Joe McCarthy most satisfying of all. Like Hearst, like McCarthy, Sokolsky sought revenge for perceived slights at the hands of the Respectables—and like Hearst and McCarthy, Sokolsky had no sense of decency.

Sokolsky appears to have had many deep and genuine friendships with Asians, both Chinese and Japanese. His first wife was a West Indian of Chinese ancestry and he wrote movingly on problems of race in treaty port China and against Oriental exclusion laws in the United States. He was not a racist, at least not in the same sense that his countrymen were and remain racists. Toward the Chinese, however, he revealed a familiar ambivalence. Too often his correspondence with other Americans referred to the childlike ways of the Chinese, describing them as ungrateful children who required a firm hand. Chinese were not dogs, but they were not quite the equals of adult American males. Sokolsky had come among the Chinese people seeking to be the Great White Father. As a Jew who reached China via Petrograd he had been viewed with intense suspicion by Americans and Europeans in the treaty ports and it was among the Chinese he sought status. Among these backward people he would be a leader: the man who would teach them how to organize a revolution and become the power behind the throne. Fat Georgie, the Jewish Rasputin of China, aspired to Borodin's role before anyone in the Comintern had conceived of it. And in the early 1920s, when Western-educated Chinese found other Westerners in China aloof, Sokolsky was there to drink, swap stories, and dance with the Soongs, C. T. Wang, Eugene Chen, and others. There he found himself welcome in centers of wealth and power from which he had been excluded in Western society. It was heady stuff and young Sokolsky ran from one Kuomintang leader to another, from one minor war lord to another, offering his services and dreaming grand dreams.

In his early years in China, Sokolsky indicated little interest in American policy toward Asian countries. He helped Chinese students with the organization of the May Fourth Movement, and sympathized with their opposition to Japanese imperialism, but he does not appear to have envisioned a role for the United States in the controversy. When Lamont came to China to discuss the Consortium with Chinese authorities, Sokolsky's role as intermediary between Lamont and the Chinese students was designed to call attention to himself rather than to support or oppose the Consortium. During the mid-1920s, as Sokolsky became identified with the American Chamber of Commerce in Shanghai, with the British *North China Daily News,* and with George Bronson Rea and Japanese interests in China, his interest in American policy increased. For the duration of the Chinese Nationalist revolution he asked the United States to be firm in its dealings with China and more responsive to Japanese needs on the Asian mainland. After his return to the United States in 1931, American policy during the Japanese occupation of Manchuria became his primary concern. Again he stressed Japan's needs while urging the United States to let the Chinese and Japanese solve the problem bilaterally. Central to his argument was a demand for greater realism in American foreign policy: avoid moral judgments while concentrating on the pursuit of tangible benefits.

The great foreign policy debates on questions of American intervention in World War II came at a time when Sokolsky was identified with the conservative Midwestern wing of the Republican Party. Because he was a Jew, perhaps also because he was a cosmopolitan relative to his compatriots, he seemed less reluctant to support Great Britain against Germany than did his friends Herbert Hoover and Col. Robert R. McCormick of the *Chicago Tribune.* Nonetheless, Sokolsky did not wander far in advance of the party line, remaining intensely nationalist and anti-interventionist. When war came he initially endorsed the administration's Europe first strategy, but a swing through the Midwest at McCormick's side during the election campaign of 1942 brought him quickly into the Asia First camp. As the war progressed, Sokolsky became increasingly critical of Roosevelt's strategic decisions and, toward the end of the war, openly apprehensive of Soviet intentions. Before the shooting stopped, he was preparing for the next battle with the Soviet Union.

Sokolsky had an unusually clear understanding of the early years of the Chinese Communist movement and had written some of the best analyses of the movement and its prospects available in English prior to the Yenan era. The possibility of a Chinese Communist victory over Chiang had not troubled him and a China that might constitute a threat to the United States was beyond his comprehension. But as part of the process by which he became a "star-spangled spieler for capitalism,"[6] communism anywhere became immoral and the distinctions between various communist movements that he had described in the early 1930s were ignored. When the Truman administration proved itself ready and able to combat the Soviet threat it perceived in Europe, Sokolsky and his friends, deprived of one issue, turned their attention to the administration's acquiescence in Mao's victory in China. The "betrayal" of China became the issue with which they worked to destroy the Democrats—and Sokolsky did all he could to distort the issue for partisan advantage. When, in 1805, Thomas Jefferson spoke of the "artillery of the press" being levelled against his administration "charged with whatsoever its licentiousness could devise or dare," he surely had in mind the workings of men like George Sokolsky.[7]

While Sokolsky was in China, from 1918 to 1931, he had little access to the American people. He was able to submit his opinions on various issues, generally relating to China's internal affairs, through private channels, especially through American officials like Cunningham, Drysdale, Magruder, and MacMurray—and through their use of his columns. Although he served as a "stringer" for several American newspapers, they published his articles infrequently, more often than not without a byline. He had less opportunity to influence public opinion than he did to influence decision-makers.

After his return to the United States in 1931, until the denouement of the Manchurian affair in 1933, Sokolsky's lines of access changed as he wrote over fifty articles for the *New York Times,* several others for important journals like the *Atlantic Monthly* and *Christian Century,* published *Tinder Box of Asia* and lectured before groups interested in world affairs in various parts of the country. For those Americans interested in issues of foreign policy, especially of American-East Asian relations, for the "attentive public," Sokolsky had become a major source of information and analysis. On the single issue of East Asian politics, Sokolsky qualified as a national opinion maker.

After several years in which he spoke increasingly on behalf of the business interests that retained him, and wrote sparingly, Sokolsky became a columnist for the *New York Herald Tribune* in 1935. He wrote primarily on

6. *Time,* quoted in *Current Biography* (New York, 1941), 805.

7. Quoted by James Reston in the *Artillery of the Press* (New York, 1967), vii.

domestic affairs, as a critic of Roosevelt and the New Deal. In the middle and later 1930s he became involved in Republican Party politics, associating himself with more conservative elements within the party and gaining access to Republican leaders like Hoover. In the late 1930s, as part of his campaign on behalf of conservative capital, he joined forces with Isaac Don Levine and J. B. Matthews, men who once had been committed radicals, in an effort to discredit the New Deal. At a time when the House Un-American Activities Committee was flailing aimlessly at a communist menace its members could not comprehend, Sokolsky decided to give it direction, recommending to the chairman, Martin Dies, that he call in Matthews. Matthews had an extraordinary wealth of information about communist-front activities, much of it from first-hand experience, much of it accurate—and the Dies Committee had both direction and the material with which to follow it.[8]

From 1937 to 1941 Sokolsky had his own radio program, sponsored by the National Association of Manufacturers. In 1940, when he moved from the *Herald Tribune* to the *New York Sun,* his column was syndicated, enlarging his audience. Picked up by Hearst King features in 1944, the column became available to millions of Americans all over the United States. In the late 1930s and 1940s he was an opinion-maker on a national level, able to lead on a wide variety of domestic as well as foreign policy issues. In Rosenau's terms he had become a national multi-issue opinion-maker, known to far more Americans than either Greene or Lamont. Within conservative circles, within a specific segment of the attentive public, he was highly regarded. His columns, especially after the Hearst connection, and most obviously his editorials for the *New York Mirror,* were directed at arousing the mass public as well. But his emergence as a spokesman for conservative Republicanism during an era of Democratic hegemony barred him from direct access to foreign policy decision-makers, from the kind of intimacy he had enjoyed with American officials in China. He did gain access, however, to conservative Congressmen, puffing them in his columns, campaigning for them, providing them with issues with which to gain public attention. Dies and McCarthy were only his most notorious successes.

In the late 1940s, Sokolsky's primary target was the mass public, which he sought to arouse in order to swamp the Truman administration. He

8. Heywood Broun, *New Republic,* XCV (June 22, 1938), 185 and XCVII (January 25, 1939), 339; Walter Goodman, *The Committee* (New York, 1968), 35.

did not write subtly, about complexities, but rather appealed to the fears of generally unorganized and passive segments of the society, people generally unconcerned about issues of foreign policy. His opinions were rejected by men like Dean Acheson, so he tried to discredit them in his columns and editorials. Of most importance, he worked to create a milieu in which the Truman administration could not act as it saw fit because of apprehensions of public outrage. A poorly informed public came to mistrust the Truman administration, to suspect it of being irresolute in its relations with the Soviet Union, and Sokolsky fed this mistrust. The public, especially anticommunist Catholics, was shaken out of its passivity in the crisis atmosphere of the late 1940s and, perceiving a threat from communism, within and without, placed restraints on the Truman administration's policy. In East Asia the administration could not extricate itself completely from the Chinese civil war and when the Communists drove Chiang from the mainland, it could not recognize the People's Republic of China. Whatever other reasons existed for Truman's policies toward China from 1948 to 1950, public and Congressional attitudes such as those Sokolsky had worked to create defined the limits within which policy was determined. When the government ignored Kohlberg's charges against the IPR, when the *Amerasia* case was discounted, Sokolsky kept these affairs alive in his columns and editorials. He and Kohlberg provided McCarthy with the information upon which the Senator based his charges.

Kohlberg rather than Sokolsky was the essential man for the attack on the IPR and the general line associated with the so-called "China Lobby," but it was Sokolsky who had access to the public. It was Sokolsky who published the charges. It was Sokolsky who was able to provide publicity for his friend Kohlberg and who, supported by Fulton Lewis, Jr. and Westbrook Pegler, provided the claque for Joe McCarthy. Among Hearst's columnists, among columnists of the far Right generally, Sokolsky was the acknowledged expert on East Asia. To him accrued the privilege of leading the assault on the Truman administration's policies toward China.

Before it was all over, George Sokolsky had made his way high up the ladder. At his death he was eulogized by ex-president Herbert Hoover.[9] The People's Republic of China was still unrecognized by the United States, still deprived of its rightful place in the United Nations. Hiss, Lattimore, Ser-

9. *New York Times*, December 14, 1962, p. 16.

vice, and all the others remained in disrepute. A Democratic administration, headed by the son of Sokolsky's old friend, Joe Kennedy, predicated its East Asian policies, in Southeast Asia as well as China, on the fear of being labelled soft on communism. The media had given Sokolsky power and he used it in his quest for status as a means of destroying other symbols of status, as represented by the likes of Alger Hiss, of the well-born Protestant establishment. For Sokolsky—and perhaps also for Kohlberg, Roy Cohn, and McCarthy—the opportunity to link the likes of Hiss and Acheson, the "striped-pants snobs" in the State Department with communism and homosexuality was revenge on an establishment to which, by birth, he was denied admission.

Three Americans found themselves in China—at a time when the United States was emerging as the world's leading power, at a time of transition between the Pax Brittanica and the Pax Americana, at a time when American thought about the affairs of East Asia was of more consequence than ever before.

For Roger Greene, China defined a mission, provided a way to serve without commitment to church or flag. In finding China he found himself—found a life that could be both meaningful and comfortable. And when the Rockefellers made his position in Peking untenable, he spent the forced leisure of his last years trying to help the Chinese people by influencing the policy of his government. He represented a strain of Americans, religious in the nineteenth century, more secular in the twentieth, missionaries and educators who worked for the creation of a modern China. Few outside this group were ever deeply involved in Chinese affairs. Few within the group had Roger Greene's opportunities to influence American policy.

For Thomas Lamont, China offered little. His involvement in China, in East Asia, was pressed on him by his government—and he found his profits not in China but in Japan. Just as Greene's commitment reflected the degree to which missionaries and educators had identified with Chinese aspirations, so Lamont's indifference reflected the relationship between China and the business community in the United States. Lamont had great personal power, commensurate with the power of big business in American society. But neither Lamont nor American business collectively ever developed an important stake in China. Neither evidenced much concern about the course of Chinese modernization or showed interest in rescuing China from Japan in the 1930s.

Indeed, in the 1920s, Lamont was a leader in an effort to align American political interests in East Asia with the economic interests he was developing in Japan. He failed largely because Japanese militarism alienated Americans. He was himself alienated from Japan by the assassinations of Inoue and Dan, by the thwarting of his hopes for a liberal Japan.

With Lamont's withdrawal, Greene and his friends were virtually unopposed in their efforts to influence American policy and opinion toward East Asia. In the absence of a major economic stake in East Asia, missionaries, scholars, and journalists were the most common submitters of opinion. And when American businessmen developed an important stake in Japan, the Japanese military made it impossible for their country's American friends to plead Japan's cause.

For Sokolsky, China was one step on the way to "making it." A special breed, he was an adventurer skilled in living by his wits, in using available men and material to serve his own cause, "no one's hero but his own."[10] The treaty ports attracted many such men—part-time journalists, publicists, entrepreneurs, and political advisors. With varying degrees of fidelity they interpreted China for Americans and Europeans, exhibiting what may have passed for Western manners among the Chinese. Sokolsky spent an eventful twelve years in China, doing neither much good nor much harm. He gave those who supported him a fair return on their money and provided American officials—and in 1931 and 1932 the American public—with useful insights into the affairs of East Asia. The ease with which he subsequently immersed himself in other matters reflected the superficiality of his involvement in China. In America he played the game much as he had in China, seeking out those who could reward him with money and power and serving them as best he could. Whether it was China or America, Shanghai or New York, it was the game and not the locale that mattered.

Republican China was an especially attractive place for men like Greene and Sokolsky. Unlike Japan, it was a country too weak to control its own affairs. It was not a part of the British or French empires, like so much of the rest of the world. It was a country where an American could range freely, exercising his talents for good or evil to the fullest. But the very fluidity of Chinese affairs left China unattractive to the Lamonts, to men who prized stability—a safe investment.

10. Quote is from description of Sokolsky by Harold Isaacs in letter to author, October 24, 1972.

The activities of Greene and Sokolsky in China were not peculiarly American. There were Englishmen playing similar roles, especially in the nineteenth century. British bankers like Addis were different from Lamont in that years before, in Ch'ing China, they had been able to invest with profit. But in the 1920s, Addis was no more eager than Lamont to lend money to the Chinese. The activities of Greene, Lamont, and Sokolsky reveal more about the opportunities that existed on the periphery of Chinese society than about Americans. And the coming of the People's Republic closed that era of opportunity, left no scope for foreign friends who would help China on their own terms.

None of these Americans had a profound impact on China. Only Greene's contribution to medical education could be considered of any consequence in China's long struggle to modernize. But all three men played important roles in the shaping of American policy toward East Asia—and their careers illustrate several ways in which private citizens in democratic societies can affect the course of international relations.

Lamont was of tremendous importance as an individual. In the interwar period there was no businessman of comparable stature and ability. Without him the Consortium agreement might never have been reached. There might not have been the rapproachement with Japan that cleared the way for the Washington Conference. In the fall of 1940, when business leaders were far less willing than the rest of the American people to impose economic sanctions on Japan, it was Lamont, friend of Japan, who declared to the nation that the time for sanctions had come.

Greene and Sokolsky mattered less as individuals than as representatives of specific patterns of interaction with the Chinese. Greene was representative of a cadre of American friends of China who could be relied upon to elicit public support when China was in need. At the time of the Nationalist revolution, Kellogg's rejection of MacMurray's recommendations reflected public and Congressional pressures that Greene, A. L. Warnshuis, Leighton Stuart, and their friends aroused. American policy mirrored alternatives Greene had offered to Nelson Johnson, Kellogg's principal advisor on China. Similarly, the relentless pressure of Greene, Harry Price, and their associates from 1938 to 1941 focused public attention on economic sanctions as a way of responding to Japanese imperialism. Public and Congressional pressures were generated which Roosevelt long resisted. But once he yielded to the demand for sanctions, these pressures enormously complicated efforts to reach a modus vivendi with Japan in the closing months of 1941. And in the late 1940s Sokolsky and his friends demonstrated how unscrupulous journalists could stir and manipulate the anxieties of an ill-informed mass public—creating an atmosphere in which the administration perceived limits on its freedom to act toward China.

The Communist victory in the Chinese civil war closed off opportunities for private forays into Chinese affairs, but did not end private efforts to influence American-East Asian relations. As the years passed without relations between the People's Republic of China and the United States, however, participants with experience in China were fewer. The missionaries, educators, and journalists who once worked in China ceased to be the public's principal source of information, ceased to be the principal opinion submitters. A new generation of scholars, without experience on mainland China, vied with government officials to shape the views of the public, of Congress, and ultimately of the men with the power to decide American policy. Whether their wisdom would lead to a better informed public or to superior policy was a moot question involving many other variables, but it was clear that the perspective of men and women who had worked in Republican China, with a weak and disunited China, was gone.

# Appendix

THE following is a list of Americans with regular opportunity to offer opinions on East Asian affairs to the American public or to decision-makers in the years 1900 to 1950.

Abbott, John J. (1871–1942). Chicago banker. Interested in loans to China during and immediately after World War I. In 1919 he arranged a $5 million loan to the Chinese government on which that government subsequently defaulted. He was a member of the managing board of the American Group of the second Consortium and regarded favorably by J. V. A. MacMurray.

Abend, Hallett (1884–1955). Journalist. Correspondent for *New York Times* in China 1927–1941. Won Pultizer Prize in 1940. Contributor to popular magazines including *Saturday Evening Post, Readers Digest, Look,* and *Cosmopolitan.* Author of *Tortured China* (1930), *Can China Survive?,* with Anthony J. Billingham (1936), *Chaos in Asia* (1939), *Japan Unmasked* (1941), *Ramparts of the Pacific* (1942), *My Life in China, 1926–1941* (1943). Lectured widely.

Adams, Brooks (1848–1927). Historian. Author of *The Law of Civilization and Decay* (1895), *American Economic Supremacy* (1900), *The New Empire* (1902). Alleged to be an important influence on Theodore Roosevelt and American policy toward East Asia at the turn of the century. See Walter LaFeber, *The New Empire* (1963), and Marilyn B. Young, *The Rhetoric of Empire* (1968).

Alsop, Joseph (1910– ). Journalist. Syndicated columnist and contributor to popular magazines like *Saturday Evening Post, Atlantic Monthly,* and *New Yorker.* With Chennault in China during World War II. Alleged to have access to major political figures beginning with Franklin D. Roosevelt.

Barnett, Eugene E. (1888–1970). Missionary. Served in China 1910–1936. Became General Secretary of YMCA in 1941. Father of A. Doak and Robert Barnett. Active in Foreign Policy Association and UNESCO. Corresponded frequently with Stanley Hornbeck.

Bashford, James W. (1849–1919). Methodist Bishop. Discussed policy toward China with Presidents Roosevelt, Taft, and Wilson. Had access to secretaries of state in those administrations. Wrote *Awakening of China* (1906), *China and Methodism* (1907), *China: An Interpellation* (1916).

Bisson, Thomas A. (1900– ). Writer. Taught in China 1924–1928. Became Foreign Policy Association's research specialist on East Asia in 1929, contributing numerous articles to the Association's *Bulletin* and *Reports*. Also contributed many articles to *Amerasia*, the *New Republic*, the *New York Times*, and scholarly journals like the *American Political Science Review* and *Pacific Affairs*. Author of *Japan in China* (1938) and *America's Far Eastern Policy* (1945).

Blakeslee, George H. (1871–1954). Historian. Taught at Clark University for forty-four years. Active in IPR and President of board of directors of World Peace Foundation. Served many times on assignments for Department of State: technical advisor to American Delegation at Washington Conference, 1921; counsel to American member of Lytton Commission, 1932; and American delegate to Far East Advisory Commission, 1945–1946. Author of many articles and books including *The Pacific Area—An International Survey* (1929) and *Conflicts of Policy in the Far East* (1934). A close confidant of Stanley Hornbeck.

Buck, Pearl (1892–1973). Novelist. Her books and the motion pictures based on them probably did more to shape American views of China than the work of any other single person. Author of many books and articles in popular journals. Best known for *The Good Earth* (1931), a Book-of-the-Month Club selection which won the Pulitzer Prize.

Byas, Hugh (1875–1945). Journalist. A Scot who served as *New York Times* correspondent in Tokyo, 1927–1941. Lectured at Yale after reaching the United States in 1941. Wrote *The Japanese Enemy* (1942) and *Government by Assassination* (1942).

Carter, Edward C. (1878–1954). Administrator. One of founders of Institute of Pacific Relations. Served as Secretary of the American Council, 1926–1933 and as Secretary-General of the International IPR, 1933–1946. See John N. Thomas, *Institute of Pacific Relations—Asian Scholars and American Politics* (1974).

Chamberlin, William H. (1897–1969). Journalist. East Asian correspondent for *Christian Science Monitor*, 1935–1939. Contributor to popular magazines like *Atlantic Monthly*, *Current History*, *Foreign Affairs*, and *Fortune*. Author of many books, including *Japan Over Asia* (1937). In 1941 joined Committee on Pacific Relations, a group advocating the appeasement of Japan. Contributing editor of *New Leader* and editorial contributor to *Wall Street Journal*, beginning in 1945.

Clark, Grover (1891–1938). Writer, publisher. Taught in Japan 1918–1920 and in China 1920–1927. Owner and publisher of *Peking Leader* 1921–1929. Peking correspondent for *Christian Science Monitor* 1924–1929. Published many articles in popular and scholarly journals including *Annals*, *Asia*, *Current History*, *New Republic*, and *Outlook*. Author of *Economic Rivalries in China* (1932) and *The Great Wall Crumbles* (1935).

Clyde, Paul H. (1896– ). Historian. Author of *Japan's Pacific Mandate* (1935), *United States Policy Toward China, Diplomatic and Public Documents, 1939–1940* (1940), and *The Far East: A History of the Impact of the West on Eastern Asia* (1948). In 1941 joined Committee on Pacific Relations, a group advocating the appeasement of Japan.

Colegrove, Kenneth (1886–1975). Political scientist. Author of *Militarism in Japan* (1936). Editorial board of *Far Eastern Quarterly,* 1940–1949. Consultant to OSS 1943–1945, to MacArthur's headquarters, Tokyo, 1946, and to Department of State, 1949.

Crane, Charles R. (1858–1939). Chicago industrialist. Appointed Minister to China in 1909 but resigned before taking up his post. Financial supporter of Woodrow Wilson and advisor to Wilson administration on East Asian affairs. Patron of George Marvin, Thomas Millard, and Paul Reinsch. Served as Minister to China, 1920–1921. Founder of Institute of Current World Affairs.

Crow, (Herbert) Carl (1883–1945). Writer, businessman. Journalist in China and Japan, 1911–1917. Far Eastern representative of Committee on Public Information (Creel Committee), 1917–1918. Owned advertising agency in Shanghai, 1919–1937. Directed anti-Communist campaign in China. Returned to United States in 1938 and joined sponsors of American Committee for Non-Participation in Japanese Aggression. Contributed many articles to popular journals such as *Outlook* and *World's Work.* Author of *Japan and America* (1915), the best-selling *400 Million Customers* (1937), and *The Chinese Are Like That* (1938).

DeForest, John H. (?–1911). Missionary. Went to Japan in 1874 under auspices of American Board. Wrote many articles for *Independent* and *Missionary Review.* Described as missionary from Japan to the United States and decorated by Japanese government for dispelling anti-Japanese misconceptions among Americans.

Dennett, Tyler (1883–1949). Historian. Visited East Asia as journalist for religious publications. Chief, Division of Publications, Department of State, 1924–1929, and Historical Advisor, Department of State, 1929–1931. Contributed numerous articles to scholarly and popular journals. Author of *The Democratic Movement in East Asia* (1918), *Americans in East Asia* (prepared as staff paper for American delegation to Washington Conference) (1922), *Roosevelt and the Russo-Japanese War* (1925), and the Pulitzer Prize-winning *John Hay* (1933). See Dorothy Borg, "Two Historians of the Far Eastern Policy of the United States: Tyler Dennett and A. Whitney Griswold," in D. Borg and S. Okamoto (eds.), *Pearl Harbor as History* (1973).

Dewey, John (1859–1952). Philosopher. Taught in China in 1920. Wrote many articles on China and American policy toward China during the 1920s for *Asia, Current History,* and especially for the *New Republic.* Author of *Letters from China and Japan* (1920) and *Impressions of the Revolutionary World, Mexico-China-Turkey* (1929). Source of U.S. government information on Bolshevism in China in 1920.

Drought, James M. (1896–1943). Missionary. With Maryknoll Society in China, 1924–1926. Central figure in "John Doe Associates" effort to avert war between Japan and the United States in 1941. See R. J. C. Butow, *The John Doe Associates* (1974).

Durdin, Tillman (1907– ). Journalist. Reporter for *Shanghai Evening Post,* 1930–1932, and managing editor, *China Press,* 1932–1937. Wrote for *New York Times* beginning 1937. Close to several Foreign Service officers in China, including John P. Davies.

Egan, Martin (1872–1938). Journalist, publicist. Started with *San Francisco Chronicle.* Went to Manila during Spanish-American War, covered Boxer uprising. Headed AP bureau in Tokyo 1904–1907. Joined J. P. Morgan and Company in 1913 and accompanied Lamont to Japan and China in 1920. Worked closely with Lamont, drafting letters, speeches, and articles on East Asian affairs.

Fairbank, John K. (1907– ). Historian. With OSS, 1941–1942. Special assistant to American Ambassador, Chungking, 1942–1943. With OWI, Washington, 1944–1945, and Director, USIS in China, 1945–1946. Author of *The United States and China* (1948). Contributed articles to popular journals like *Atlantic Monthly, Current History, Foreign Affairs, Nation,* and the *New Republic.*

Field, Frederick V. (1905– ). Writer. Secretary of American Council of IPR, 1934–1940, co-editor of *Amerasia,* 1937–1947, sometime correspondent for *Daily Worker.* Author of *American Participation in the China Consortiums* (1931), *Behind the Far Eastern Conflict,* with Joseph Barnes (1933), and *China's Greatest Crisis* (1945).

Fitch, George A. (1883– ) and Geraldine (?– ). Missionaries, publicists. George Fitch and his second wife, Geraldine, served as missionaries in China and publicists for the Chinese government in the United States. Born in China, he was a YMCA secretary and active in a variety of public service affairs in China from 1909 to 1945. He was affiliated with Frederick McKee's Committee to Defend America by Aiding Anti-Communist China. She was a leading figure in the American Committee for Non-Participation in Japanese Aggression, formed her own Emergency Committee for a Complete Embargo in 1941, and later served on the executive board of the American China Policy Association.

Fleisher, Benjamin W. (1870–1946) and Wilfred (1897– ). Journalists. Father and son identified with the *Japan Advertiser,* which they owned 1908–1940. Wilfred was at various times a correspondent for the *New York World, New York Times,* and *New York Herald Tribune.* He was with ABC radio, 1942–1946, and wrote *Volcanic Island* (1941), *Our Enemy Japan* (1942), and *What to Do with Japan* (1945).

Foord, John (1844–1922). Journalist. Organized American Asiatic Association in 1898 and edited its journal 1898–1917. Editor of *Journal of Commerce,* 1902–1922, known especially for his editorials on East Asia. Joined with Willard Straight to create *Asia* in 1917, serving as editor until his death.

Forman, Harrison (1904– ). Writer, lecturer, explorer. Represented *New York Herald Tribune* in China during World War II. Author of *Report from Red China* (1945), *Changing China* (1948), and *Blunder in Asia* (1950). See Kenneth E. Shewmaker, *Americans and Chinese Communists, 1927–1945* (1971).

Garside, B. A. (1894– ). Missionary. Served in China, 1922–1926. Secretary, China Union Universities, New York, 1927–1932; Executive Secretary, Associated Boards of Christian Colleges in China, 1932–1941. Served as vice-chairman of American Committee for Non-Participation in Japanese Aggression, 1938–1941, and as Executive Secretary, United China Relief, 1941–1942. Worked with American Bureau for Medical Aid to China and with United Services to China, Inc., during World War II.

Gilbert, Rodney (1889–1968). Journalist. Went to China in 1912 as medicine salesman, stayed until 1929 as reporter for *North China Daily News.* Editorial staff, *New York Herald Tribune,* 1929–1944. Dean, School of Journalism, Chungking, China, 1944–1946. Under pseudonym "Heptisax," wrote column for *Herald Tribune,* 1946–1949.

Goodwin, William J. (1896–1957). Lobbyist. Press consultant to Chinese News Service, New York, 1949. Source for Congressional investigations of alleged Communist activities within Department of State.

Gould, Randall C. (1898– ). Journalist. Wrote for *Japan Times,* 1923–1924. Represented United Press in East Asia, 1925–1931. Editor, *Shanghai Evening Post and Mercury,* 1931–1941. Correspondent in China for *Christian Science Monitor,* 1932–1941 and *Monitor's* chief Far Eastern correspondent, 1939–1941. Author of *Chungking Today* (1941) and *China in the Sun* (1946). Returned to Shanghai after World War II.

Griffis, William E. (1843–1928). Writer, lecturer. Taught in Japan, 1870–1874. Wrote many articles for popular journals like *Harper's Weekly, Missionary Review, North American Review,* and *Outlook.* Author of *The Japanese Nation in Evolution* (1907), *China's Story in Myth, Legend, Art and Annals* (1911), *Hepburn of Japan* (1913), *The Mikado* (1915), and many other books.

Griswold, A. Whitney. (1906–1963). Historian. Contributed numerous articles to popular and scholarly journals including *Annals, Asia, Events, Foreign Affairs, Harper's,* and the *Yale Review.* Author of *The Far Eastern Policy of the United States* (1938). In 1941 joined Committee on Pacific Relations, a group advocating appeasement of Japan. See Borg, "Two Historians of the Far Eastern Policy of the United States: Tyler Dennett and A. Whitney Griswold," in Borg and Okamoto (ed.) *Pearl Harbor as History* (1973).

Gulick, Sidney L. (1860–1945). Missionary, publicist. Served in Japan, 1887–1913. Secretary, Department of International Justice and Good-Will of Federal Council of Churches of Christ in America, 1914–1934. Active with National Committee on Japanese-American Relations, 1921–1934. Author of many books on Japan, including *Evolution of the Japanese* (1903), *White Peril in the Far East* (1905), *The American-Japanese Problem* (1914), *America and the Orient* (1916), *Problems of the Pacific and the Far East* (1921), *The Winning of the Far East* (1923) and *Toward Understanding Japan* (1935).

Hall, Josef W. (Upton Close) (1894–1960). Writer, lecturer, radio commentator. In East Asia 1916–1922 as journalist, adventurer. Lectured at University of Washington on Oriental affairs, 1922–1926. Wrote on Asian affairs for *New York Journal American* and *New York Times,* contributed to popular journals like *American Mercury, Cosmopolitan, Readers Digest,* and *Saturday Evening Post.* Author of *Land of the Laughing Buddha* (1925), *Outline History of China,* with H. H. Gowen (1926), *The Revolt of Asia* (1927), *Eminent Asians* (1929), and *Challenge* (1934). Lectured widely in addition to regular radio broadcasts.

Hanson, Haldore (1912– ). Journalist. Taught in Chinese colleges, 1934–1937. With AP in China 1936–1939. Contributed articles to journals like *Amerasia* and *Pacific Affairs.* Author of *Humane Endeavor: Story of the China War* (1939). Served with Department of State, beginning 1949. See Shewmaker, *Americans and Chinese Communists* (1971).

Harriman, E. H. (1848–1909). Railroad builder, financier. Interested in extending his railroad empire to East Asia from 1905 to his death. Tried unsuccessfully to purchase South Manchuria Railway and then became involved in Willard Straight's schemes for building new lines in Manchuria. See Michael H. Hunt, *Frontier Defense and the Open Door* (1973).

Hume, Edward H. (1876–1957). Missionary doctor. Central figure in establishment of Yale-in-China in 1904. Headed medical service in Changsha, 1904–1926. Served on national board of American Committee for Non-Participation in Japanese Aggression and as chairman of China Famine Relief. His *Doctors East, Doctors West: An American Physician's Life in China* won the Norton Prize.

Isaacs, Harold R. (1910– ). Journalist. Reporter for *China Press, New York Times,* and *Shanghai Evening Post,* 1928–1931. Associate editor *Newsweek* in Washington, China, Southeast Asia, and New York, 1943–1950. Author of *Tragedy of the Chinese Revolution* (1938) and *No Peace for Asia* (1947).

Jaffe, Philip J. (1897– ). Editor of *Amerasia,* 1937–1947. Wrote *New Frontiers in Asia* (1945) and edited English edition of Chiang Kai-shek, *China's Destiny and Chinese Economic Theory* (1947). Indicted and pleaded guilty in *Amerasia* case.

Jenks, Jeremiah W. (1856–1929). Economist. Visited British and Dutch colonies in East Asia on behalf of War Department in 1901. Appointed by President Roosevelt to commission on international exchange, visiting China, Japan, and the Philippines in 1903. Founded Far Eastern Bureau, 1913. Member, China Society of America and chairman, research committee of IPR. Contributed articles to popular journals such as *North American Review, Outlook, Review of Reviews, Scribner's,* and *World's Work.*

Judd, Walter H. (1898– ). Missionary doctor, lobbyist. Served as medical missionary in China for ten years between 1925 and 1938. From 1938 to 1940 lectured around the United States under auspices of American Committee for Non-Participation in Japanese Aggression. Gave 1,400 speeches in 46 states, one of which was broadcast on America's Town Meeting of the Air and printed in the *Reader's Digest.* Subsequently elected to Congress.

Kennan, George (1845–1924). Journalist, lecturer. Covered Russo-Japanese War for *Outlook.* Served on staff of both *Outlook* and *McClure's.* Wrote many articles on East Asian affairs, mostly for *Outlook.* Corresponded with President Roosevelt about American relations with Japan. Author of *E. H. Harriman's Far Eastern Plans* (1917).

Kohlberg, Alfred (1887–1960). Businessman, lobbyist. Importer of Chinese textiles and frequent visitor to China from 1916 to 1950. Initiated attack on leadership of IPR. Prominent in American China Policy Association. Advisor to Senator Joseph McCarthy. See Thomas, *The Institute of Pacific Relations* (1974), and Joseph Keeley, *The China Lobby Man: The Story of Alfred Kohlberg* (1969).

Latourette, Kenneth S. (1884–1968). Historian. Taught in China, 1909–1912. Wrote many books, including *A History of Christian Missions in China* (1929), and *The Chinese: Their History and Culture* (1934).

Lattimore, Owen (1900– ). Writer. Editor of *Pacific Affairs,* 1934–1941. Appointed by President Franklin Roosevelt as advisor to Chiang Kai-shek in 1941. With OWI, 1942–1944, and accompanied Vice President Wallace to China in 1944. Appointed by President Truman as advisor to E. W. Pauley on latter's mission to Tokyo in 1945. Contributed articles to popular journals like *Asia, Atlantic Monthly,* and *New Republic.* Author of *Manchuria—Cradle of Conflict* (1932), *Inner Asian Frontiers* (1940), *Making of Modern China,* with Eleanor Lattimore (1944), and *Solution in Asia* (1945).

Linebarger, Paul M. W. (1871–1939). Lawyer, publicist. U.S. judge in Philippines, 1901–1907. Legal advisor to Sun Yat-sen, 1907–1925. Advisor to government of Chiang Kai-shek, 1930–1936 with lobbying assignment in United States, 1930–1931. Writings include *Sun Yat-Sen and the Chinese Republic* (1924), *Our Common Cause with China Against Communism and Imperialism* (1927), and *A Commentary on the San Min Chu I* (1931).

Lobenstine, Edwin C. (1872–1958). Missionary. Served in China for thirty-five years, beginning 1898. Involved in arrangements for missionary participation in rural reconstruction under the Kuomintang regime, especially arrangements between Chiang Kai-shek and George Shepherd. With China Medical Board, 1935–1945. Unofficial advisor to American Committee for Non-Participation in Japanese Aggression.

Lockwood, W. W. (1906– ). Writer. Born in Shanghai. Research secretary, American Council, IPR, 1935–1940, and Executive Secretary, 1941–1943. Consultant to U.S. Office of Export Control, 1941. Served with OSS in 1943 and Department of State in 1946. Wrote many scholarly articles and edited *Our Far Eastern Record* (1940).

Luce, Henry R. (1898–1967). Publisher. Born in China and lived there until age 14. Publisher of *Time, Fortune, Life*. Created "March of Time" motion picture newsreel. Frequent visitor to China and steadfast supporter of Chiang Kai-shek. Unofficial supporter of American Committee for Non-Participation in Japanese Aggression and of American China Policy Association. His wife served as president of the latter organization.

McCormick, Frederick (?–1951). Journalist. Covered Boxer War for *Harper's Weekly* and Russo-Japanese War for the Associated Press. In East Asia for AP 1905, 1907–1910, 1917–1922. Radio commentator specializing in Pacific affairs. Contributed to popular journals like *Forum, Outlook,* and *Scribner's*. Author of *The Flowery Republic* (1913) and *The Menace of Japan* (1917).

McKee, Frederick C. (1891–1961). Businessman, lobbyist. Involved in various business enterprises including caskets, limestone, and railroads. Active in American Committee for Non-Participation in Japanese Aggression, League of Nations Association, Council on Foreign Relations, Committee to Defend America by Aiding the Allies. Served as National Director of the Committee for a Boycott Against Japan and both created and operated the China Emergency Committee and the Committee to Defend America by Aiding Anti-Communist China.

Martin, W. A. P. (1826–1916). Missionary, writer. Lived in China for sixty-six years, beginning in 1850. Wrote countless articles and books, including *Lore of Cathay* (1912), *Siege in Peking* (1900), *A Cycle of Cathay* (1887), and *Awakening of China* (1907).

Marvin, George (1873–1955). Journalist, editor. Briefly vice consul at Mukden under Willard Straight and employed in public relations capacity for Imperial Government of China. Served as secretary to the American Group of the first Consortium. Wrote articles for popular journals like *Asia, New Republic,* and *Outlook*. Washington editor for *World's Work*.

Millard, Thomas F. (1868–1942). Journalist, publicist. Founder of *China Press* and *China Weekly Review* and sometime representative of *New York Times* in China. Advisor to Chinese delegation at Paris Peace Conference and Washington Conference. Advisor to Chinese Government 1929–1935. Author of *The New Far East* (1906), *America and the Far Eastern Question* (1909), *Our Eastern Question* (1916), *Democracy and the Eastern Question* (1919), *Conflict of Policies in Asia* (1924), *China—Where It Is Today and Why* (1928), and *The End of Extraterritoriality in China* (1931).

Moore, Frederick (1877–1951?). Journalist, publicist. Associated Press correspondent in China, 1910–1915. Managing editor of *Asia,* 1917–1918. Served as advisor to Japanese Foreign Office, 1921–1926. Represented *New York Times* in China and Japan in 1927. Advisor to Japanese Government during 1930s. Author of *With Japan's Leaders* (1942).

Mott, John R. (1865–1955). Missionary leader. Foreign secretary of YMCA, 1898–1915, and General Secretary of the International Committee, 1915–1931. From 1921 to 1942 served as chairman of International Missionary Council. Wrote extensively on missions work. Participated in National Council of Churches effort to end extraterritoriality in China in 1926. Corecipient of Nobel Peace prize in 1946.

O'Laughlin, John C. (1873–1949). Journalist. Confidant of President Theodore Roosevelt. Served as go-between for Roosevelt and Japanese Ambassador in 1905 and helped arrange Root-Takahira agreement. Washington correspondent for *Chicago Tribune*, then *Chicago Herald*, 1905–1917. Briefly served as Assistant Secretary of State in 1909. Publisher of *Army-Navy Journal* at time of death. See Charles E. Neu, *An Uncertain Friendship* (1967).

Peffer, Nathaniel (1890–1964). Writer, lecturer. Journalist in East Asia for approximately twenty-five years, beginning in 1911. Wrote many articles for popular journals like *Asia*, *Harper's Weekly*, *Nation*, and *New Republic*. Author of *The White Man's Dilemma* (1927), *China: The Collapse of a Civilization* (1930), *Must We Fight in Asia?* (1935), *Prerequisite to Peace in the Far East* (1942), and *America's Place in the World* (1945).

Powell, John B. (1886–1947). Journalist, lobbyist. Joined Millard in 1917 on what was then called *Millard's Review*. Took over *Review* in 1922 and renamed it the *China Weekly Review*. Lobbied in the United States for Chinese businessmen. President of American China Policy Association in 1946. Author of *My Twenty-five Years in China* (1945).

Price, Frank (1895–  ). Missionary. Taught in China 1915–1918. Worked with Chinese Labor Corps in France, 1918–1919. Served as missionary in China, 1923–1952, active in war relief in W. China, 1939–1945. With his brother Harry participated in creation of the American Committee for Non-Participation in Japanese Aggression. Also established the China Information Service. Wrote many articles, especially for *Christian Century*. Translated Sun Yat-sen's *Three Principles of the People* (1927). Author of *The Rural Church in China* (1938) and *China Rediscovers the West* (1939).

Price, Harry B. (1905–  ). Economist, lobbyist. Went to China with Financial Mission to Chinese Government, 1929. Taught in Peking, 1932–1937. Executive Secretary of American Committee for Non-Participation in Japanese Aggression, 1938–1941. Treasurer, director of China Defense Supplies, Inc., 1941–1944. Served as assistant director of UNRRA mission in China, 1944–1948. Consultant to China Division of Economic Cooperation Administration, 1948–1949.

Rawlinson, Frank J. (1871–1937). Missionary. Editor of *Chinese Recorder*. Represented *Christian Century* in China and wrote many articles for that journal and for others, like *Current History* and *Missionary Review*. Author of *The Chinese Idea of the Supreme Being* (1928) and *Chinese Ethical Ideals* (1934).

Rea, George Bronson (1869–1936). Publicist. Founded *Far Eastern Review* in 1904. Sometime advisor to Chinese government officials. Lobbyist for American Chamber of Commerce, China, 1927–1929. Counsellor, Ministry of Foreign Affairs, Manchukuo, 1932–1936.

Reinsch, Paul S. (1869–1923). Political economist, diplomat, publicist. Served as Minister to China, 1913–1919, resigning to lecture and write in criticism of American policy toward China. Spent last years as an advisor to Chinese Government. Author of many scholarly articles and books, including *World Politics at the End of the Nineteenth Century as Influenced by the Oriental Situation* (1900), *Intellectual Currents in the Far East* (1911), and *An American Diplomat in China* (1922).

Rosinger, Lawrence K. (1915– ). Writer. Joined IPR research staff in 1948. Wrote articles for *Foreign Policy Reports* and *New Republic*. Author of *Deadlock in China* (1940), *The Changing Far East,* with William C. Johnstone (1943), *China's Crisis* (1945), *China's Wartime Politics* (1945), and *Forging a New China* (1948).

Roth, J. Andrew (1919– ). Writer. Onetime *Amerasia* researcher, indicted and subsequently cleared in *Amerasia* case. Wrote many articles for *Nation*. Author of *Dilemma in Japan* (1945).

Rowe, David (1905– ). Political scientist. Born in China, served with OSS there 1941–1942. Served also as special assistant to American Ambassador, Chungking, 1941–1942. Author of *China Among the Powers* (1945).

Rowell, Chester (1867–1948). Editor. Editor of *San Francisco Chronicle* from 1932 to his death. Pacific coast leader of Committee to Defend America by Aiding the Allies and important supporter of Greene's efforts on behalf of China. Prominent Republican, close to Hiram Johnson. Claimed access to every President since Grant.

Schiff, Jacob (1847–1920). Banker. Senior partner of Kuhn, Loeb, and Company. Supporter of E. H. Harriman's railroad ventures. Floated $200-million bond issue for Japanese Government during the Russo-Japanese War.

Shepherd, George W. (1894– ). Missionary. Born in New Zealand, reached China via United States in 1917. Very close to Chiang Kai-shek, who chose him to direct Christian rural reconstruction experiment in Kiangsi. Travelled to United States 1937–1938 and again in 1939 to raise funds for China. Wrote and spoke on behalf of Chinese government throughout World War II. See James C. Thomson, Jr., *While China Faced West* (1969).

Smedley, Agnes (1894–1950). Writer. Went to China as correspondent for German newspaper in 1928. Wrote articles for *American Mercury, Asia, Nation,* and *New Republic*. Author of *Chinese Destinies* (1933), *China's Red Army Marches* (1934), *China Fights Back* (1938), and *Battle Hymn of China* (1943), a Book-of-the-Month Club selection.

Smith, Arthur H. (1845–1932). Missionary. Went to China in 1872. Served on editorial board of *Chinese Recorder*. Contributed many articles to *Missionary Review* and *Outlook*. Author of *Chinese Characteristics* (1890), *China in Convulsion* (1901), *The Uplift of China* (1907), and *China and America Today* (1907).

Snow, Edgar (1905–1972). Journalist. Reached East Asia in 1928 and stayed twelve years, working for the *China Weekly Review* and the *New York Sun*. Contributed articles to popular journals like *Asia, Current History, Fortune, Look,* and the *Saturday Evening Post*. Author of the *Far Eastern Front* (1933), *Red Star Over China* (1938), *Battle for Asia* (1941). President Franklin Roosevelt evidenced interest in his work.

Speer, Robert (1867–1947). Presbyterian lay leader. Lay secretary of Board of Foreign Missions. Served as honorary vice-chairman of American Committee for Non-Participation in Japanese Aggression. Contributed articles to *Missionary Review*. Wrote many books, including *Missions and Politics in Asia* (1896).

Steele, Archibald T. (1903– ). Journalist. Correspondent for *New York Times* in Manchuria, North China, 1932–1933. Worked in China for Associated Press 1933–1935, for *Chicago Daily News* 1937–1945. Covered Chinese affairs for *New York Herald Tribune*, beginning 1945.

Stewart, Maxwell S. (1900– ). Economist, writer. Taught in China, 1923–1930. With research staff of Foreign Policy Association, 1931–1934. Associate editor of the *Nation*, 1934–1947. Edited pamphlet series for the American Council of the IPR, 1942–1943, 1946–1948. Chairman of American Friends of the Chinese People and member of national board of American Committee for Non-Participation in Japanese Aggression.

Straight, Willard (1880–1918). Entrepreneur, diplomat. Worked briefly for Chinese Imperial Maritime Customs Service and for the United States Department of State. Also served briefly as correspondent for Reuters and the Associated Press. His interest in railroads in Manchuria led to involvements with E. H. Harriman, J. P. Morgan and Company, and the American International Corporation. See Herbert Croly, *Willard Straight* (1924), and Michael H. Hunt, *Frontier Defense and the Open Door* (1973).

Strawn, Silas (1866–1946). Lawyer, business executive. Important Chicago businessman who served as President of the American Bar Association, 1927–1928 and as President of the United States Chamber of Commerce, 1931–1932. Appointed American commissioner for conference on Chinese tariff in 1925 and on commission on extraterritoriality, of which he was chairman, 1925–1926.

Stuart, J. Leighton (1876–1962). Missionary, diplomat. Born in China, returned in 1904 to begin twenty-five years as teacher and administrator in Peking. Active in campaign for treaty revision in 1920s. Appointed American Ambassador to China in 1946.

Taylor, George E. (1905– ). Historian. Studied and taught in China, 1930–1939. Served with OWI, 1942–1945 and with Department of State, 1946. Author of *Struggle for North China* (1941), *America in the New Pacific* (1942), and *Changing China* (1942).

Treat, Payson (1879–1972). Historian. Appears to have held first professorship in Far Eastern history in the United States. Author of *Early Diplomatic Relations between the United States and Japan, 1853–1865* (1917), *Japan and the United States, 1853–1921* (1921), *Diplomatic Relations between the United States and Japan, 1853–1895* (1932) and *Diplomatic Relations between the United States and Japan, 1895–1905* (1938). In 1941 joined Committee on Pacific Relations, a group advocating the appeasement of Japan.

Utley, Freda (1898– ). Writer, lecturer. Correspondent in East Asia for British newspapers. Consultant to Chinese Supply Commission, 1944–1945, for *Readers Digest* in China, 1945–1946. Wrote many articles for popular journals like *Asia, Living Age,* and *Nation*. Author of *Japan's Feet of Clay* (1936), *Japan's Gamble in China* (1937), *China at War* (1939), *Last Chance in China* (1940), and *Lost Illusion* (1948). Active with American China Policy Association.

Vanderlip, Frank (1864–1937). Banker. Served as Assistant Secretary of Treasury under McKinley. Prominent with National City Bank of New York. Became interested in extending American banking interests abroad when branch banking was permitted under the Federal Reserve Act. Obtained control of International Development Corporation with branches in East Asia. From 1919 to 1924 travelled to Japan and worked in the United States to improve relations with Japan.

Warnshuis, A. L. (1877–1958). Missionary. Served in China for twenty years. Senior secretary of International Missions Council. Trustee of Yenching and other missionary colleges in China. President of Foreign Missions Conference of North America, 1943–1944. Contributed articles to journals like *Annals, Christian Century,* and *Missionary Review.* Instrumental in having the "Porter" resolution brought before Congress in 1927. See Wesley Fishel, *The End of Extraterritoriality in China* (1952).

White, Theodore H. (1915– ). Writer. Chief, China bureau of *Time,* 1939–1945. Editor, *New Republic,* 1947. With Annalee Jacoby, wrote *Thunder Out of China* (1946), a Book-of-the-Month Club selection. Edited *The Stilwell Papers* (1948).

Willoughby, Westel W. (1867–1945). Political scientist. Advisor to Chinese government, 1916–1917, at Washington Conference 1921–1922, and at Geneva Opium Conference 1924–1925. In frequent contact with American diplomats on questions of China's affairs. Occasional contributor to popular journals like *North American Review.* Author of many scholarly publications including *Foreign Rights and Interests in China* (1920), *China at the Conference* (1922), *The Sino-Japanese Controversy and the League of Nations* (1935), and *Japan's Case Re-Examined* (1940).

Young, Arthur N. (1890– ). Economist. Economic advisor to Department of State, 1922–1929. Financial advisor to Chinese Government, 1929–1937. Director, Chinese National Aviation Corporation, 1937–1945. In frequent contact with American diplomats and with his former colleagues in the Department of State. Author of *China's Economic and Financial Reconstruction* (1947).

# Bibliography


## I. *Manuscript collections*

A. PRINCIPAL COLLECTIONS:

Files of the American Committee for Non-Participation in Japanese Aggression, Littauer Center, Harvard University
Files of the Committee to Defend America by Aiding the Allies, Princeton University
Papers of Roger Sherman Greene, Houghton Library, Harvard University
Papers of Stanley K. Hornbeck, Hoover Institution
Papers of Thomas W. Lamont, Baker Library, Harvard University
Papers of J. V. A. MacMurray, Princeton University
Papers of George E. Sokolsky, Columbia University
Transcripts (1956 and 1962) of George E. Sokolsky, Oral History Collection, Columbia University
Files of the U.S. Department of State, National Archives

B. OTHER COLLECTIONS OF VALUE:

Transcript of L. C. Goodrich, Oral History Collection, Columbia University
Transcript of J. B. Grant, Oral History Collection, Columbia University
Papers of Joseph G. Grew, Houghton Library, Harvard University
Papers of Nelson T. Johnson, Library of Congress
Transcript of Nelson T. Johnson, Oral History Collection, Columbia University
Papers of William Phillips, Houghton Library, Harvard University
Papers of W. W. Rockhill, Houghton Library, Harvard University
Papers of Franklin D. Roosevelt, Franklin D. Roosevelt Library
Reports of U.S. Military Attachés, China, National Archives
Files of the U.S. Senate Committee on Foreign Relations, National Archives
Papers of Oswald Garrison Villard, Houghton Library, Harvard University
Papers of Harriet Welling, University of Chicago
Papers of William Allen White, Library of Congress

C. COLLECTIONS AVAILABLE ON MICROFILM

Great Britain, Foreign Office, Confidential Prints

Diary of Marquis Kido Koichi, International Military Tribunal

Diaries of Henry L. Stimson, Yale University

## II. *Published sources cited or otherwise of value*

A. DOCUMENTS, NEWSPAPERS

Great Britain, *Documents on British Foreign Policy, 1919–1939,* 1st series

U.S. Department of State, *Papers Relating to the Foreign Relations of the United States*

*New York Times,* 1905–1950

B. ARTICLES, BOOKS, AND THESES

Abend, Hallett. *My Life in China, 1926–1941*. New York: Harcourt, Brace, 1943.

Adams, Henry. *The Education of Henry Adams*. New York: Modern Library, 1931.

Asada Sadao. "Japan and the United States, 1915–1925." Ph.D. dissertation, Yale University, 1962.

Beale, Howard K. *Theodore Roosevelt and the Rise of America to World Power*. Baltimore: Johns Hopkins Press, 1956.

Booker, Edna Lee. *News is My Job*. New York: Macmillan, 1940.

Borg, Dorothy. *American Policy and the Chinese Revolution, 1925–1928*. New York: American Institute of Pacific Relations and Macmillan, 1947.

—— *The United States and the Far Eastern Crisis of 1933–1938*. Cambridge, Massachusetts: Harvard University Press, 1964.

Borg, Dorothy, and Okamoto, Shumpei (eds.). *Pearl Harbor as History: Japanese-American Relations, 1931–1941*. New York: Columbia University Press, 1973.

Bowers, John Z. "The Founding of Peking Union Medical College: Policies and Personalities." *Bulletin of the History of Medicine,* XLV (1971), 305–21, 409–29.

Buckley, Thomas H. *The United States and the Washington Conference, 1921–1922*. Knoxville: University of Tennessee Press, 1970.

Cantril, Hadley (ed.). *Public Opinion, 1935–1946*. Princeton: Princeton University Press, 1951.

Chang Tao-hsing. *International Controversies Over the Chinese Eastern Railway*. Shanghai: Commercial Press, 1936.

Cook, Fred. *The Nightmare Decade*. New York: Random House, 1971.

Cohen, Bernard C. *The Public's Impact on Foreign Policy*. Boston: Little, Brown, 1973.

Cronon, E. David (ed.). *The Cabinet Diaries of Josepheus Daniels, 1913–1921*. Lincoln: University of Nebraska Press, 1963.

Curry, Roy Watson. *Woodrow Wilson and Far Eastern Policy, 1913–1921*. New York: Bookman Associates, 1957.

Divine, Robert A. *Illusion of Neutrality*. Chicago: University of Chicago Press, 1962.

—— *The Reluctant Belligerent.* New York: John Wiley, 1966.
Erikson, Erik H. *Gandhi's Truth.* New York: W. W. Norton, 1969.
Esthus, Raymond A. *Theodore Roosevelt and Japan.* Seattle: University of Washington Press, 1966.
Feis, Herbert. *The Diplomacy of the Dollar, 1919–1932.* Baltimore: Johns Hopkins Press, 1950.
Ferguson, Mary E. *China Medical Board and Peking Union Medical College.* New York: China Medical Board, 1970.
Field, Frederick V. *American Participation in the China Consortiums.* New York: Institute of Pacific Relations, 1931.
Friedman, Donald J. *The Road From Isolation.* Cambridge, Massachusetts: East Asian Research Center, Harvard University, 1968.
Gallup, George H. *The Gallup Poll: Public Opinion, 1935–1971.* 3 volumes. New York: Random House, 1972.
Goldman, Eric F. *The Crucial Decade—And After.* New York: Vintage, 1960.
Goodman, Walter. *The Committee.* New York: Farrar, Straus & Giroux, 1968.
Greene, Evarts B. *A New-Englander in Japan.* Boston: Houghton Mifflin, 1927.
Griffiths, Robert. *Politics of Fear.* Lexington: University of Kentucky Press, 1970.
Healy, David. *US Expansionism.* Madison: University of Wisconsin Press, 1970.
Heinrichs, Waldo H. *American Ambassador.* Boston: Little, Brown, 1966.
—— "Bureaucracy and Professionalism in the Development of American Career Diplomacy," in John Braeman, et al., *Twentieth Century American Foreign Policy.* Columbus, Ohio: Ohio State University Press, 1971.
Hennigar, Nancy A. "The United States, Great Britain, and Japan's Special Interests in Manchuria, 1917–1923." M.A. thesis, Michigan State University, 1975.
Hodgson, Godfrey. "The Establishment," *Foreign Policy,* 10 (1973), 3–40.
Hunt, Michael H. "The American Remission of the Boxer Indemnity: A Reappraisal," *Journal of Asian Studies,* XXXI (1972), 539–59.
—— *Frontier Defense and the Open Door.* New Haven: Yale University Press, 1973.
Irick, Robert L. "The Chinchow-Aigun Railroad and the Knox Neutralization Plan in Ch'ing Diplomacy," *Papers on China,* East Asian Research Center Harvard University, XIII (1959), 80–112.
Iriye Akira. *After Imperialism.* Cambridge, Massachusetts: Harvard University Press, 1965.
—— *Pacific Estrangement.* Cambridge, Massachusetts: Harvard University Press, 1972.
Keeley, Joseph. *The China Lobby Man: The Story of Alfred Kohlberg.* New Rochelle, New York: Arlington House, 1969.
Kirwin, Harry W. "The Federal Telegraph Company: A Testing of the Open Door," *Pacific Historical Review,* XXII (1953), 271–86.

Koen, Ross Y. *The China Lobby in American Politics.* New York: Harper & Row, 1974.

Kuehnelt-Leddihn, Erik v. "Do Jews Tend Toward Communism?" *Catholic World,* CLXIV (1946), 160–62.

Lamont, Thomas W. *Across World Frontiers.* New York: Harcourt, Brace, 1951.

—— "Banking Consortium for China as a Power for Peace," *New York Times,* August 8, 1920, VII, 2.

—— "The Chinese Consortium and American Trade Relations," *Annals XCIV (1921), 87–93.*

—— "The Economic Situation in the Orient," *Proceedings of the Academy of Political Science,* IX (1921), 68–75.

—— *My Boyhood in a Parsonage.* New York: Harper, 1946.

—— "Putting China on Her Feet," *Forum,* LXIV (1920), 90–94.

—— "The World Situation," *Atlantic Monthly,* CXXIV (1919), 420–29.

Langdon, Frank, "The Japanese Policy of Expansion in China, 1917–1928," Ph.D. dissertation, University of California (1953).

Li Chien-nung. *The Political History of China, 1840–1928.* Princeton: D. Van Nostrand, 1956.

Link, Arthur S. *Wilson: The New Freedom.* Princeton: Princeton University Press, 1956.

Lipset, Seymour Martin. "The Sources of the Radical Right," in Daniel Bell (ed.), *The Radical Right.* Garden City: Doubleday, 1964.

Louis, W. Roger. *British Strategy in the Far East, 1919–1939.* Oxford: Clarendon, 1971.

Mitani Taichirō. *Nihon Seito seiji no keisei.* Tokyo: Tokyo University Press, 1967.

Nathan, Andrew J. *A History of the China International Famine Relief Commission.* Cambridge, Massachusetts: East Asian Research Center, Harvard University, 1965.

Neu, Charles E. *An Uncertain Friendship.* Cambridge, Massachusetts: Harvard University Press, 1967.

Nish, Ian H. *Alliance in Decline.* London: Athalone, 1972.

Parrini, Carl P. *Heir to Empire.* Pittsburg: University of Pittsburg Press, 1969.

Pugach, Noel. "Making the Open Door Work: Paul S. Reinsch in China, 1913–1919." *Pacific Historical Review,* XXXVIII (1969), 157–75.

Reston, James. *The Artillery of the Press.* New York: Harper & Row, 1967.

Rogin, Michael P. *The Intellectuals and McCarthy: The Radical Specter.* Cambridge: MIT Press, 1967.

Rosenau, James N. *National Leadership and Foreign Policy.* Princeton: Princeton University Press, 1963.

—— *Public Opinion and Foreign Policy.* New York: Random House, 1961.

Scholes, Walter and Mary. *The Foreign Policies of the Taft Administration.* Columbia, Missouri: University of Missouri Press, 1970.

Selle, Earl Albert. *Donald of China.* Sydney, Australia: Invincible Press, 1948.

Service, John S. *The Amerasia Papers.* Berkeley, California: Center for Chinese Studies, 1971.

Sokolsky, George E. "The American Monkey Wrench," *Atlantic Monthly*, CL (1932), 739–48.
—— "Asia for the Asiatics," *American Mercury*, LV (1942), 72–81.
—— "Catholic Missions in China," *Commonweal*, XVII (1933), 573–74.
—— "China's Defiance of Japan," *Independent*, XLIX (1919), 388–90.
—— "The China Story," *Catholic World*, CLXIX (1949), 406–11.
—— "Communism Under Four Flags," *New Outlook*, CLXI (1932), 27–31.
—— "Let's Change Our Foreign Policy," *Asia*, XXXIII (1933), 175–77.
—— "My Mixed Marriage," *Atlantic Monthly*, CLII (1933), 137–46.
—— "The Red Armies of Asia," *Asia*, XXXII (1932), 620–26.
—— "The Russo-Japanese War Myth," *American Mercury*, XXXII (1934), 80–86.
—— "Shantung Under General Ma Liang," *New York Times Current History*, XI (1919), 350–51.
—— "The Soongs of China," *Atlantic Monthly*, CLIX (1937), 185–88.
—— *Tinder Box of Asia*. Garden City, New York: Doubleday, Doran, 1932.
—— "What Matters in Missions," *Christian Century*, L (1933), 52–54.
Shewmaker, Kenneth E. *Americans and Chinese Communists, 1927–1945*. Ithaca: Cornell University Press, 1971.
Spence, Jonathan. *To Change China: Western Advisers in China, 1620–1960*. Boston: Little, Brown, 1969.
Thomas, John N. *The Institute of Pacific Relations*. Seattle: University of Washington Press, 1974.
Thomson, James C. *While China Faced West*. Cambridge, Massachusetts: Harvard University Press, 1969.
Turner, George Kibbe. "Morgan's Partners," *McClure's Magazine*, XL (1913), 25–35.
Varg, Paul A. *The Making of a Myth*. East Lansing: Michigan State University Press, 1968.
—— *Missionaries, Chinese, and Diplomats*. Princeton: Princeton University Press, 1958.
Vevier, Charles. *The United States and China, 1906–1913*. New Brunswick, New Jersey: Rutgers University Press, 1955.
Walker, W. M. "J.P. The Younger," *American Mercury*, XI (1927), 129–36.
Williams, Jesse Lynch. "How T. W. Lamont Got the Consortium Framed," *World's Work*, XLI (1921), 452–64.
Wilson, Joan Hoff. *American Business and Foreign Policy, 1920–1933*. Lexington: University of Kentucky Press, 1971.
Young, John W. "Japanese Military and the Hara Cabinet." Ph.D. dissertation, University of Washington, 1972.
Zabriskie, Edward H. *American-Russian Rivalry in the Far East, 1895–1914*. Philadelphia: University of Pennsylvania Press, 1946.

# Index

# Studies of The East Asian Institute

THE LADDER OF SUCCESS IN IMPERIAL CHINA, by Ping-ti Ho. New York: Columbia University Press, 1962.

THE CHINESE INFLATION, 1937–1949, by Shun-hsin Chou. New York: Columbia University Press, 1963.

REFORMER IN MODERN CHINA: CHANG CHIEN, 1853–1926, by Samuel Chu. New York: Columbia University Press, 1965.

RESEARCH IN JAPANESE SOURCES: A GUIDE, by Herschel Webb with the assistance of Marleigh Ryan. New York: Columbia University Press, 1965.

SOCIETY AND EDUCATION IN JAPAN, by Herbert Passin. New York: Bureau of Publications, Teachers College, Columbia University, 1965.

AGRICULTURAL PRODUCTION AND ECONOMIC DEVELOPMENT IN JAPAN, 1873–1922, by James I. Nakamura. Princeton: Princeton University Press, 1966.

JAPAN'S FIRST MODERN NOVEL: UKIGUMO OF FUTABATEI SHIMEI, by Marleigh Ryan. New York: Columbia University Press, 1967.

THE KOREAN COMMUNIST MOVEMENT, 1918–1948, by Dae-Sook Suh. Princeton University Press, 1967.

THE FIRST VIETNAM CRISIS, by Melvin Gurtov. New York: Columbia University Press, 1967.

CADRES, BUREAUCRACY, AND POLITICAL POWER IN COMMUNIST CHINA, by A. Doak Barnett. New York: Columbia University Press, 1967.

THE JAPANESE IMPERIAL INSTITUTION IN THE TOKUGAWA PERIOD, by Herschel Webb. New York: Columbia University Press, 1968.

HIGHER EDUCATION AND BUSINESS RECRUITMENT IN JAPAN, by Koya Azumi. New York: Teachers College Press, Columbia University, 1969.

THE COMMUNISTS AND CHINESE PEASANT REBELLIONS: A STUDY IN THE REWRITING OF CHINESE HISTORY, by James P. Harrison, Jr. New York: Atheneum, 1969.

HOW THE CONSERVATIVES RULE JAPAN, by Nathaniel B. Thayer. Princeton: Princeton University Press, 1969.

ASPECTS OF CHINESE EDUCATION, edited by C. T. Hu. New York: Teachers College Press, Columbia University, 1970.

DOCUMENTS OF KOREAN COMMUNISM, 1918–1948, by Dae-Sook Suh. Princeton: Princeton University Press, 1970.

JAPANESE EDUCATION: A BIBLIOGRAPHY OF MATERIALS IN THE ENGLISH LANGUAGE, by Herbert Passin. New York: Teachers College Press, Columbia University, 1970.

ECONOMIC DEVELOPMENT AND THE LABOR MARKET IN JAPAN, by Koji Taira. New York: Columbia University Press, 1970.

THE JAPANESE OLIGARCHY AND THE RUSSO-JAPANESE WAR, by Shumpei Okamoto. New York: Columbia University Press, 1970.

IMPERIAL RESTORATION IN MEDIEVAL JAPAN, by H. Paul Varley. New York: Columbia University Press, 1971.

JAPAN'S POSTWAR DEFENSE POLICY, 1947–1968, by Martin E. Weinstein. New York: Columbia University Press, 1971.

ELECTION CAMPAIGNING JAPANESE STYLE, by Gerald L. Curtis. New York: Columbia University Press, 1971.

CHINA AND RUSSIA: THE "GREAT GAME," by O. Edmund Clubb. New York: Columbia University Press, 1971.

MONEY AND MONETARY POLICY IN COMMUNIST CHINA, by Katharine Huang Hsiao. New York: Columbia University Press, 1971.

THE DISTRICT MAGISTRATE IN LATE IMPERIAL CHINA, by John R. Watt. New York: Columbia University Press, 1972.

LAW AND POLICY IN CHINA'S FOREIGN RELATIONS: A STUDY OF ATTITUDES AND PRACTICE, by James C. Hsiung. New York: Columbia University Press, 1972.

PEARL HARBOR AS HISTORY: JAPANESE-AMERICAN RELATIONS, 1931–1941, edited by Dorothy Borg and Shumpei Okamoto, with the assistance of Dale K. A. Finlayson. New York: Columbia University Press, 1973.

JAPANESE CULTURE: A SHORT HISTORY, by H. Paul Varley. New York: Praeger, 1973.

DOCTORS IN POLITICS: THE POLITICAL LIFE OF THE JAPAN MEDICAL ASSOCIA-TION, by William E. Steslicke. New York: Praeger, 1973.

THE JAPAN TEACHERS UNION: A RADICAL INTEREST GROUP IN JAPANESE POLITICS, by Donald Ray Thurston. Princeton: Princeton University Press, 1973.

JAPAN'S FOREIGN POLICY, 1868–1941: A RESEARCH GUIDE, edited by James William Morley. New York: Columbia University Press, 1974.

PALACE AND POLITICS IN PREWAR JAPAN, by David Anson Titus. New York: Columbia University Press, 1974.

THE IDEA OF CHINA: ESSAYS IN GEOGRAPHIC MYTH AND THEORY, by Andrew March. Devon, England: David and Charles, 1974.

ORIGINS OF THE CULTURAL REVOLUTION, by Roderick MacFarquhar. New York: Columbia University Press, 1974.

SHIBA KIKAN: ARTIST, INNOVATOR, AND PIONEER IN THE WESTERNIZATION OF JAPAN, by Calvin L. French. Tokyo: Weatherhill, 1974.

INSEI: ABDICATED SOVEREIGNS IN THE POLITICS OF LATE HEIAN JAPAN, by G. Cameron Hurst. New York: Columbia University Press, 1975.

EMBASSY AT WAR, by Harold Joyce Noble. Edited with an introduction by Frank Baldwin, Jr. Seattle: University of Washington Press, 1975.

REBELS AND BUREAUCRATS: CHINA'S DECEMBER NINERS, by John Israel and Donald W. Klein. Berkeley: University of California Press, 1975.

DETERRENT DIPLOMACY, edited by James William Morley. New York: Columbia University Press, 1976.

HOUSE UNITED, HOUSE DIVIDED: THE CHINESE FAMILY IN TAIWAN, by Myron L. Cohen. New York: Columbia University Press, 1976.

ESCAPE FROM PREDICAMENT: NEO-CONFUSIANISM AND CHINA'S EVOLVING POLITICAL CULTURE, by Thomas A. Metzger. New York: Columbia University Press, 1976.

JAPANESE INTERNATIONAL NEGOTIATING BEHAVIOR, by Michael Blaker. New York: Columbia University Press, 1977.

THE CHINESE CONNECTION: ROGER S. GREENE, THOMAS W. LAMONT, GEORGE E. SOKOLSKY AND AMERICAN–EAST ASIAN RELATIONS, by Warren I. Cohen. New York: Columbia University Press, 1978.